FAIRY TAIL

フェアリーテイル

29

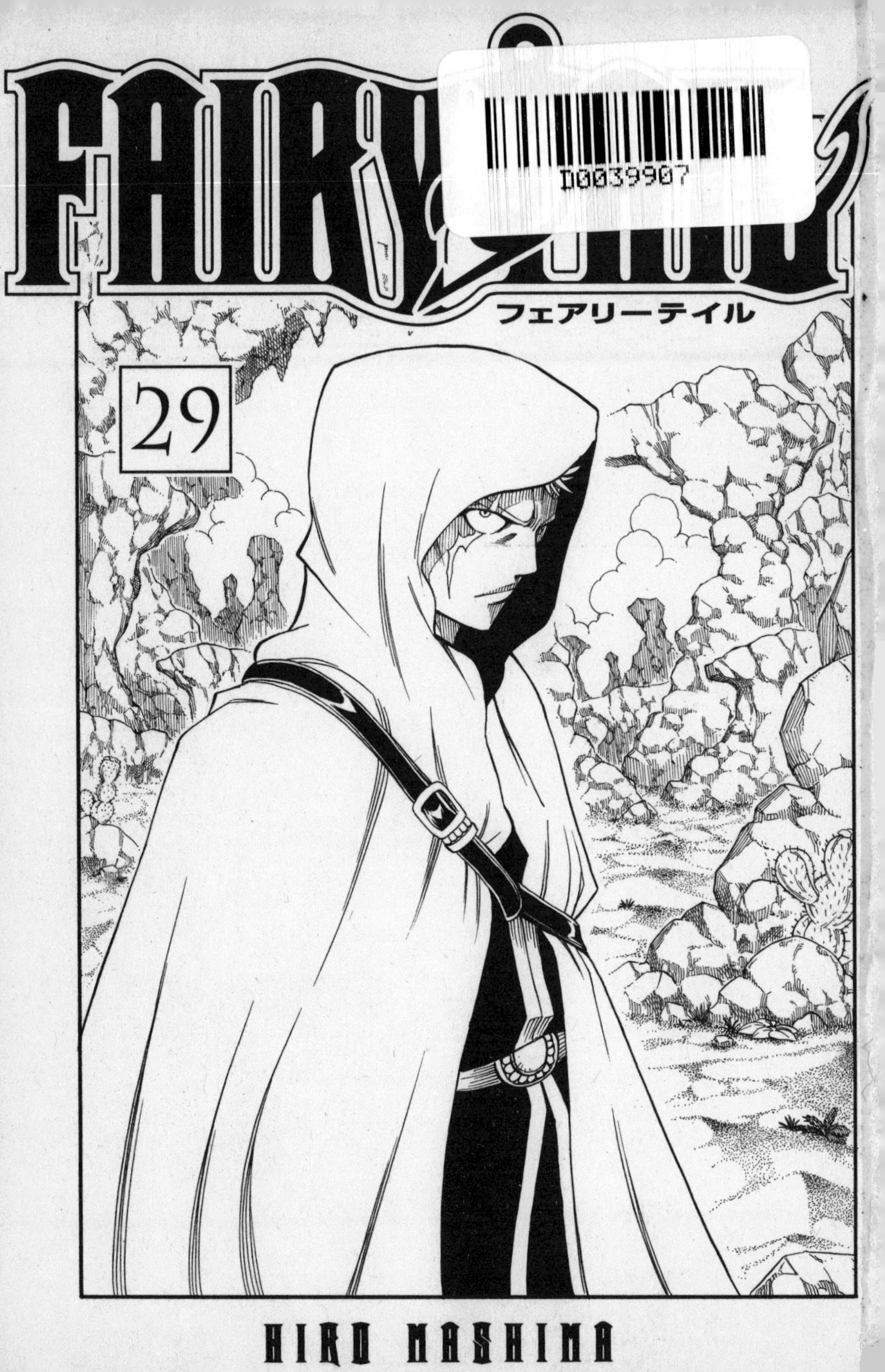

HIRO MASHIMA

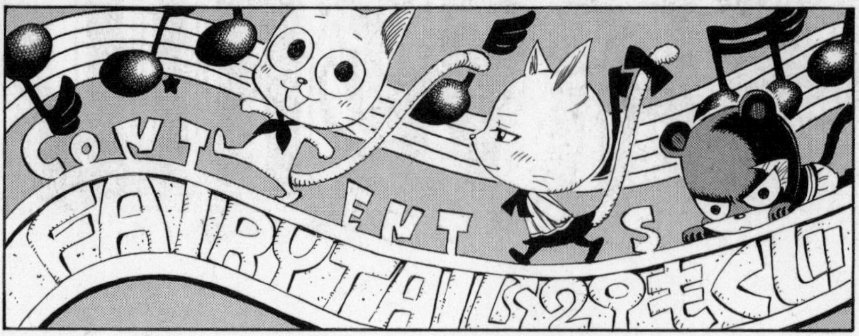
CONTENTS
FAIRY TAIL 29 もくじ

FAIRY TAIL
フェアリーテイル

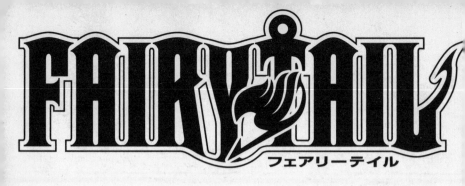

Chapter 240: Gray vs. Ultear

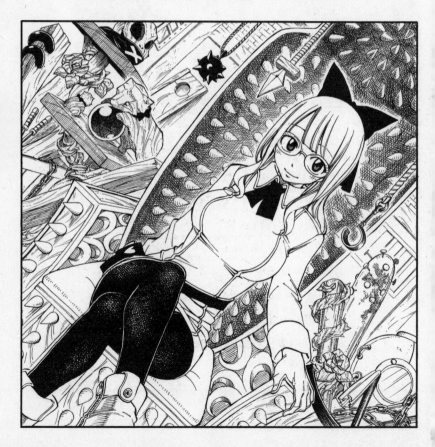

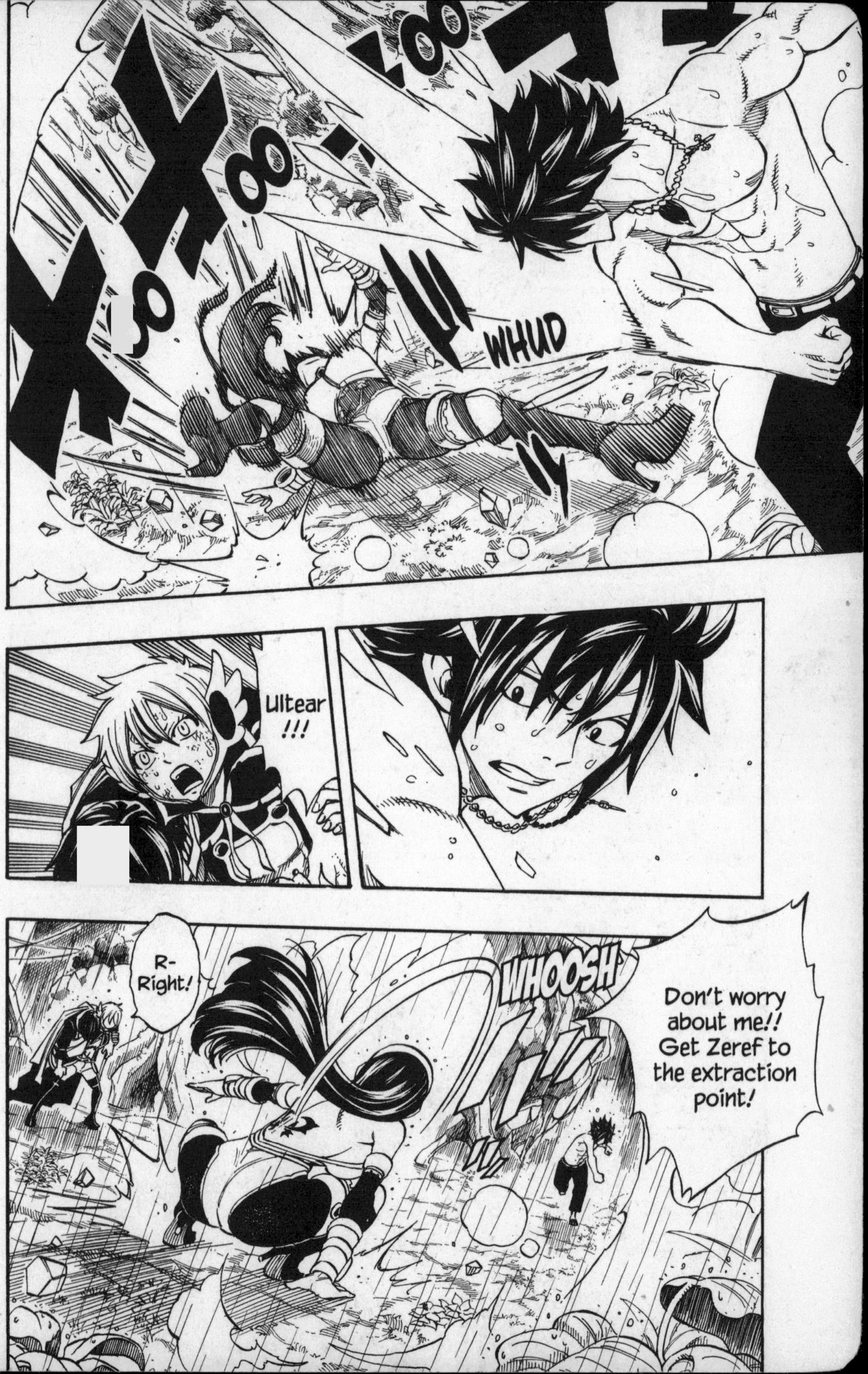
WHUD
Ultear!!!
Don't worry about me!! Get Zeref to the extraction point!
WHOOSH
R-Right!

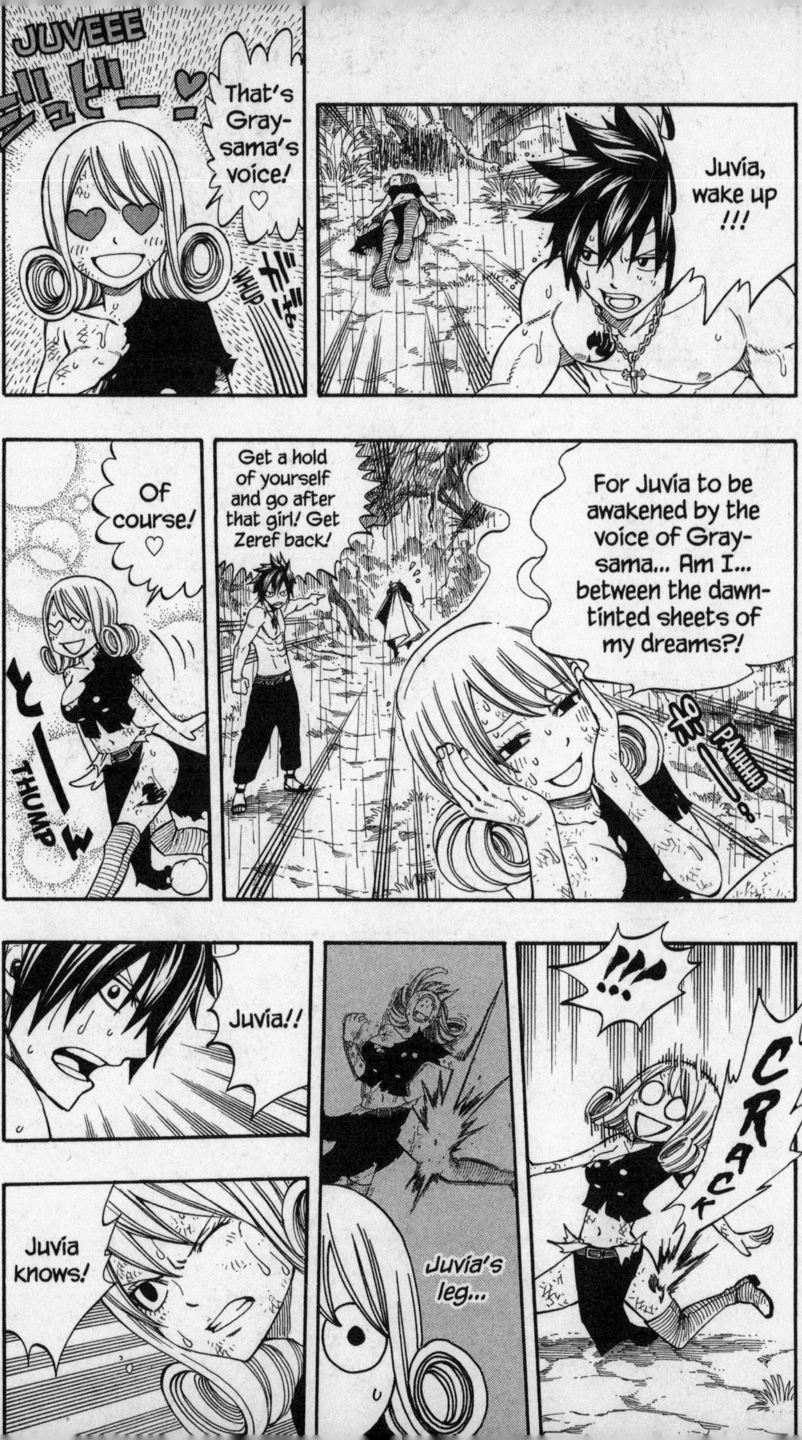
Juvia, wake up!!!
JUVEEE
ジュビーー♥
That's Gray-sama's voice! ♡
WHUP
For Juvia to be awakened by the voice of Gray-sama... Am I... between the dawn-tinted sheets of my dreams?!
PAHHH
Get a hold of yourself and go after that girl! Get Zeref back!
Of course! ♡
THUMP
!!!
CRACK
Juvia's leg...
Juvia!!
Juvia knows!

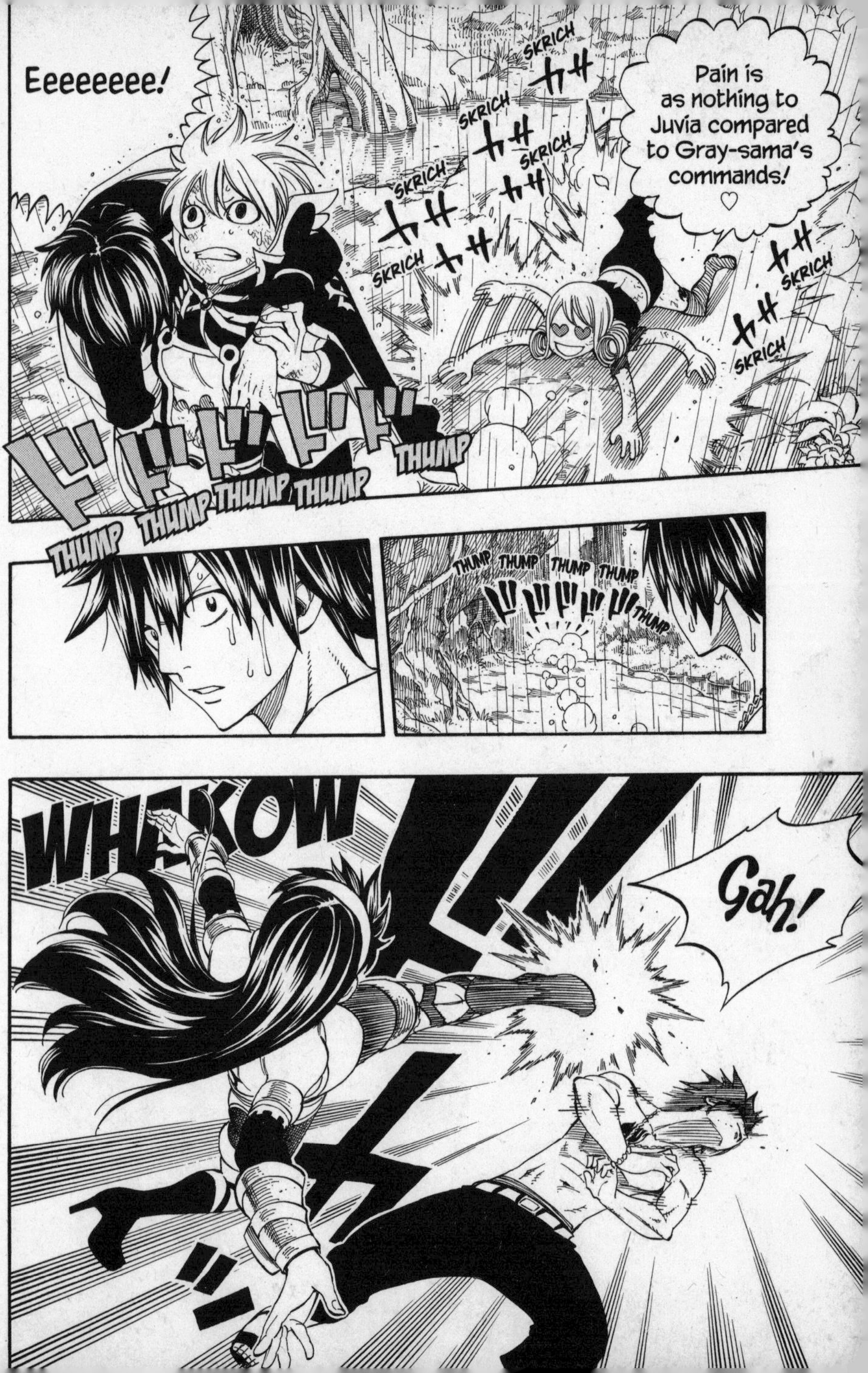
Pain is as nothing to Juvia compared to Gray-sama's commands! ♡
SKRICH
SKRICH
SKRICH
SKRICH
SKRICH
SKRICH
SKRICH
SKRICH
Eeeeeeee!
THUMP
THUMP
THUMP
THUMP
THUMP
THUMP THUMP THUMP THUMP THUMP
Gah!
WHAKOW

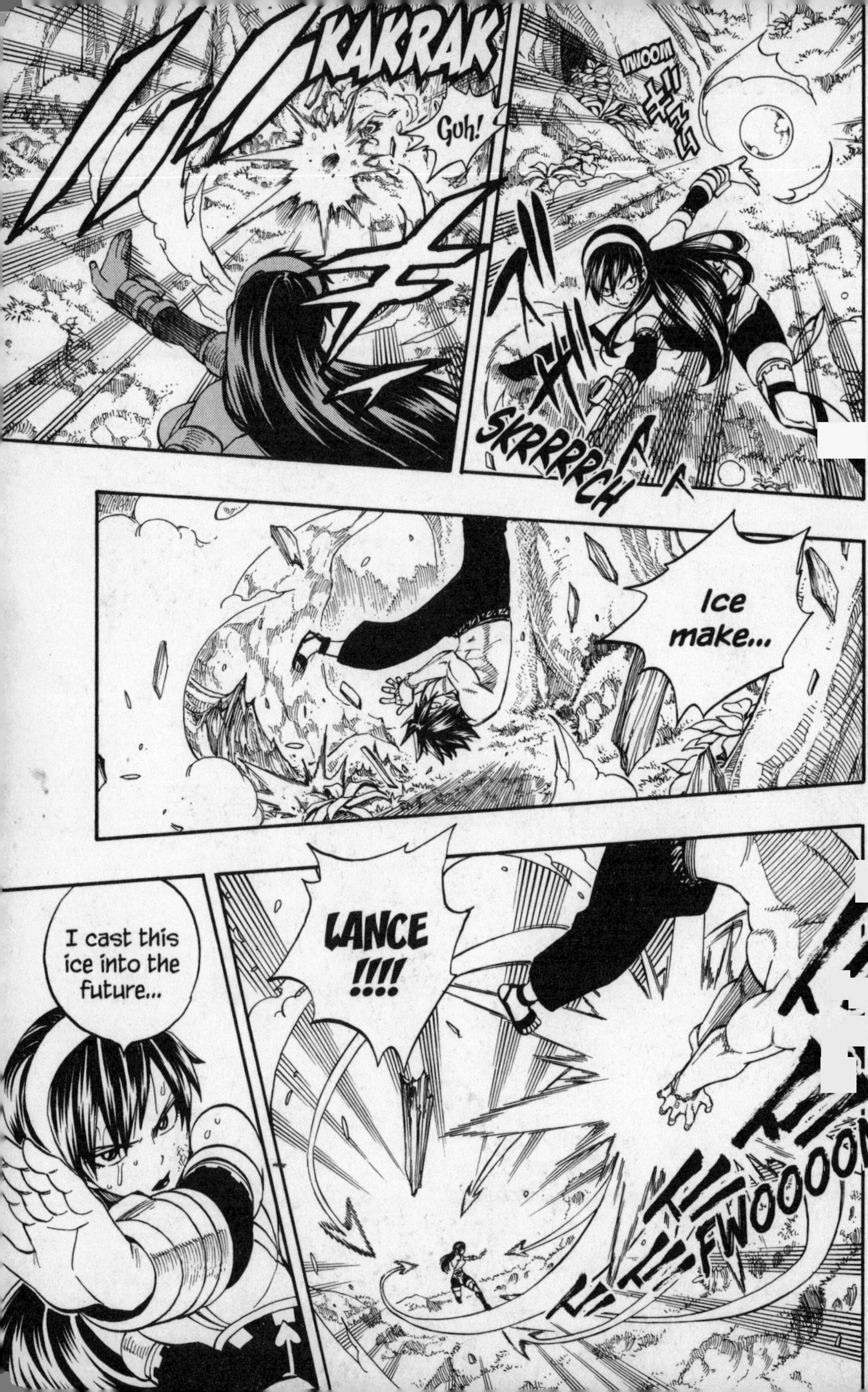
WOOM
SKRRRRCH
KAKRAK
Guh!
Ice make...
LANCE !!!!
FWOOOOM
I cast this ice into the future...

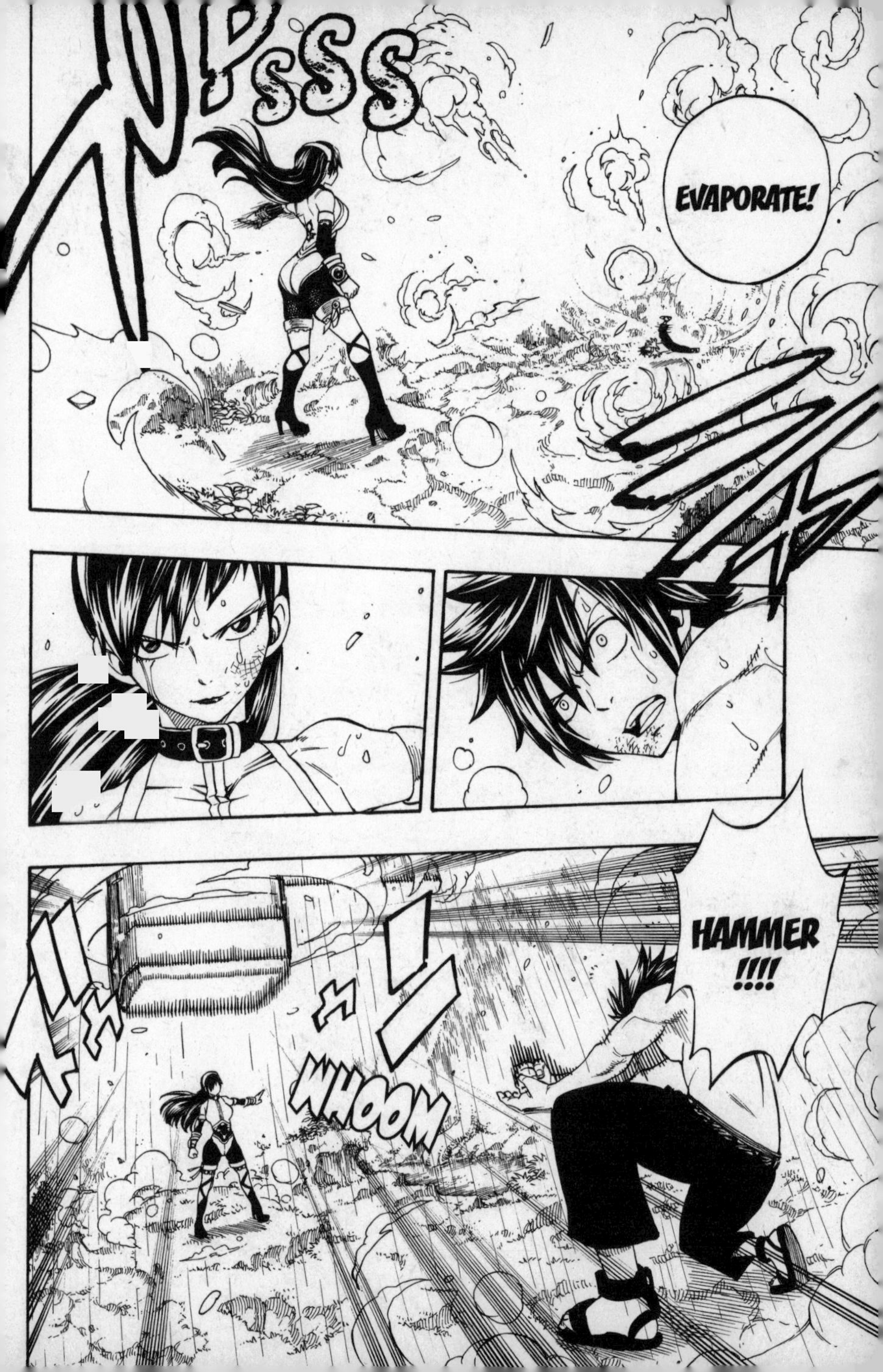
EVAPORATE!
HAMMER !!!!
WHOOM

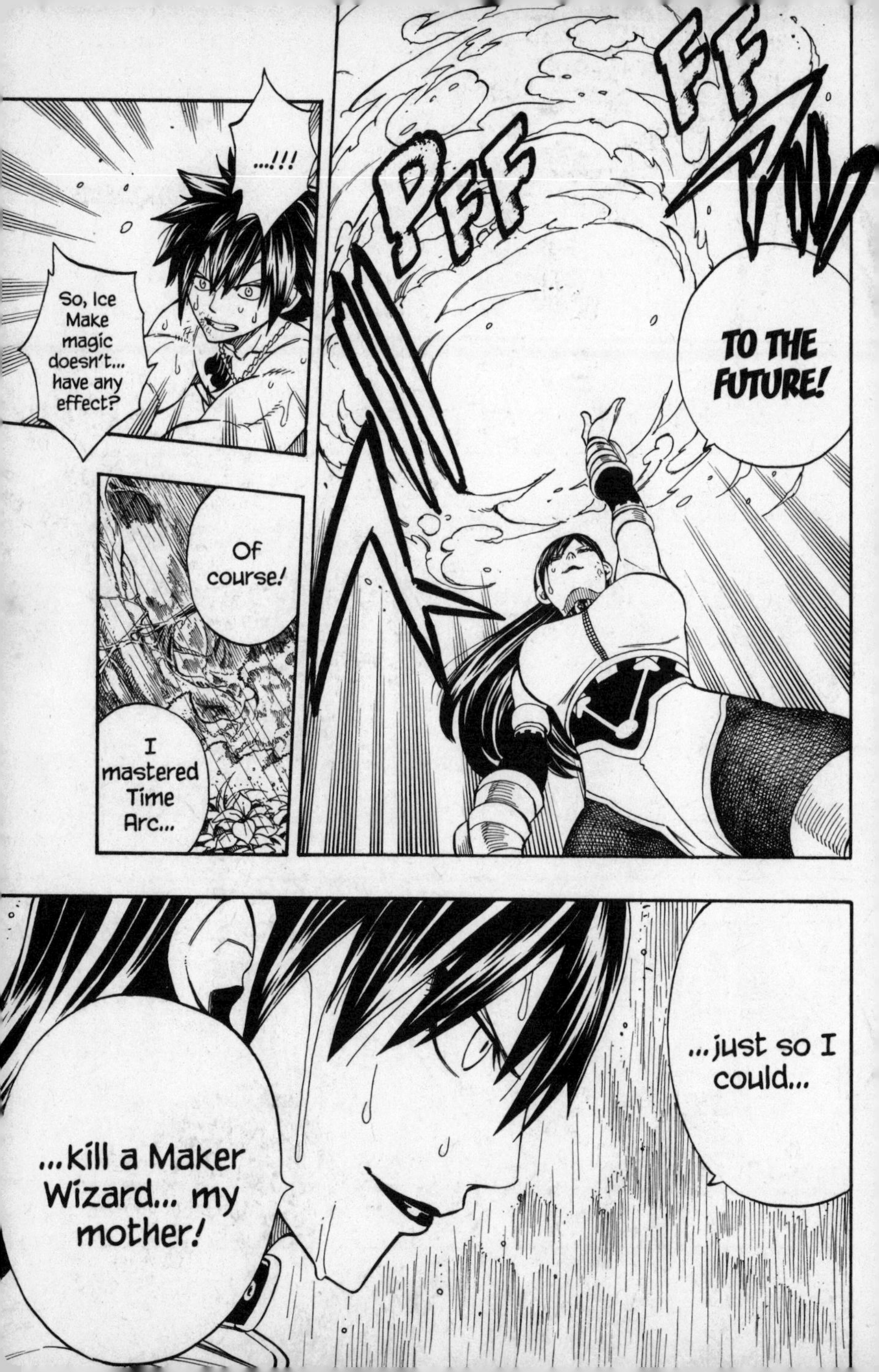
PFF
TO THE FUTURE!
...!!!
So, Ice Make magic doesn't... have any effect?
Of course!
I mastered Time Arc...
...just so I could...
...kill a Maker Wizard... my mother!

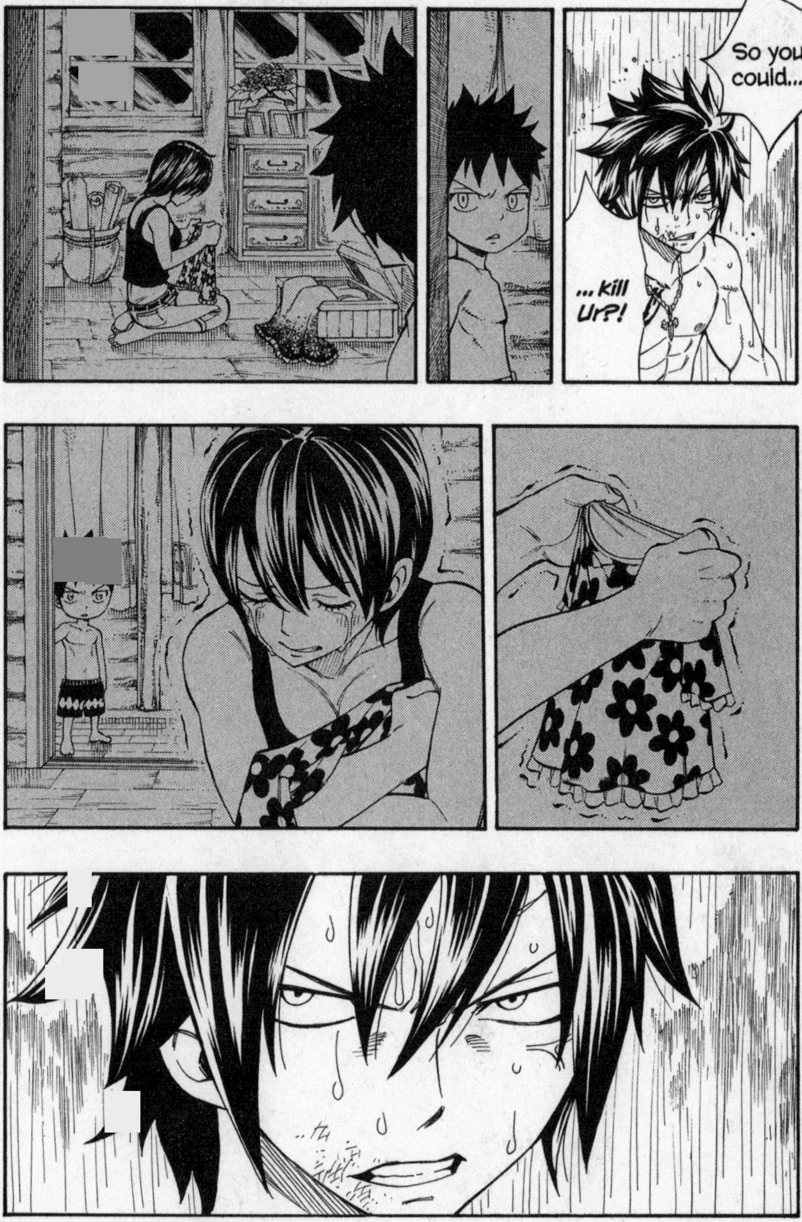
So you could...
...kill Ur?!

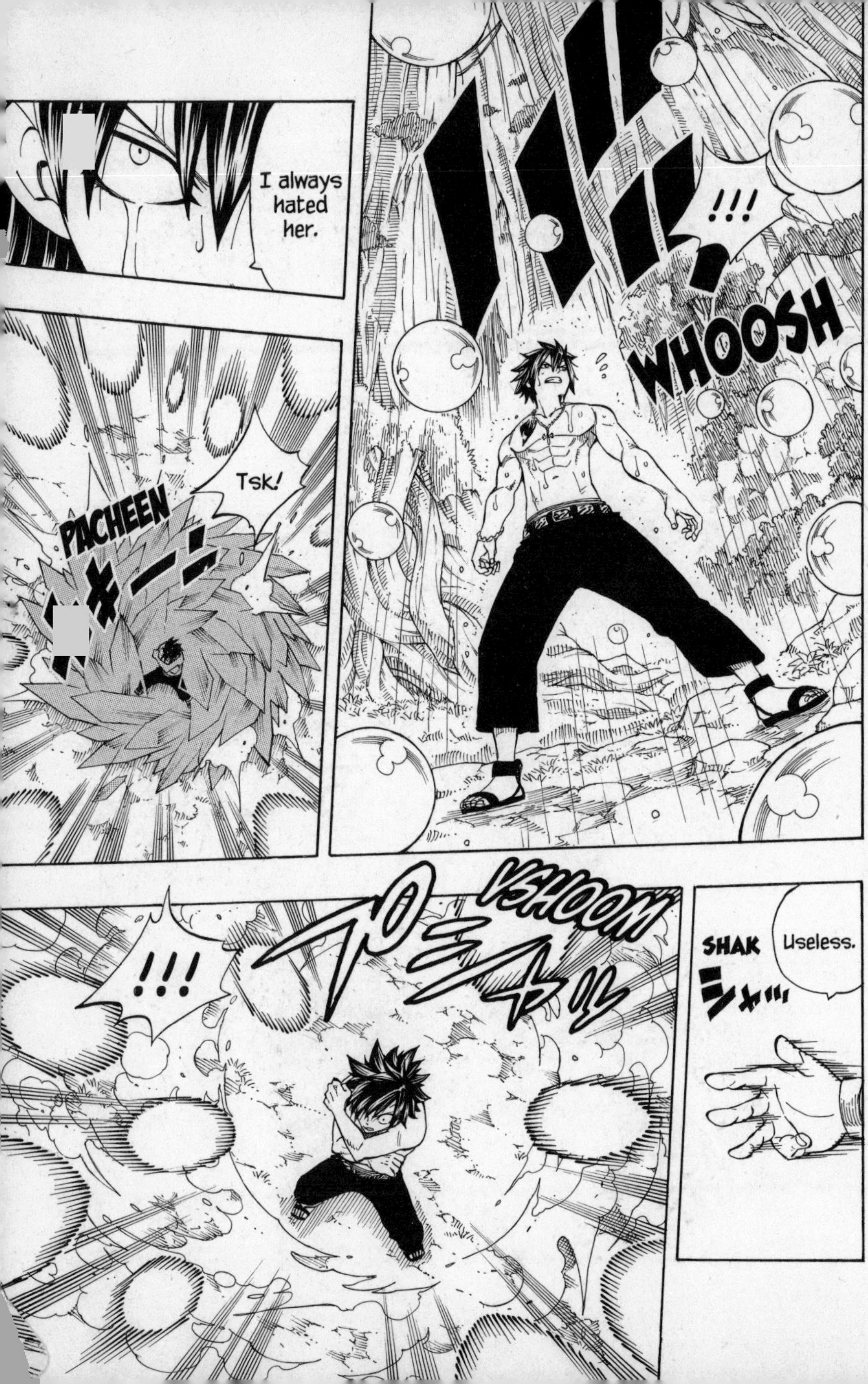
!!!
WHOOSH
I always hated her.
Tsk!
PACHEEN
SHAK
Useless.
VSHOOM
!!!

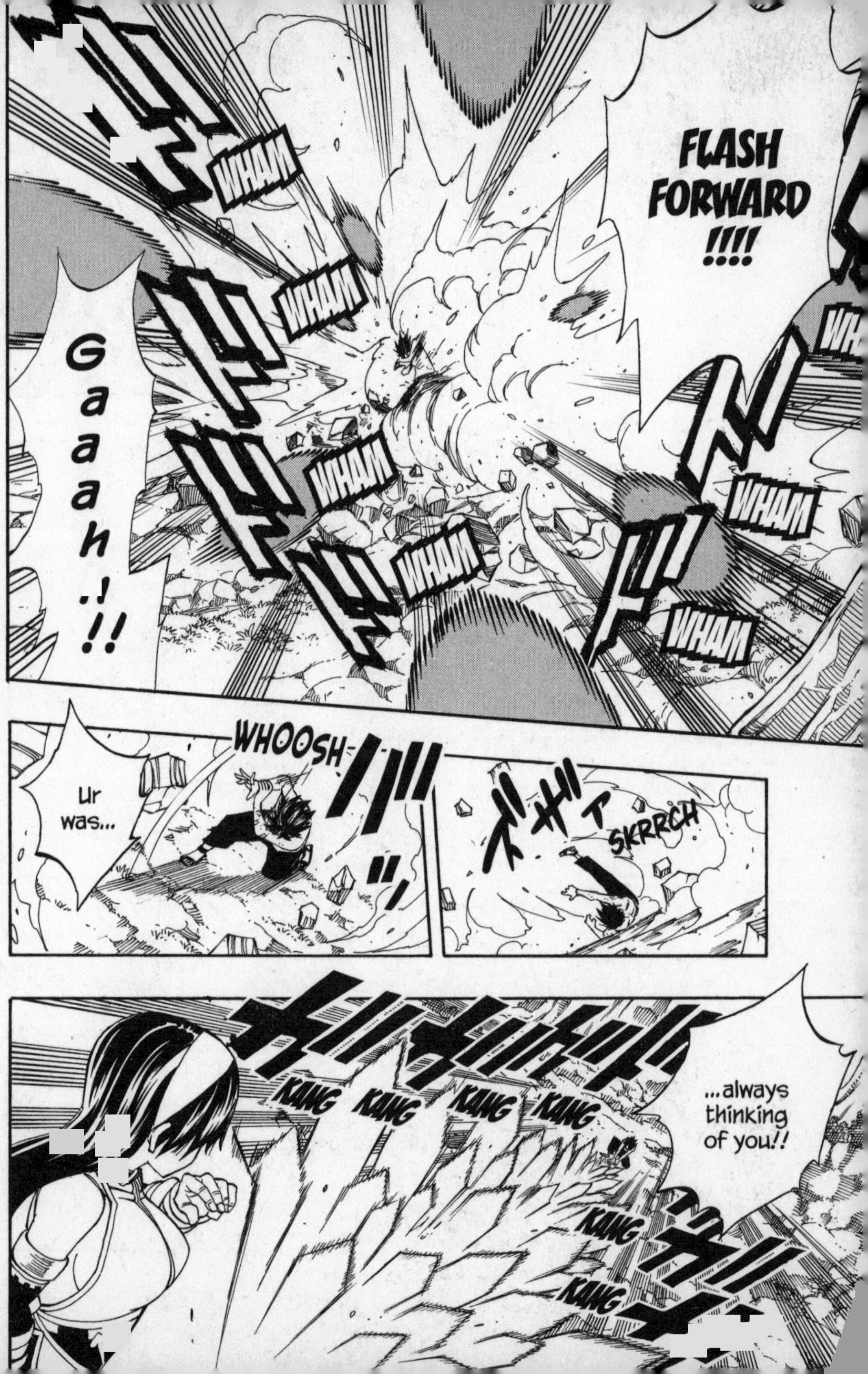
FLASH FORWARD!!!!
WHAM
WHAM
WHAM
WHAM
WHAM
WHAM
WHAM
Gaaah!!
SKRRCH
WHOOSH
Ur was...
...always thinking of you!!
KANG
KANG
KANG
KANG
KANG
KANG
KANG

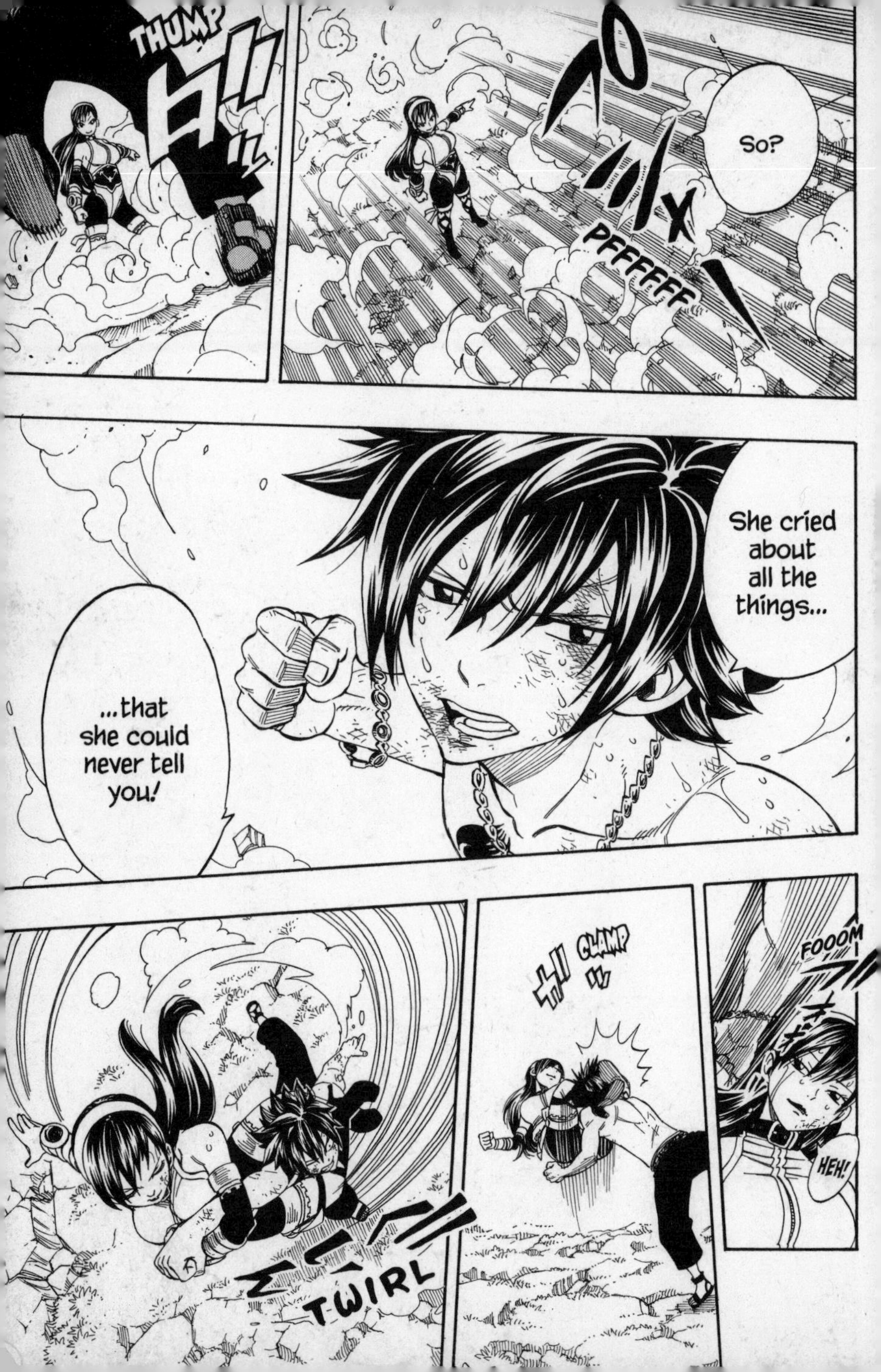
So?
PFFFFFF
THUMP
She cried about all the things...
...that she could never tell you!
FOOOM
HEH!
CLAMP
TWIRL

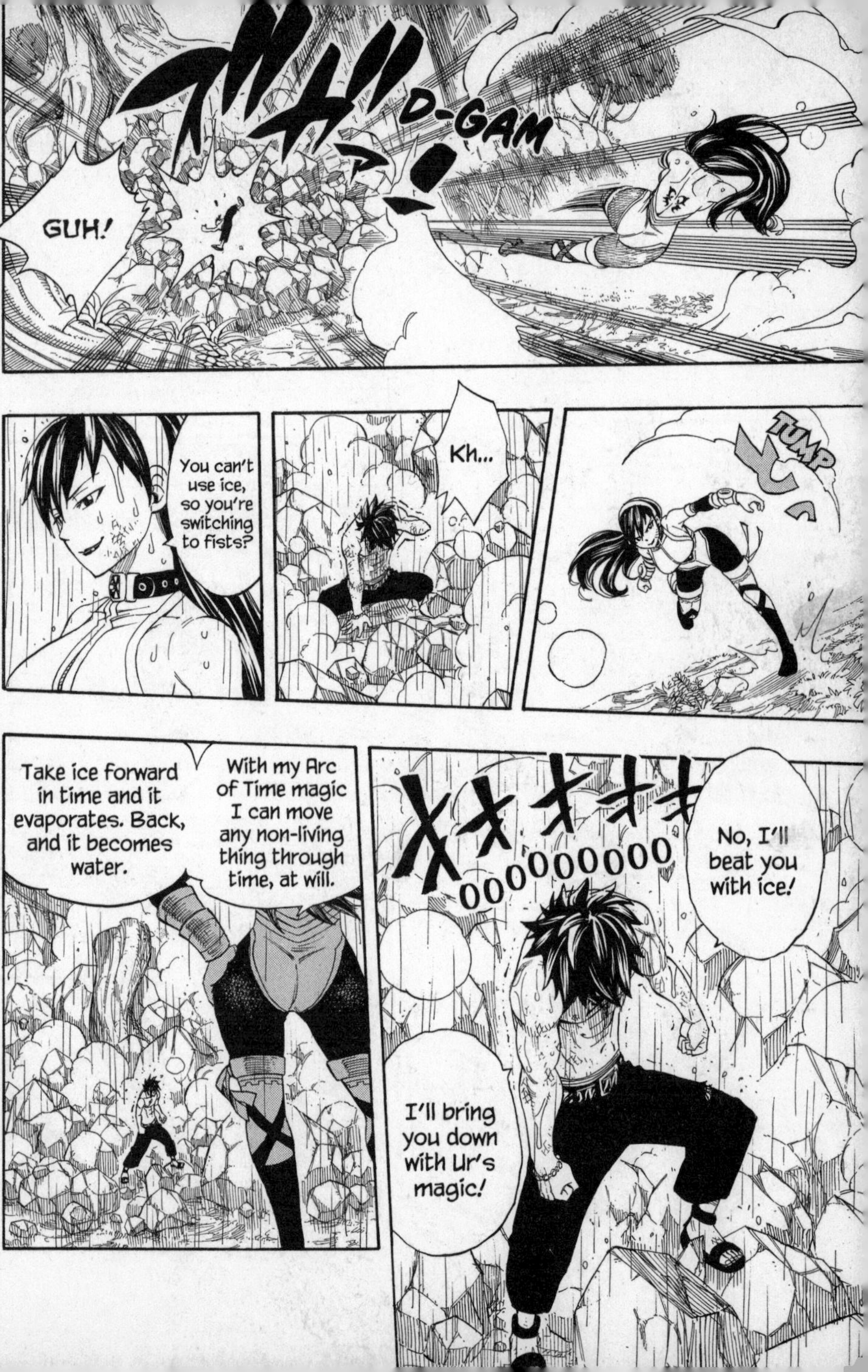
D-GAM
GUH!
TUMP
Kh...
You can't use ice, so you're switching to fists?
No, I'll beat you with ice!
I'll bring you down with Ur's magic!
With my Arc of Time magic I can move any non-living thing through time, at will.
Take ice forward in time and it evaporates. Back, and it becomes water.

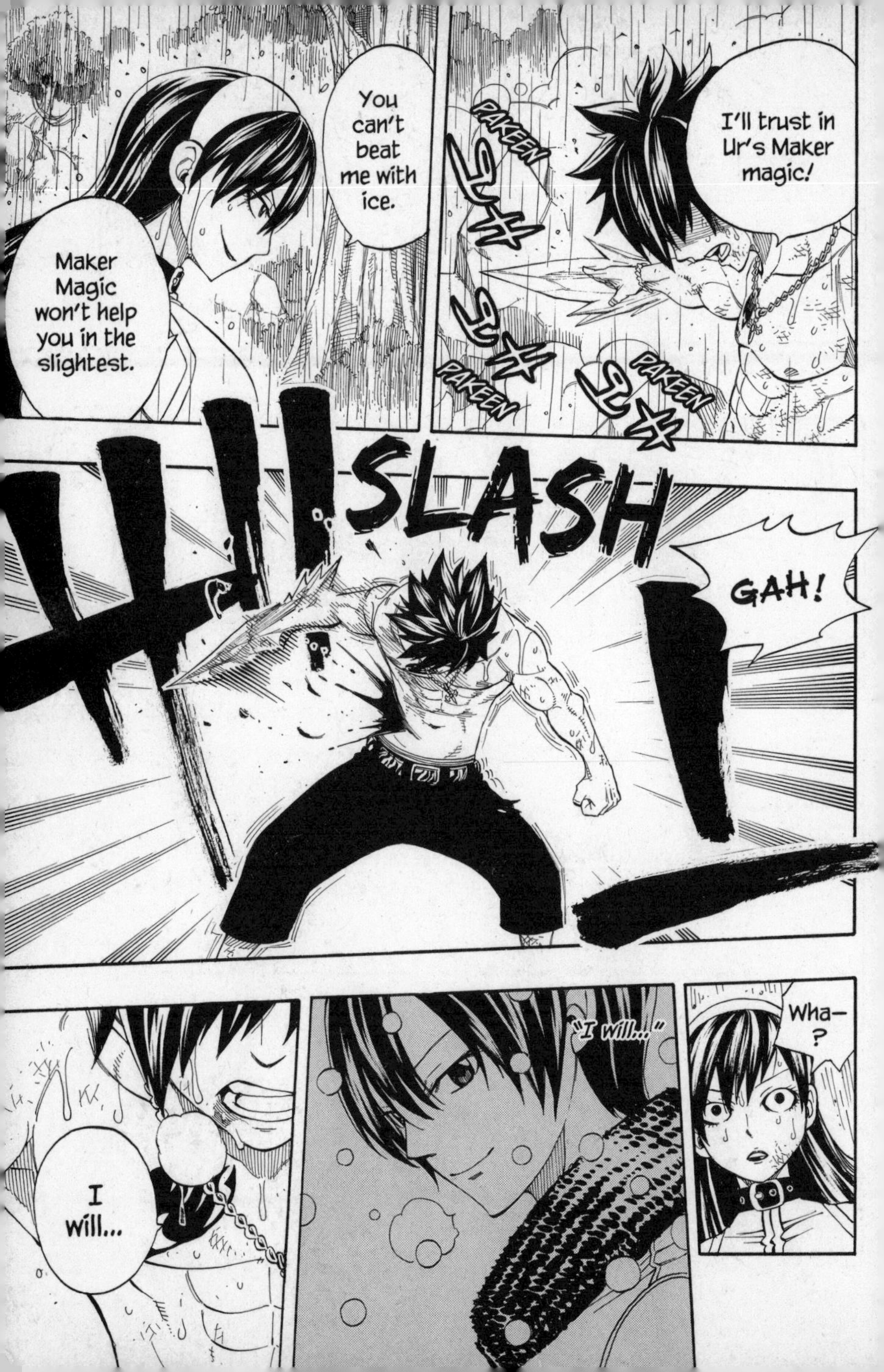
I'll trust in Ur's Maker magic!
PAKEEN
PAKEEN
PAKEEN
You can't beat me with ice.
Maker Magic won't help you in the slightest.
SLASH
GAH!
Wha-?
"I will..."
I will...

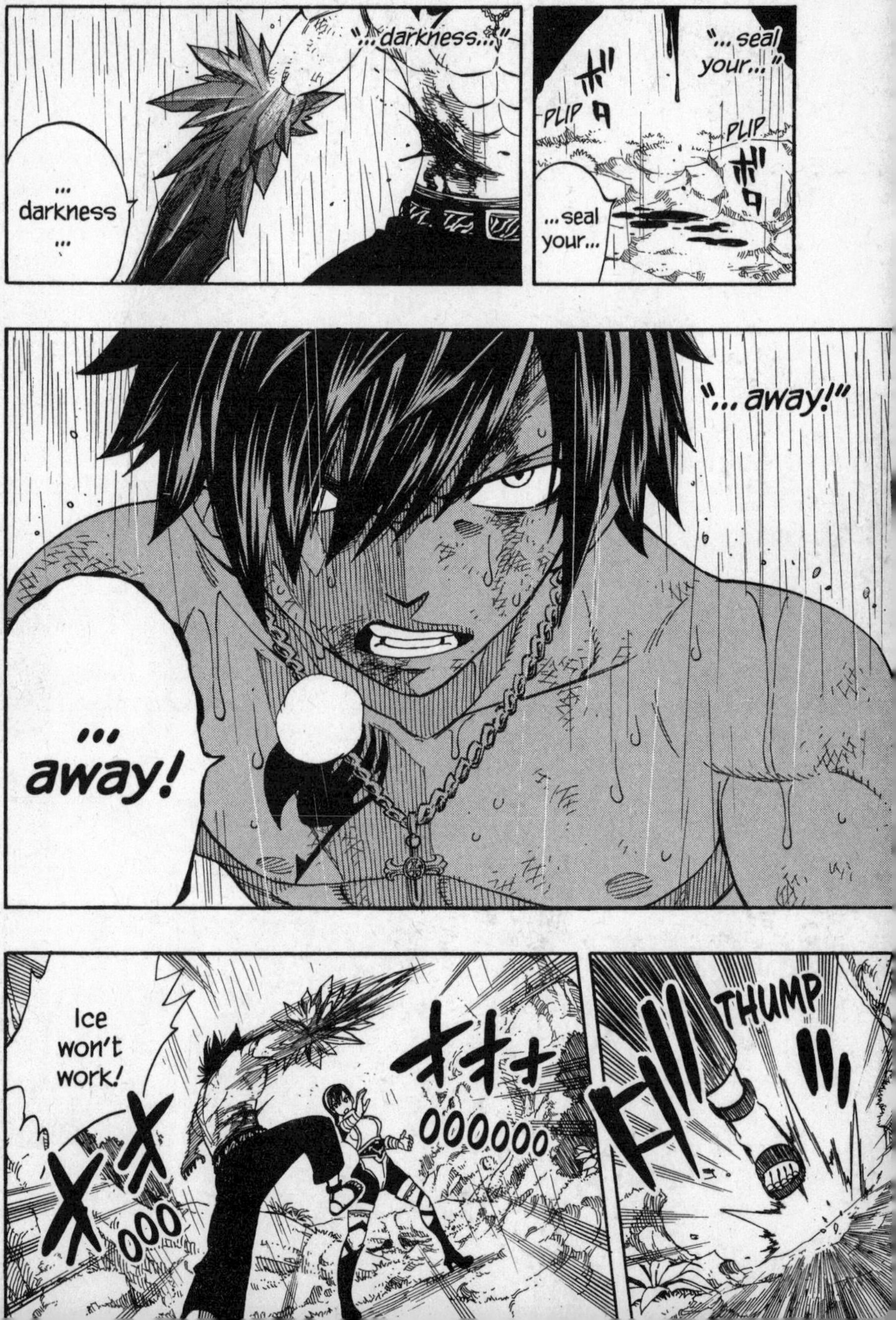
"... seal your..."
ボタ
PLIP
PLIP
ボタ
...seal your...
"...darkness..."
... darkness ...
"... away!"
... away!
THUMP
Ice won't work!
OOOOOO
OOO

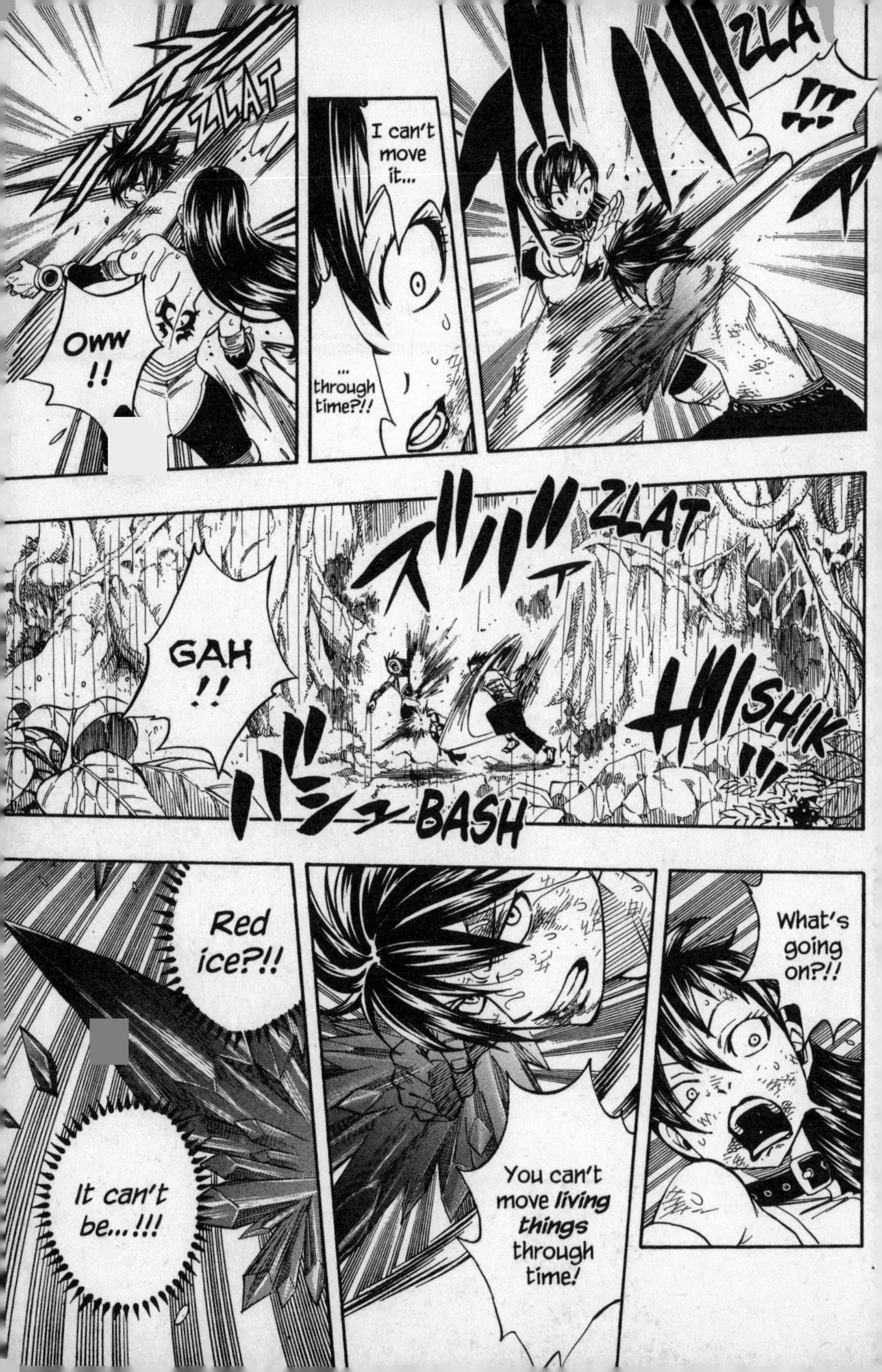
ZLA !!!
I can't move it...
... through time?!!
ZLAT
OWW !!
ZLAT
SHIK !!
GAH !!
BASH
What's going on?!!
You can't move *living things* through time!
Red ice?!!
It can't be...!!!

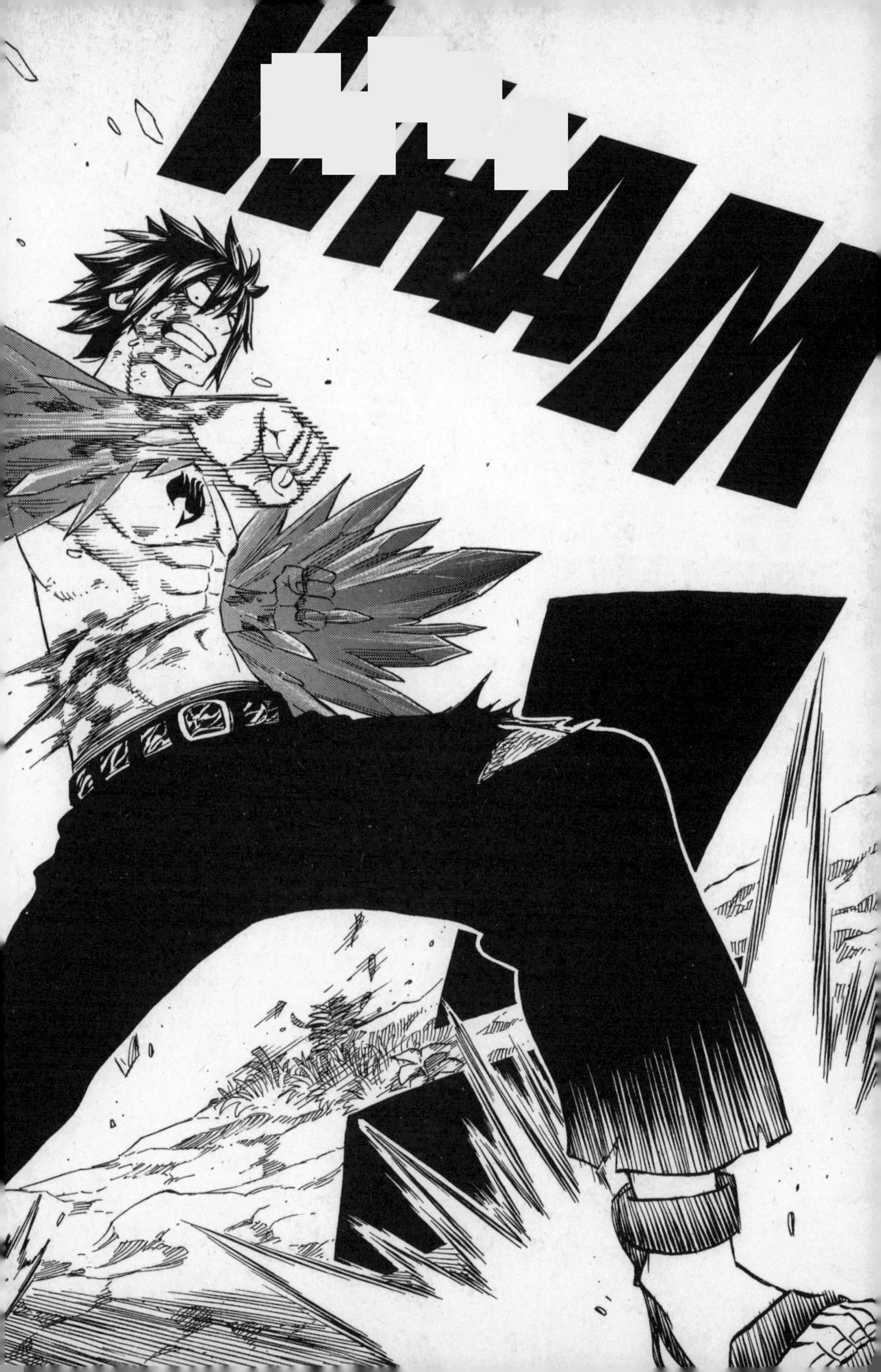

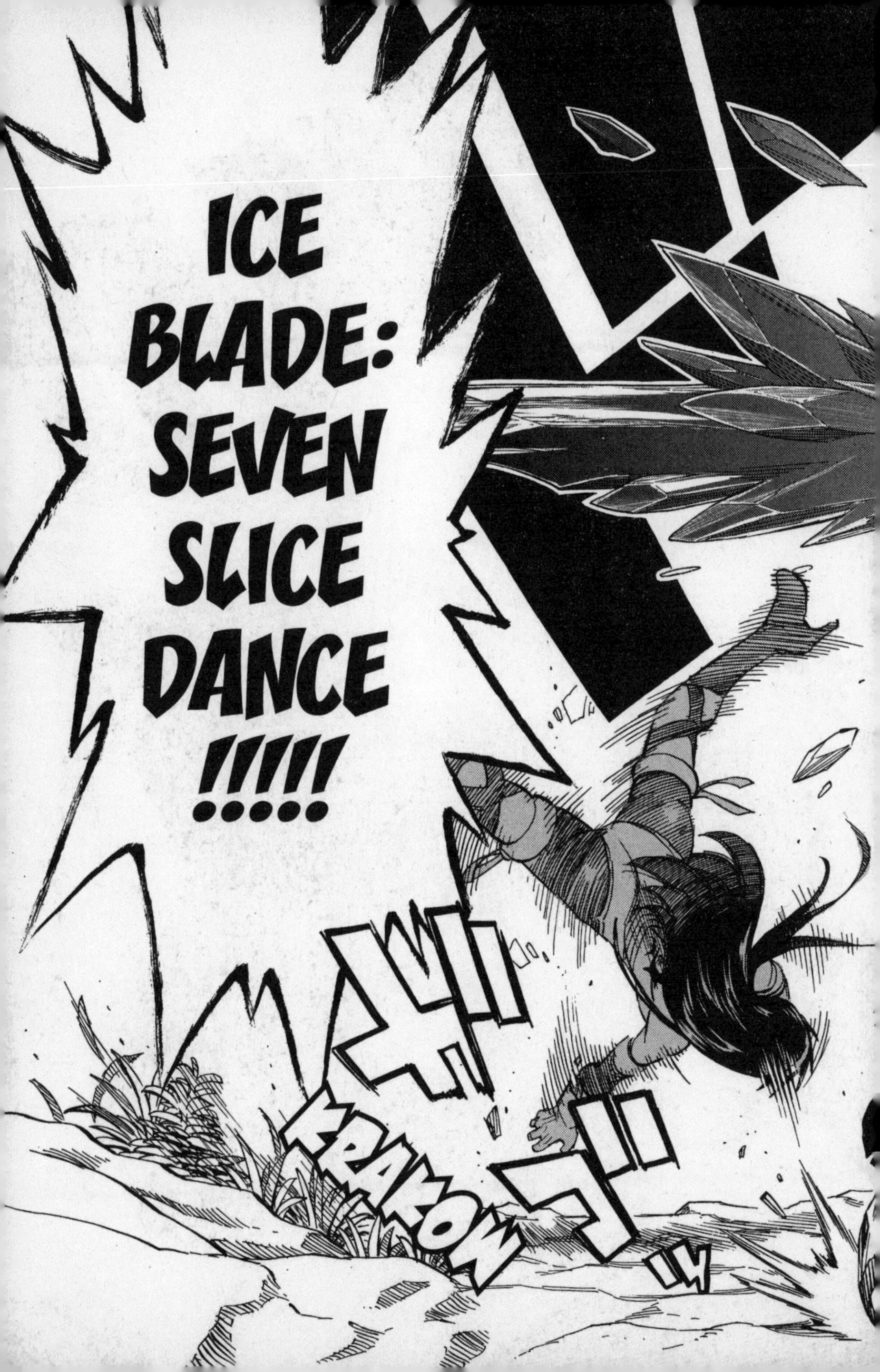
ICE BLADE: SEVEN SLICE DANCE !!!!!
KRAKOW

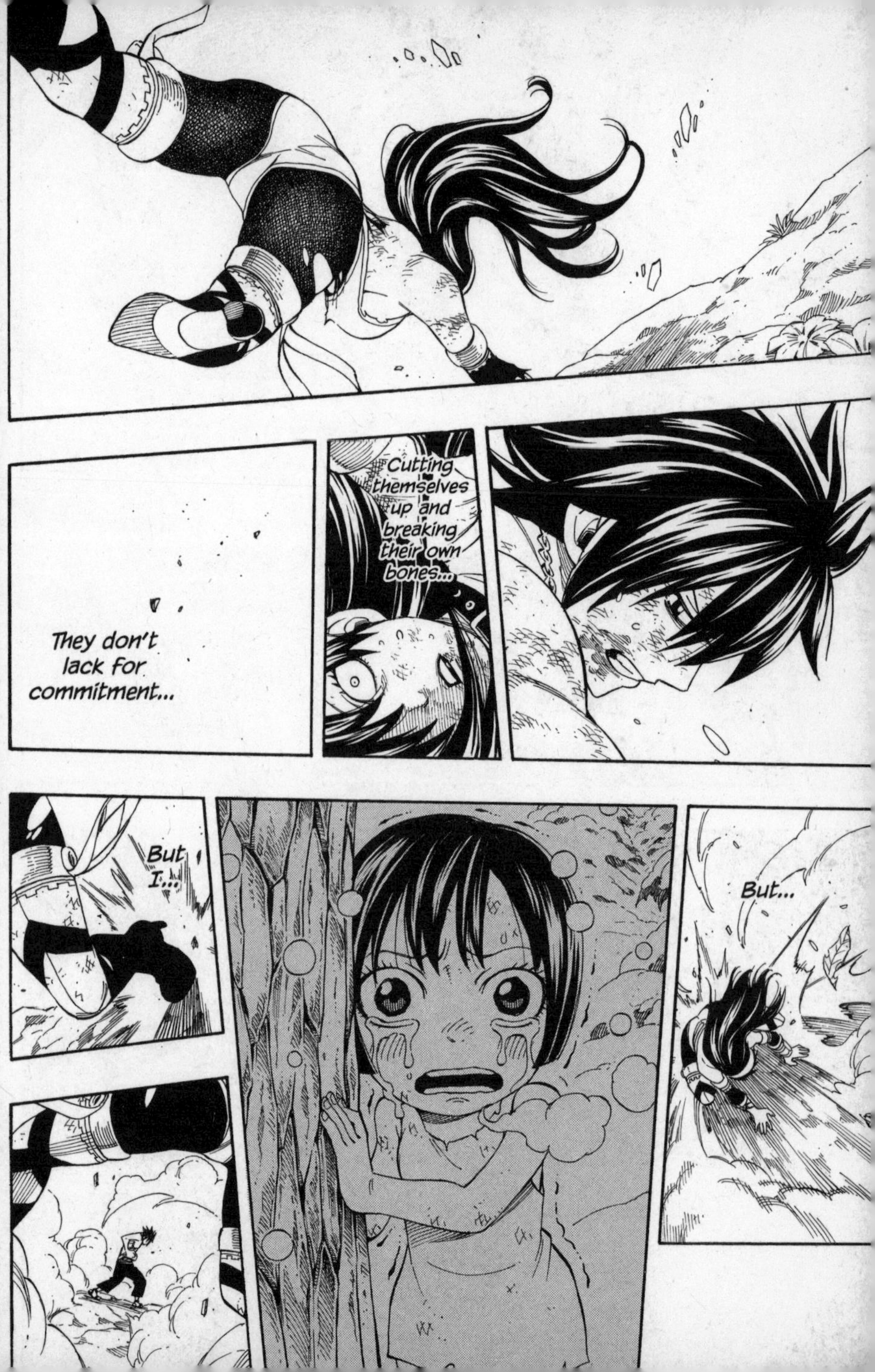
Cutting themselves up and breaking their own bones...
They don't lack for commitment...
But...
But I...

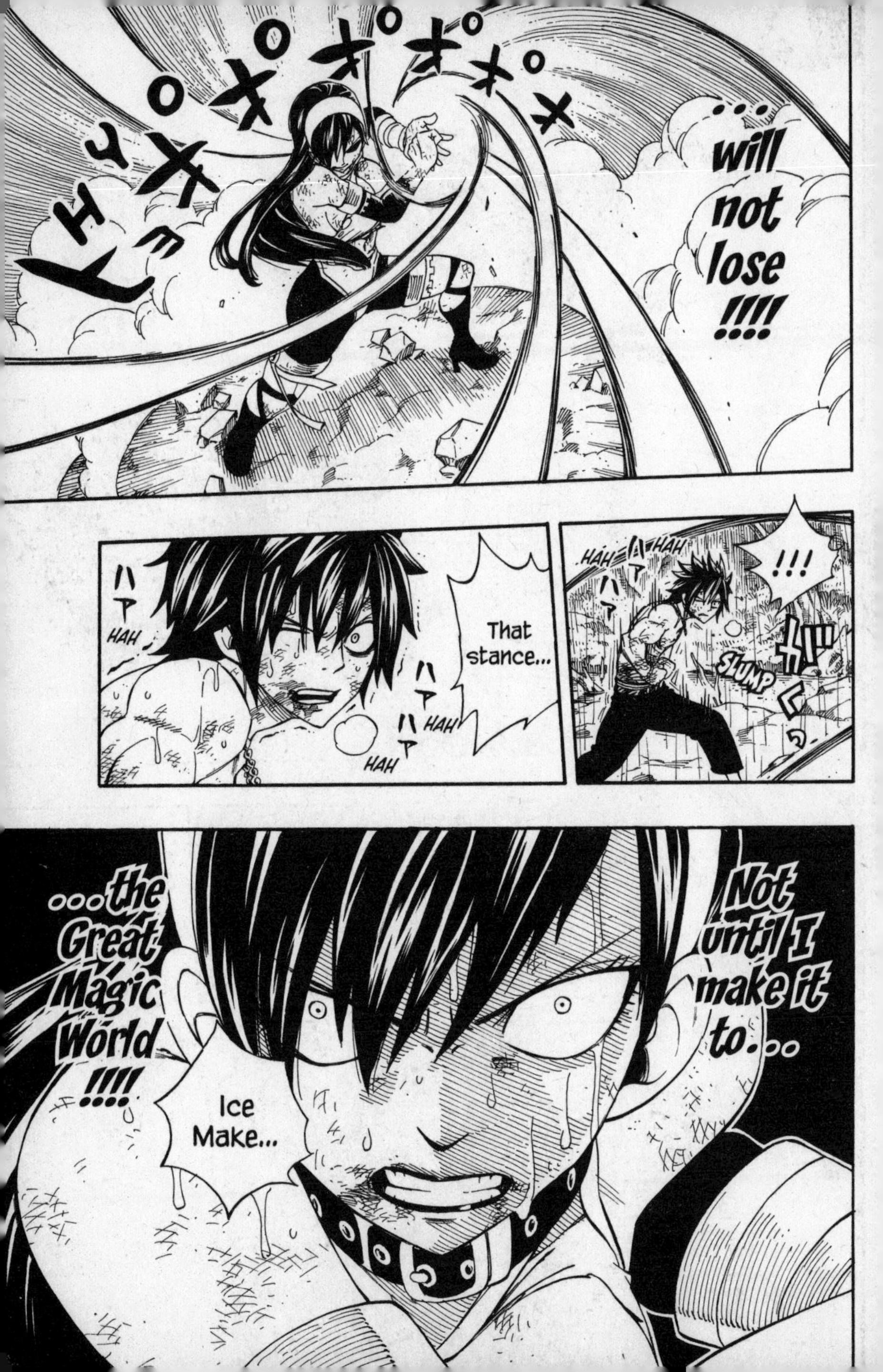
...will not lose!!!!
!!!
HAH HAH
ハァ
SLUMP
That stance...
ハァ
HAH
ハァ
HAH
ハァ
HAH
Not until I make it to...
...the Great Magic World!!!!
Ice Make...

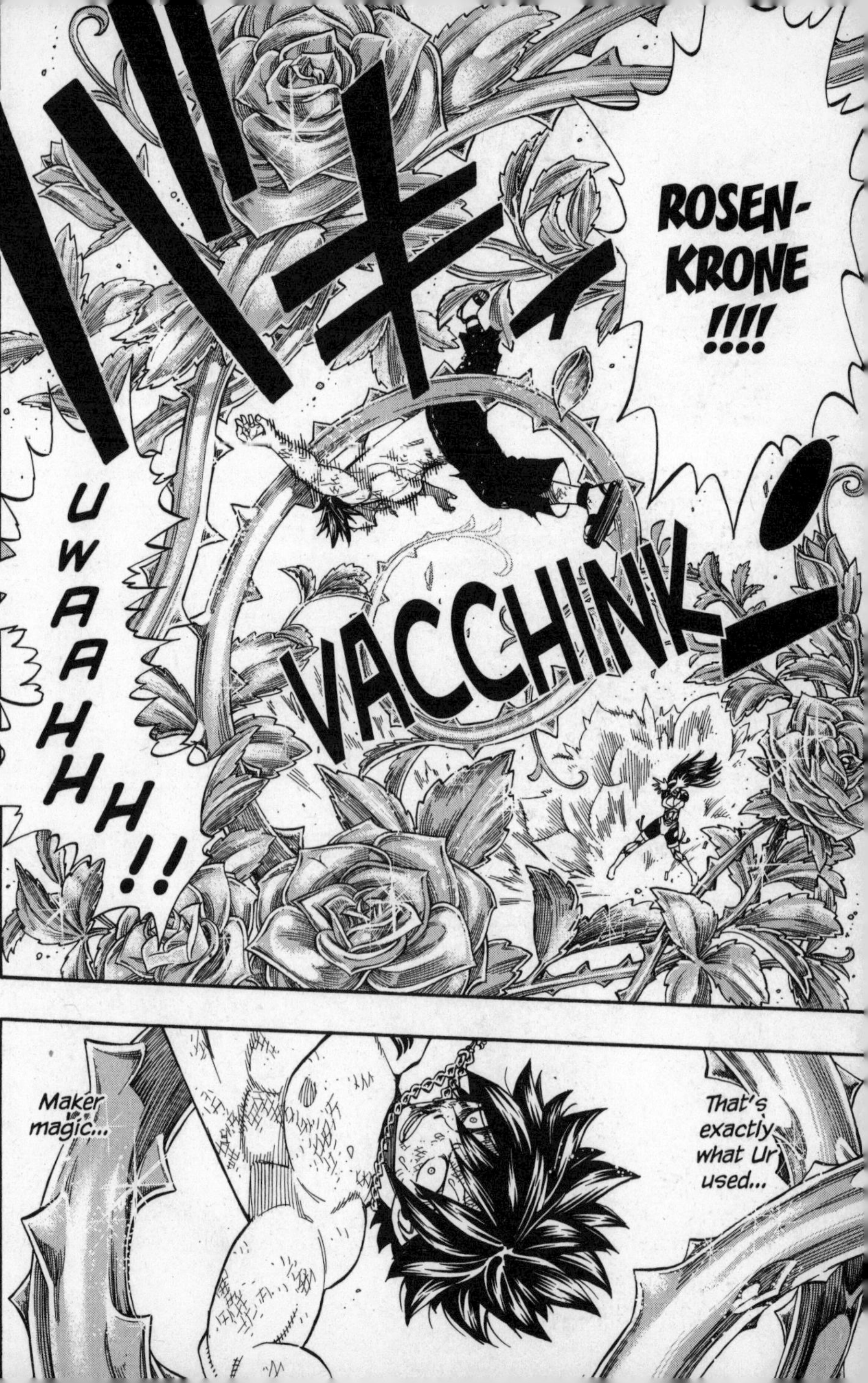
ROSEN-KRONE !!!!
VACCHINK
UWAAAHHH!!
That's exactly what Ur used...
Maker magic...

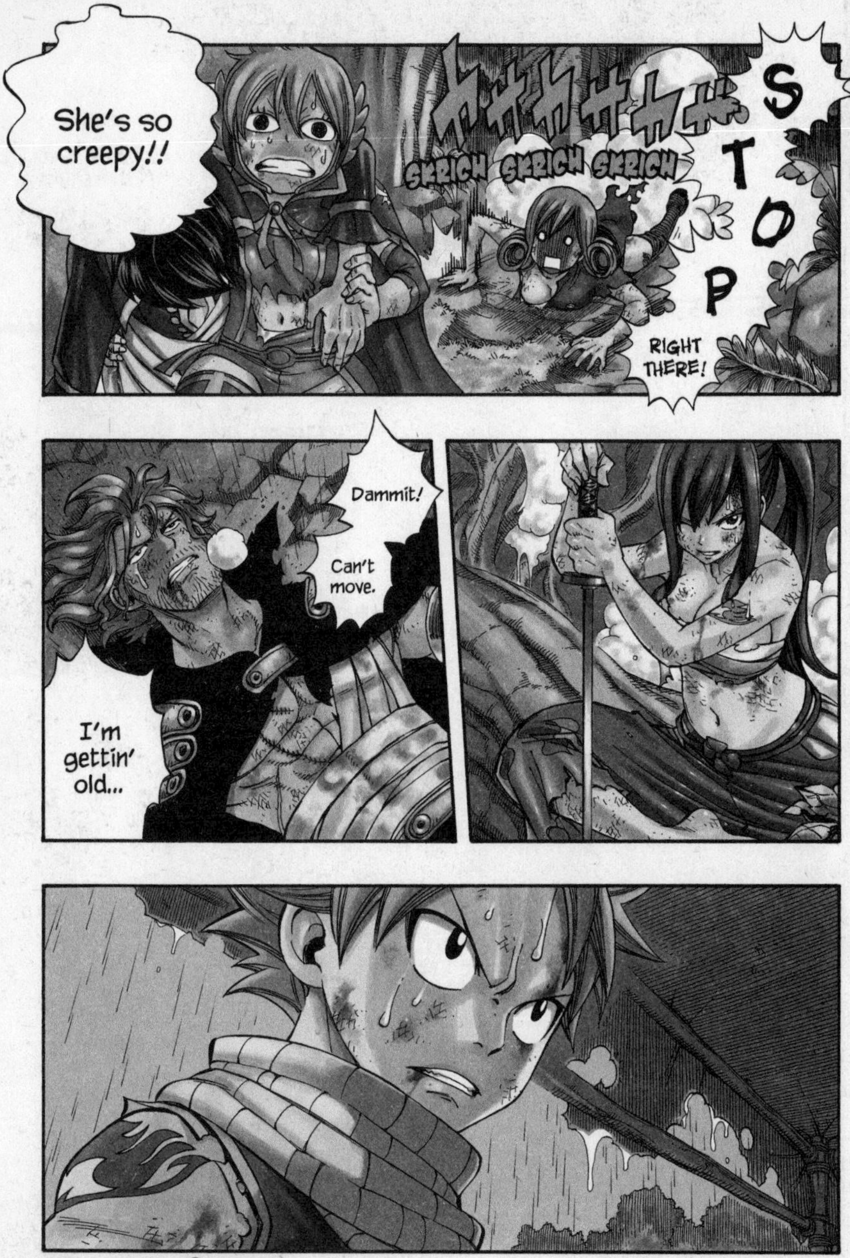
STOP
RIGHT THERE!
SKRICH SKRICH SKRICH
She's so creepy!!
Dammit!
Can't move.
I'm gettin' old...

FAIRY TAIL

Chapter 241: The Power of "Life"

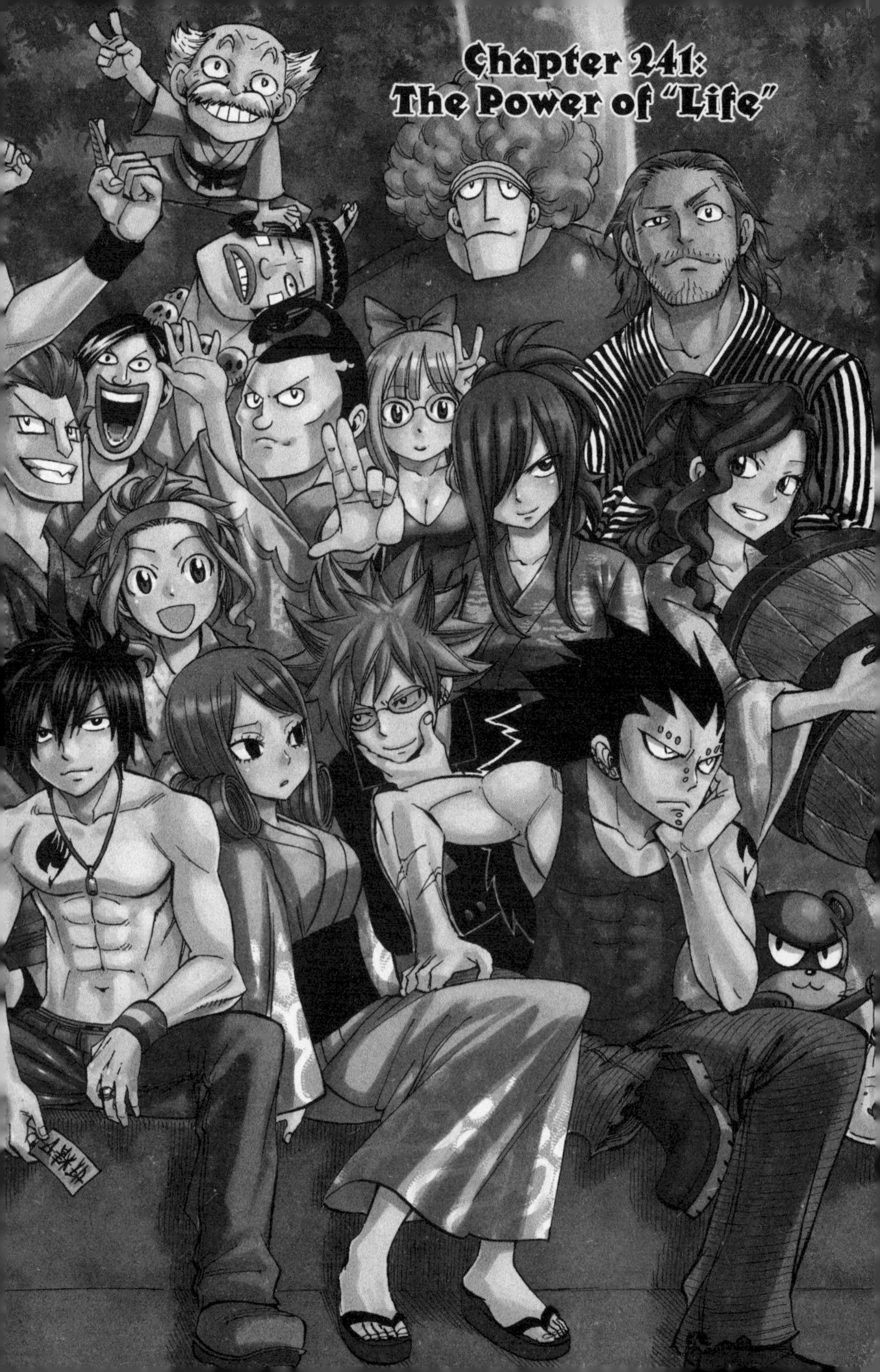

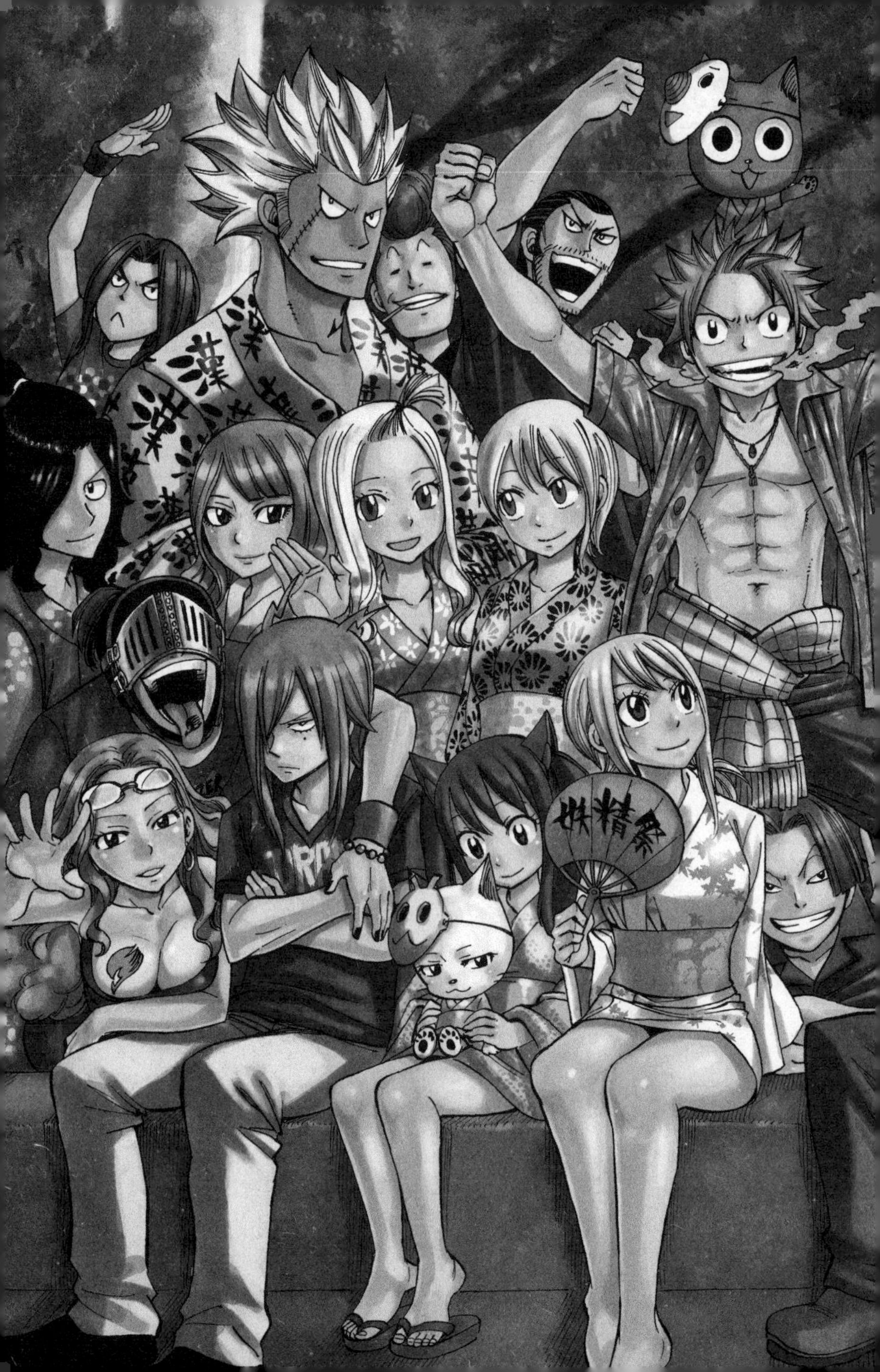
妖精祭

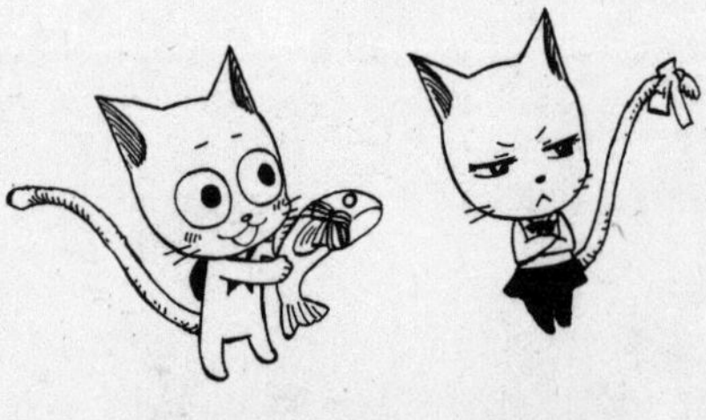

FAIRY TAIL

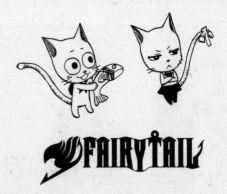

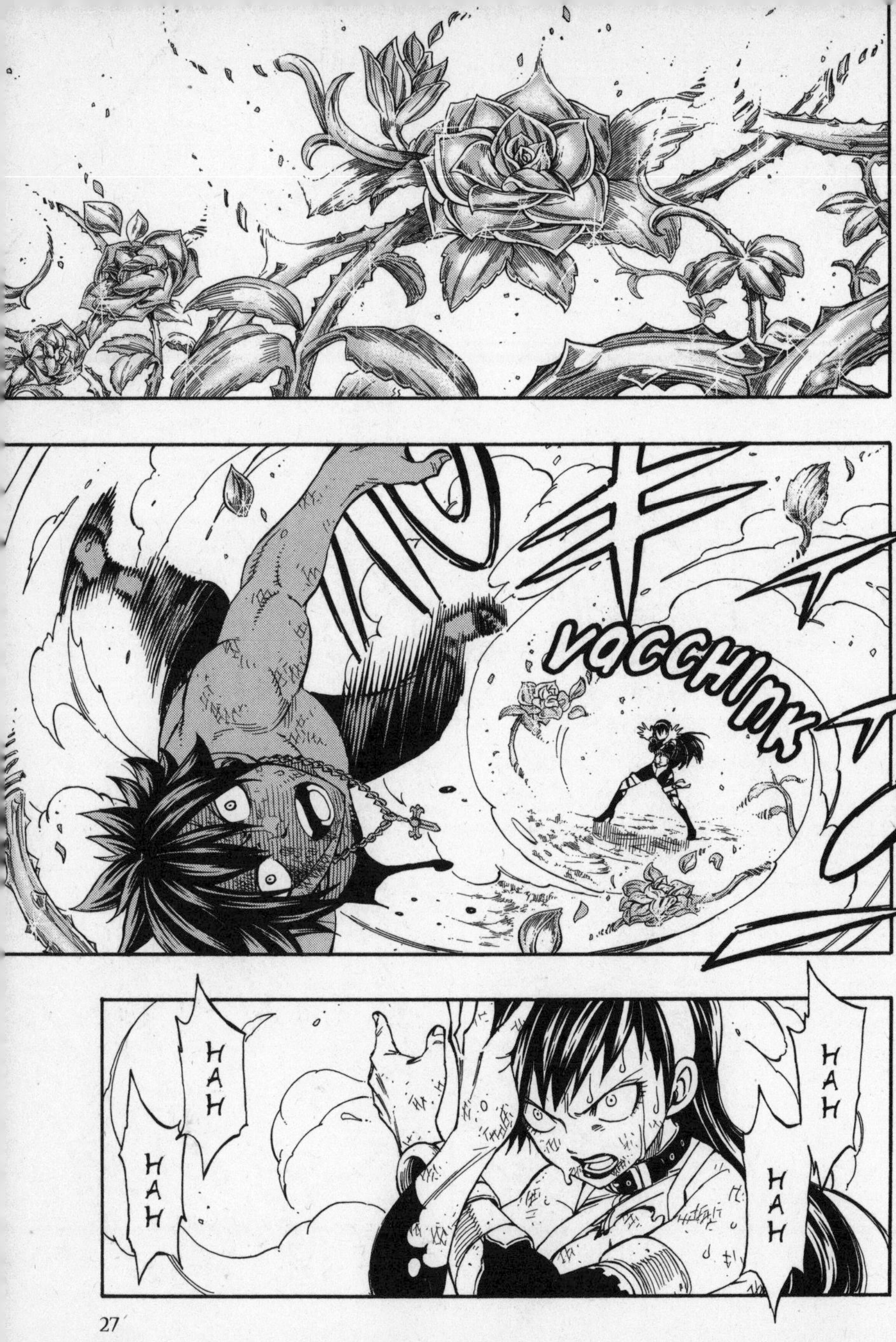
VACCHINK
HAH HAH
HAH HAH

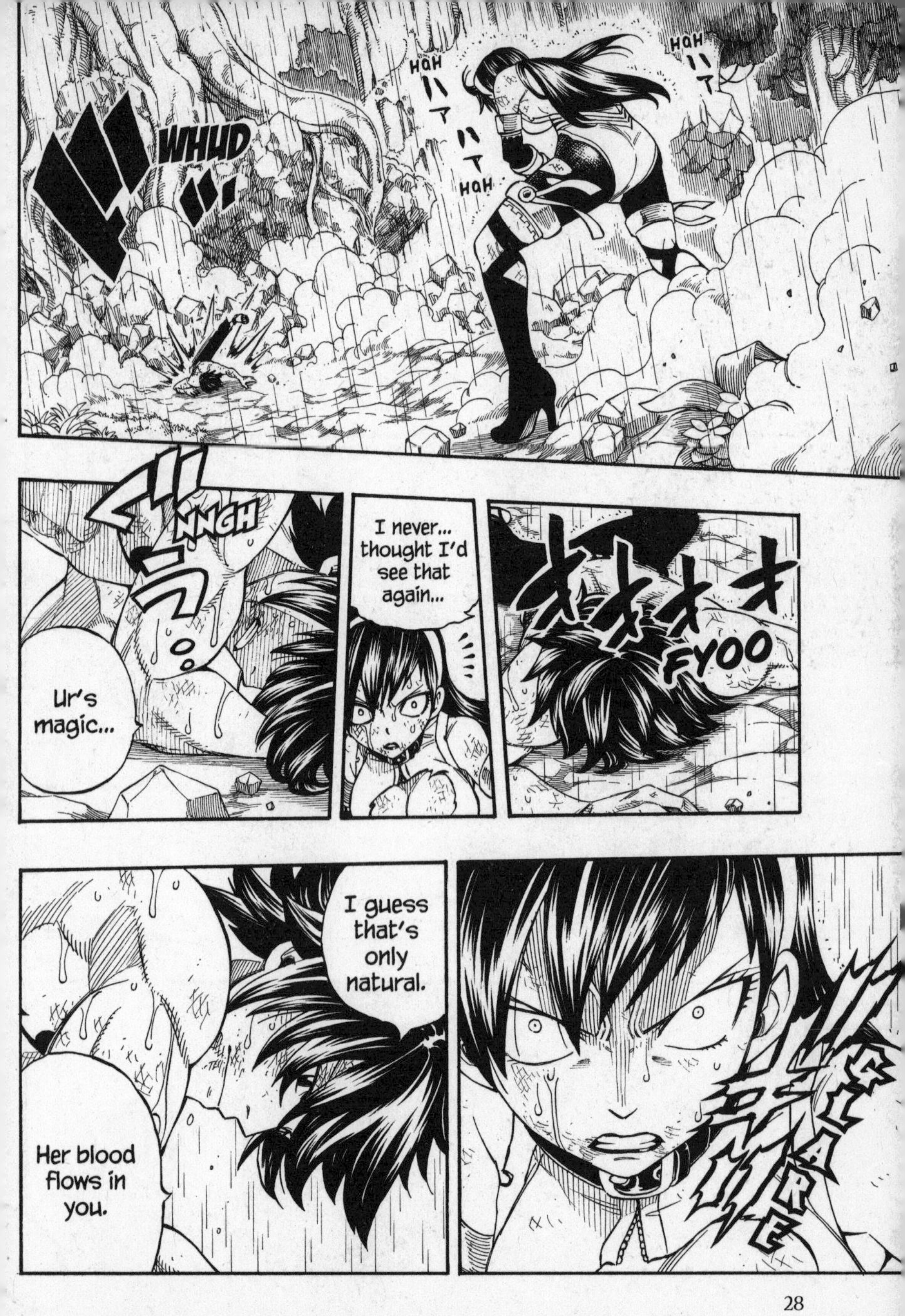

HAH
ハァ
HAH
ハァ
ハァ
HAH
WHUD
オォォォ
FYOO
I never... thought I'd see that again...
NNGH
Ur's magic...
GLARE
I guess that's only natural.
Her blood flows in you.

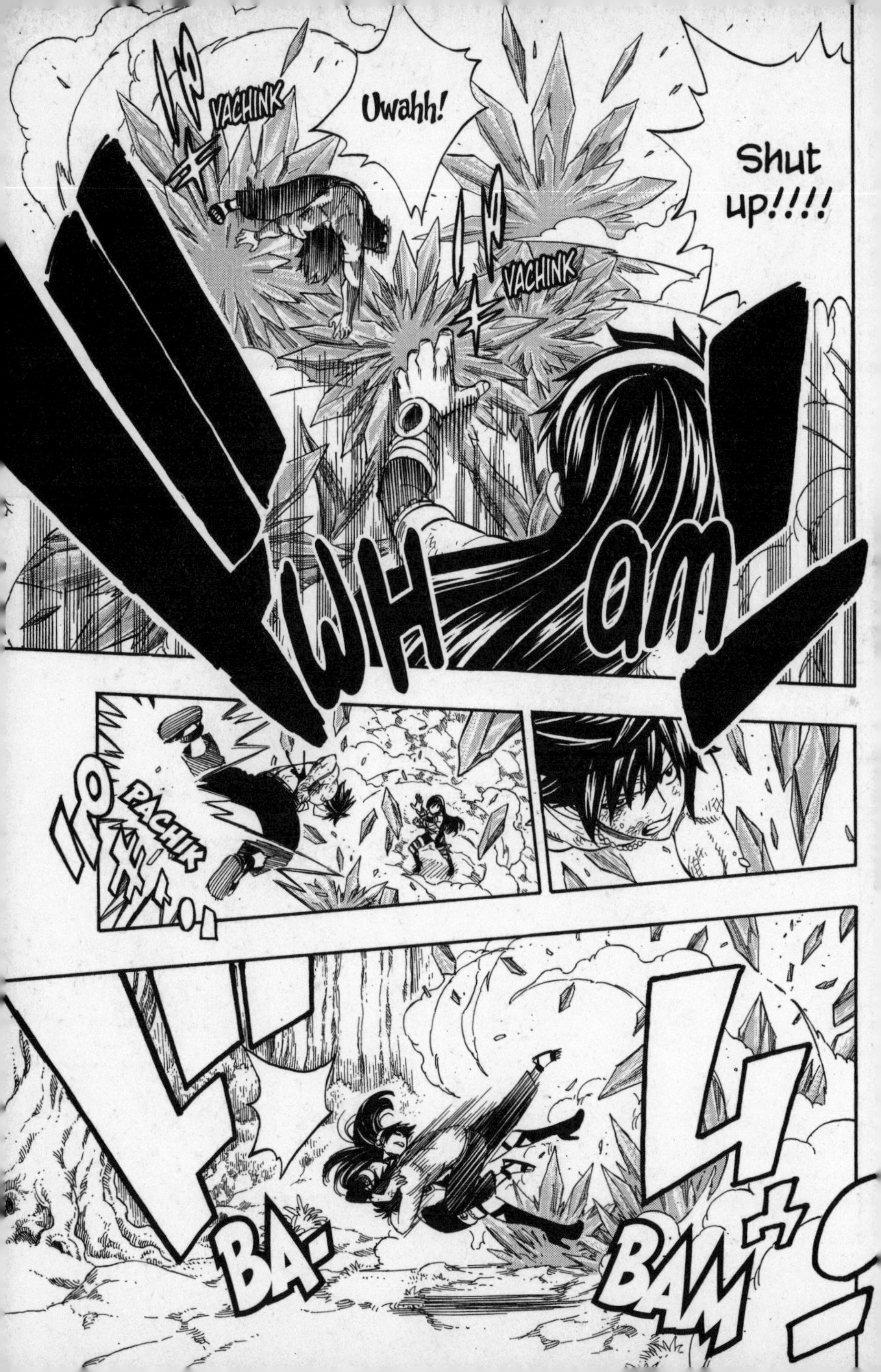
Shut up!!!!
VACHINK
Uwahh!
VACHINK
WHAM
PACHIK
BA-BAM

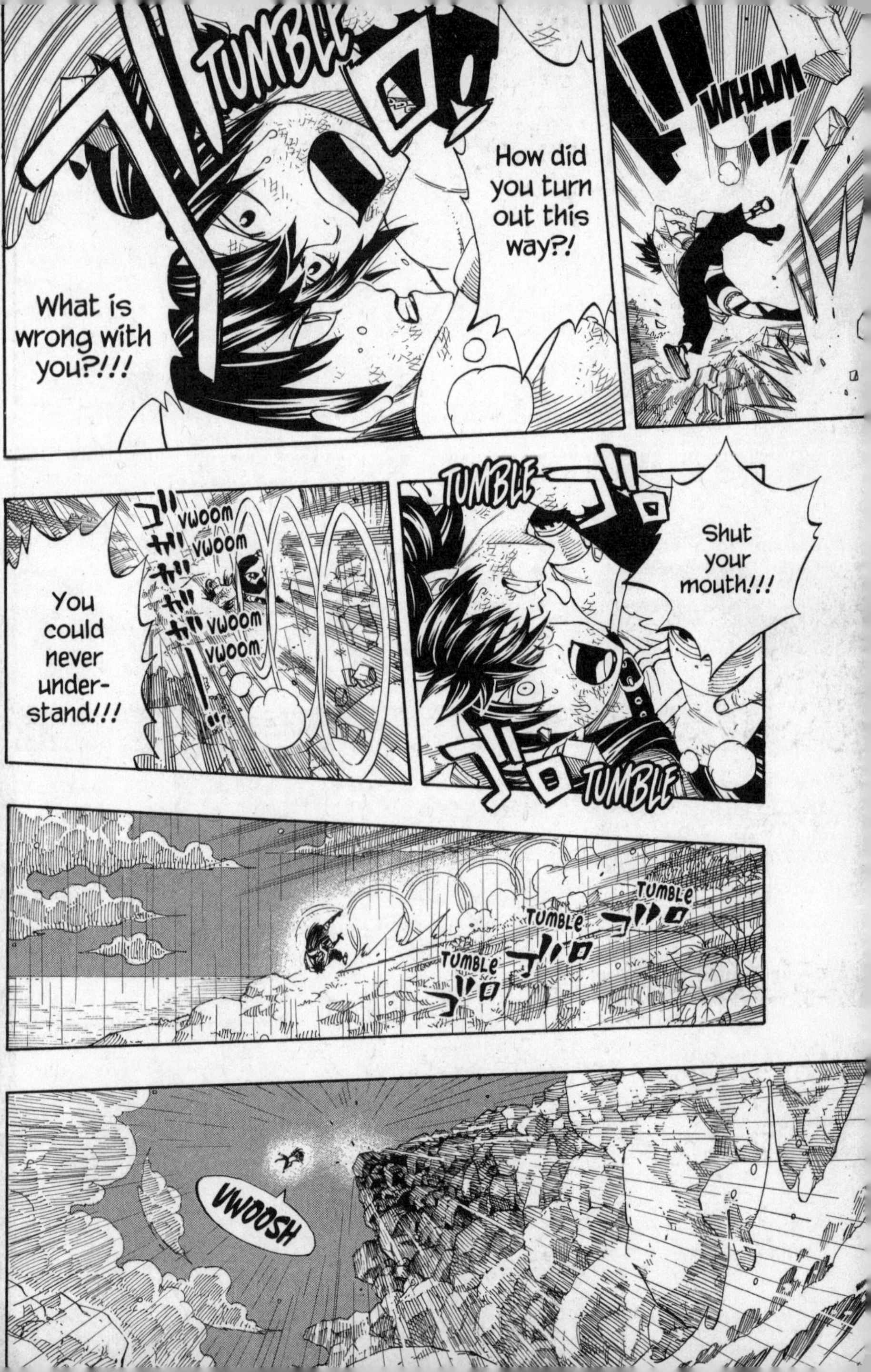

WHAM
TUMBLE
How did you turn out this way?!
What is wrong with you?!!!
TUMBLE
Shut your mouth!!!
TUMBLE
VWOOM
VWOOM
You could never under-stand!!!
VWOOM
VWOOM
TUMBLE
TUMBLE
TUMBLE
VWOOSH

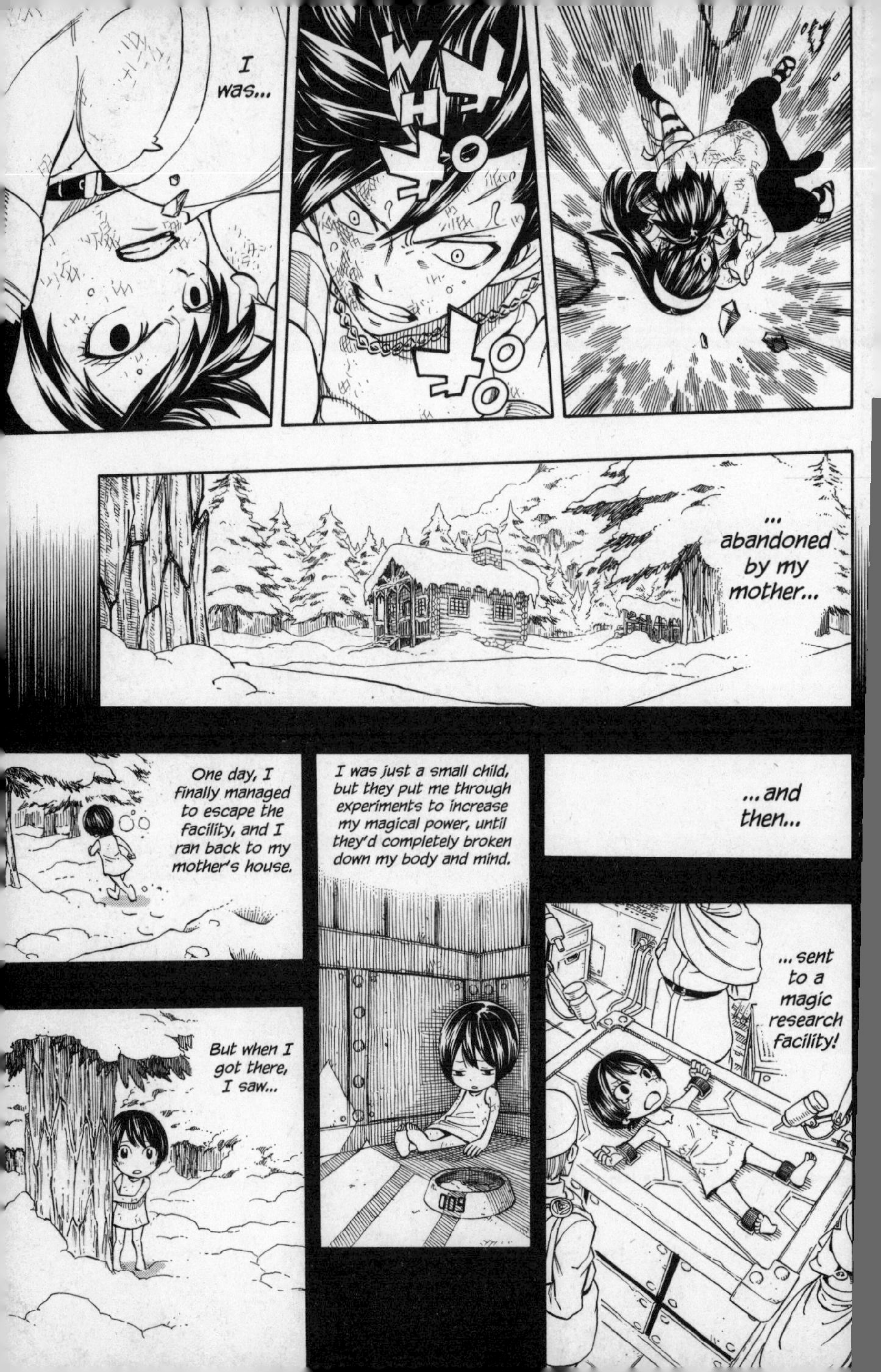
I was...
... abandoned by my mother...
...and then...
...sent to a magic research facility!
I was just a small child, but they put me through experiments to increase my magical power, until they'd completely broken down my body and mind.
One day, I finally managed to escape the facility, and I ran back to my mother's house.
But when I got there, I saw...

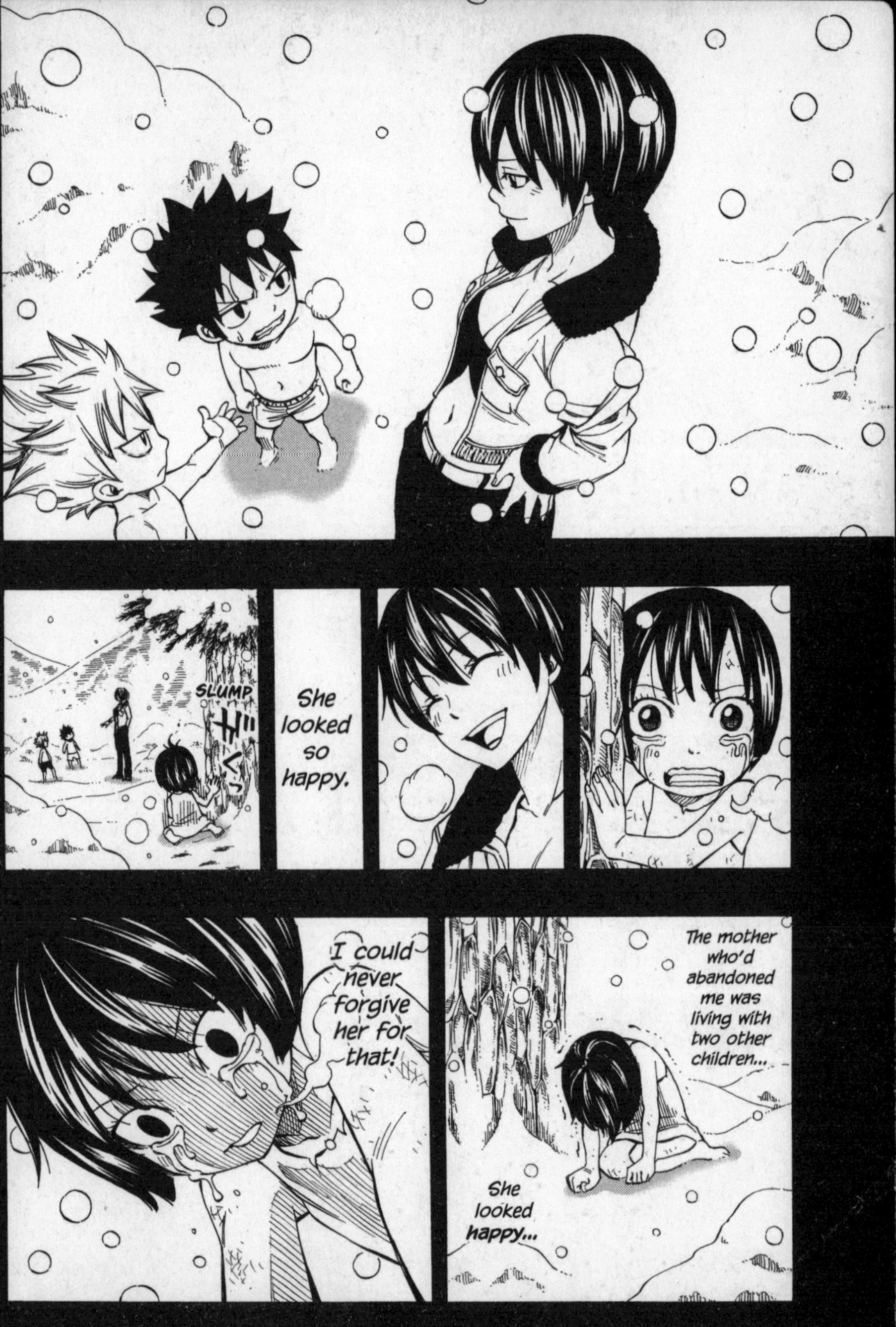
She looked so happy.
SLUMP
The mother who'd abandoned me was living with two other children...
She looked happy...
I could never forgive her for that!

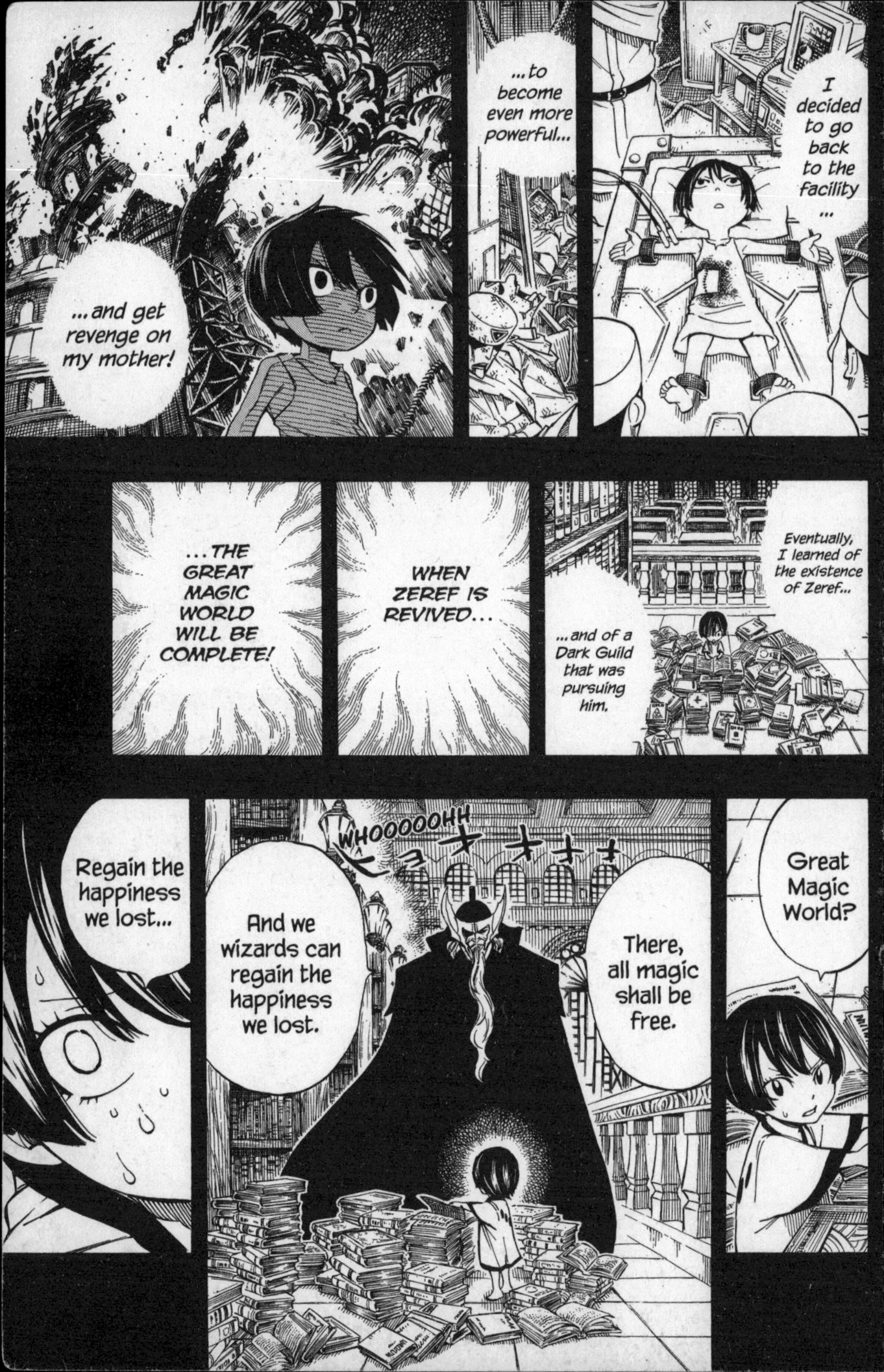
I decided to go back to the facility ...
...to become even more powerful...
...and get revenge on my mother!
Eventually, I learned of the existence of Zeref...
...and of a Dark Guild that was pursuing him.
WHEN ZEREF IS REVIVED...
...THE GREAT MAGIC WORLD WILL BE COMPLETE!
Great Magic World?
There, all magic shall be free.
WHOOOOOHH
And we wizards can regain the happiness we lost.
Regain the happiness we lost...

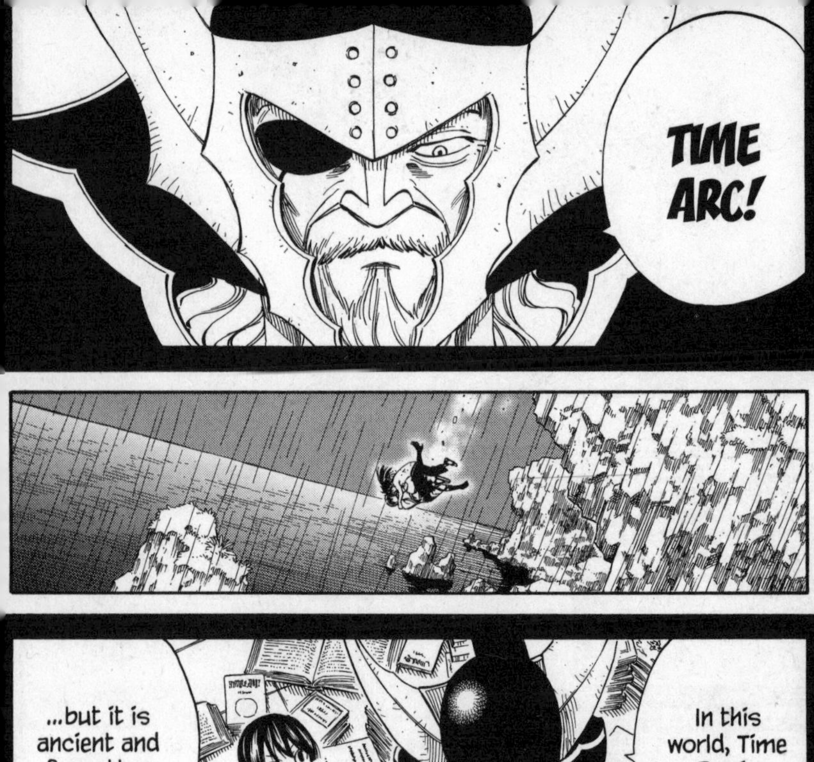
TIME ARC!
In this world, Time Arc is incomplete...
...but it is ancient and forgotten Lost Magic.
SPLOOSH

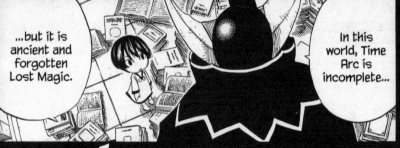

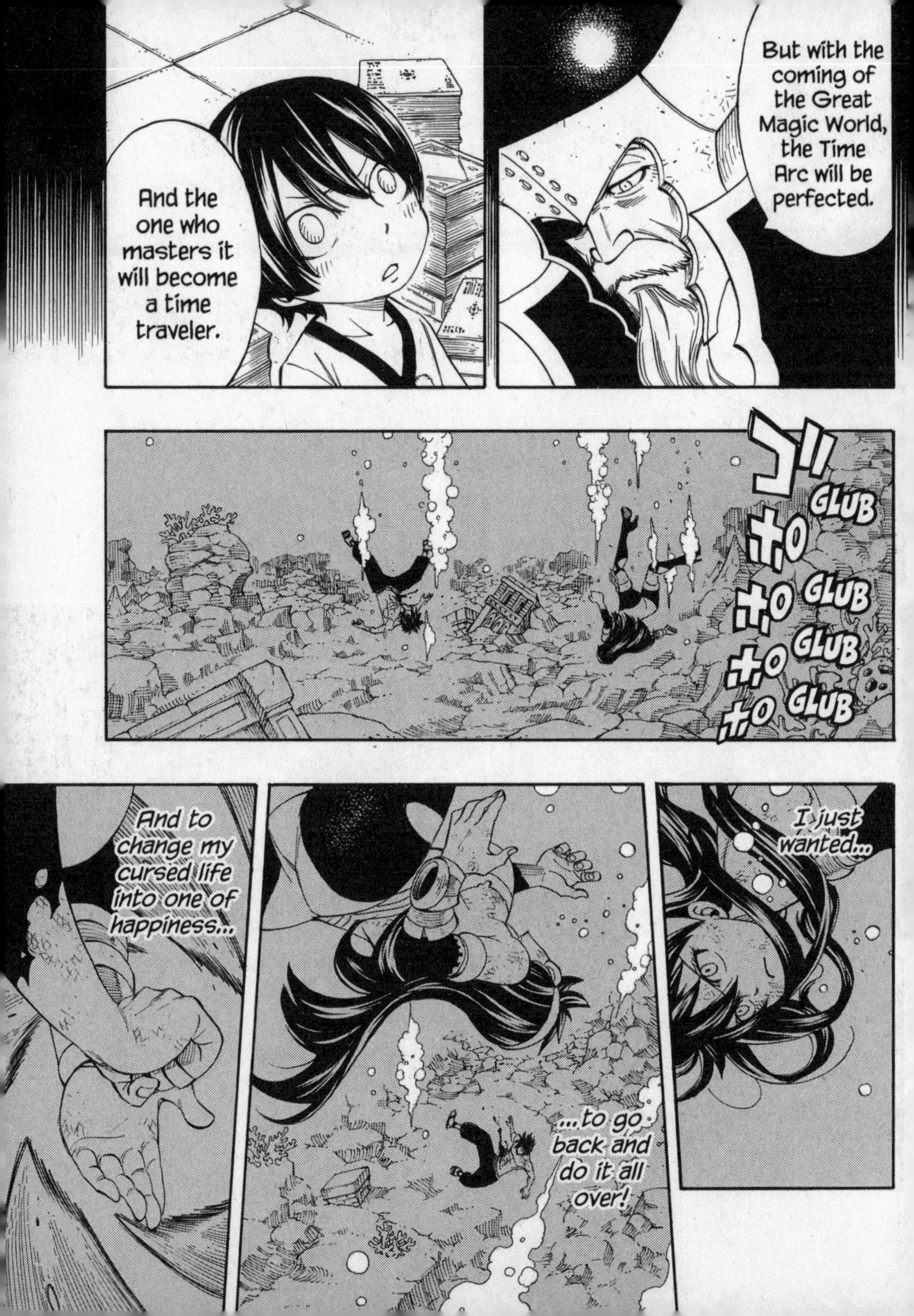
But with the coming of the Great Magic World, the Time Arc will be perfected.
And the one who masters it will become a time traveler.
GLUB
GLUB
GLUB
GLUB
I just wanted...
...to go back and do it all over!
And to change my cursed life into one of happiness...

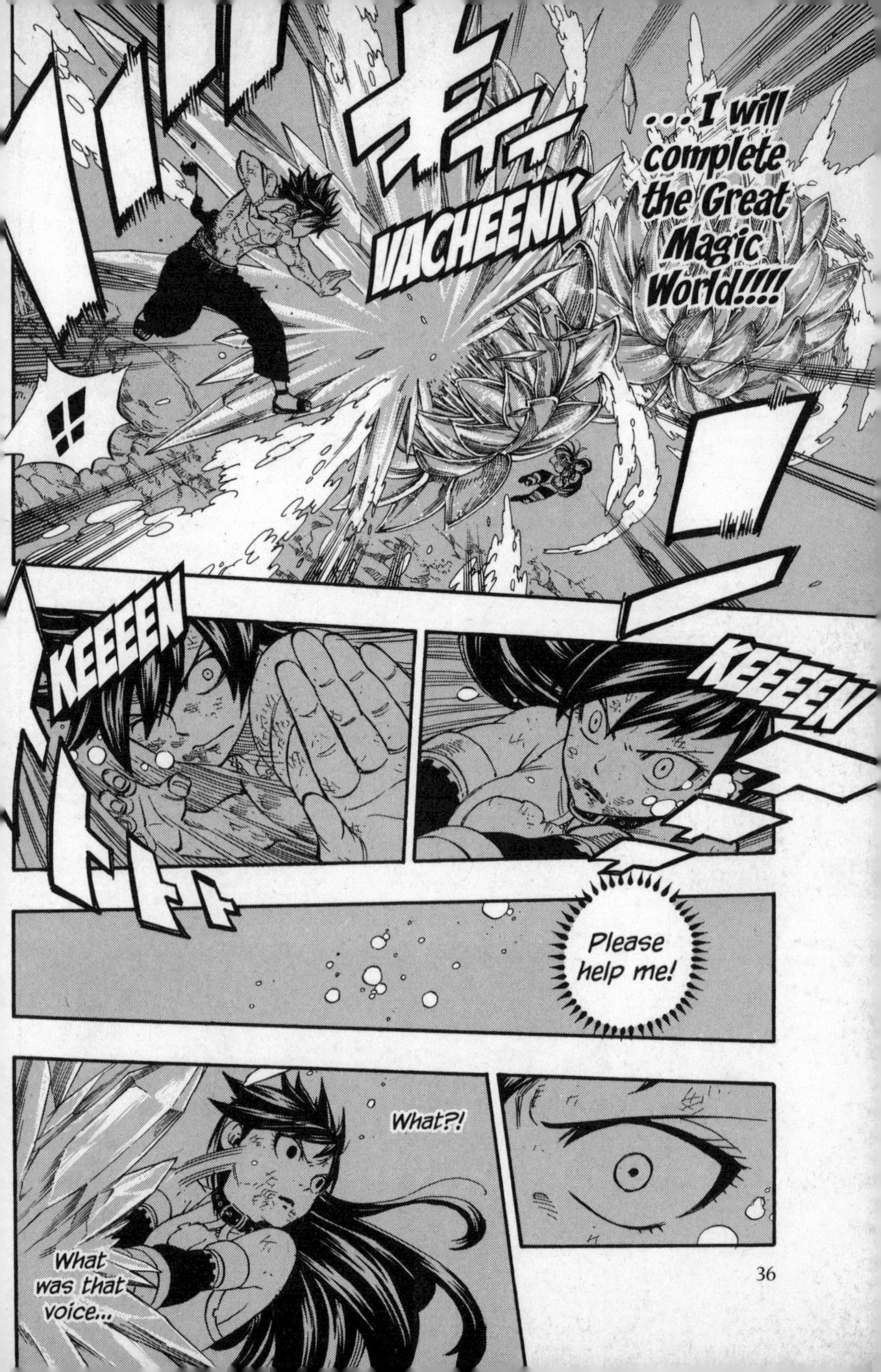
...I will complete the Great Magic World!!!!
VACHEENK
!!
KEEEEN
KEEEEN
Please help me!
What?!
What was that voice...

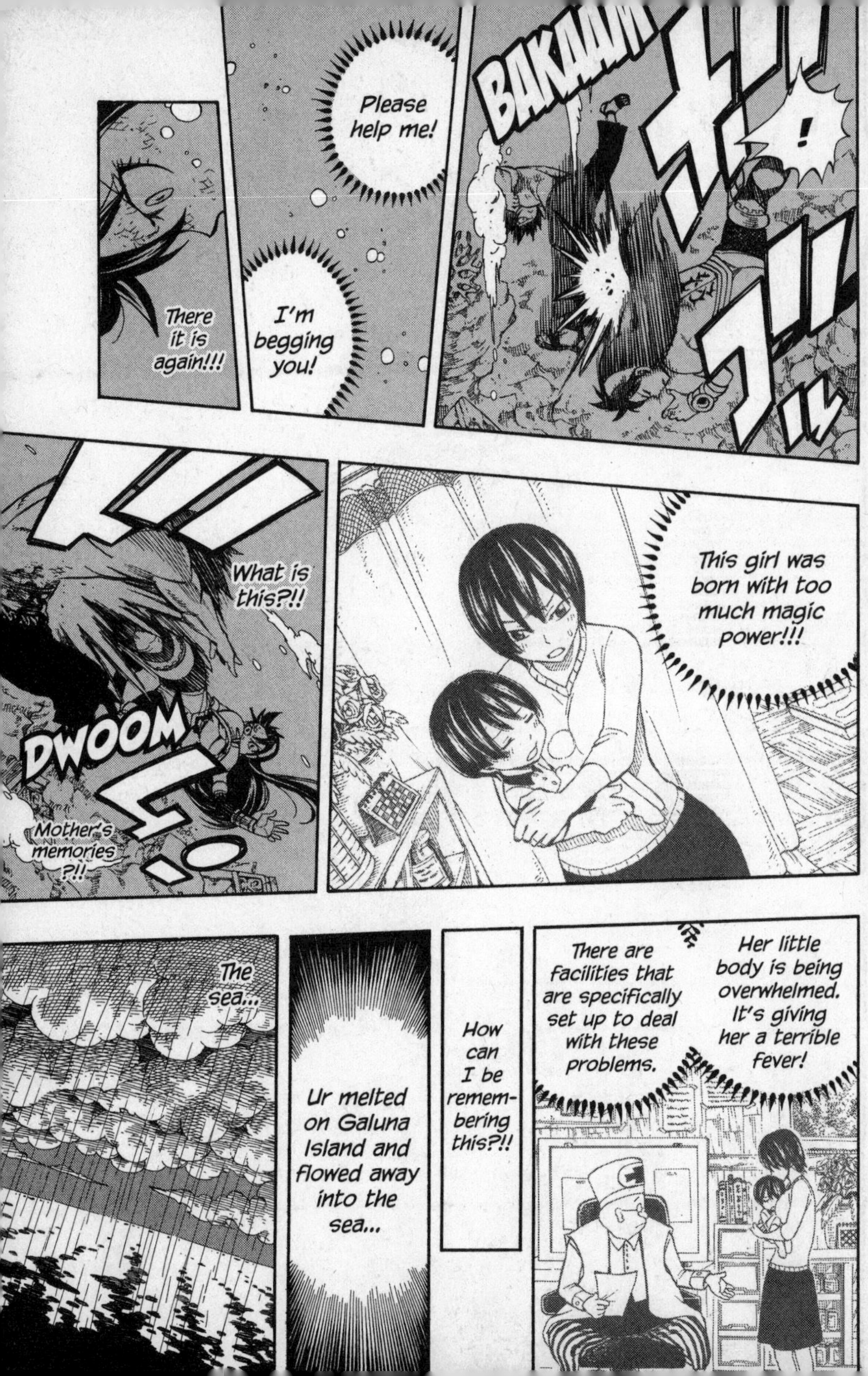
BAKAAM
!
Please help me!
I'm begging you!
There it is again!!!
This girl was born with too much magic power!!!
What is this?!!
DWOOM
Mother's memories ?!!
Her little body is being overwhelmed. It's giving her a terrible fever!
There are facilities that are specifically set up to deal with these problems.
How can I be remem-bering this?!!
Ur melted on Galuna Island and flowed away into the sea...
The sea...

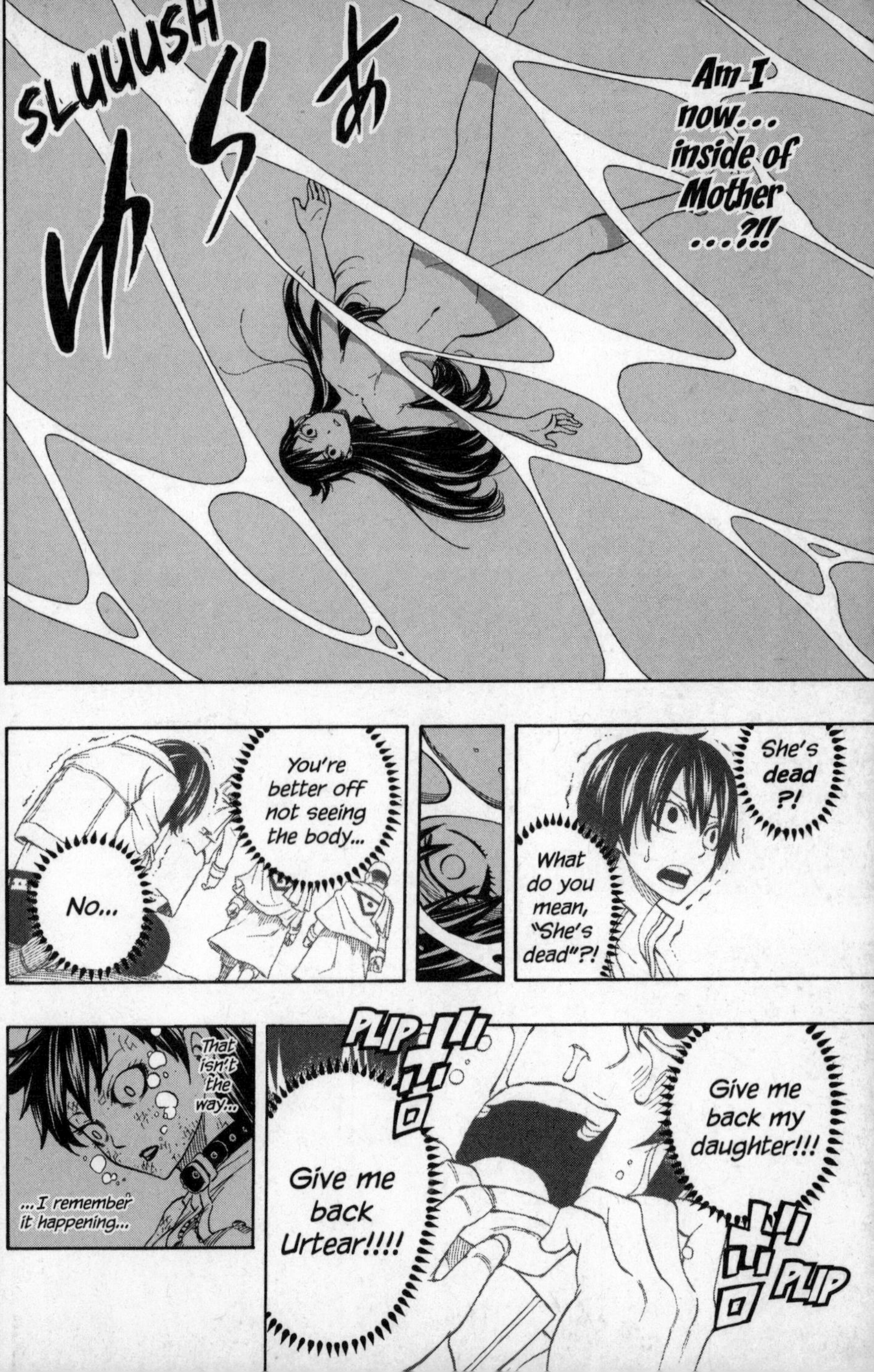
Am I now... inside of Mother ...?!!
SLUUUSH
ゆらあ
She's dead?!
What do you mean, "She's dead"?!
You're better off not seeing the body...
No...
PLIP
Give me back my daughter!!!
Give me back Urtear!!!!
PLIP
That isn't the way...
...I remember it happening...

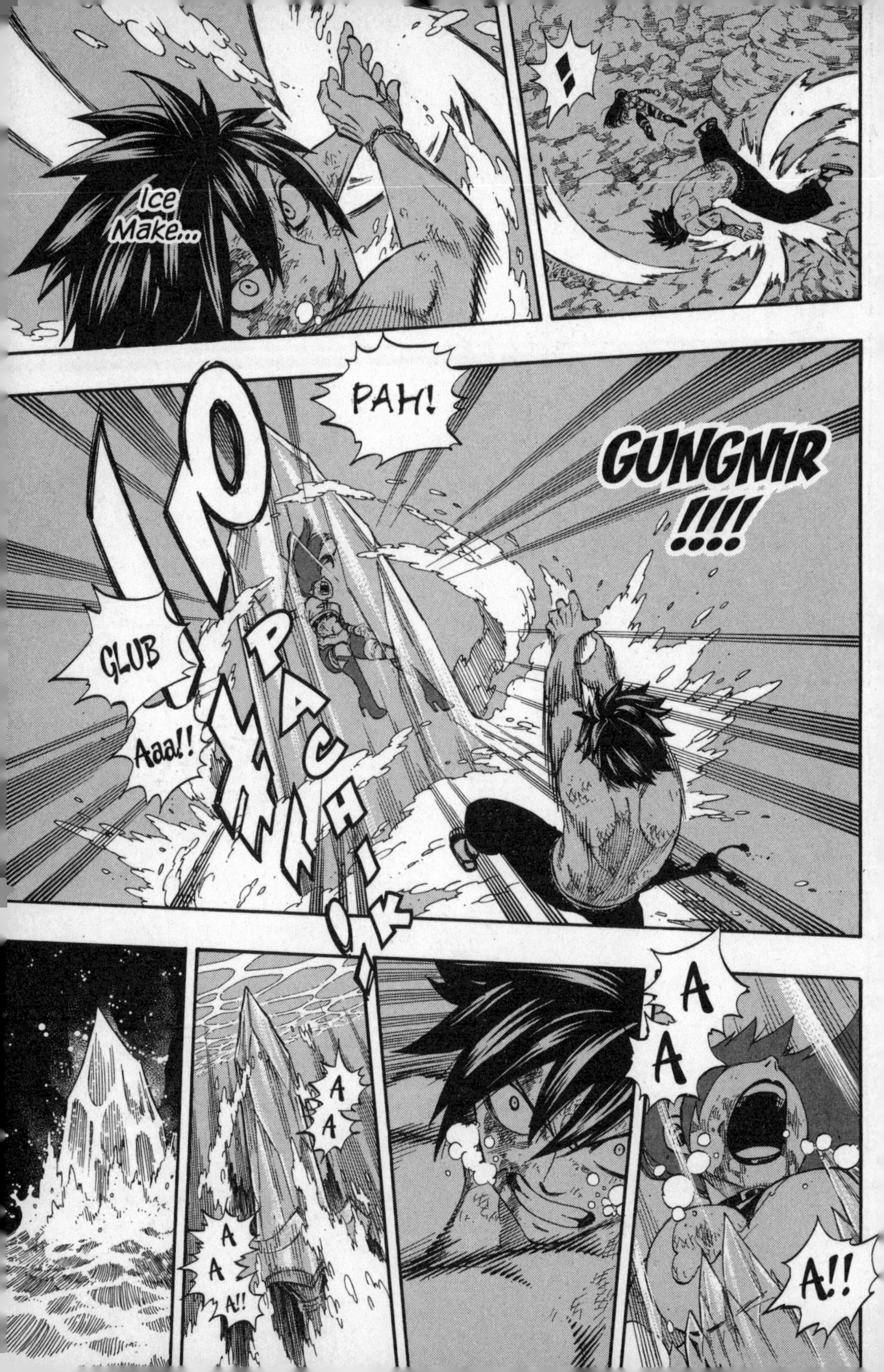
!
Ice Make...
GUNGNIR!!!!
PAH!
PACHIK!!
GLUB
Aaa!!
A
A
A!!
A
A
A
A
A!!

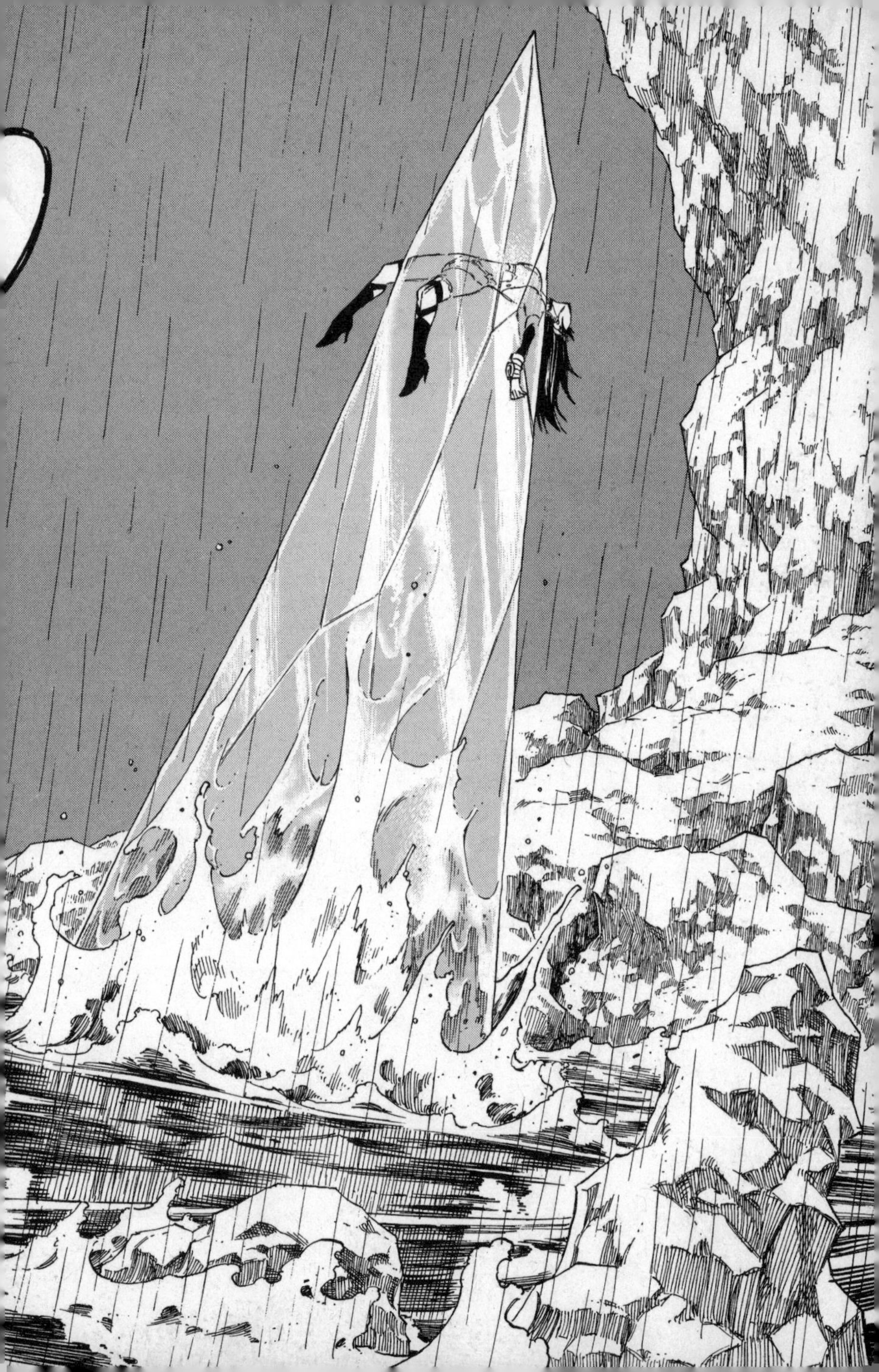

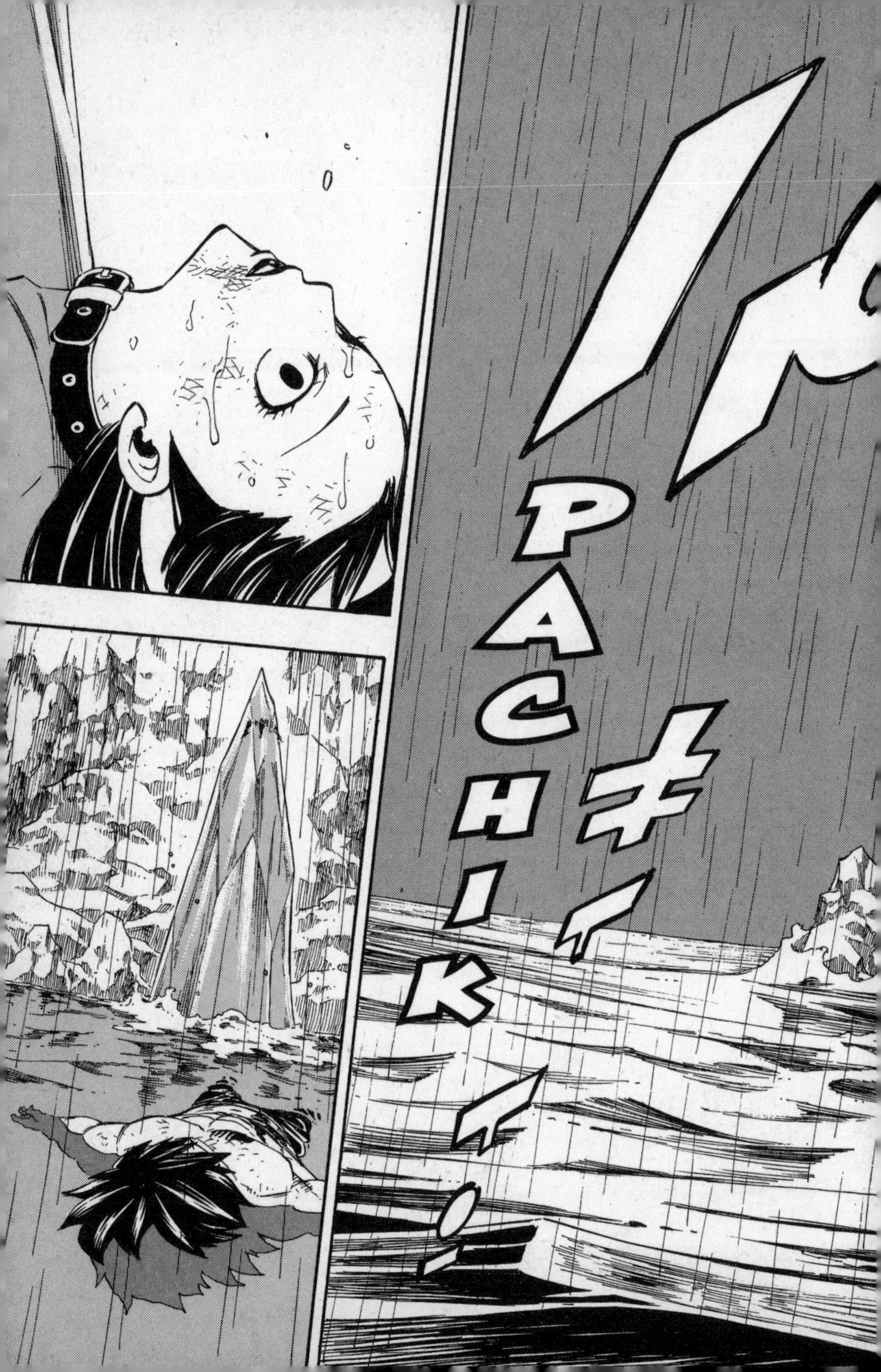
PACHIK

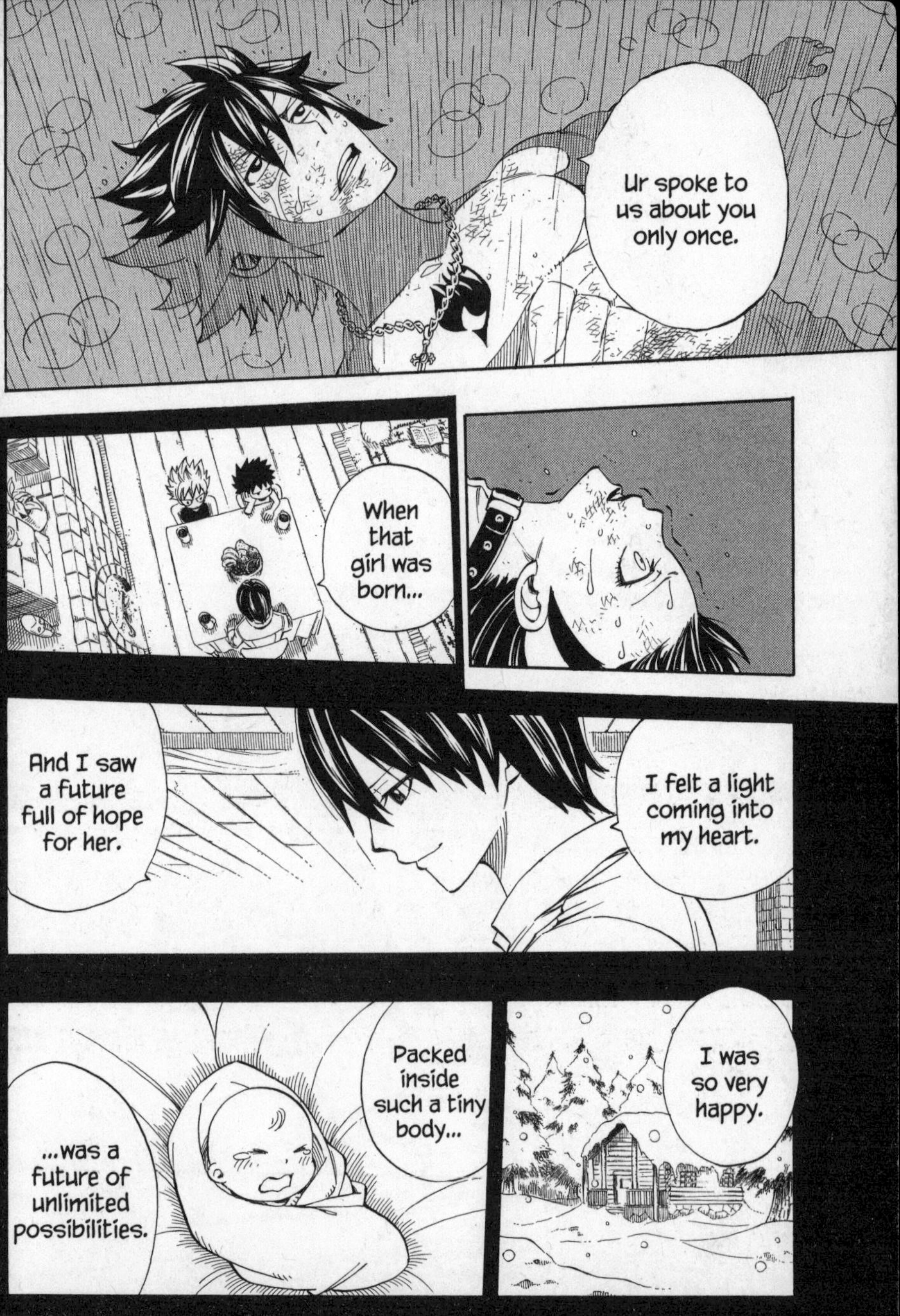
Ur spoke to us about you only once.
When that girl was born...
I felt a light coming into my heart.
And I saw a future full of hope for her.
I was so very happy.
Packed inside such a tiny body...
...was a future of unlimited possibilities.

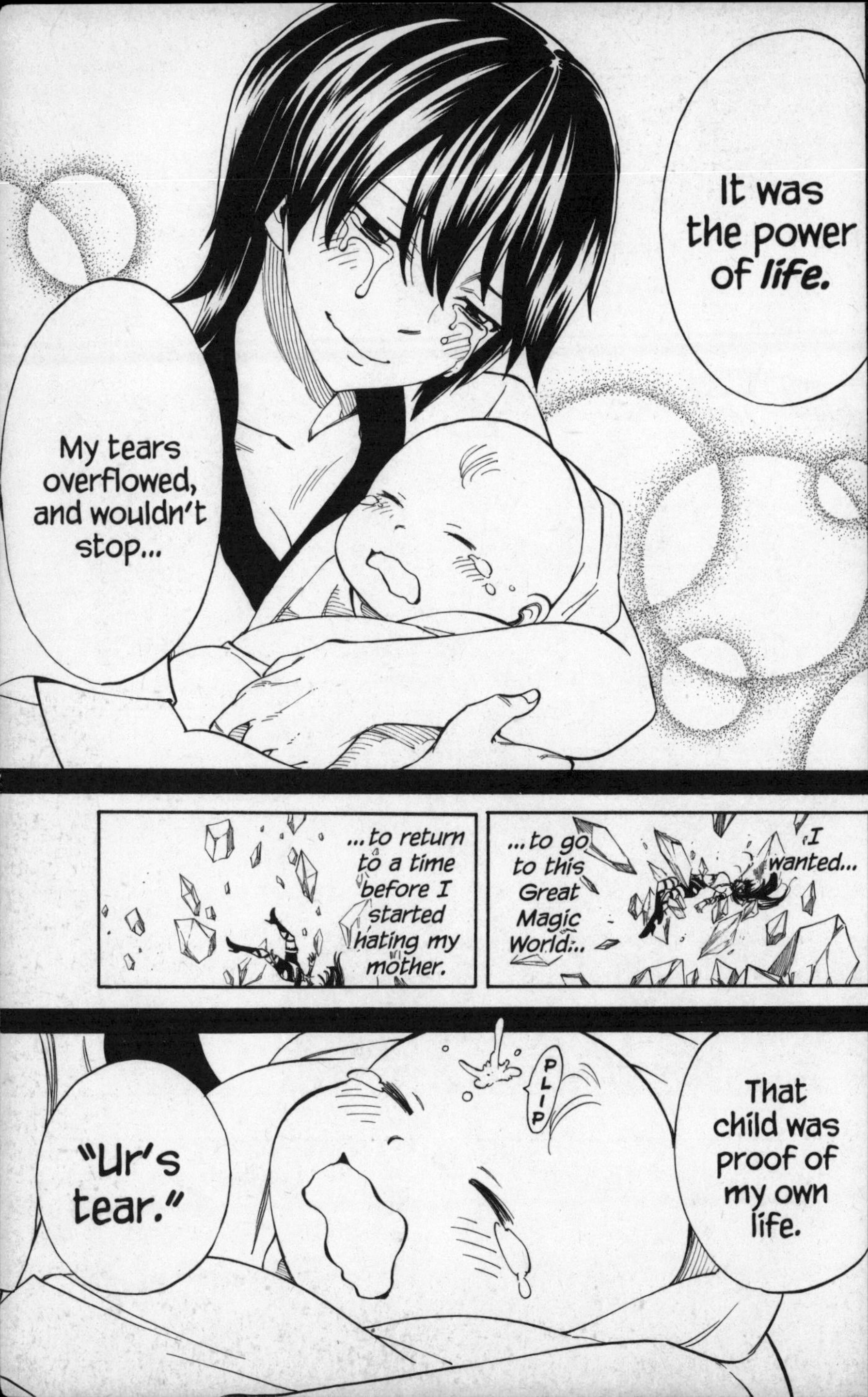
It was the power of life.
My tears overflowed, and wouldn't stop...
I wanted...
...to go to this Great Magic World...
...to return to a time before I started hating my mother.
That child was proof of my own life.
PLIP
"Ur's tear."

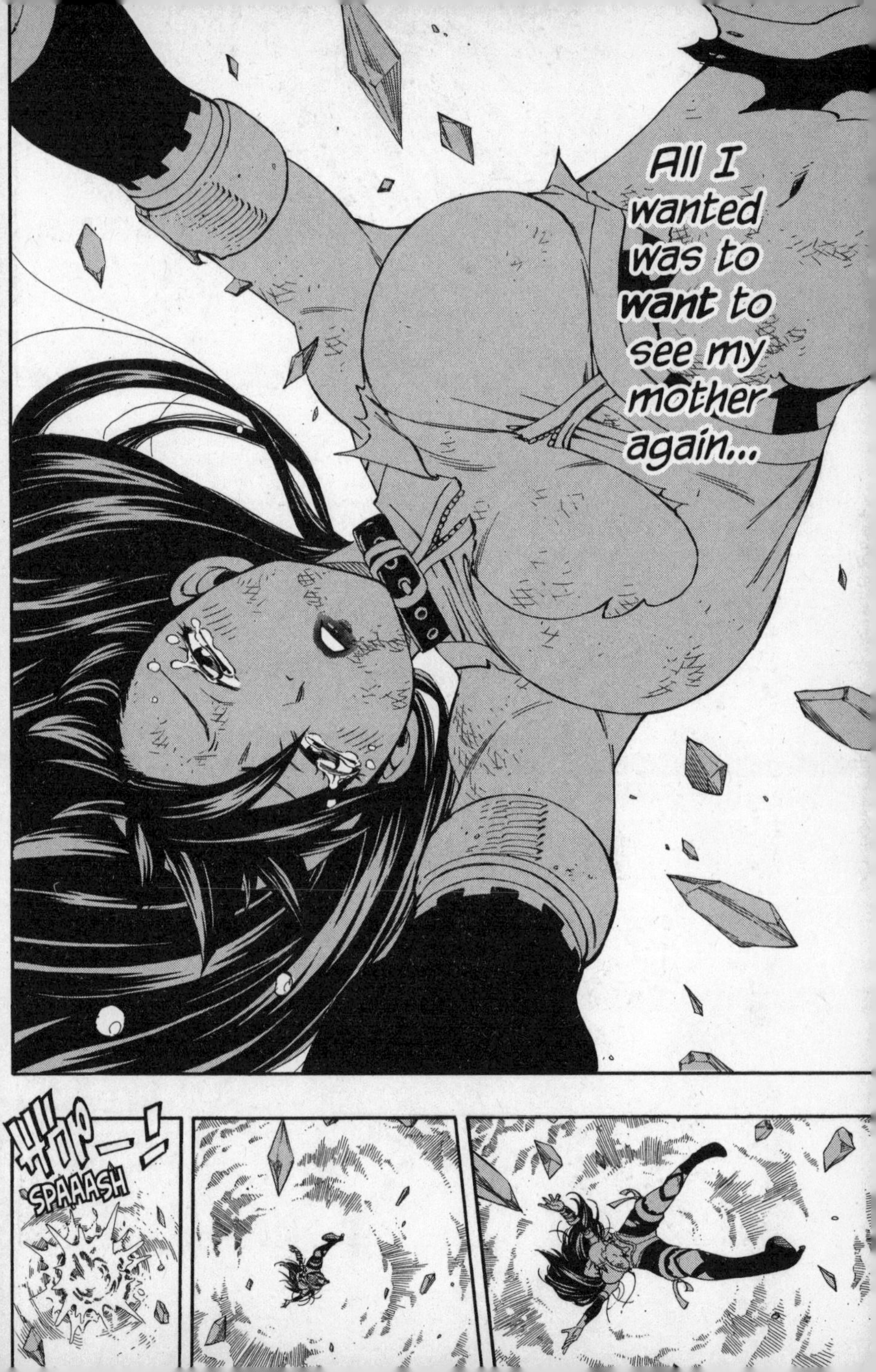
All I wanted was to want to see my mother again...
SPAAASH

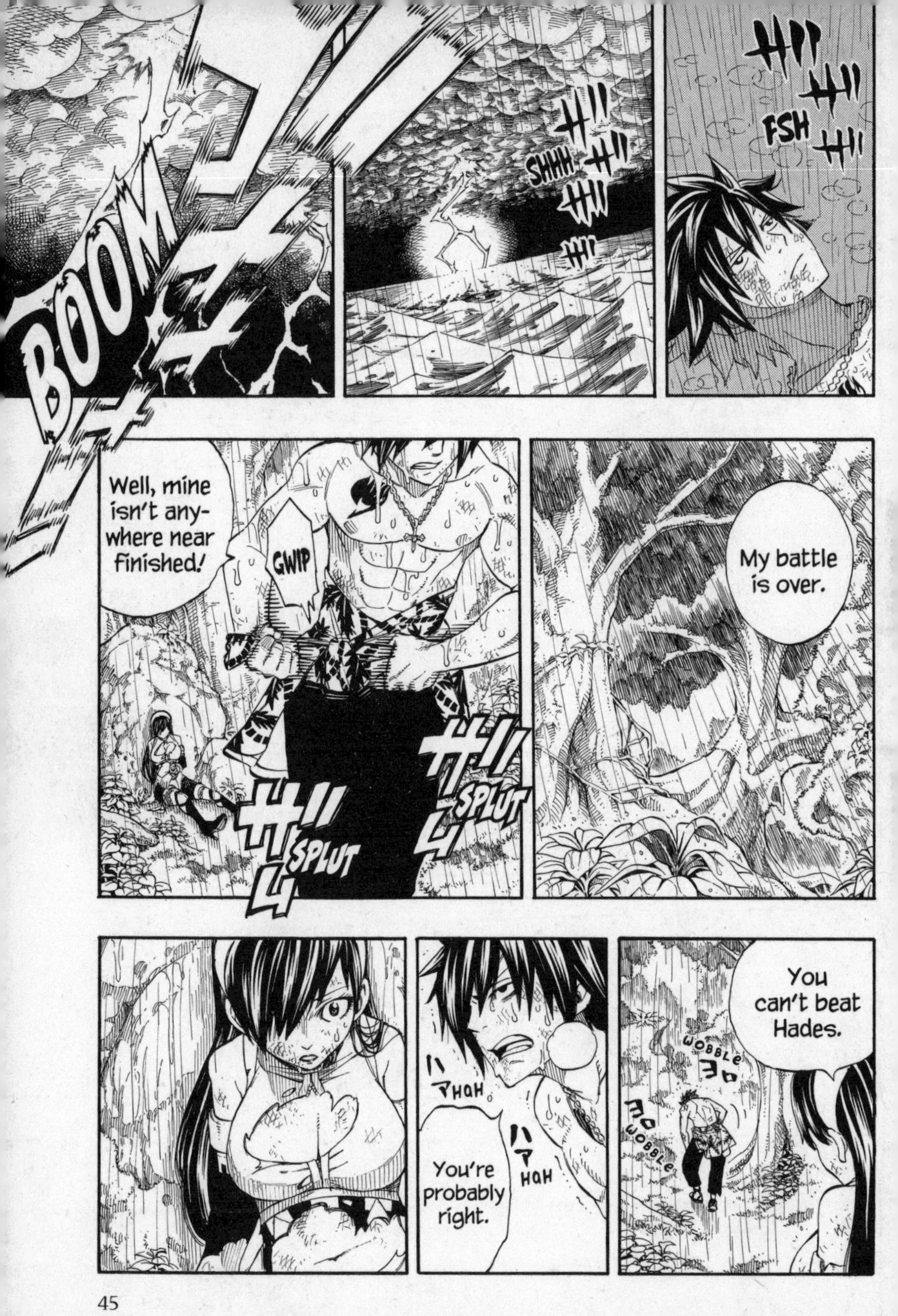
FSH
SHHH
BOOM
My battle is over.
Well, mine isn't anywhere near finished!
GWIP
SPLUT
SPLUT
You can't beat Hades.
ヨロ WOBBLE
ヨロ WOBBLE
ハァ HAH
ハァ HAH
You're probably right.

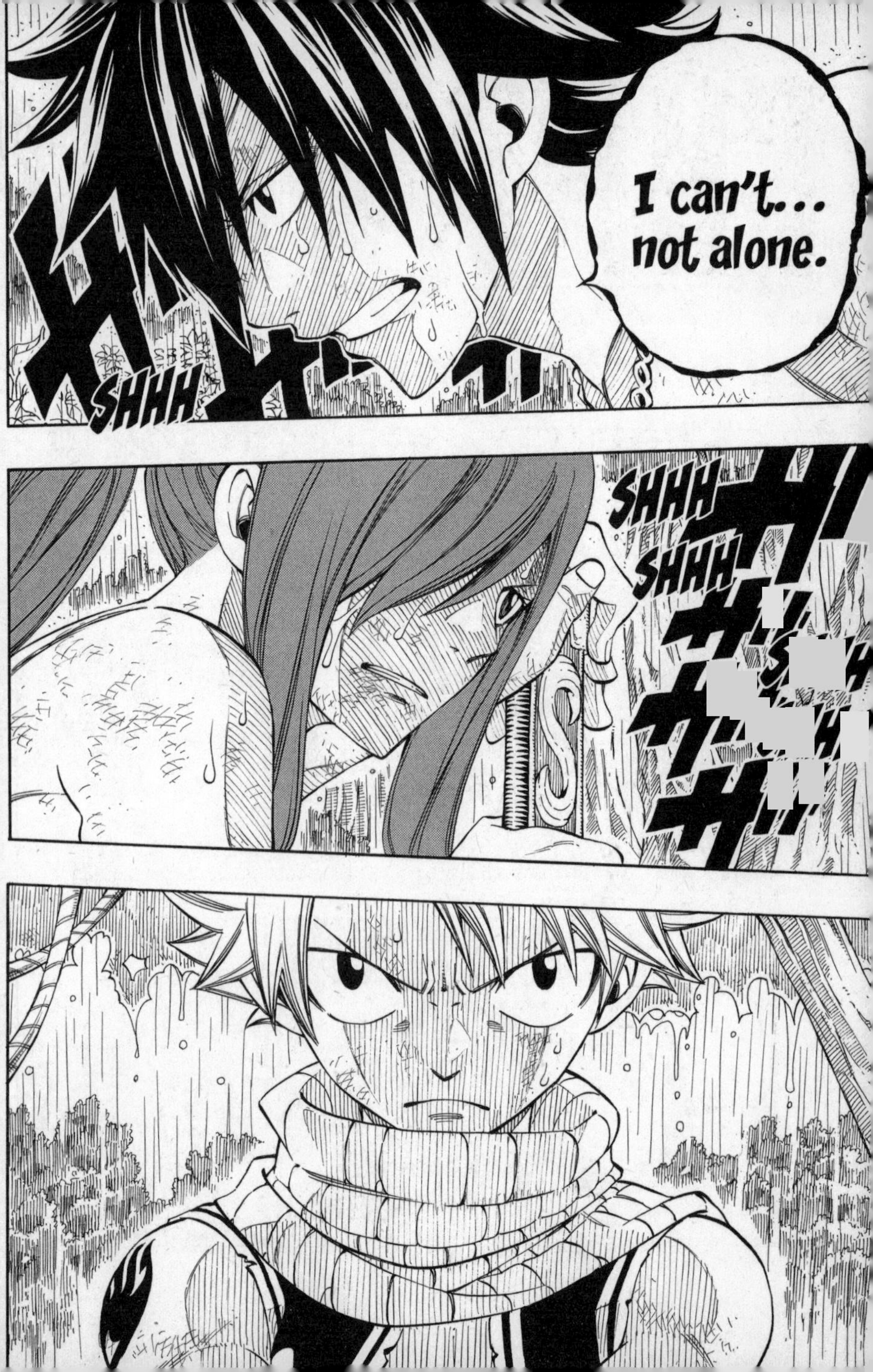
I can't... not alone.
SHHH
SHHH
SHHH

フェアリーテイル

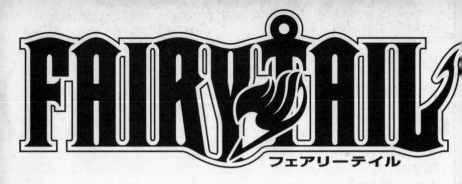

Chapter 242: Acnologia

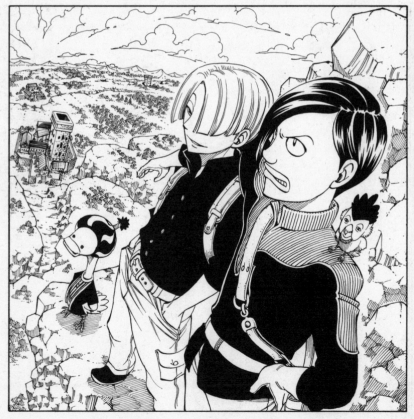

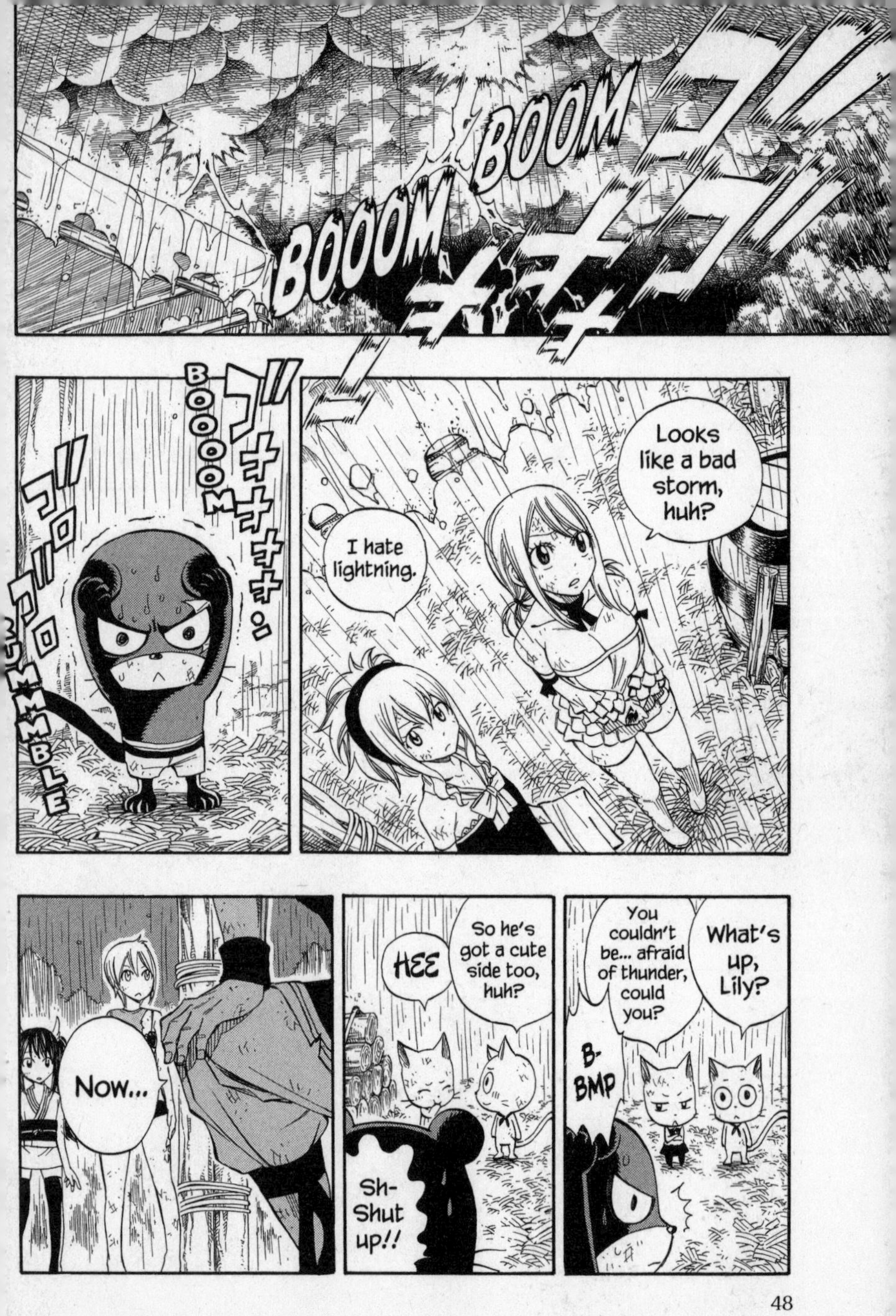
BOOM
BOOM
BOOOM
BOOOOOM
RUMMMBLE
Looks like a bad storm, huh?
I hate lightning.
What's up, Lily?
You couldn't be... afraid of thunder, could you?
B-BMP
So he's got a cute side too, huh?
HEE
Sh-Shut up!!
Now...

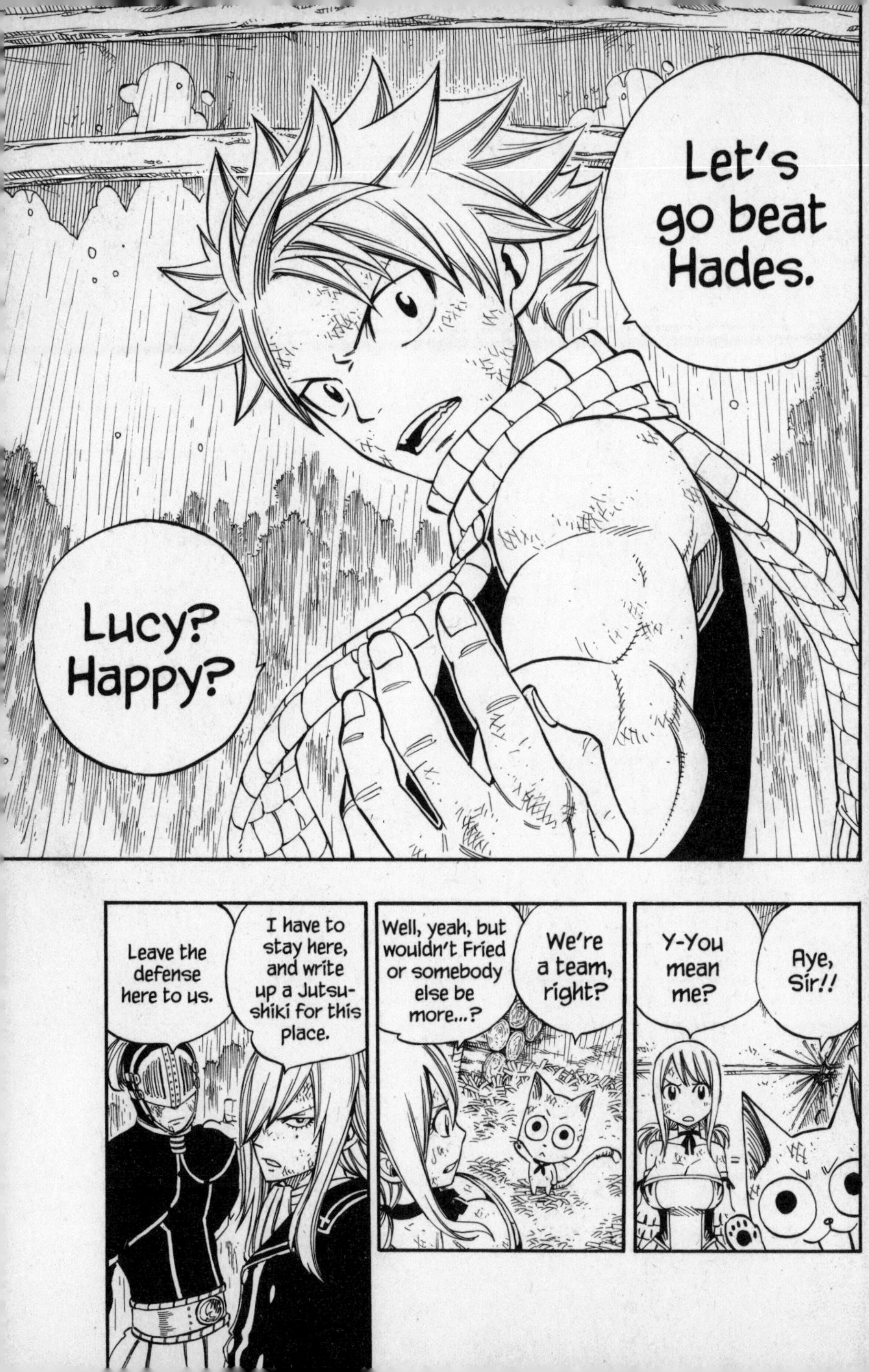
Let's go beat Hades.
Lucy? Happy?
Aye, Sir!!
Y-You mean me?
We're a team, right?
Well, yeah, but wouldn't Fried or somebody else be more...?
I have to stay here, and write up a Jutsu-shiki for this place.
Leave the defense here to us.

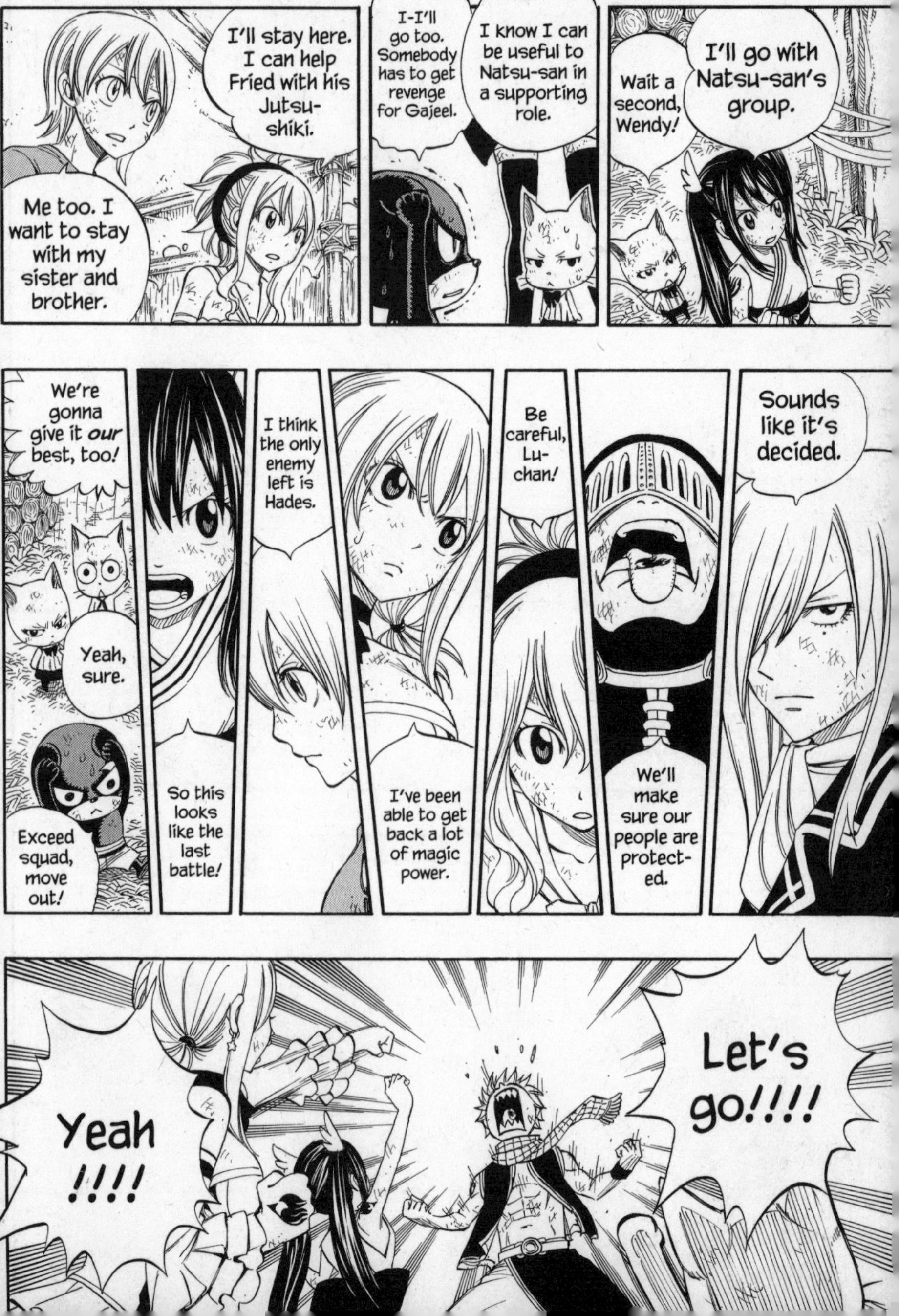
I'll go with Natsu-san's group.
Wait a second, Wendy!
I know I can be useful to Natsu-san in a supporting role.
I-I'll go too. Somebody has to get revenge for Gajeel.
I'll stay here. I can help Fried with his Jutsu-shiki.
Me too. I want to stay with my sister and brother.
Sounds like it's decided.
We'll make sure our people are protect-ed.
Be careful, Lu-chan!
I've been able to get back a lot of magic power.
I think the only enemy left is Hades.
So this looks like the last battle!
We're gonna give it *our* best, too!
Yeah, sure.
Exceed squad, move out!
Let's go!!!!
Yeah !!!!

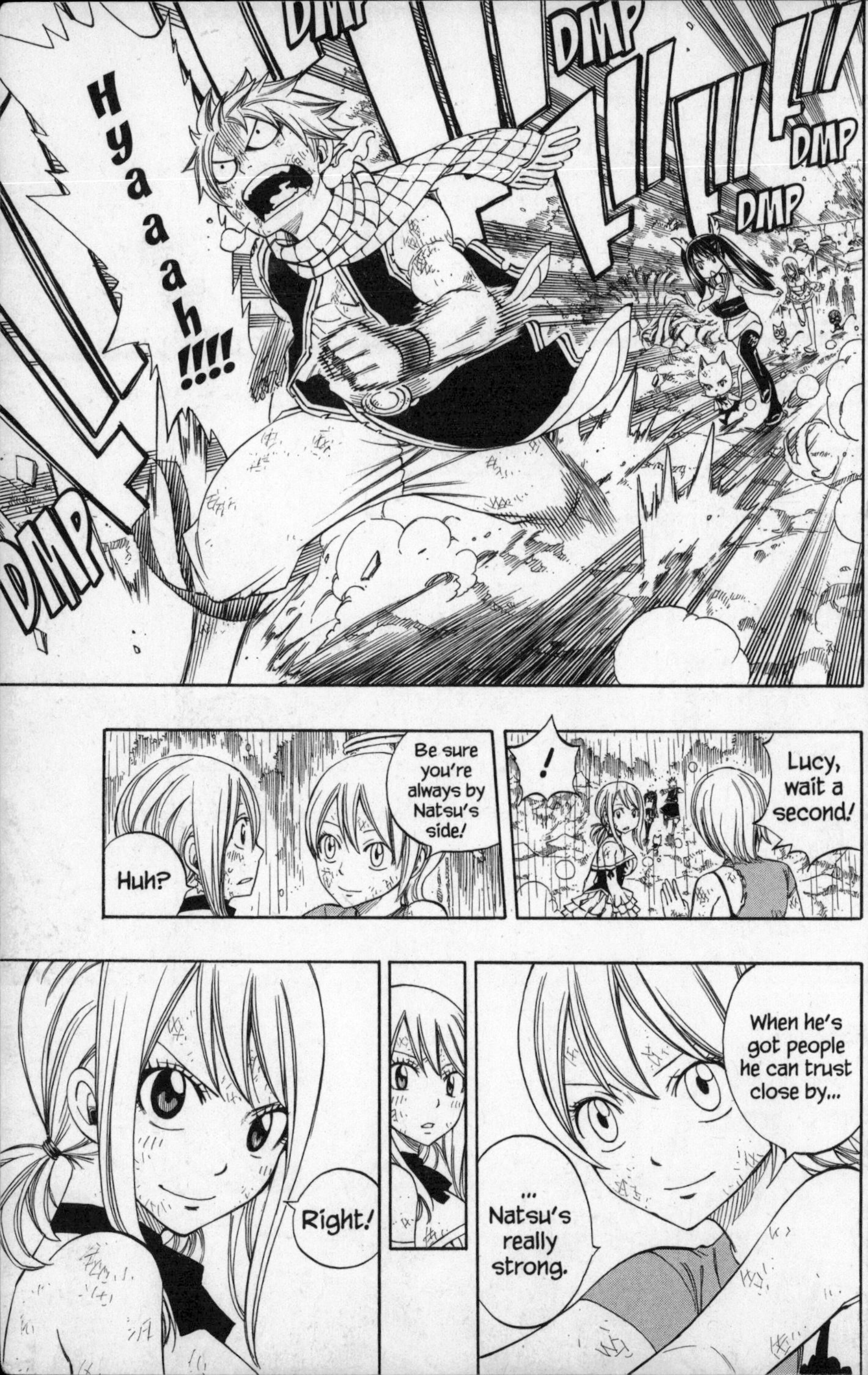
DMP
DMP
DMP
DMP
Hyaaah!!!!
DMP
!
Lucy, wait a second!
Be sure you're always by Natsu's side!
Huh?
When he's got people he can trust close by...
... Natsu's really strong.
Right!

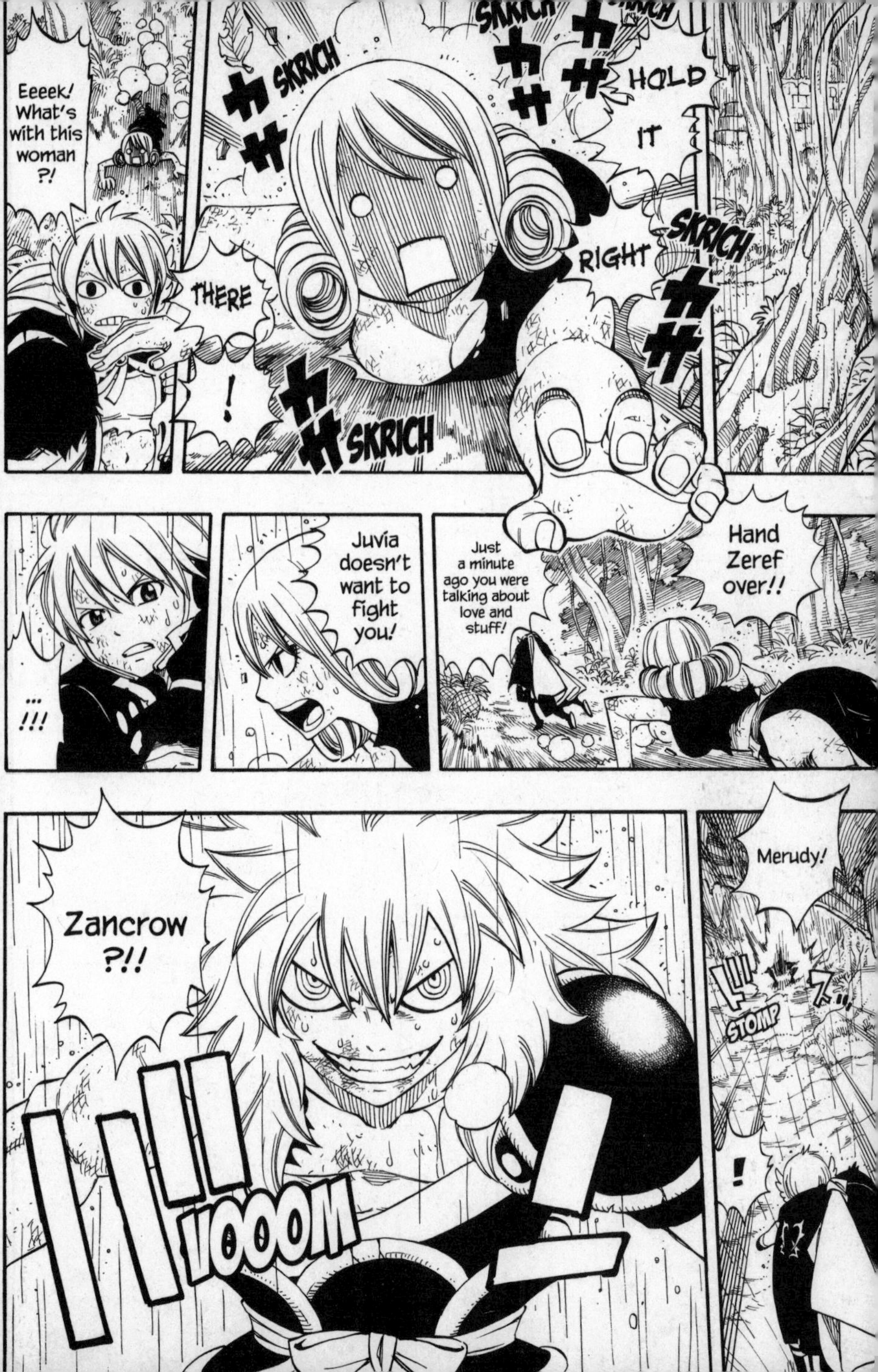
SKRICH
SKRICH
HOLD IT RIGHT THERE!
SKRICH
SKRICH
SKRICH
Eeeek! What's with this woman?!
Hand Zeref over!!
Just a minute ago you were talking about love and stuff!
Juvia doesn't want to fight you!
...!!!
Merudy!
STOMP
!
Zancrow?!!
VOOOM

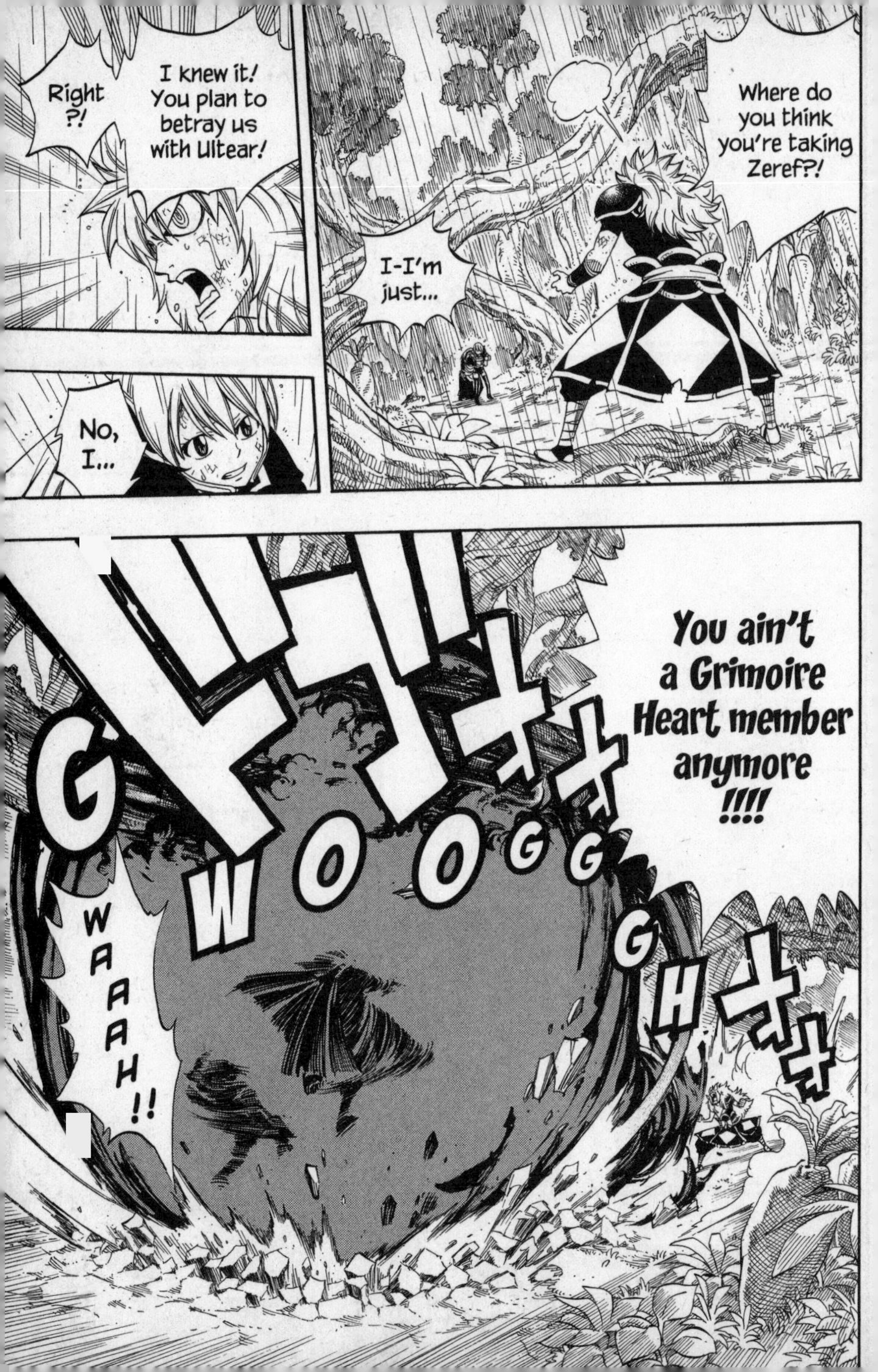

Where do you think you're taking Zeref?!
I-I'm just...
Right?!
I knew it! You plan to betray us with Ultear!
No, I...
You ain't a Grimoire Heart member anymore!!!!
GWOOGGGH
WAAAAH!!

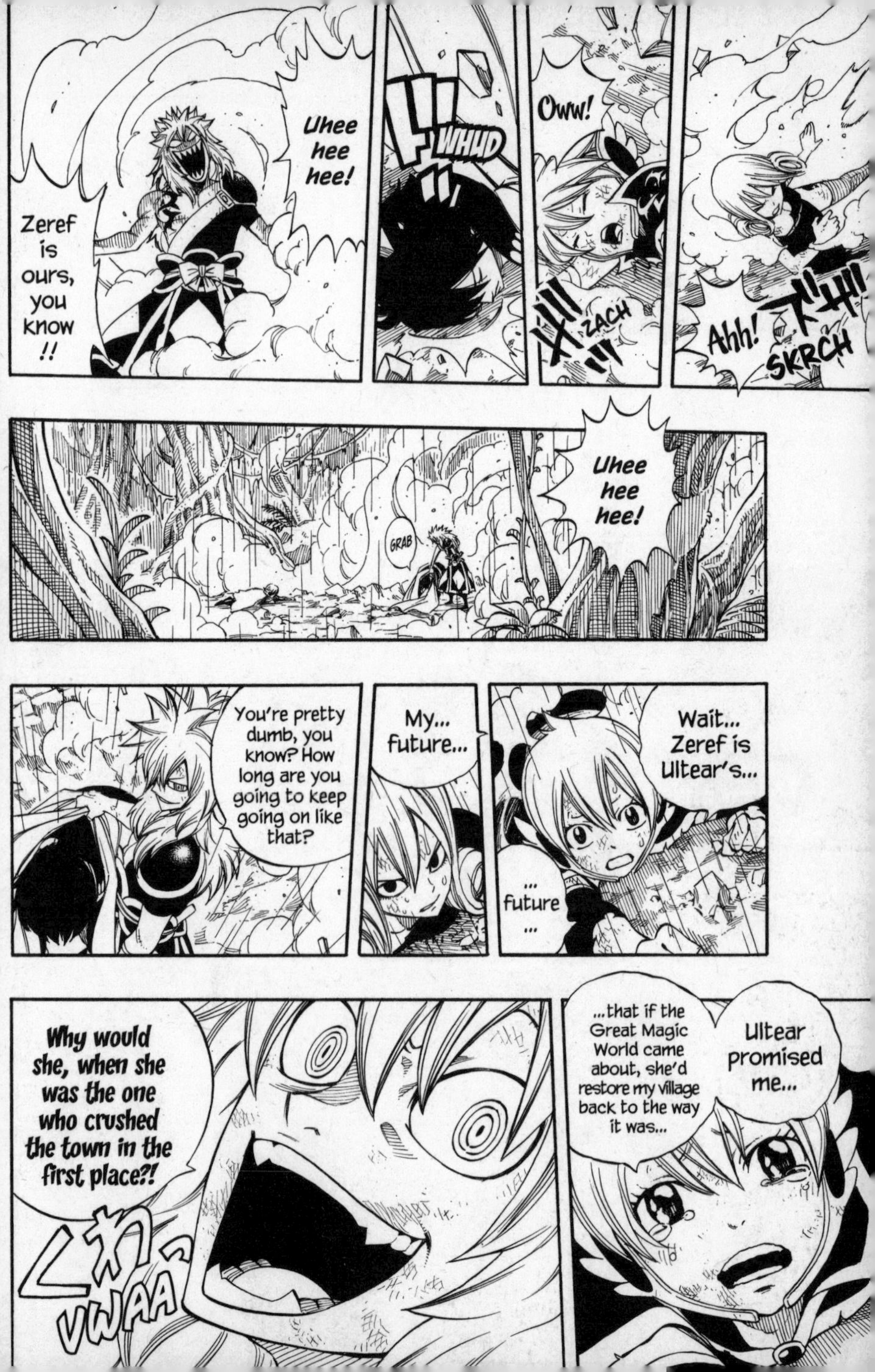
Ahh!
SKRCH
Oww!
ZACH
WHUD
Uhee hee hee!
Zeref is ours, you know !!
Uhee hee hee!
GRAB
Wait... Zeref is Ultear's...
... future ...
My... future...
You're pretty dumb, you know? How long are you going to keep going on like that?
Ultear promised me...
...that if the Great Magic World came about, she'd restore my village back to the way it was...
Why would she, when she was the one who crushed the town in the first place?!
くわっ
VWAA

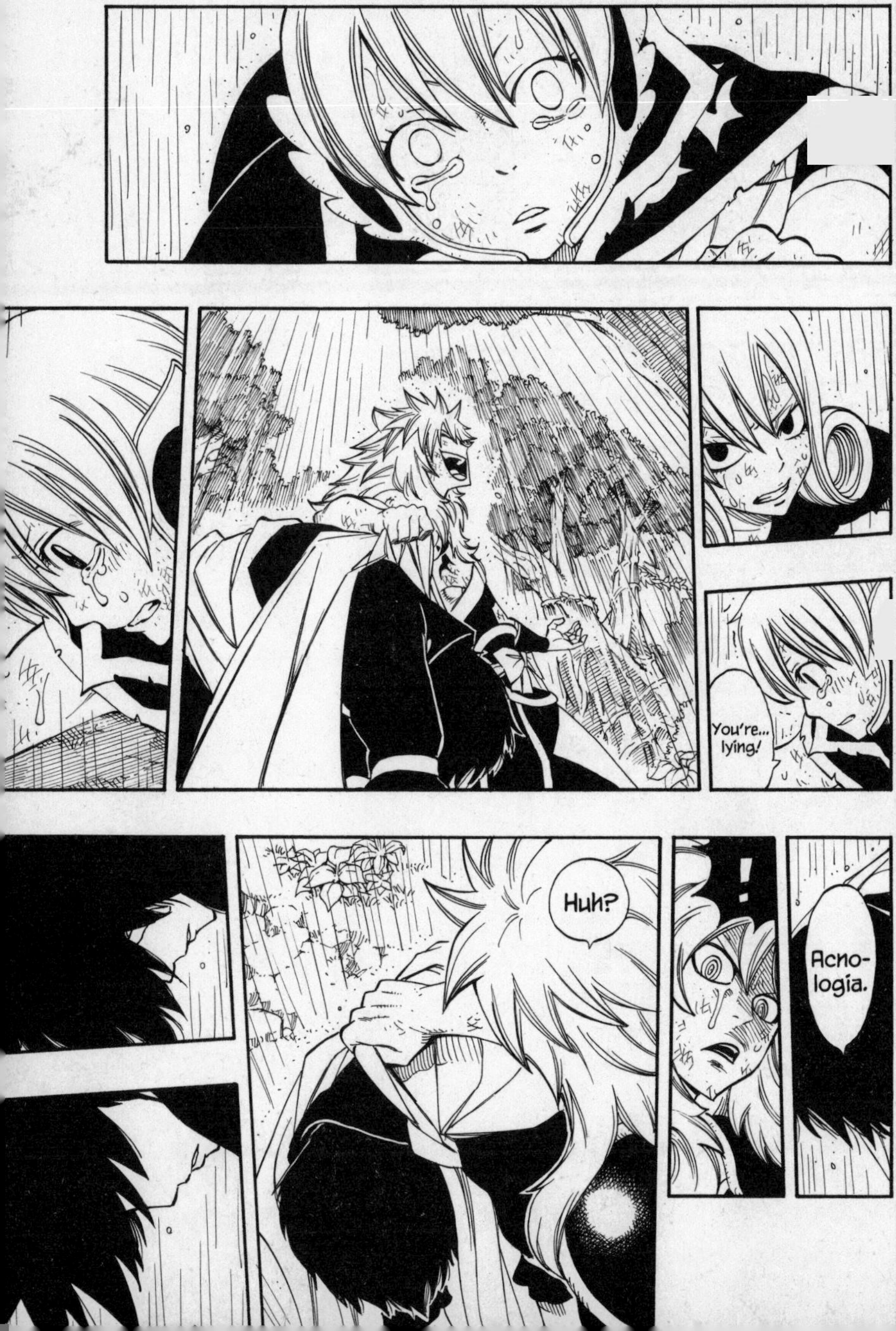
You're... lying!
Acno-logia.
!
Huh?

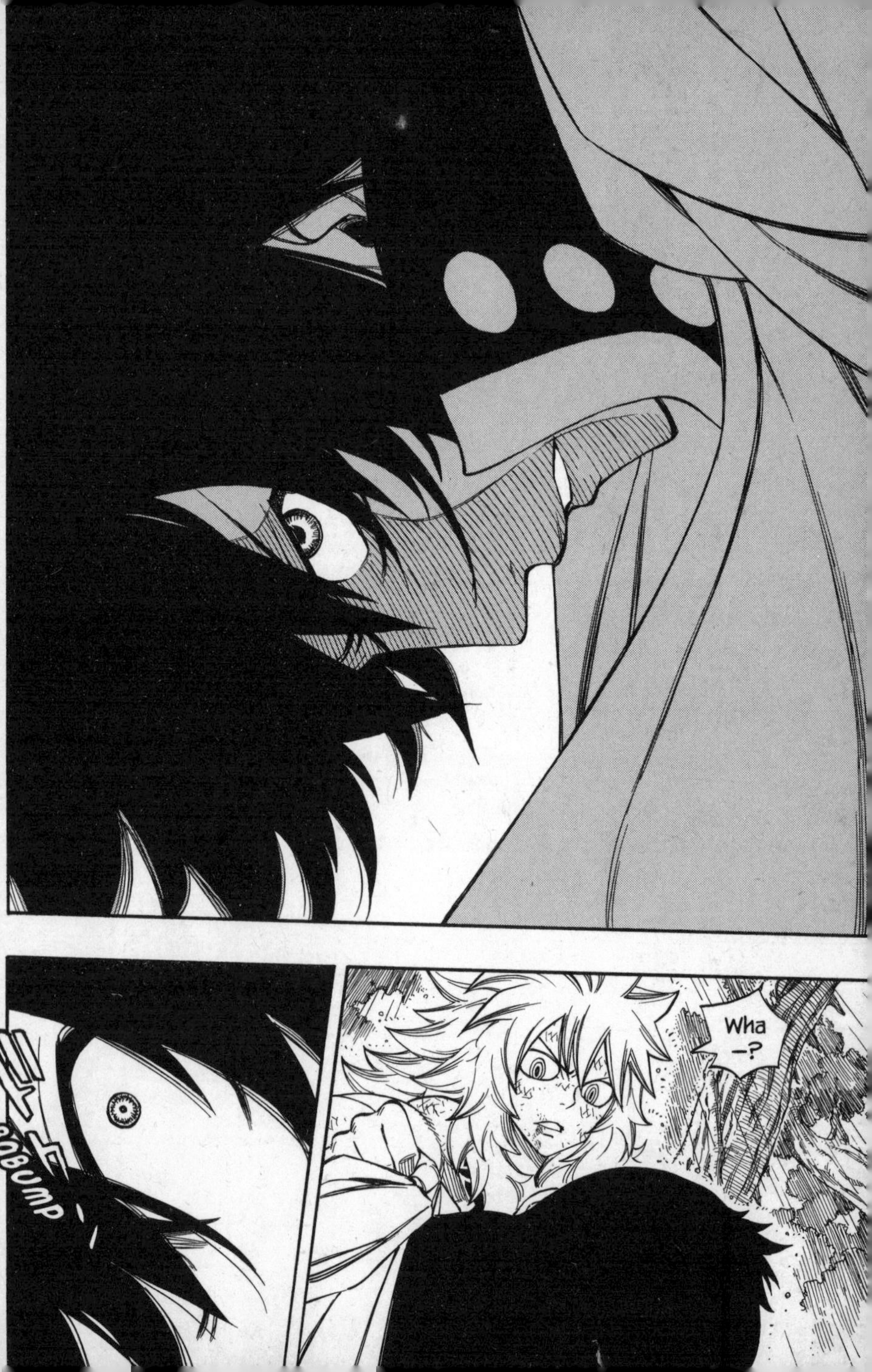
Wha
—?
BUMP

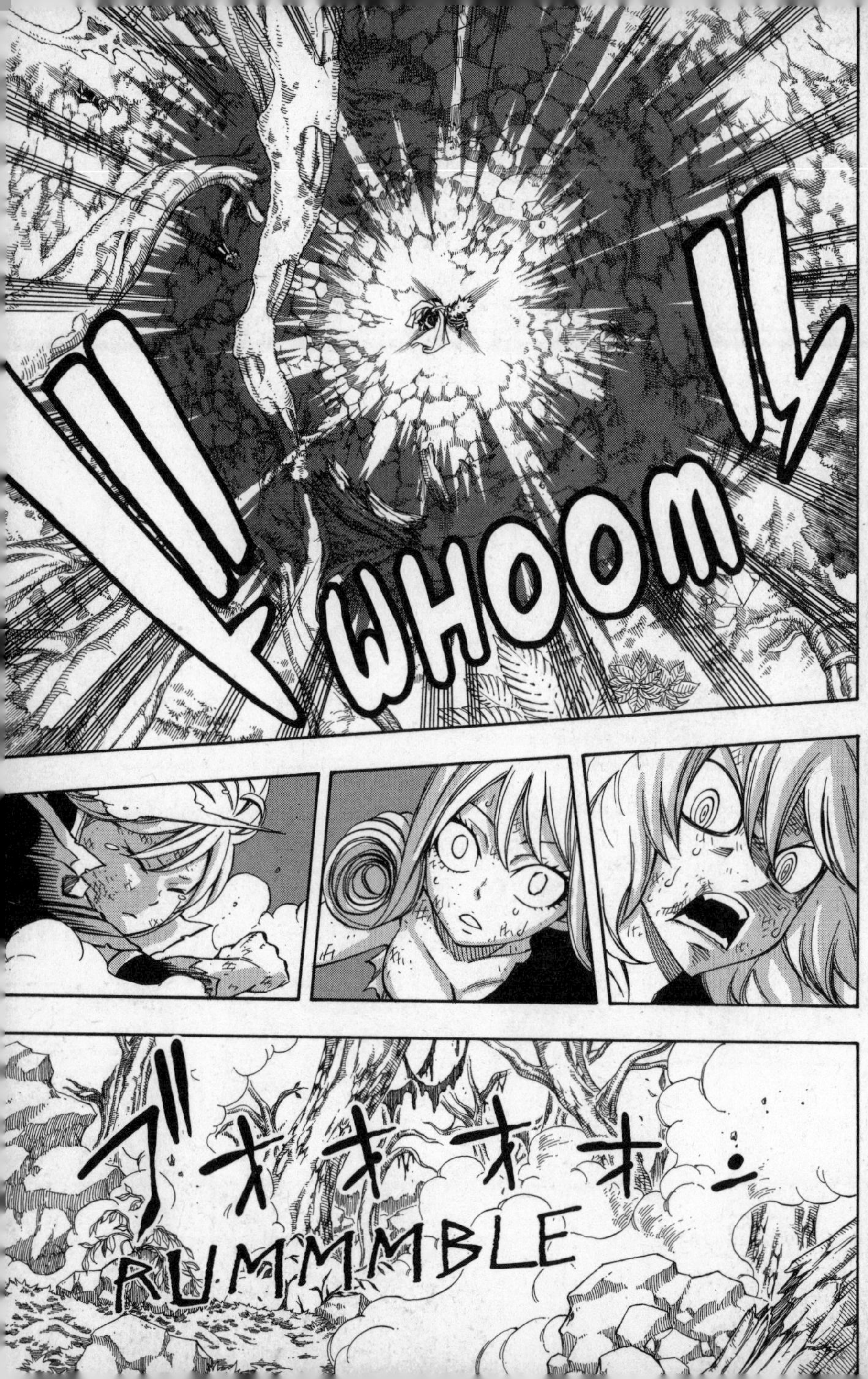

WHOOM
ゴオオオオ…
RUMMMBLE

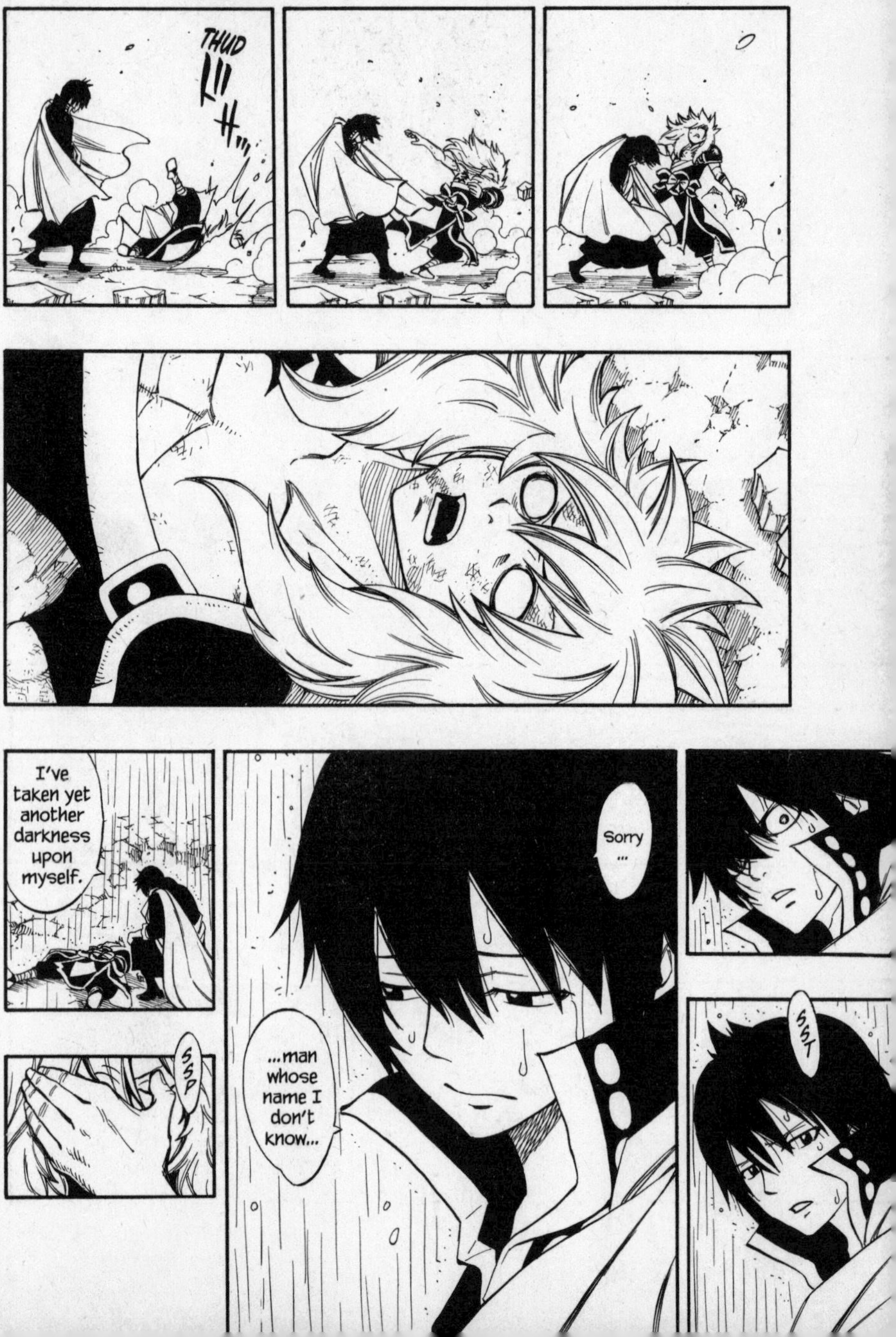
THUD
SST
Sorry...
...man whose name I don't know...
I've taken yet another darkness upon myself.
SSP

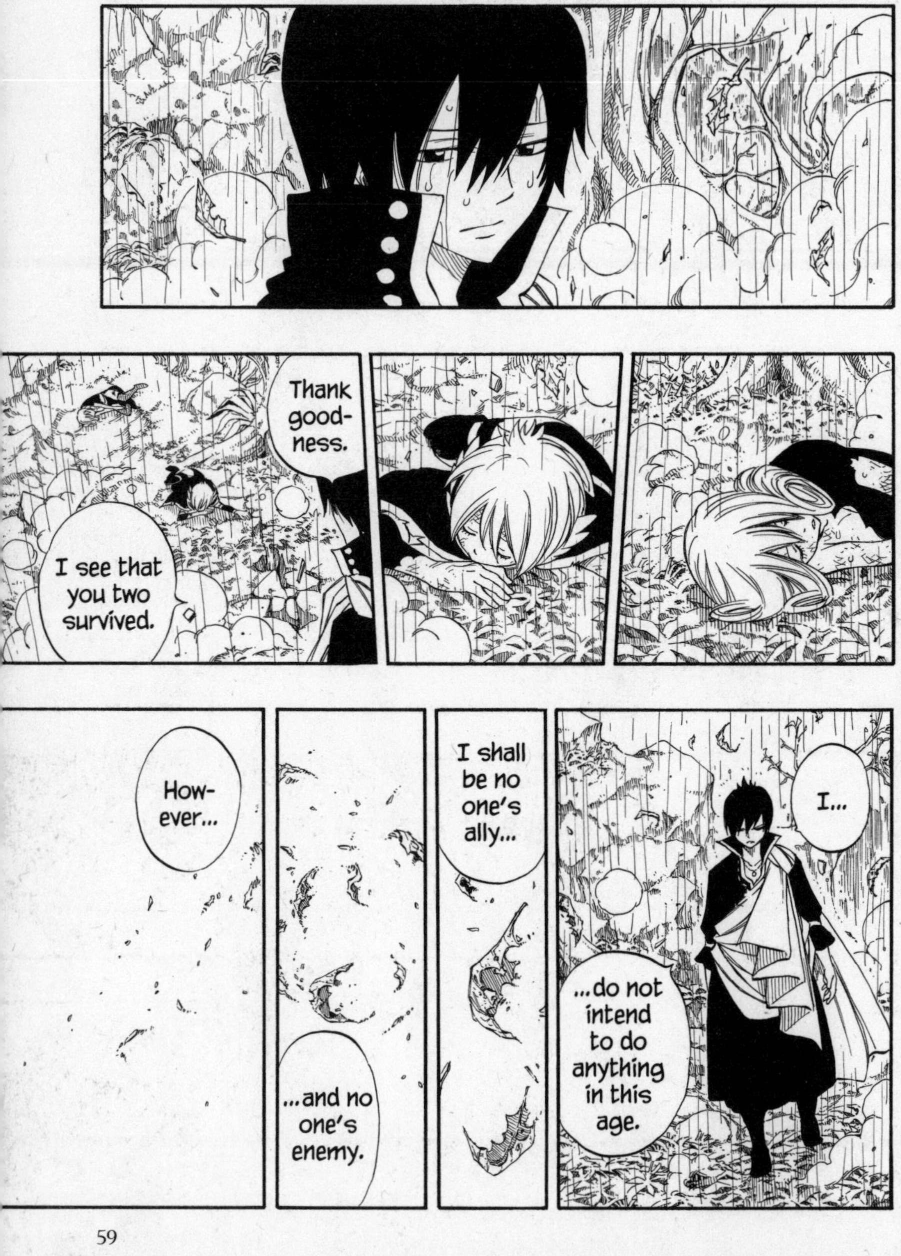
Thank goodness.
I see that you two survived.
I...
...do not intend to do anything in this age.
I shall be no one's ally...
...and no one's enemy.
However...

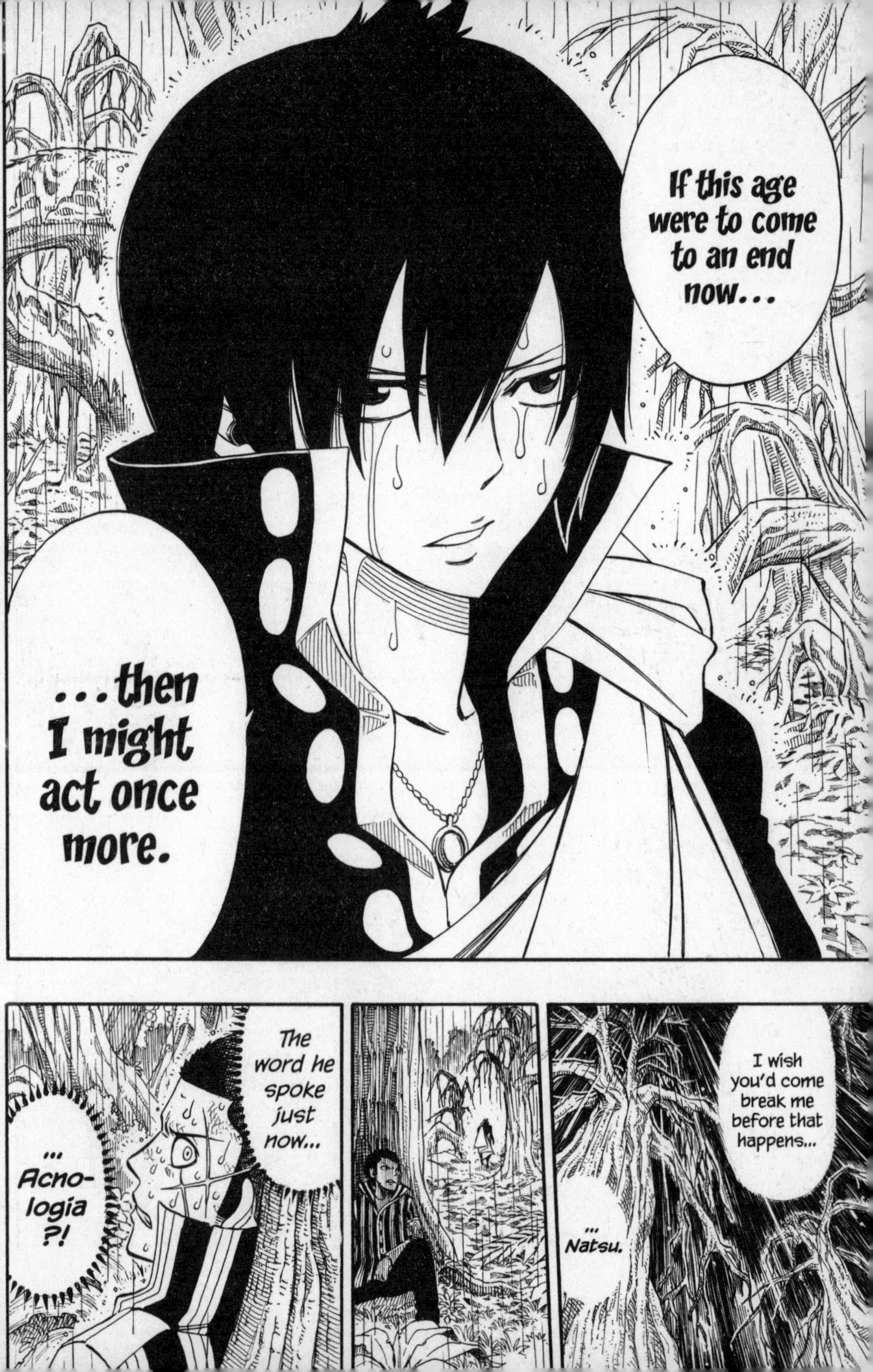
If this age were to come to an end now...
...then I might act once more.
I wish you'd come break me before that happens...
...Natsu.
The word he spoke just now...
...Acnologia?!

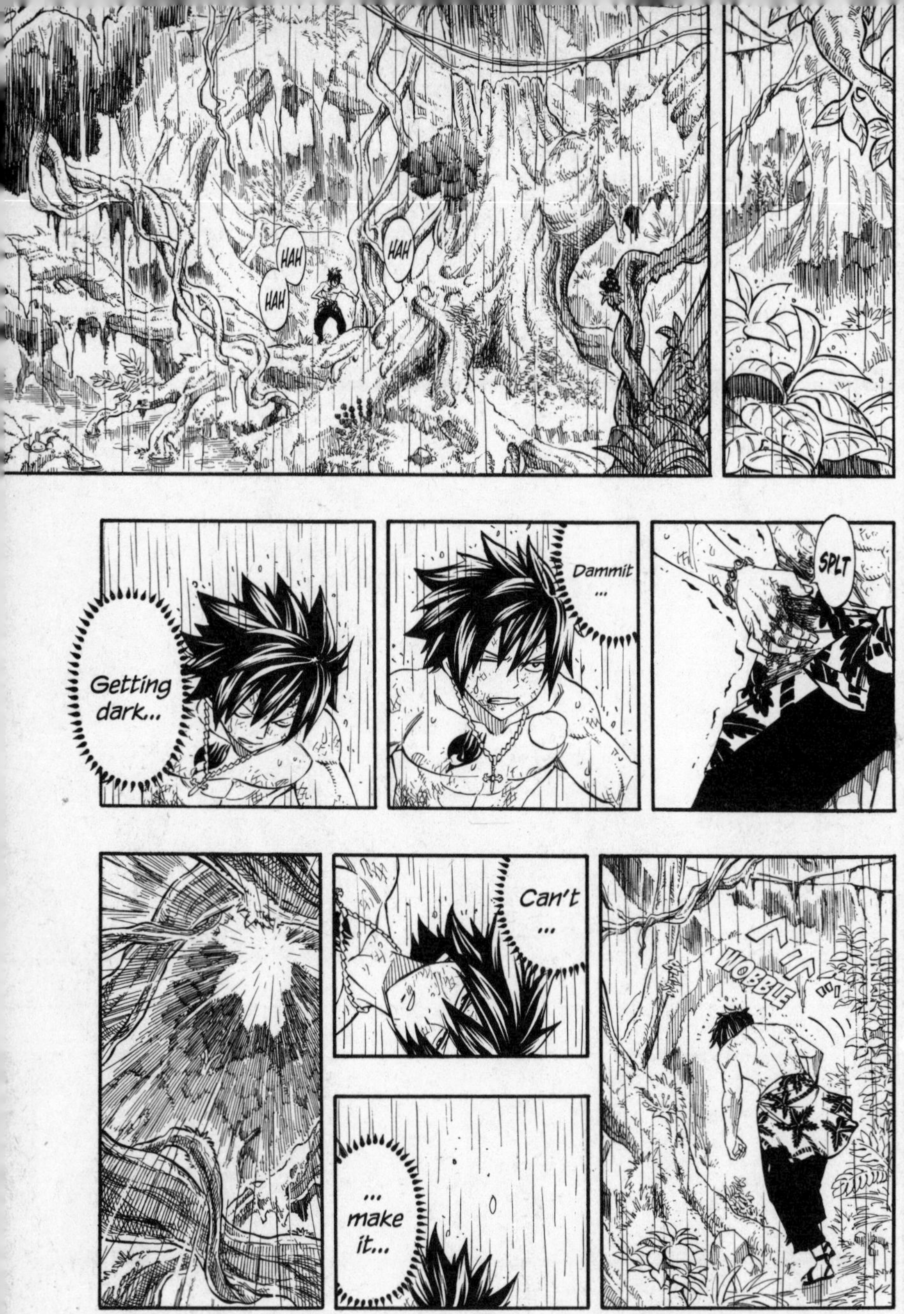
HAH
HAH
HAH
SPLT
Dammit ...
Getting dark...
WOBBLE
Can't ...
... make it...

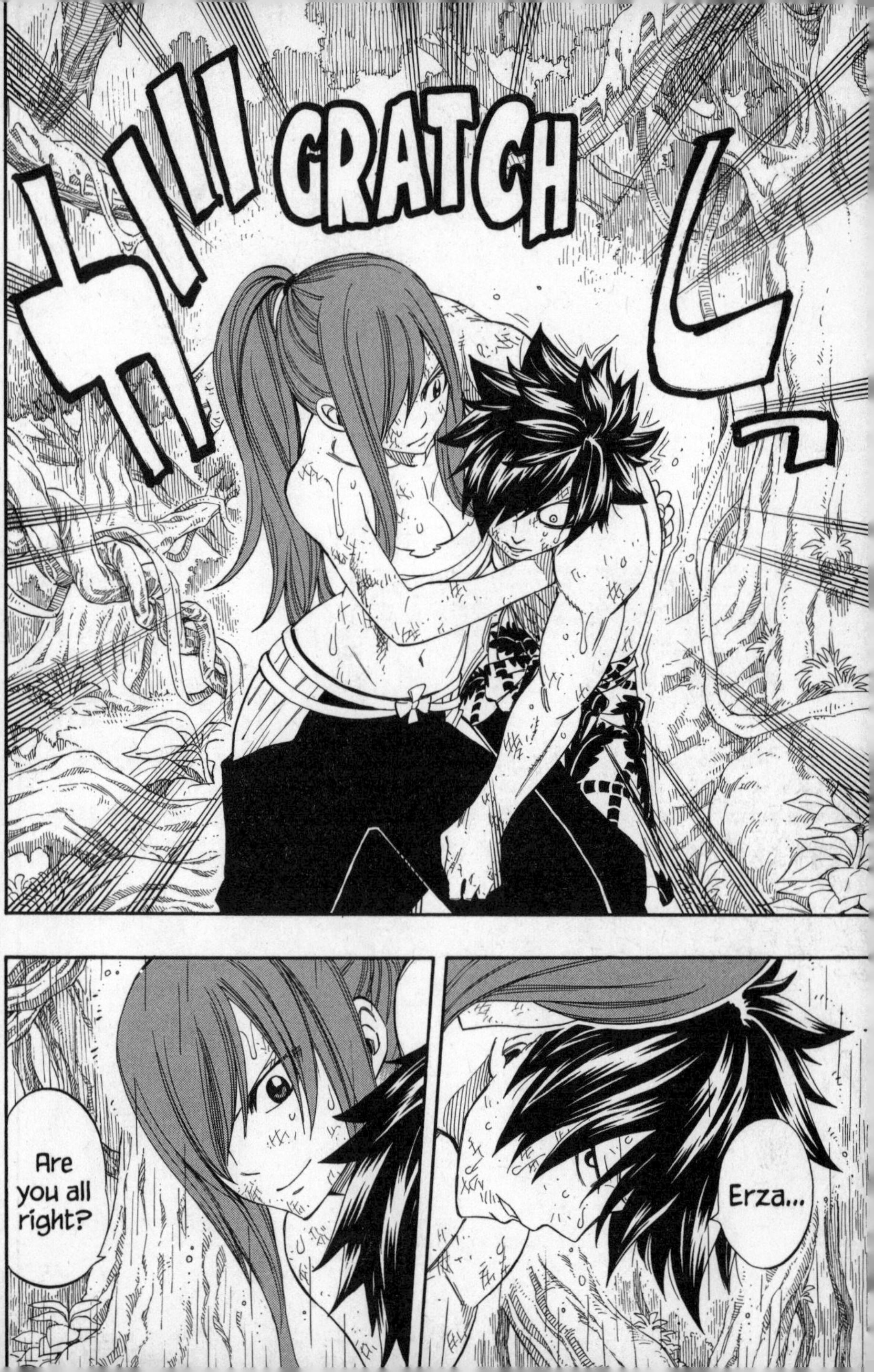
GRATCH
Erza...
Are you all right?

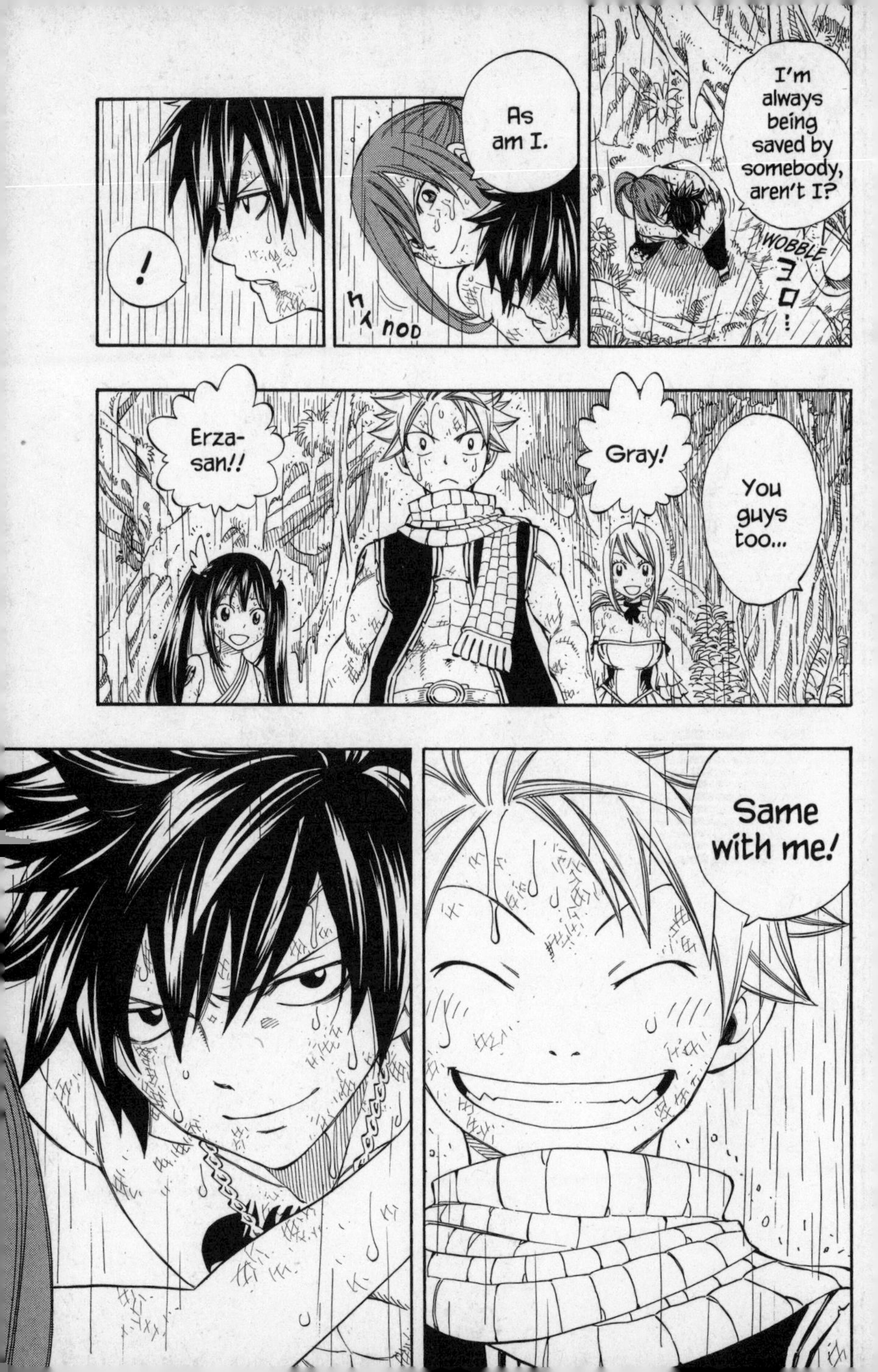
I'm always being saved by somebody, aren't I?
WOBBLE
ヨロ…
As am I.
NOD
!
Gray!
Erza-san!!
You guys too...
Same with me!

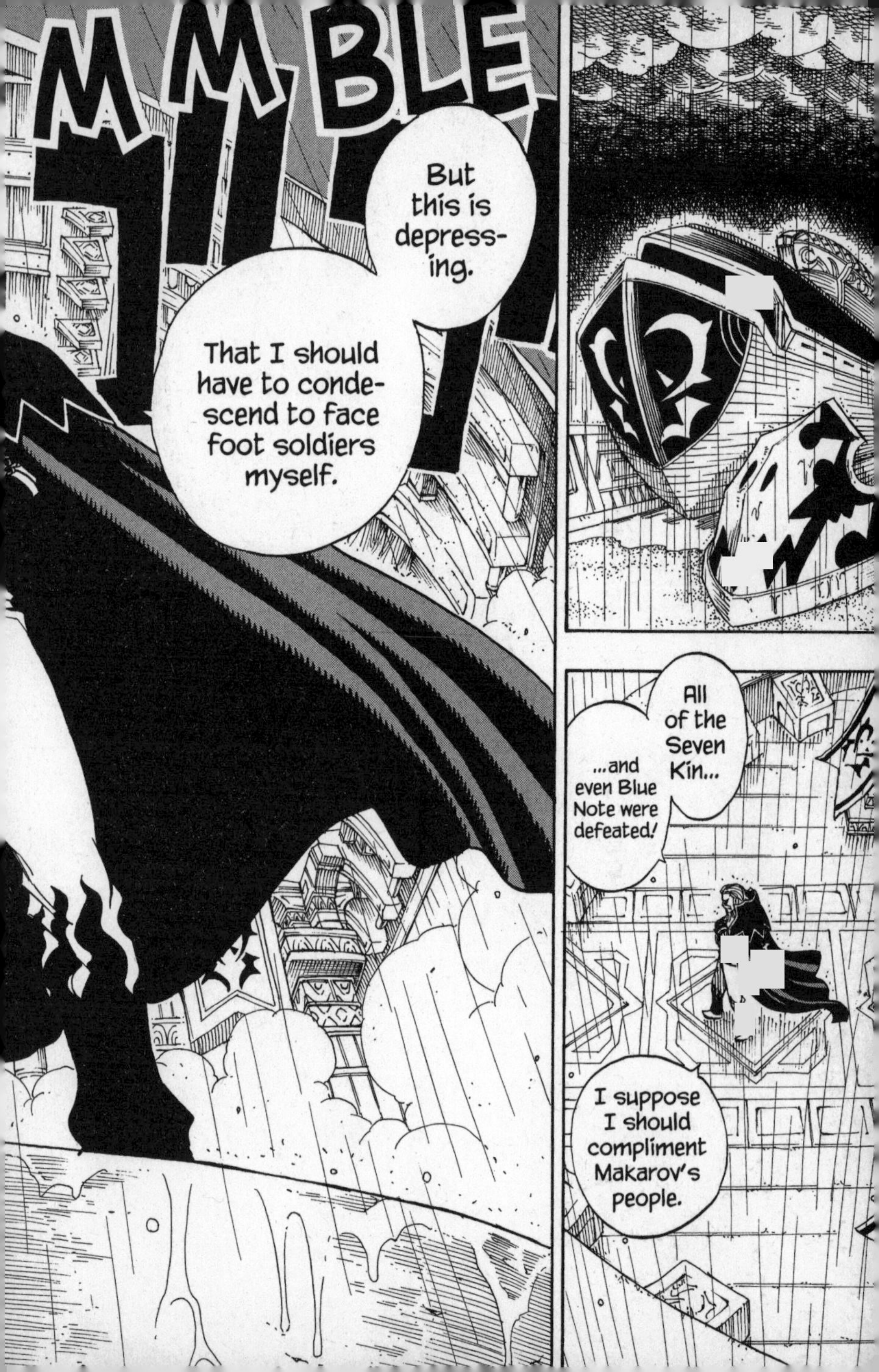
All of the Seven Kin...
...and even Blue Note were defeated!
I suppose I should compliment Makarov's people.
MMBLE
But this is depress-ing.
That I should have to conde-scend to face foot soldiers myself.

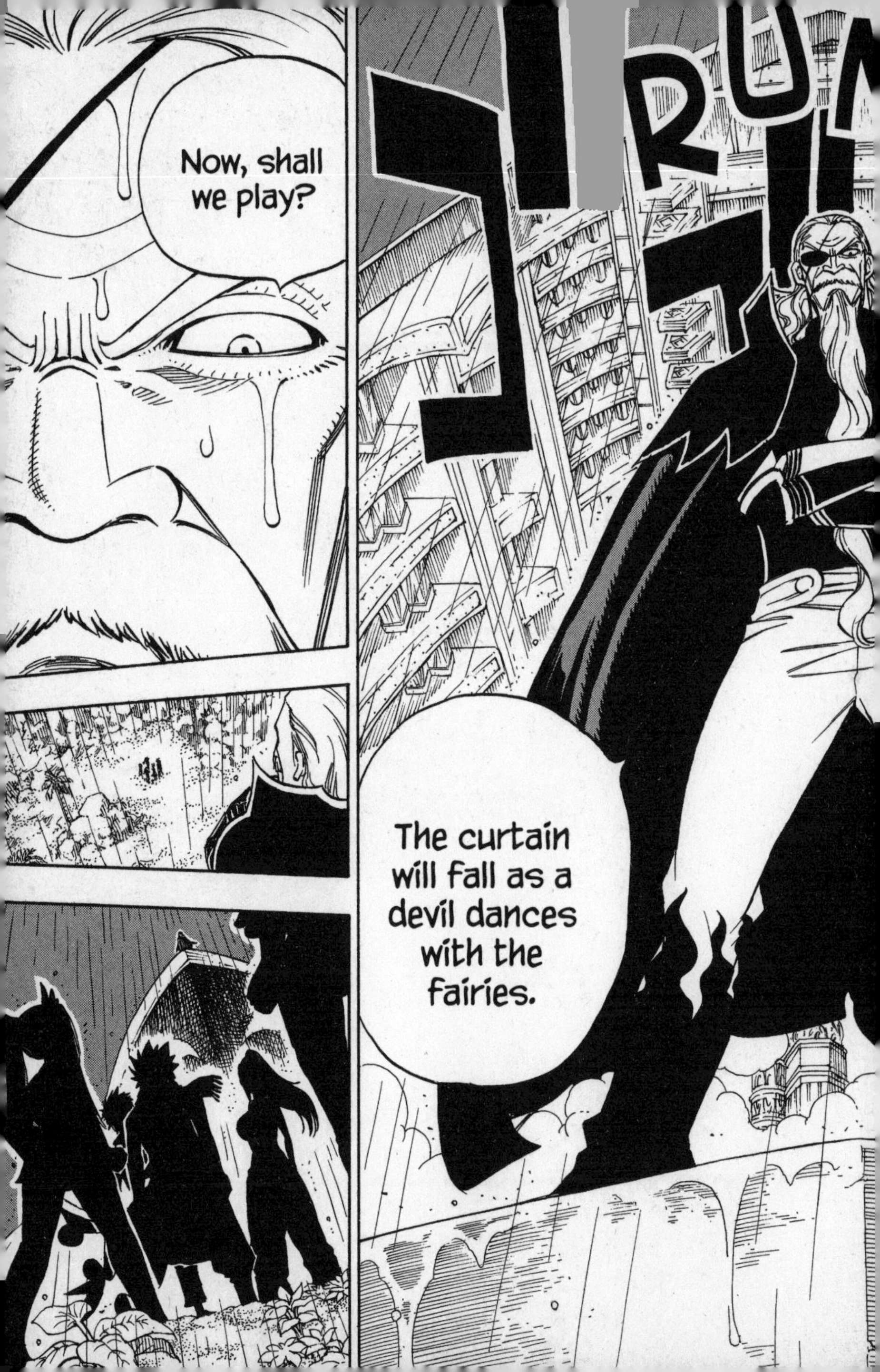
The curtain will fall as a devil dances with the fairies.
Now, shall we play?

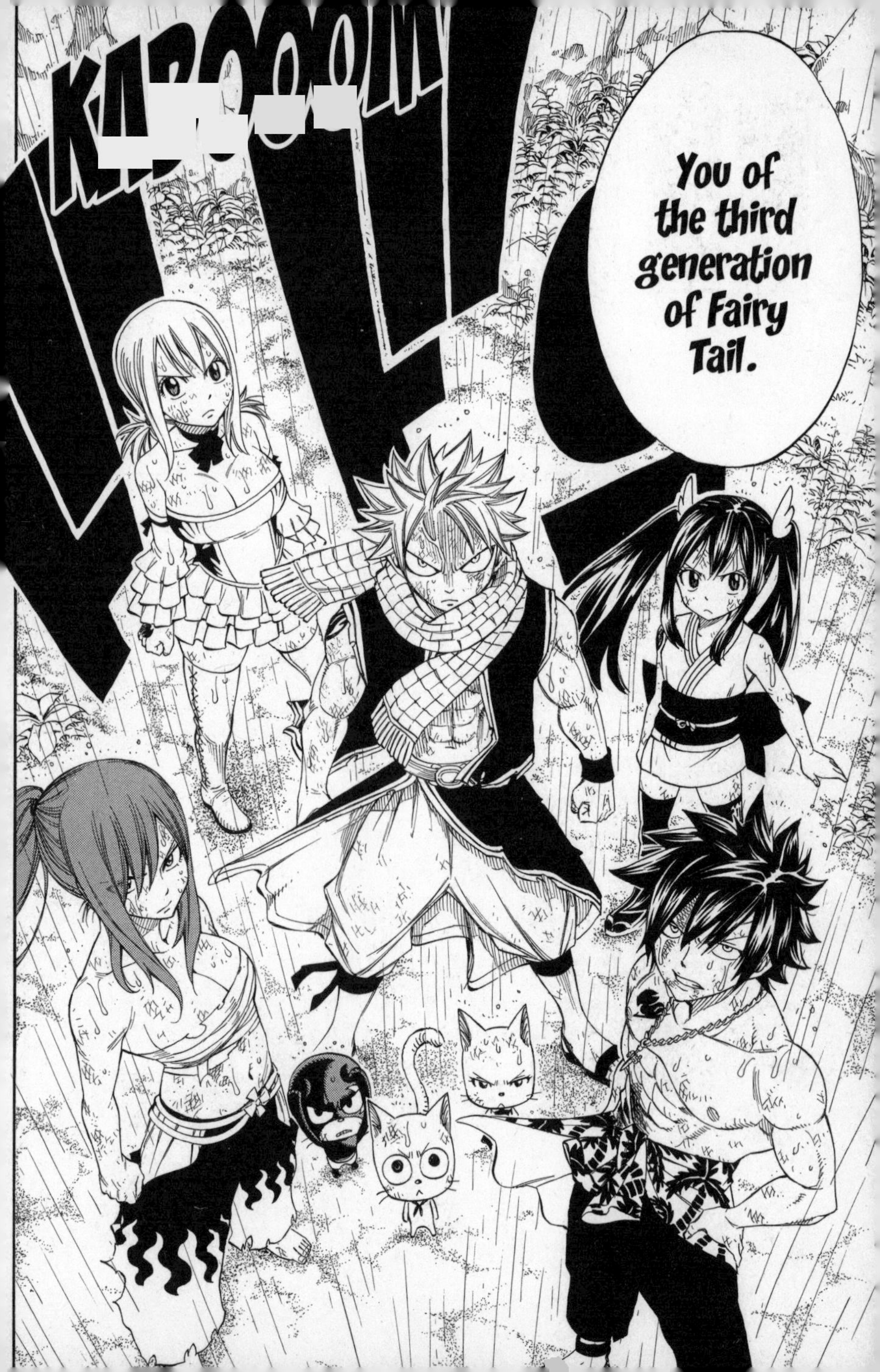
You of the third generation of Fairy Tail.

FAIRY TAIL
フェアリーテイル

Chapter 243: Errors and Experience

6000J
15,000J
Sketch Book

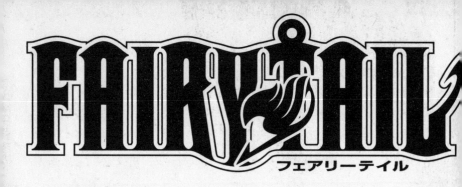

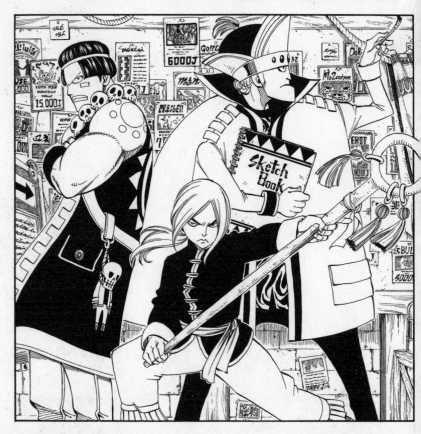

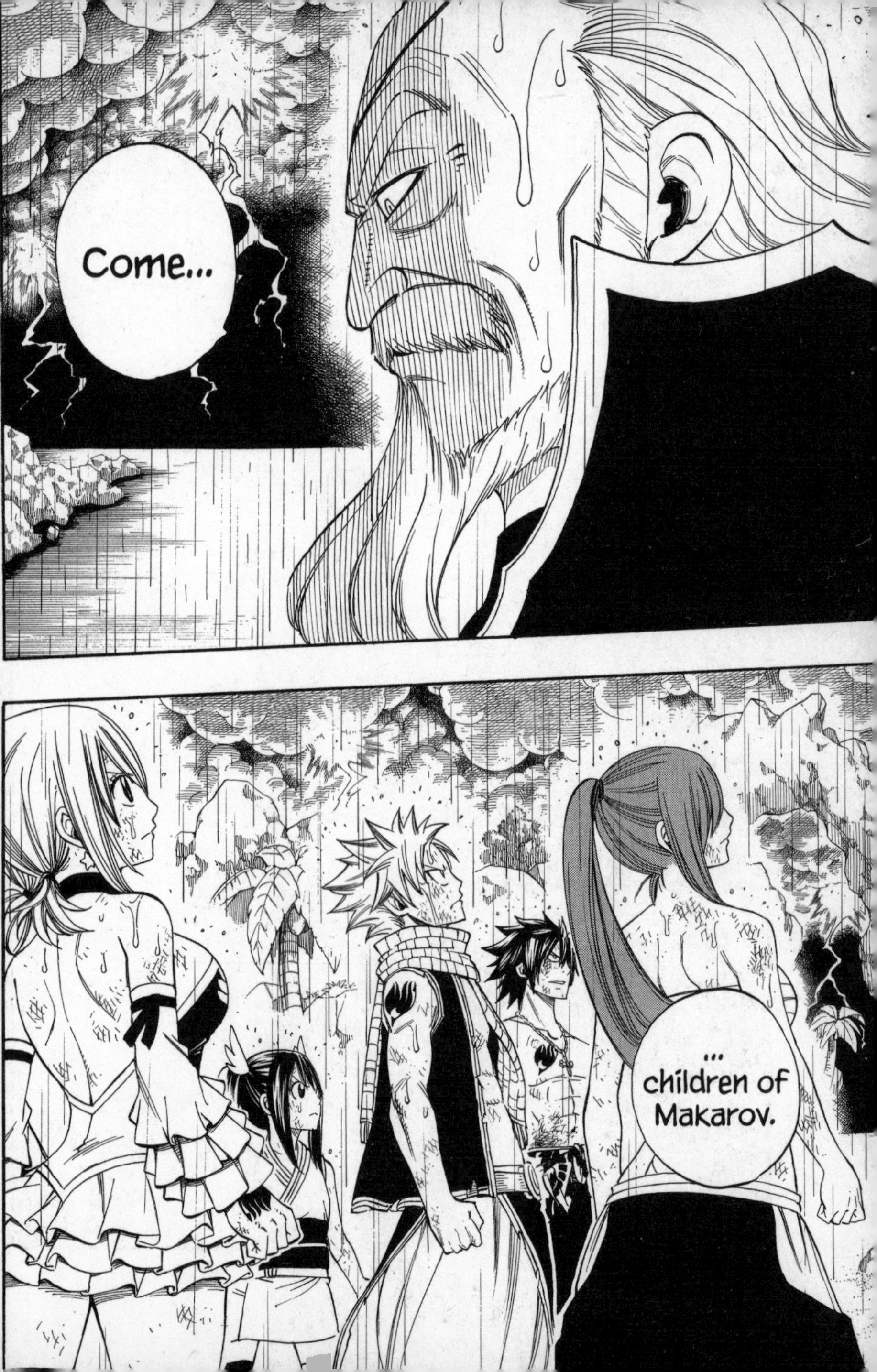
Come...
... children of Makarov.

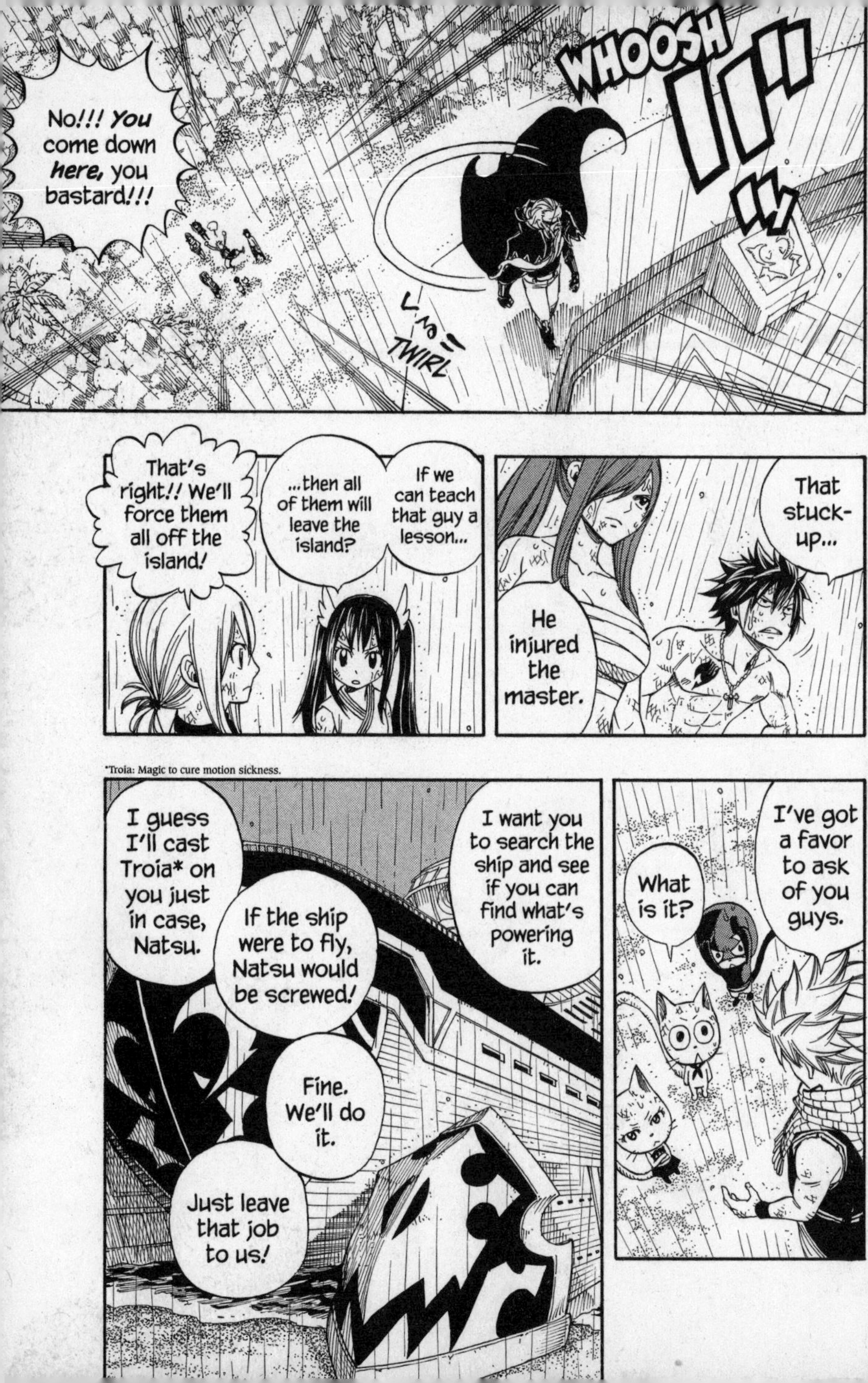
WHOOSH
No!!! You come down here, you bastard!!!
TWIRL
That stuck-up...
He injured the master.
If we can teach that guy a lesson...
...then all of them will leave the island?
That's right!! We'll force them all off the island!
I've got a favor to ask of you guys.
What is it?
I want you to search the ship and see if you can find what's powering it.
I guess I'll cast Troia* on you just in case, Natsu.
If the ship were to fly, Natsu would be screwed!
Fine. We'll do it.
Just leave that job to us!

*Troia: Magic to cure motion sickness.

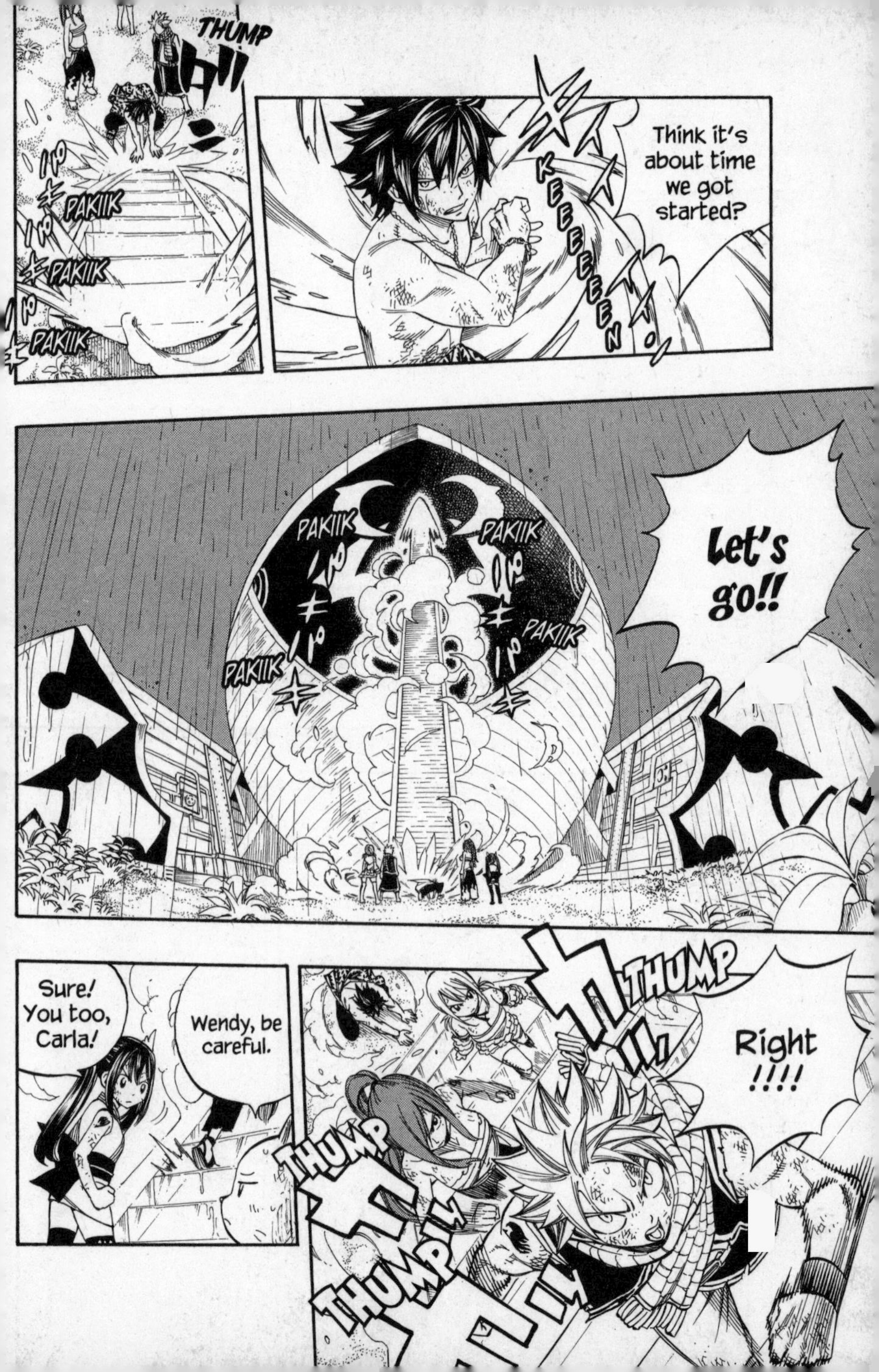
Think it's about time we got started?
KEEEEEEN
THUMP
PAKIIK
PAKIIK
PAKIIK
Let's go!!
PAKIIK
PAKIIK
PAKIIK
PAKIIK
THUMP
Right !!!!
THUMP
THUMP
Wendy, be careful.
Sure! You too, Carla!

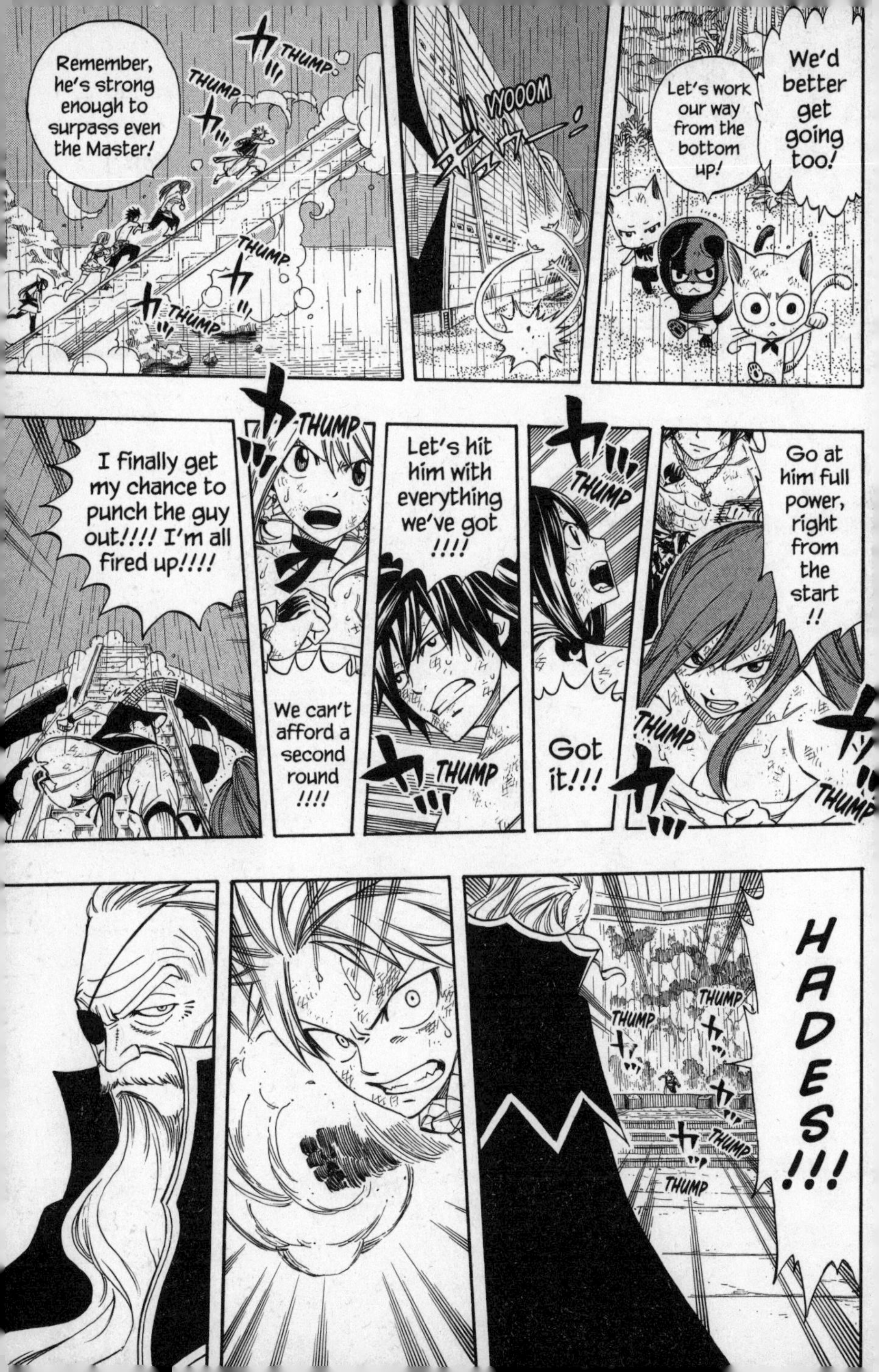
We'd better get going too!
Let's work our way from the bottom up!
VYOOOM
THUMP
THUMP
Remember, he's strong enough to surpass even the Master!
THUMP
THUMP
Go at him full power, right from the start!!
THUMP
THUMP
THUMP
Got it!!!
Let's hit him with everything we've got!!!!
THUMP
THUMP
We can't afford a second round!!!!
I finally get my chance to punch the guy out!!!! I'm all fired up!!!!
HADES!!!
THUMP
THUMP
THUMP
THUMP

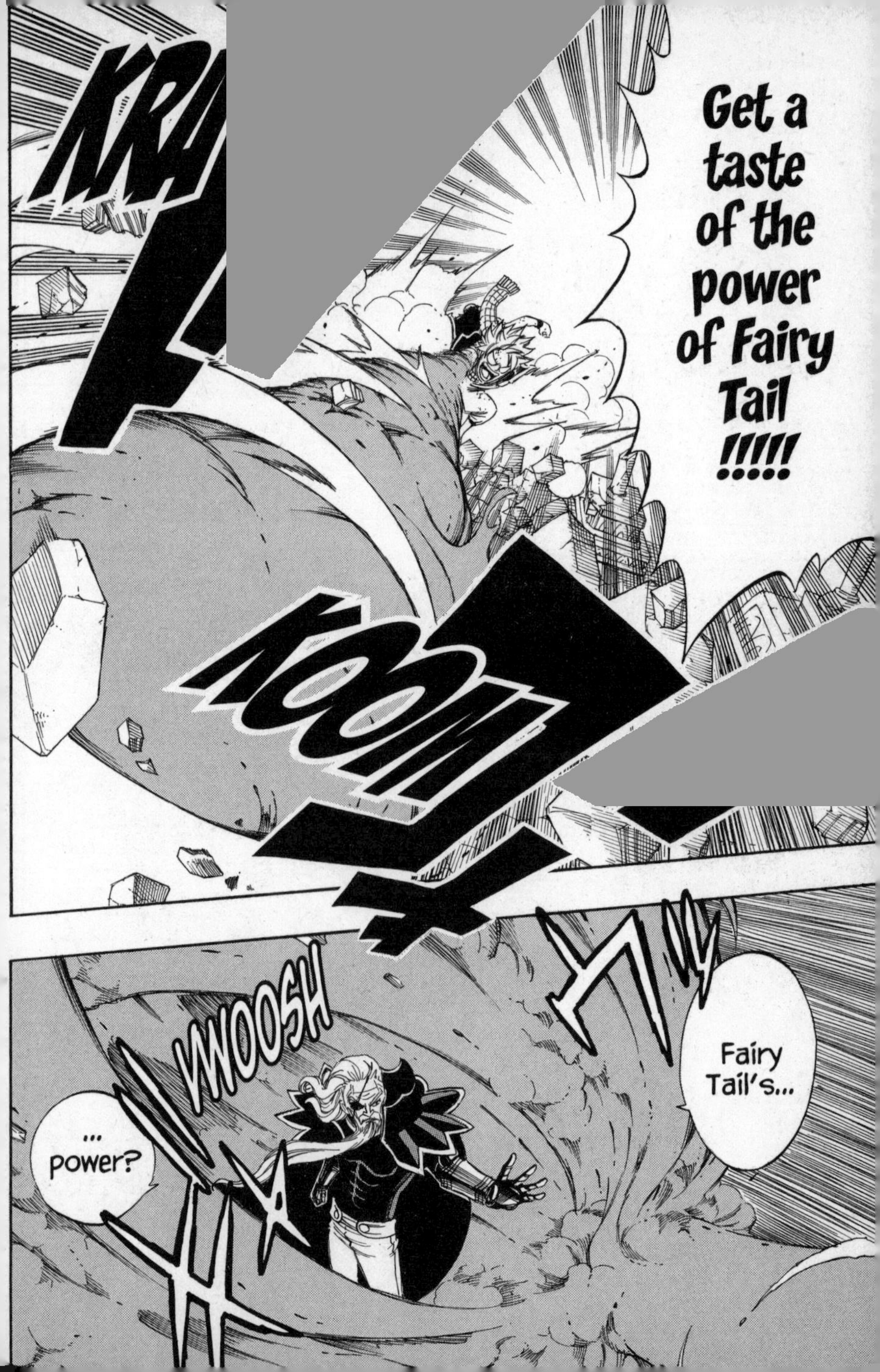
Get a taste of the power of Fairy Tail!!!!!
KRA
KOOM
Fairy Tail's...
WOOSH
... power?

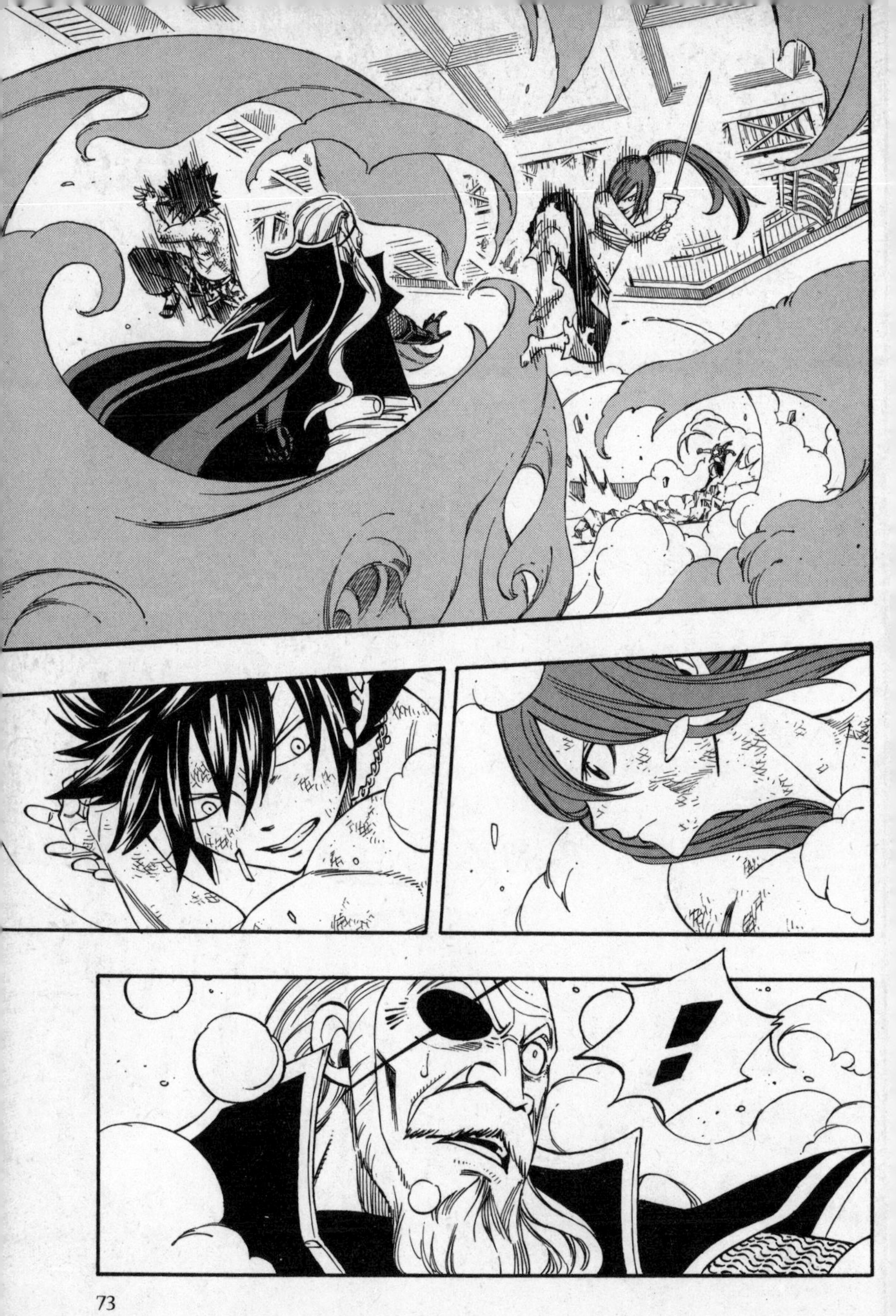
!!

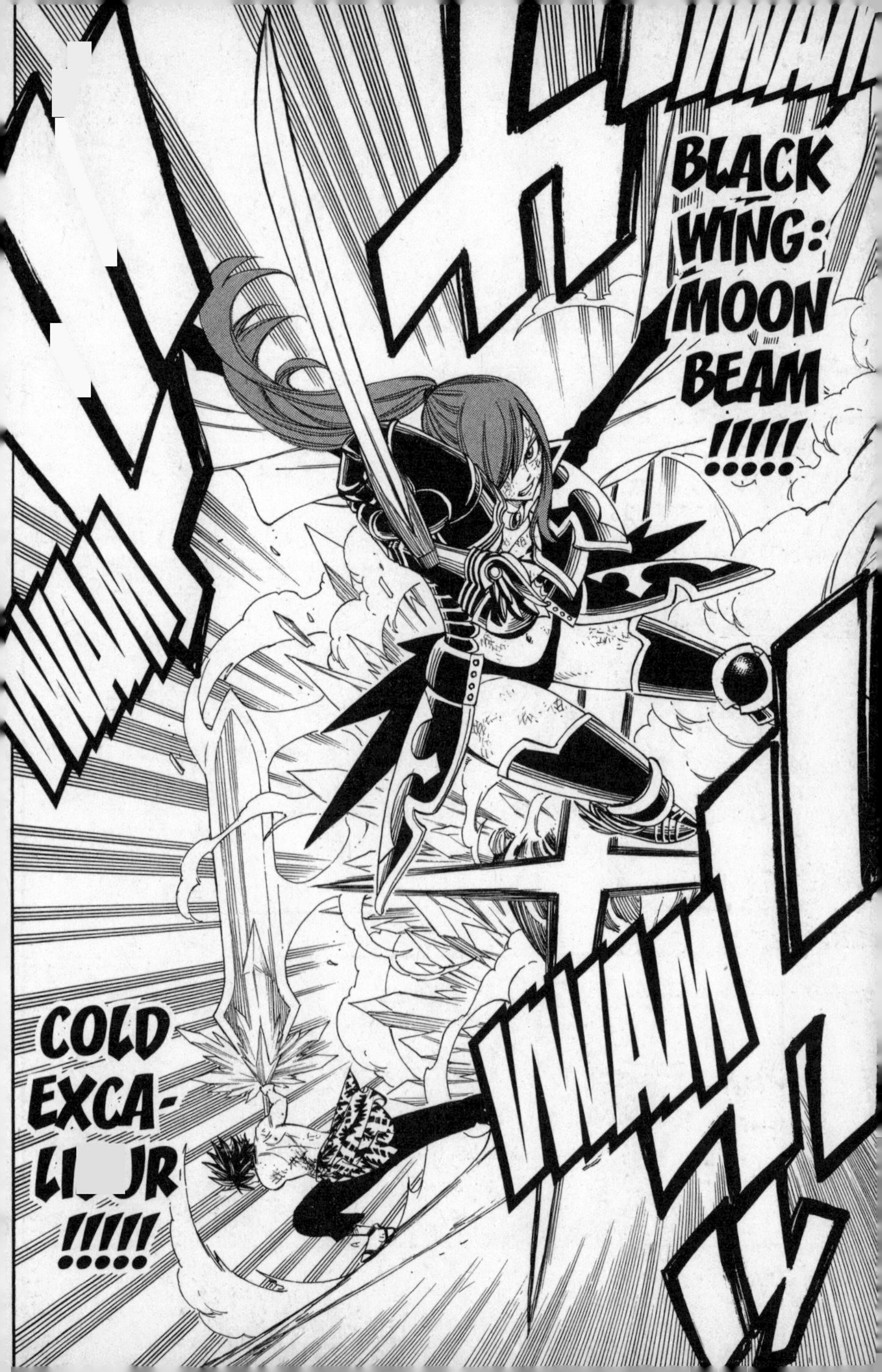
BLACK WING: MOON BEAM!!!!!
COLD EXCA-LI UR!!!!!

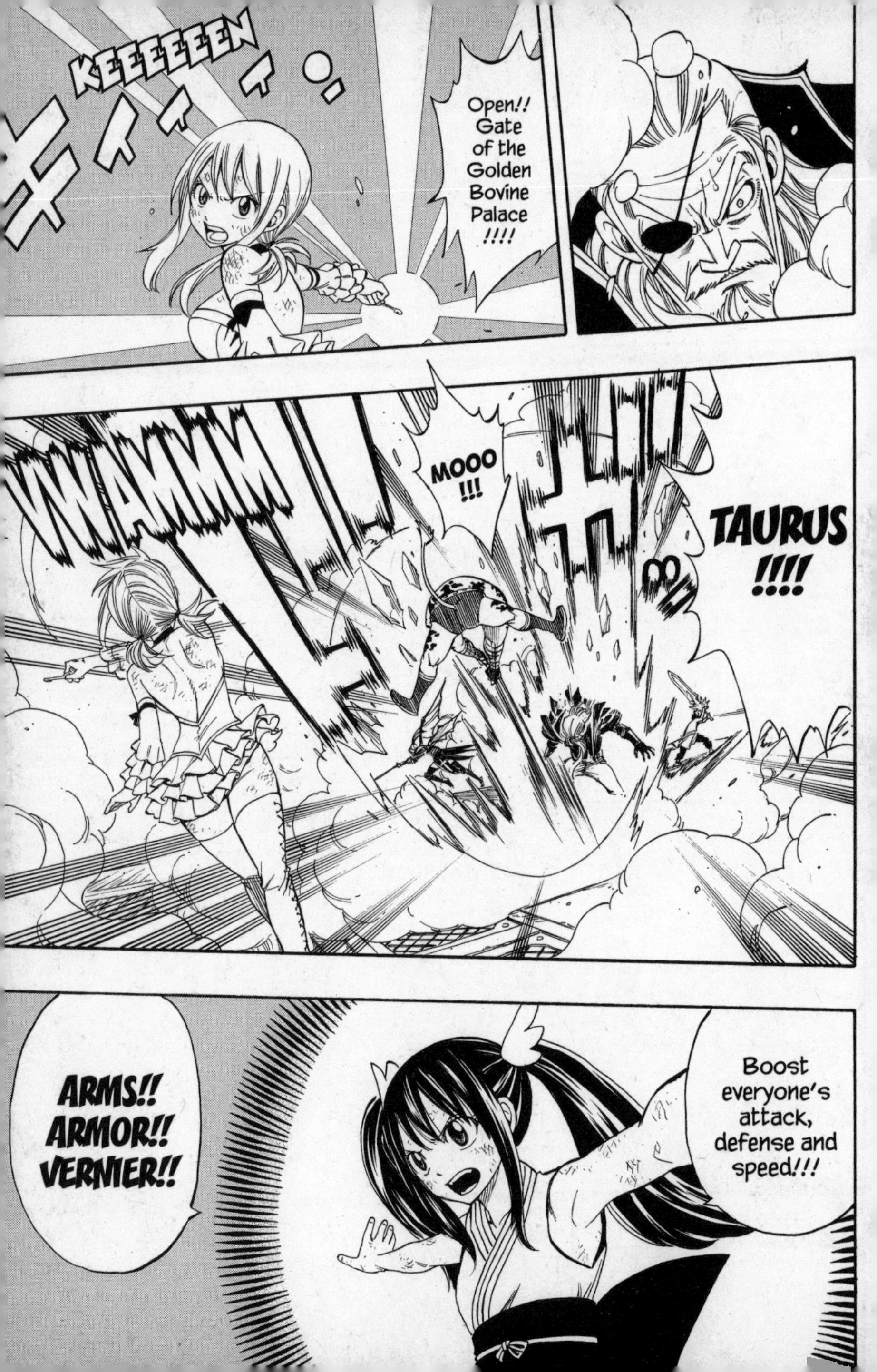
Open!! Gate of the Golden Bovine Palace !!!!
KEEEEEEN
TAURUS !!!!
MOOO !!!
VWAMMM
Boost everyone's attack, defense and speed!!!
ARMS!! ARMOR!! VERNIER!!

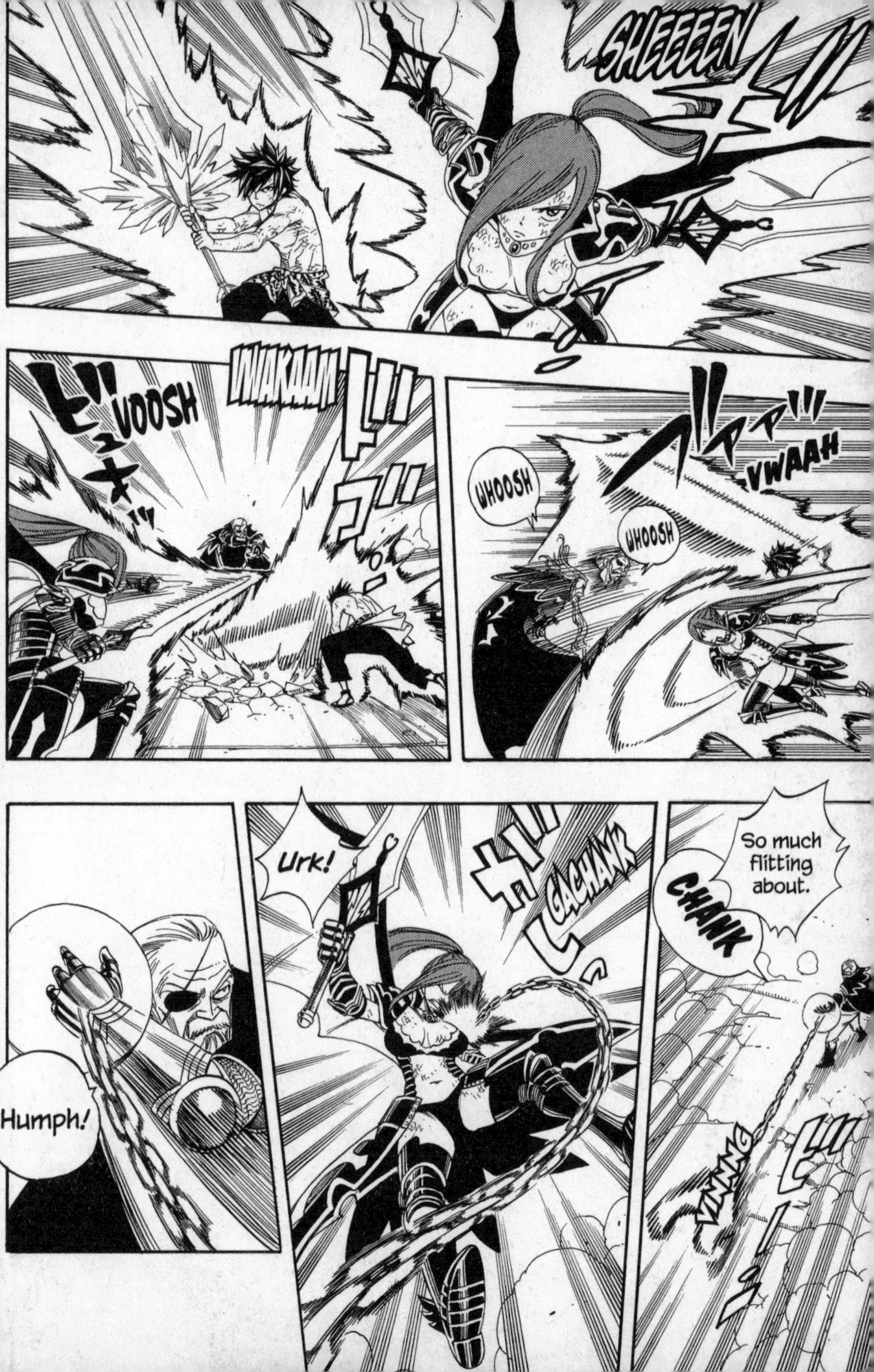
SHEEEEN
VWAAH
WHOOSH
WHOOSH
VWAKAAM
VOOSH
So much flitting about.
CHANK
VWNNG
Urk!
GACHANK
Humph!

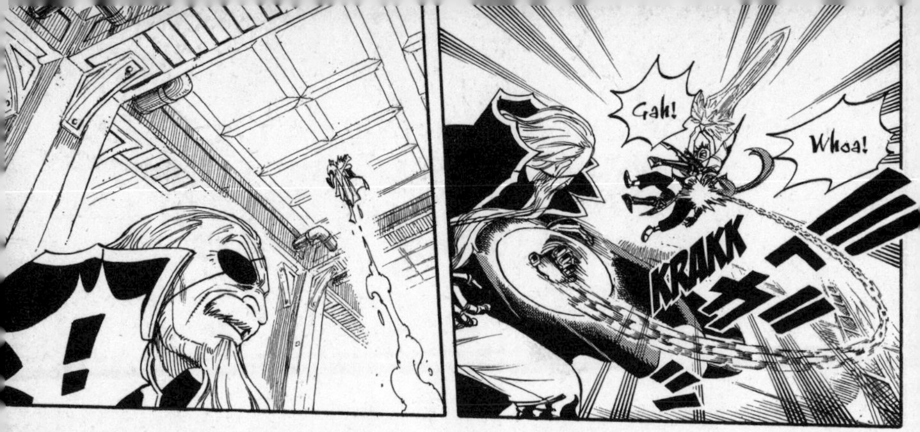
Gah!
Whoa!
KRAKK
!

*Fire Dragon's Wing Attack

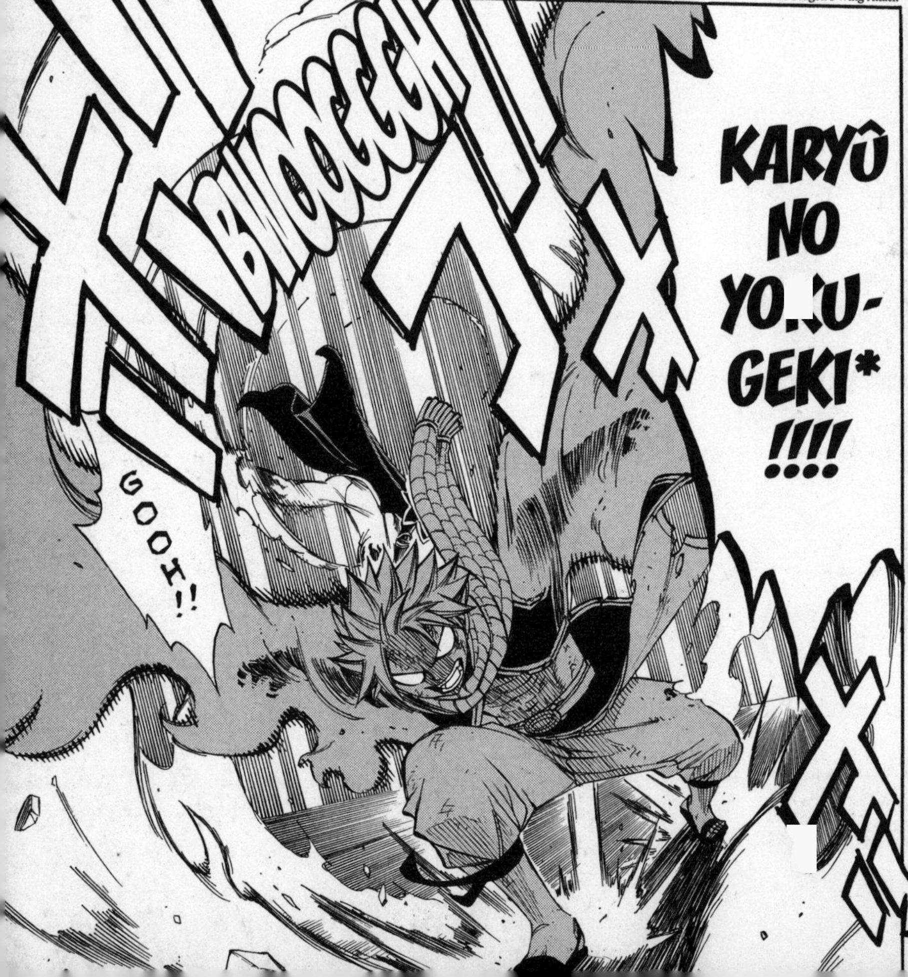
KARYÛ NO YOKU-GEKI* !!!!
BWOOCCGH
GOOH!!

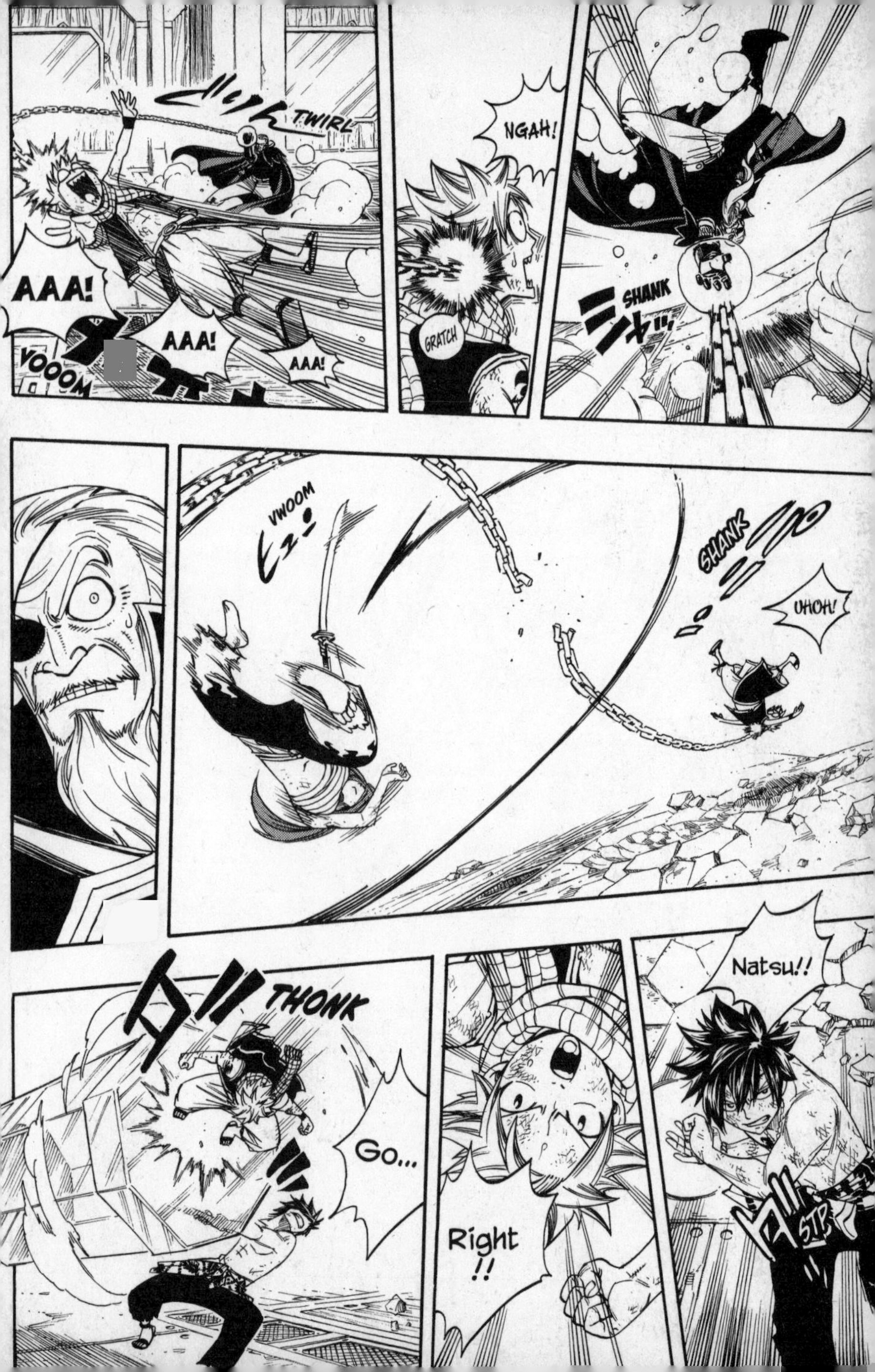
SHANK
NGAH!
GRATCH
TWIRL
AAA!
AAA!
AAA!
VOOOM
SHANK
UHOH!
VWOOM
Natsu!!
STP
Right!!
Go...
THONK

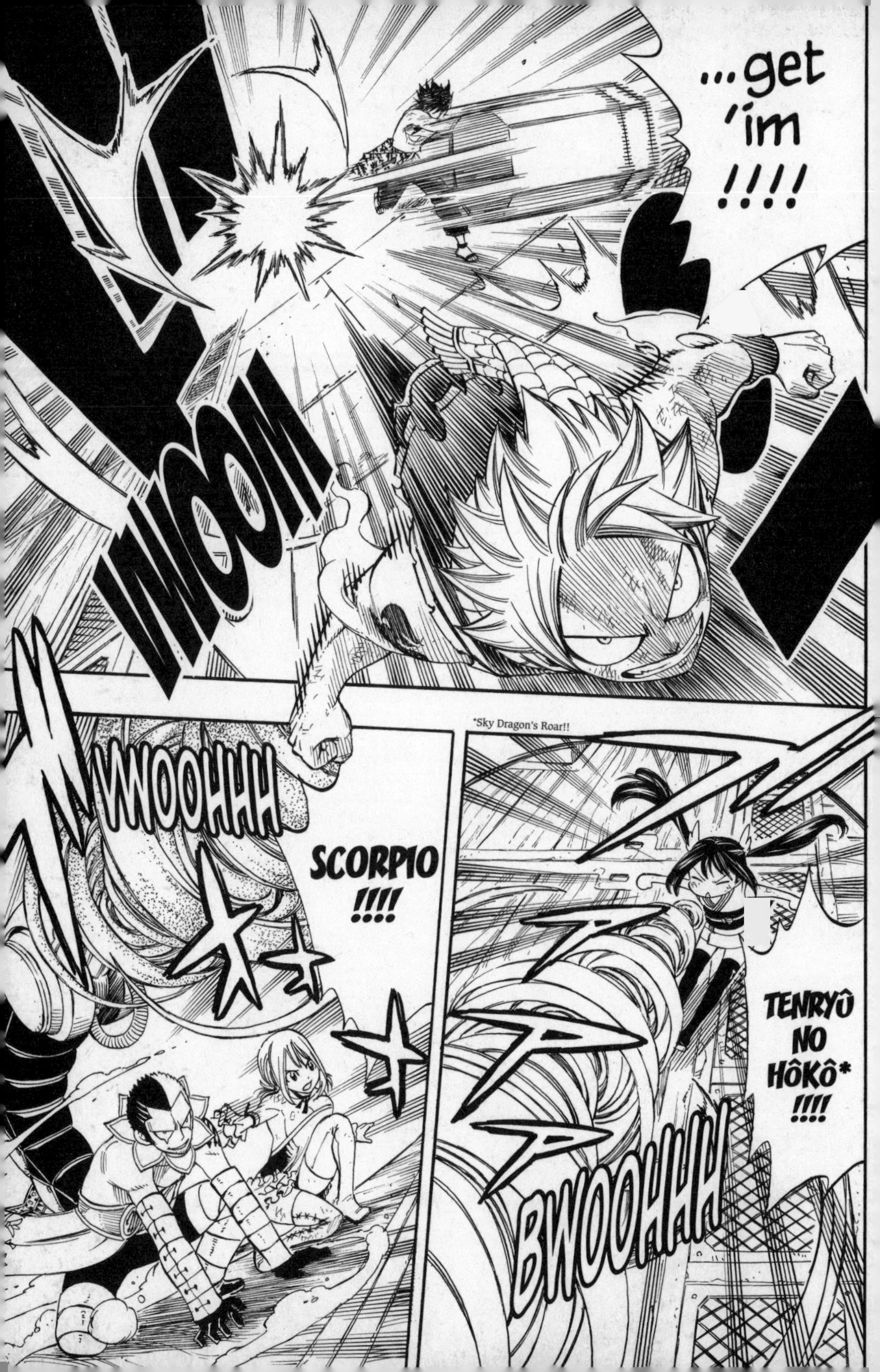
...get 'im !!!!
TENRYÛ NO HÔKÔ* !!!!
BWOOHHH
SCORPIO !!!!
*Sky Dragon's Roar!!

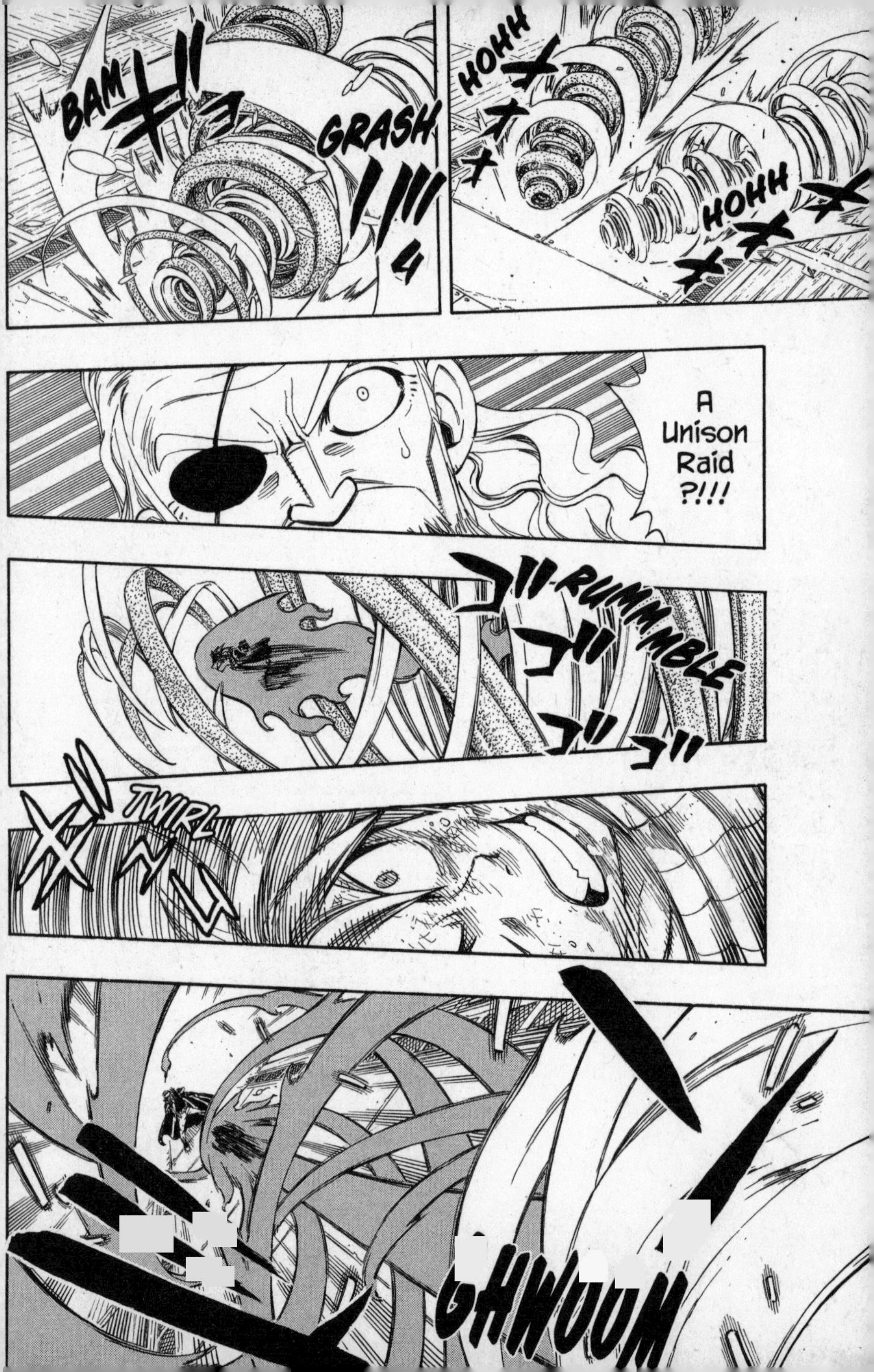
HOHH
HOHH
BAM
GRASH
A Unison Raid ?!!!
RUMMMMBLE
TWIRL
GHWOOM

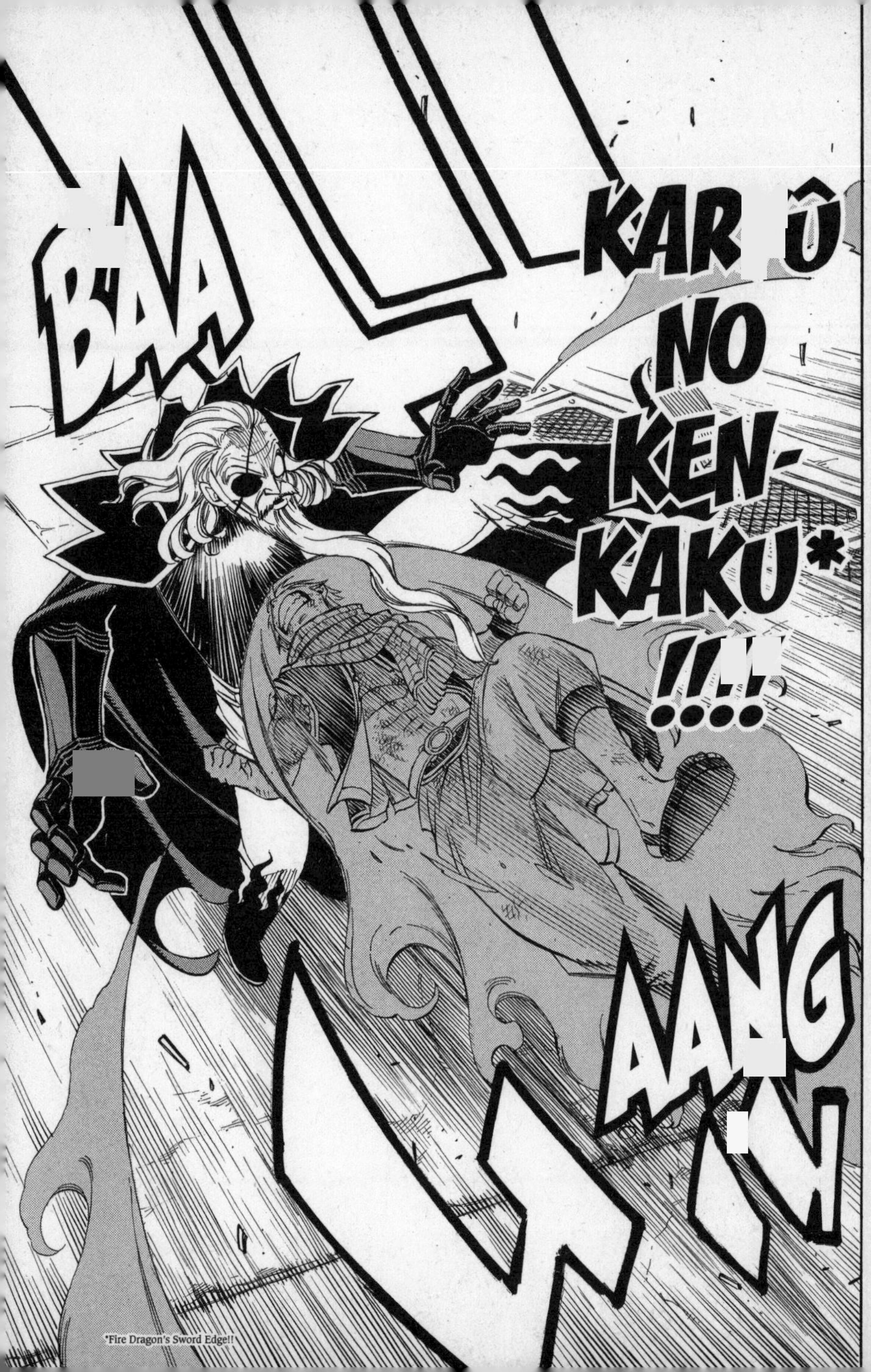
KAR Û NO KEN-KAKU*!!
BAA
AANG
*Fire Dragon's Sword Edge!!

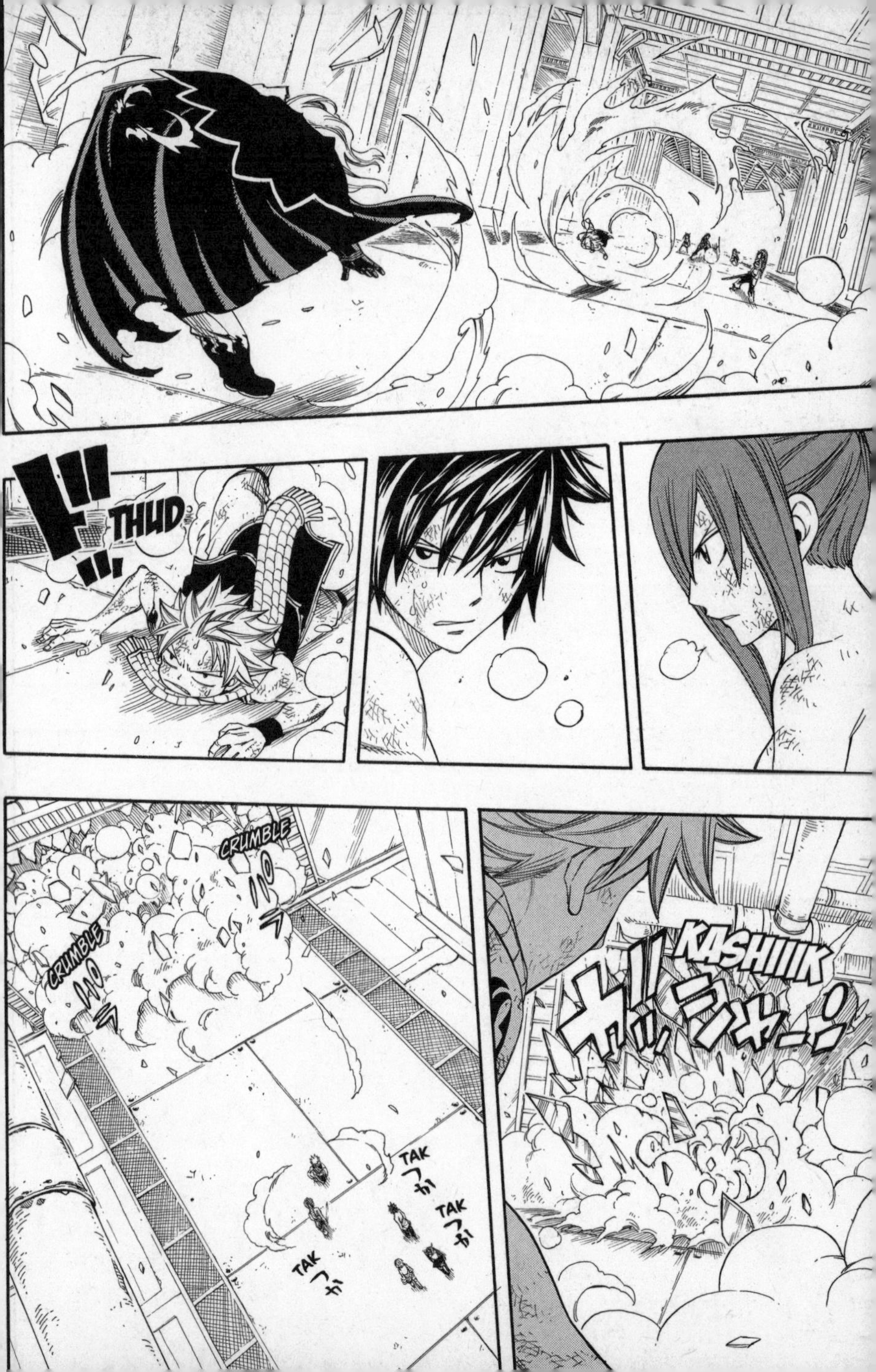
THUD
KASHIIIIK
CRUMBLE
CRUMBLE
TAK
TAK
TAK

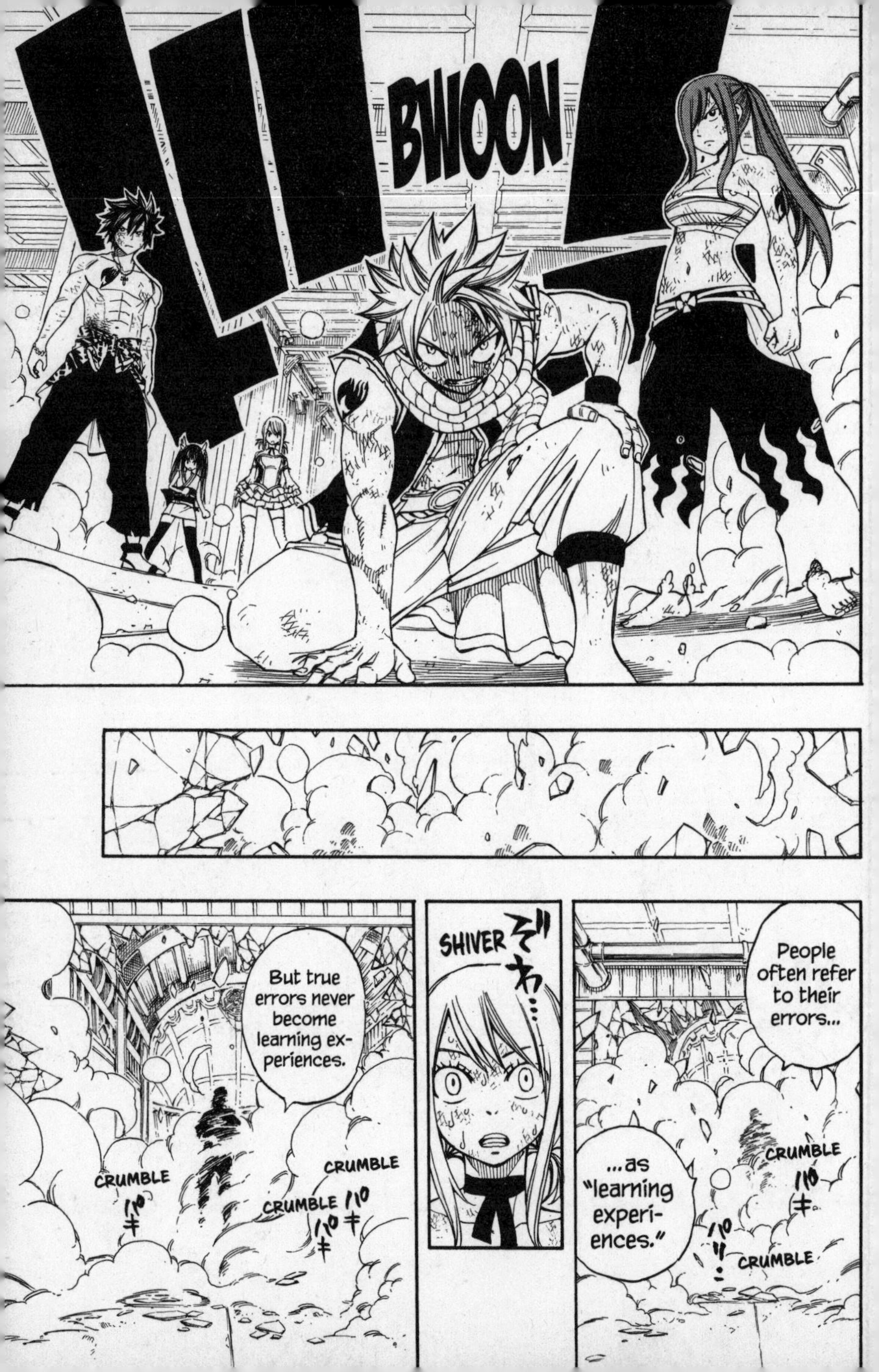
BWOON
People often refer to their errors...
...as "learning experiences."
CRUMBLE
パキ
パキ!!
CRUMBLE
SHIVER
ざわ…
But true errors never become learning experiences.
CRUMBLE
パキ
CRUMBLE
パキ
パキ
CRUMBLE
パキ

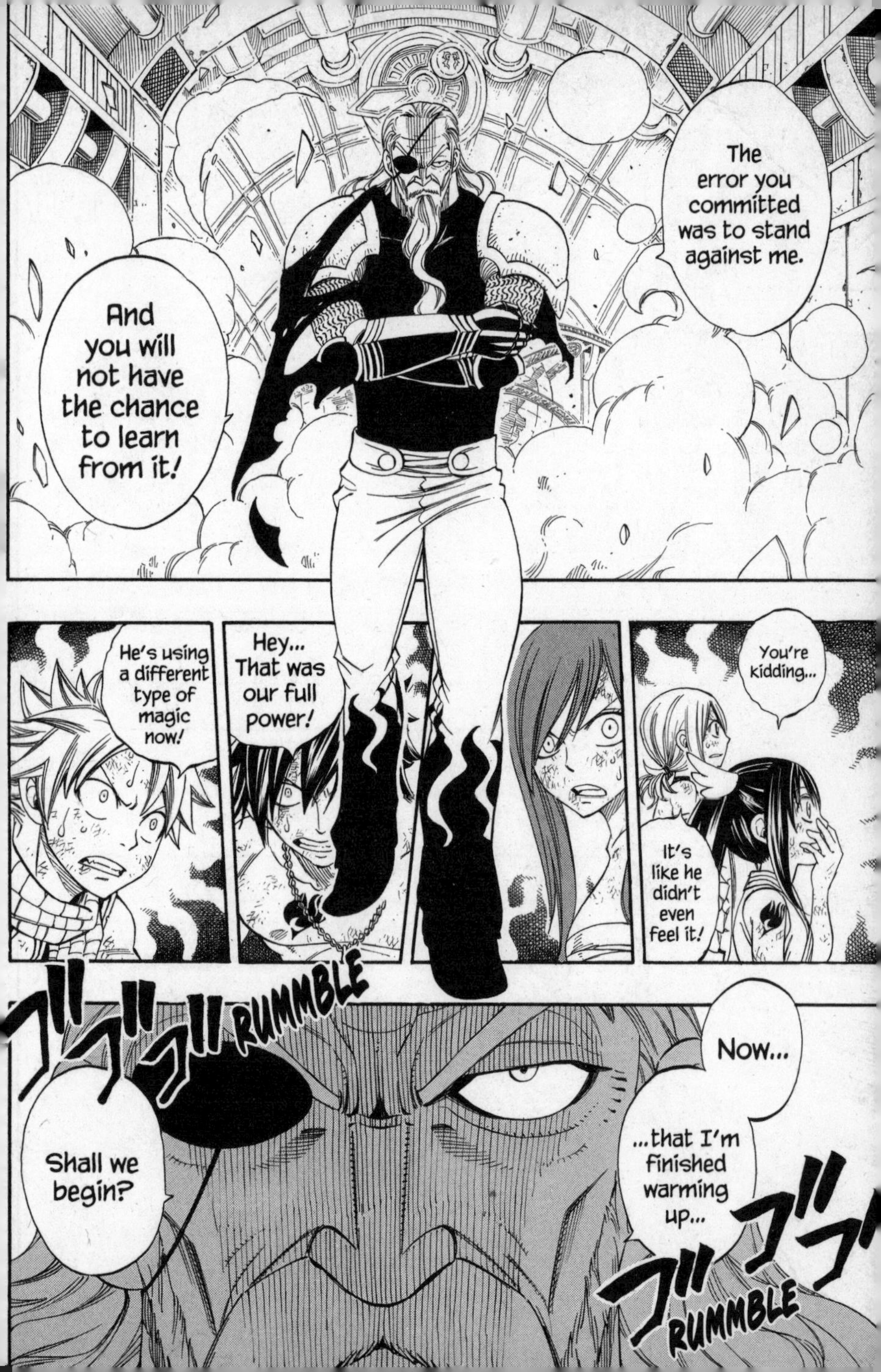
The error you committed was to stand against me.
And you will not have the chance to learn from it!
You're kidding...
It's like he didn't even feel it!
Hey... That was our full power!
He's using a different type of magic now!
Now...
...that I'm finished warming up...
RUMMBLE
Shall we begin?
RUMMBLE

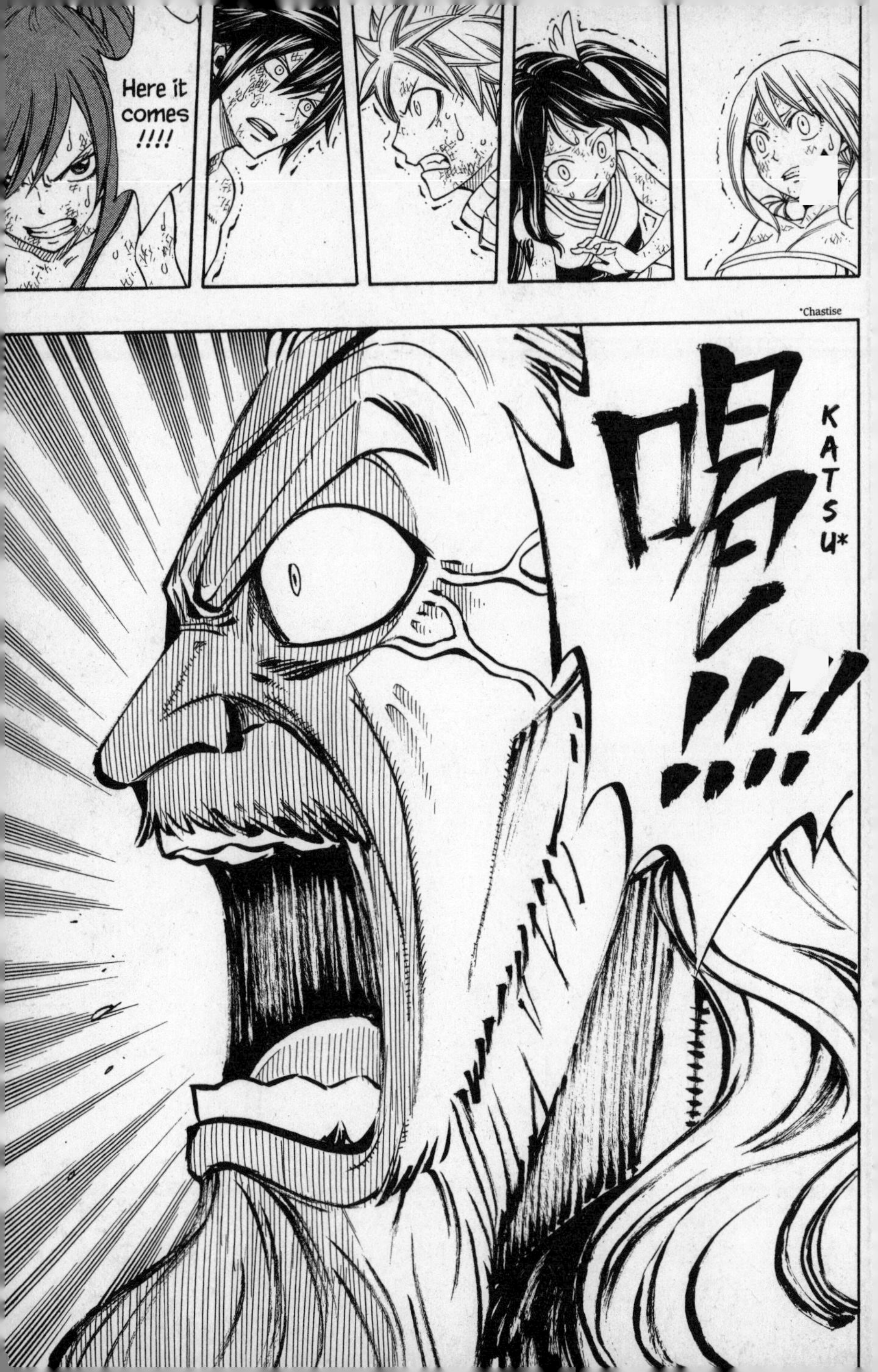
Here it comes !!!!
KATSU*
*Chastise

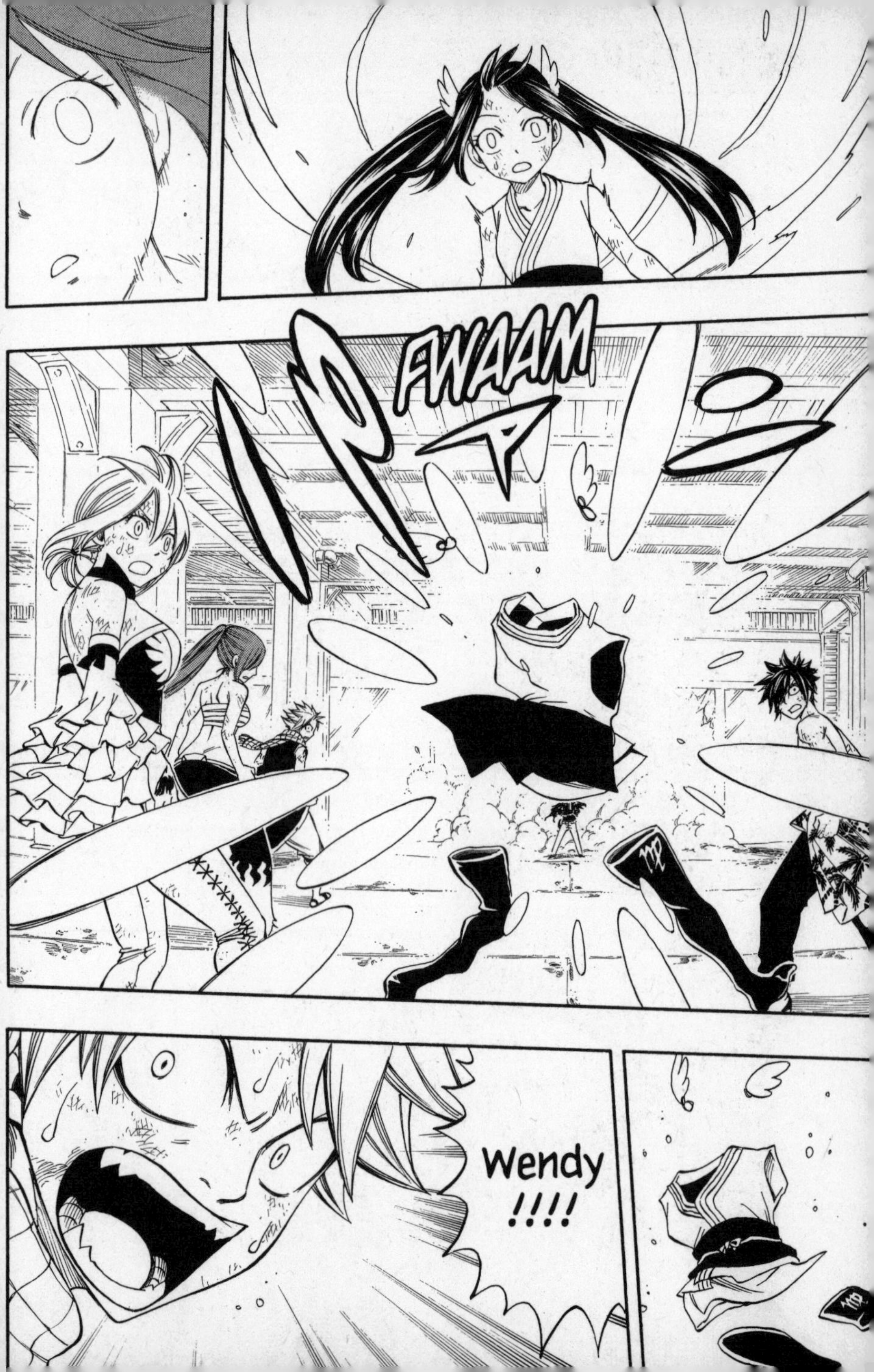
FWAAM
Wendy
!!!!

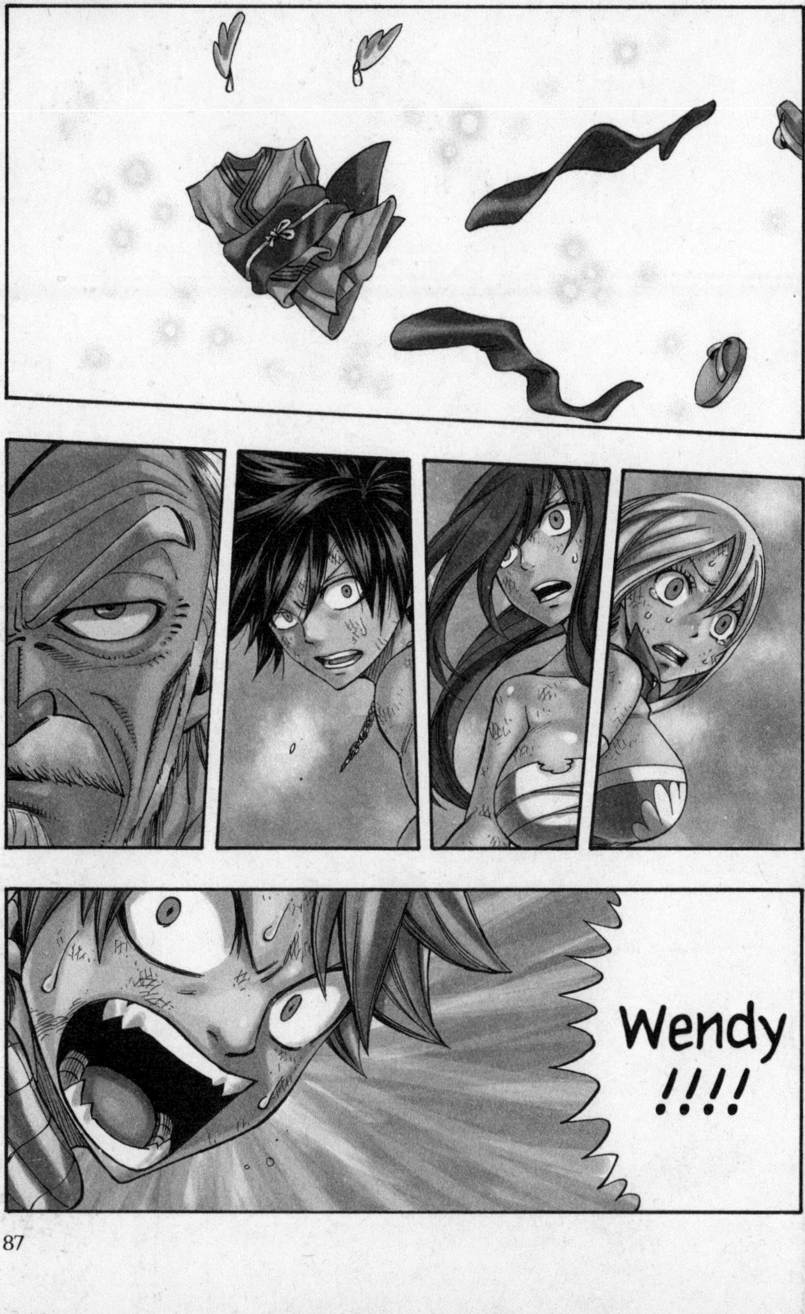
Wendy
!!!!

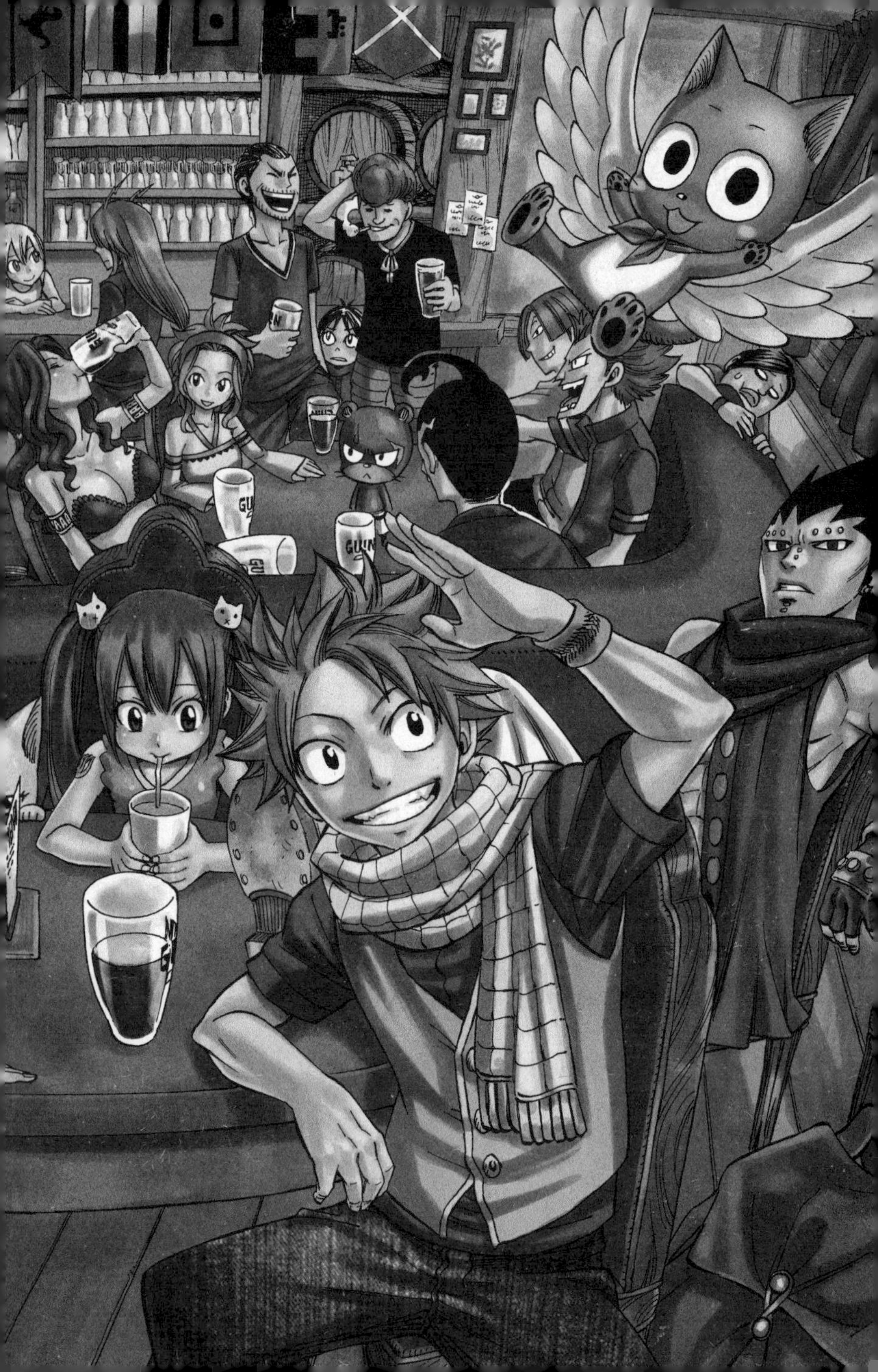

Chapter 244: The Peal of Thunder

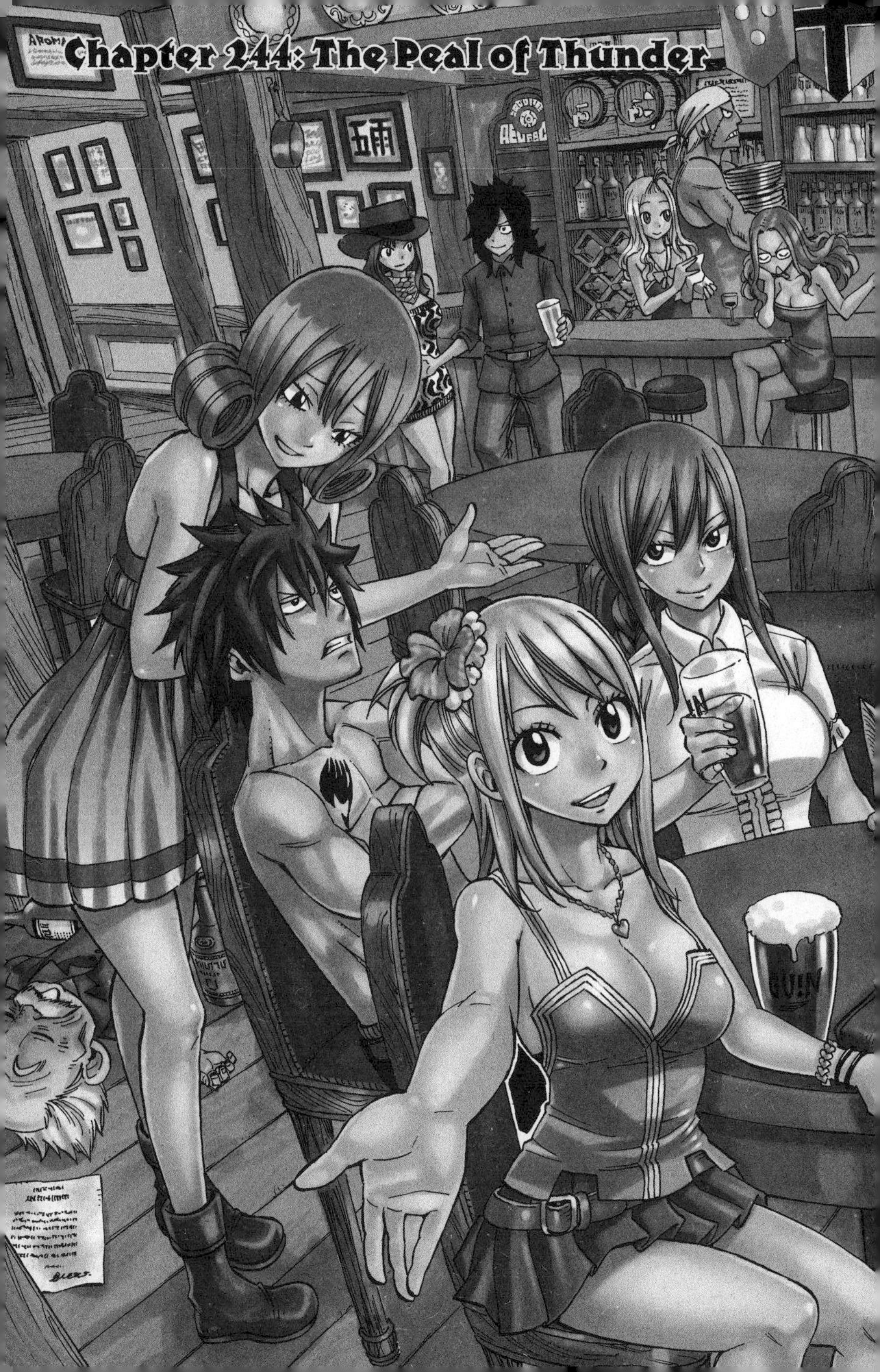

The Fairy Tail Guild is looking for illustrations! Please send in your art on a postcard or at postcard size, and do it in black pen, okay? Those chosen to be published will get a signed mini poster! ♪ Make sure you write your real name and address on the back of your illustration!

SPECIAL REJECTED COLLECTION 1

FAIRY TAIL GUILD d'ART

Recently there have been so many entries aiming at the "Rejection Corner" that we had no choice - NO CHOICE - but to do a special rejection collection.

Fukuoka Prefecture, Taiga Hayama

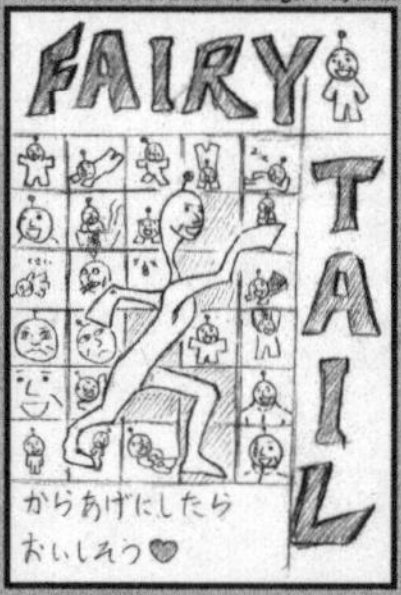
FAIRY TAIL
からあげにしたら
おいしそう♥

▲ You must not eat him. Your stomach would explode.

Okayama Prefecture, I Love to Be Rejected-san

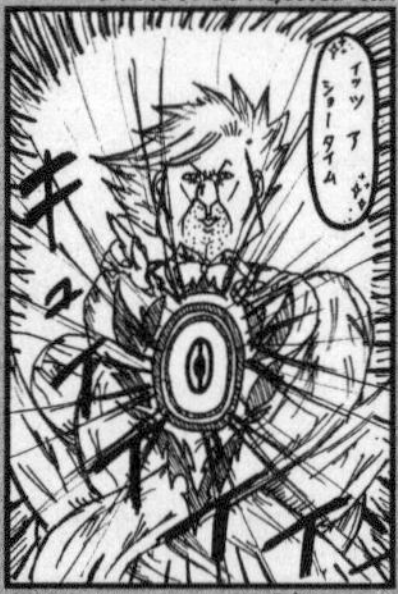

▲ Wh-What is this?! Ichiya!! Meeeen!!

Saitama Prefecture, Aa-chan

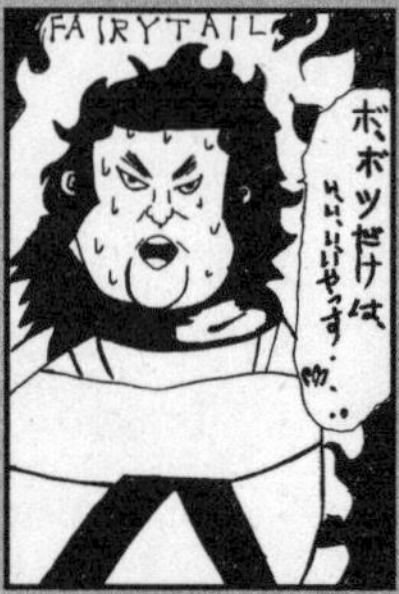
FAIRYTAIL

▲ Rejection Corner pictures of Kain have already become routine?!

Ibaraki Prefecture, Fairy

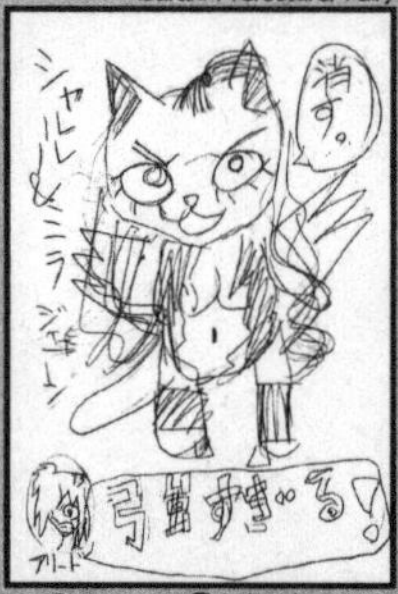

▲ Too strong? I-Is that right?

Hyogo Prefecture, Tenkō Usuda

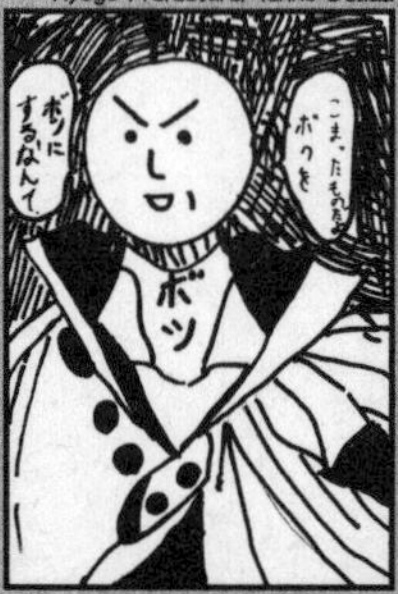

▲ Really...? Well, too bad. You're rejected.

Ibaraki Prefecture, Fuko Shimizu

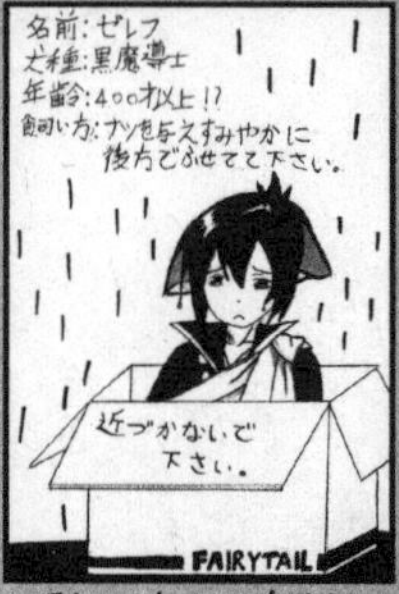
名前：ゼレフ
年齢：400才以上!?
飼い方：ナツを与えすみやかに
後方でふせてて下さい。
近づかないで
下さい。
FAIRYTAIL

▲ This one's scary! Make sure you don't adopt him!

Hokkaido, Rinoa Yoshida

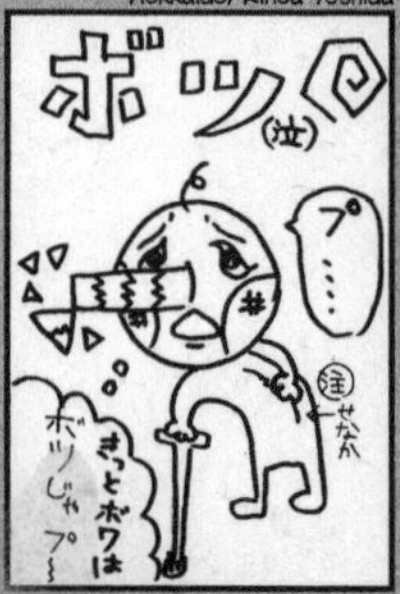
ボツ(泣)
プ……

▲ N-No, I can't...! I'm laughing!

Send to Hiro Mashima, Kodansha Comics, 451 Park Ave. South, 7th Floor, New York, NY 10016

By sending in letters or postcards you give us permission to give your name, address, postal code and any other information you include to the author as is. Please keep that in mind.

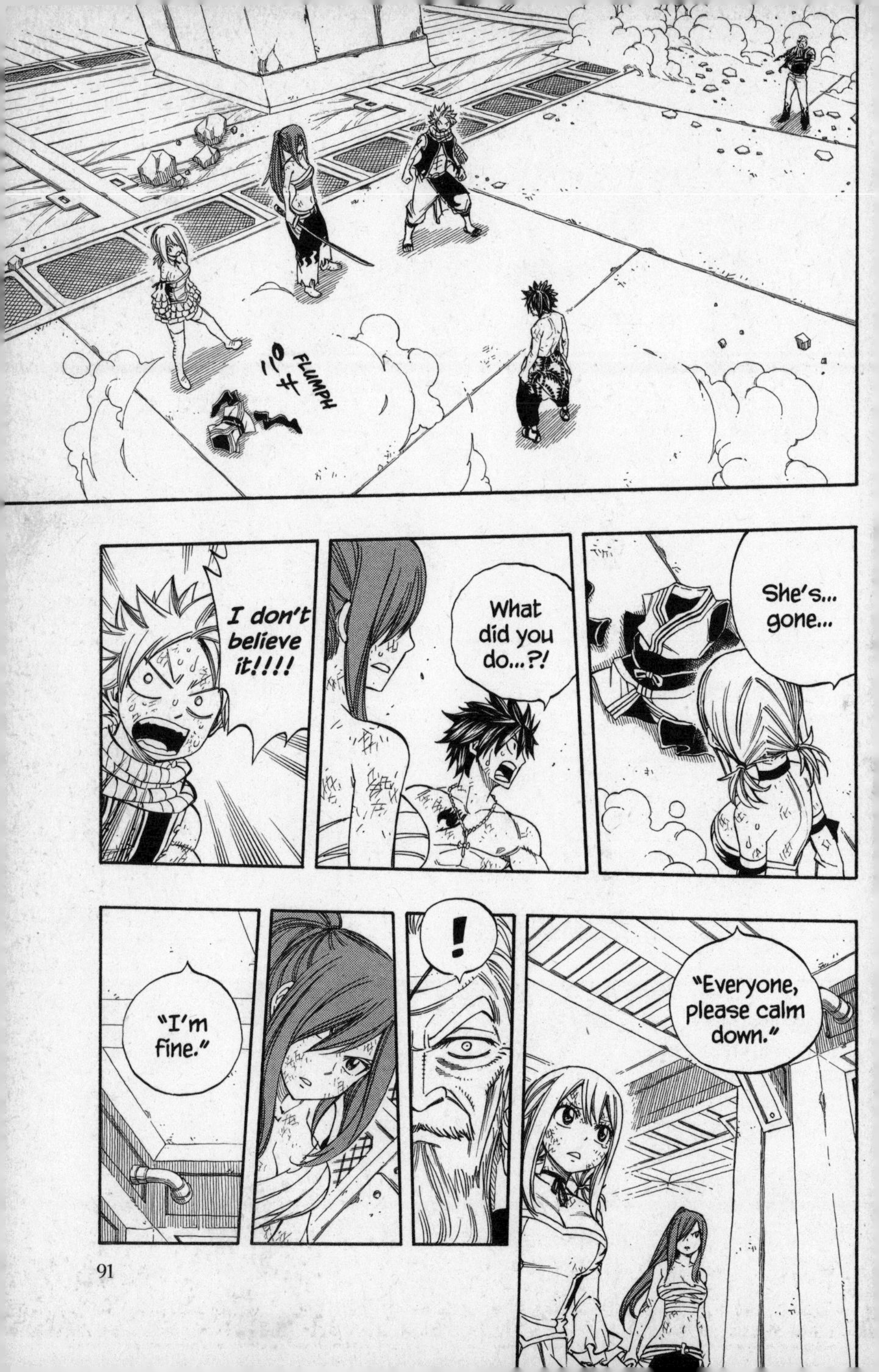
FLUMPH
"She's... gone..."
What did you do...?!
I don't believe it!!!!
"Everyone, please calm down."
!
"I'm fine."

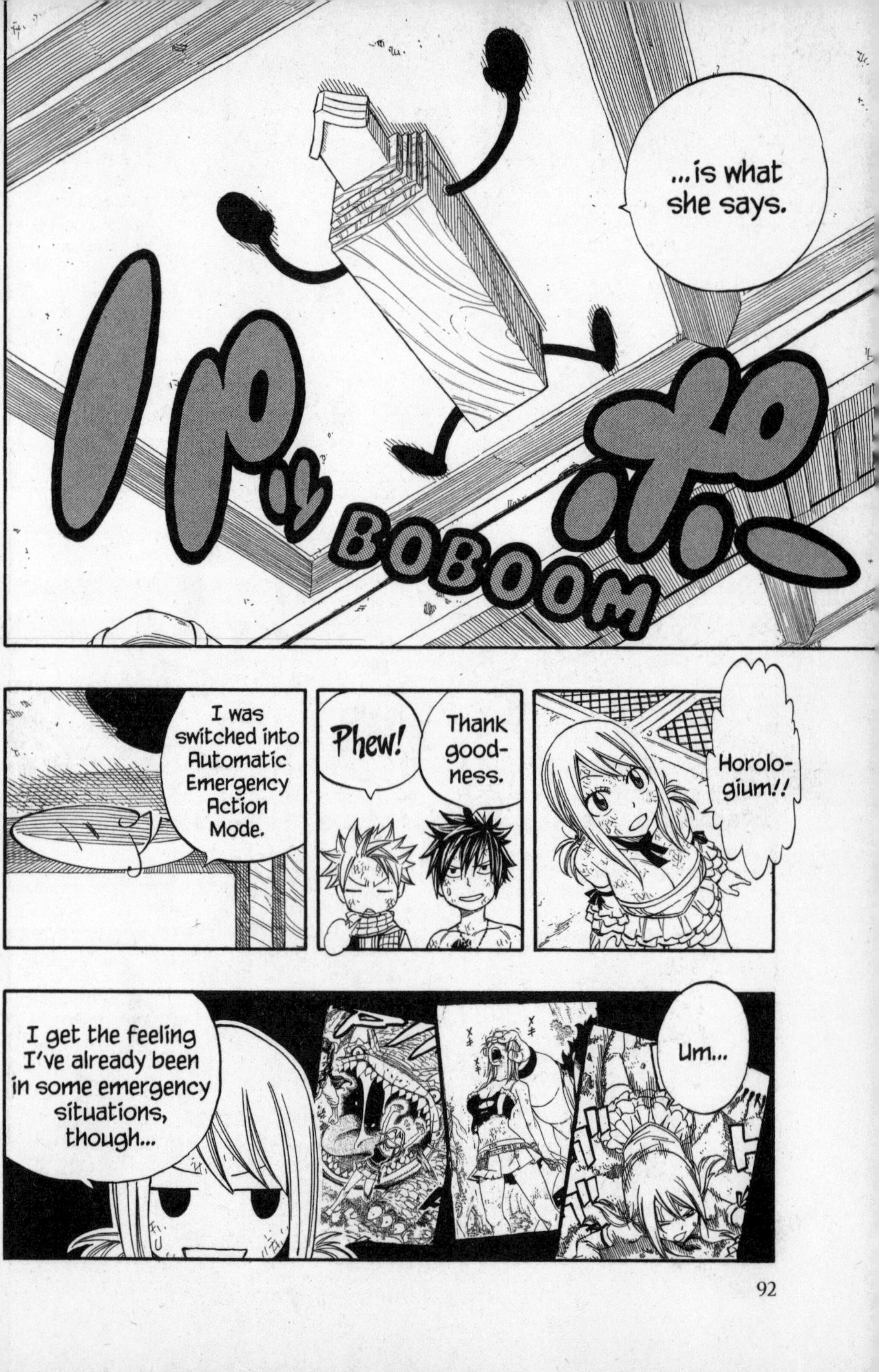
...is what she says.
BOBOOM
Horolo-gium!!
Thank good-ness.
Phew!
I was switched into Automatic Emergency Action Mode.
Um...
I get the feeling I've already been in some emergency situations, though...

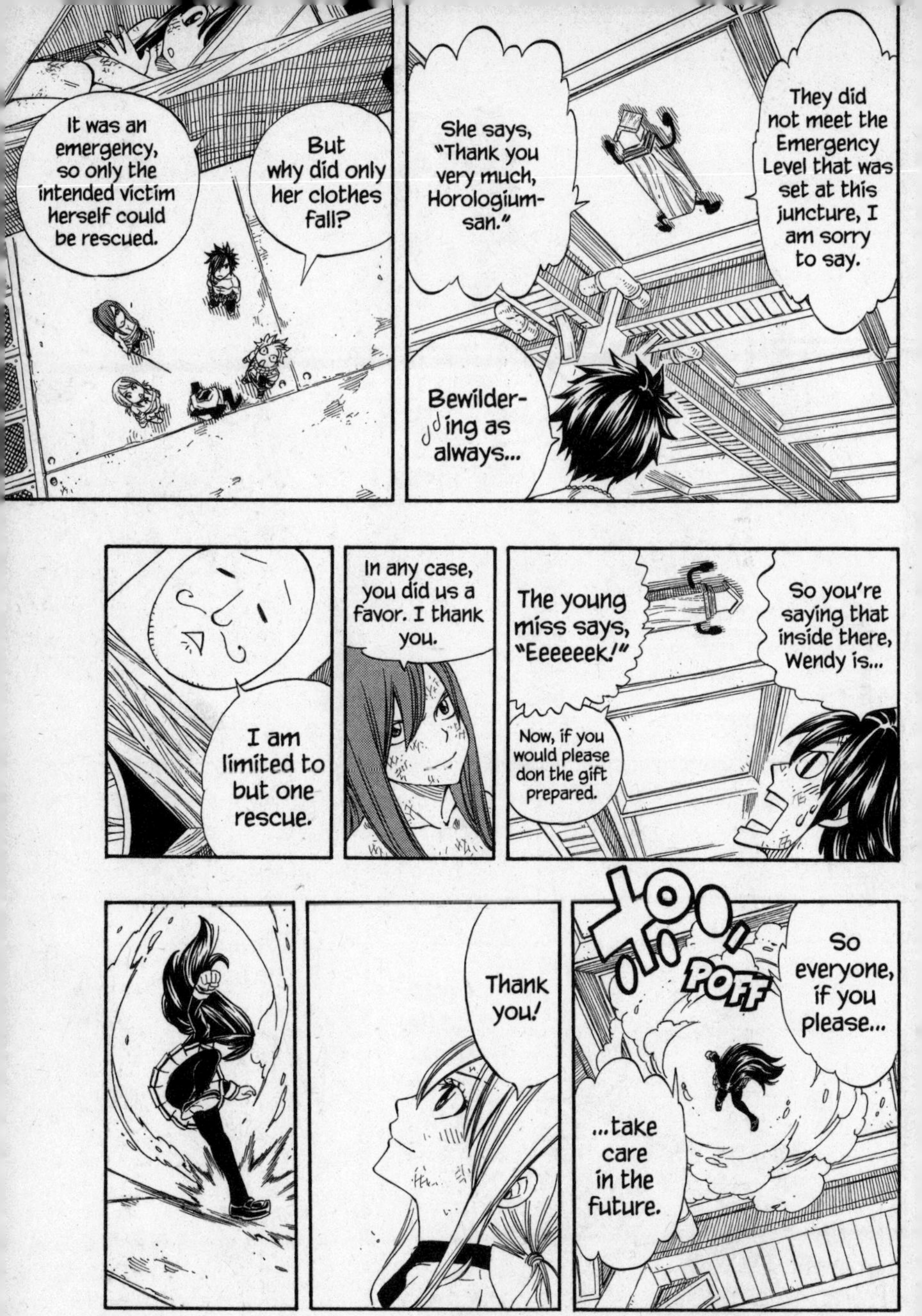
They did not meet the Emergency Level that was set at this juncture, I am sorry to say.
She says, "Thank you very much, Horologium-san."
Bewilder-ing as always...
But why did only her clothes fall?
It was an emergency, so only the intended victim herself could be rescued.
So you're saying that inside there, Wendy is...
The young miss says, "Eeeeeek!"
Now, if you would please don the gift prepared.
In any case, you did us a favor. I thank you.
I am limited to but one rescue.
So everyone, if you please...
POFF
...take care in the future.
Thank you!

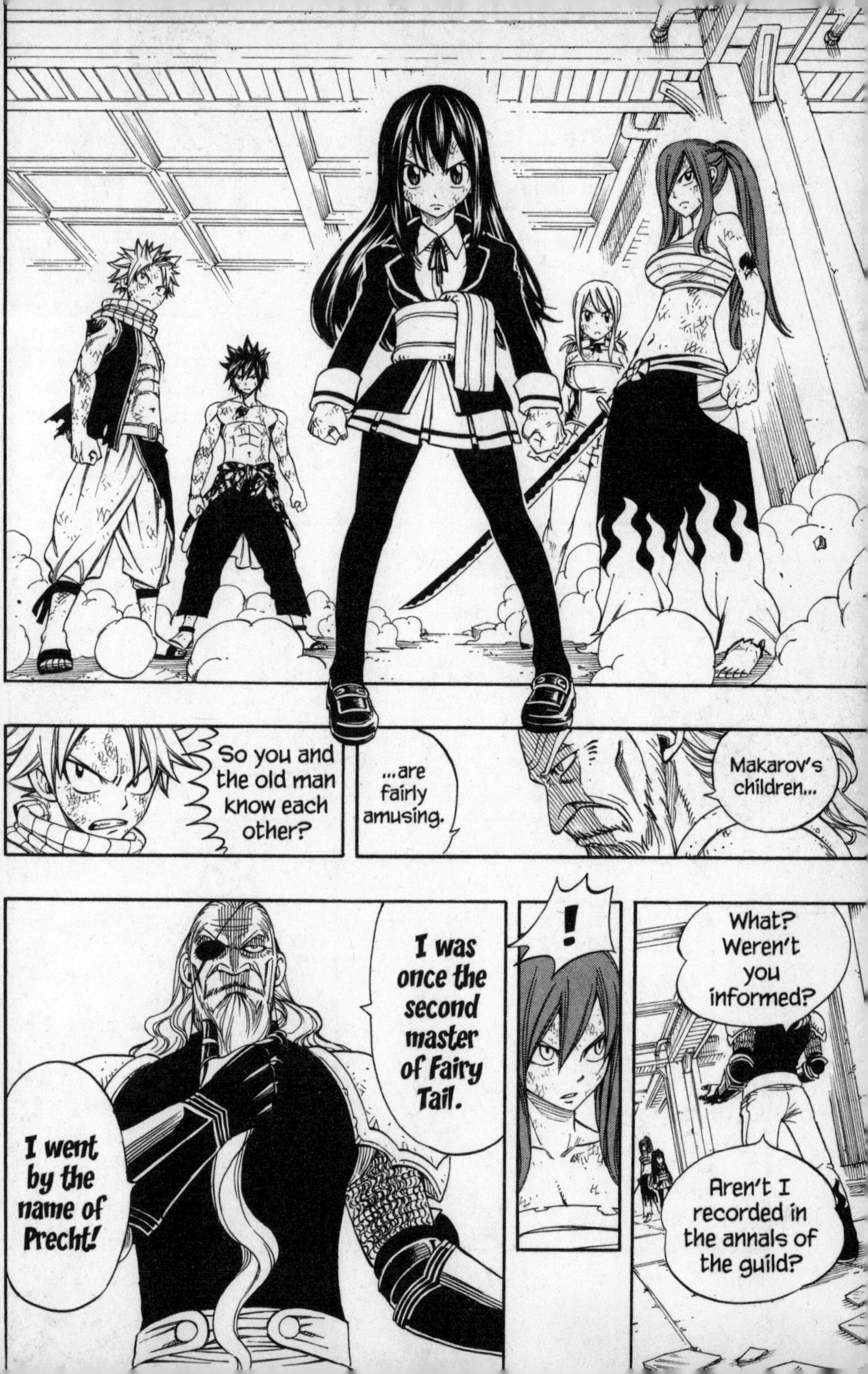
Makarov's children...
...are fairly amusing.
So you and the old man know each other?
What? Weren't you informed?
Aren't I recorded in the annals of the guild?
!
I was once the second master of Fairy Tail.
I went by the name of Precht!

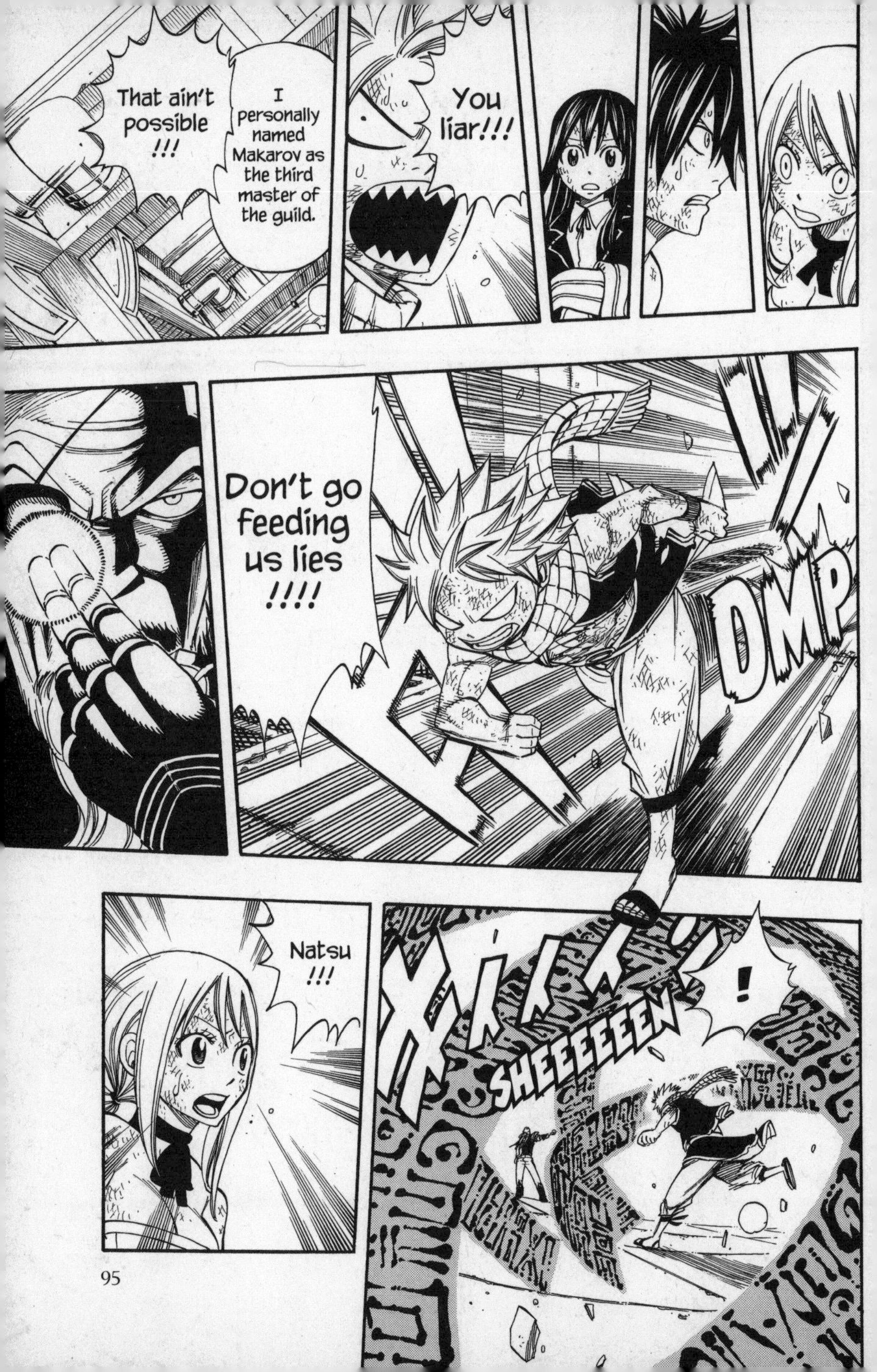
You liar!!!
I personally named Makarov as the third master of the guild.
That ain't possible!!!
DOMP
Don't go feeding us lies!!!!
!
SHEEEEEEN
Natsu!!!

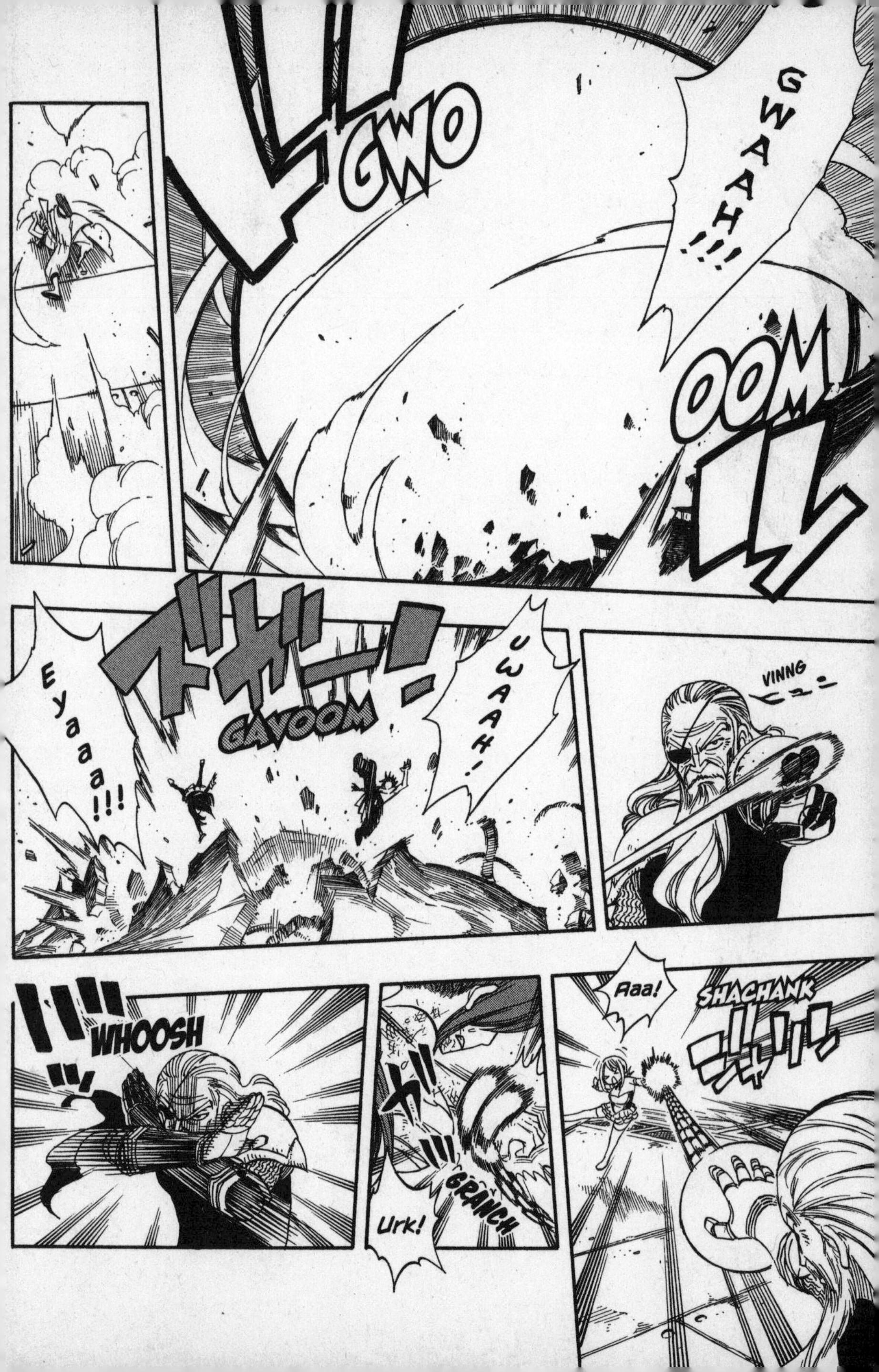
GWAAAH!!!!
GWO
OOM
VINNG
UWAAAH!
GAVOOM
Eyaaa!!!
Aaa!
SHACHANK
GRANCH
Urk!
WHOOSH

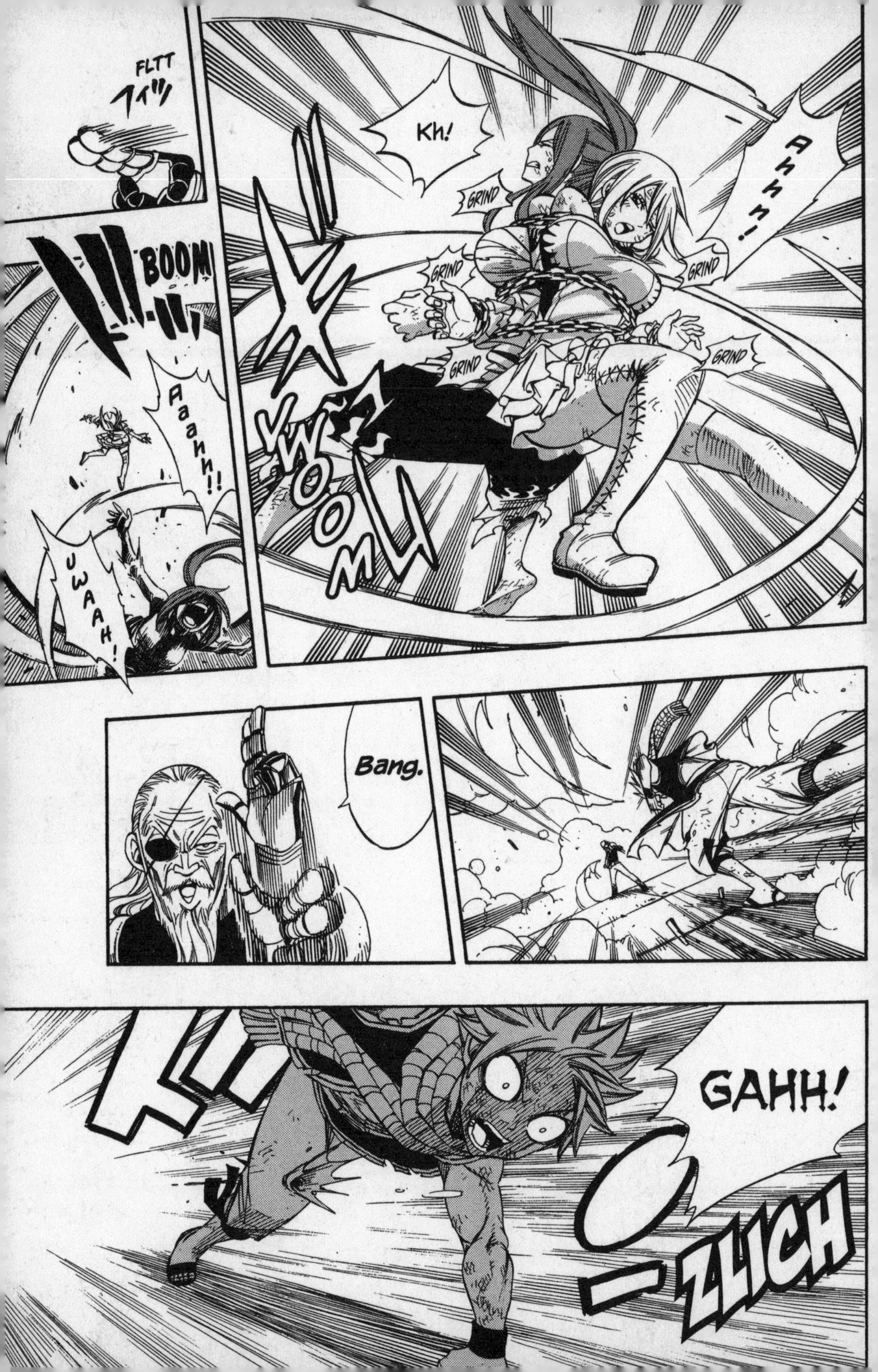
Ahhn!
Kh!
GRIND
GRIND
GRIND
GRIND
GRIND
VWOOM
FLTT
フィッ
BOOM
Aaahh!!
UWAAH!
Bang.
GAHH!
ZLICH

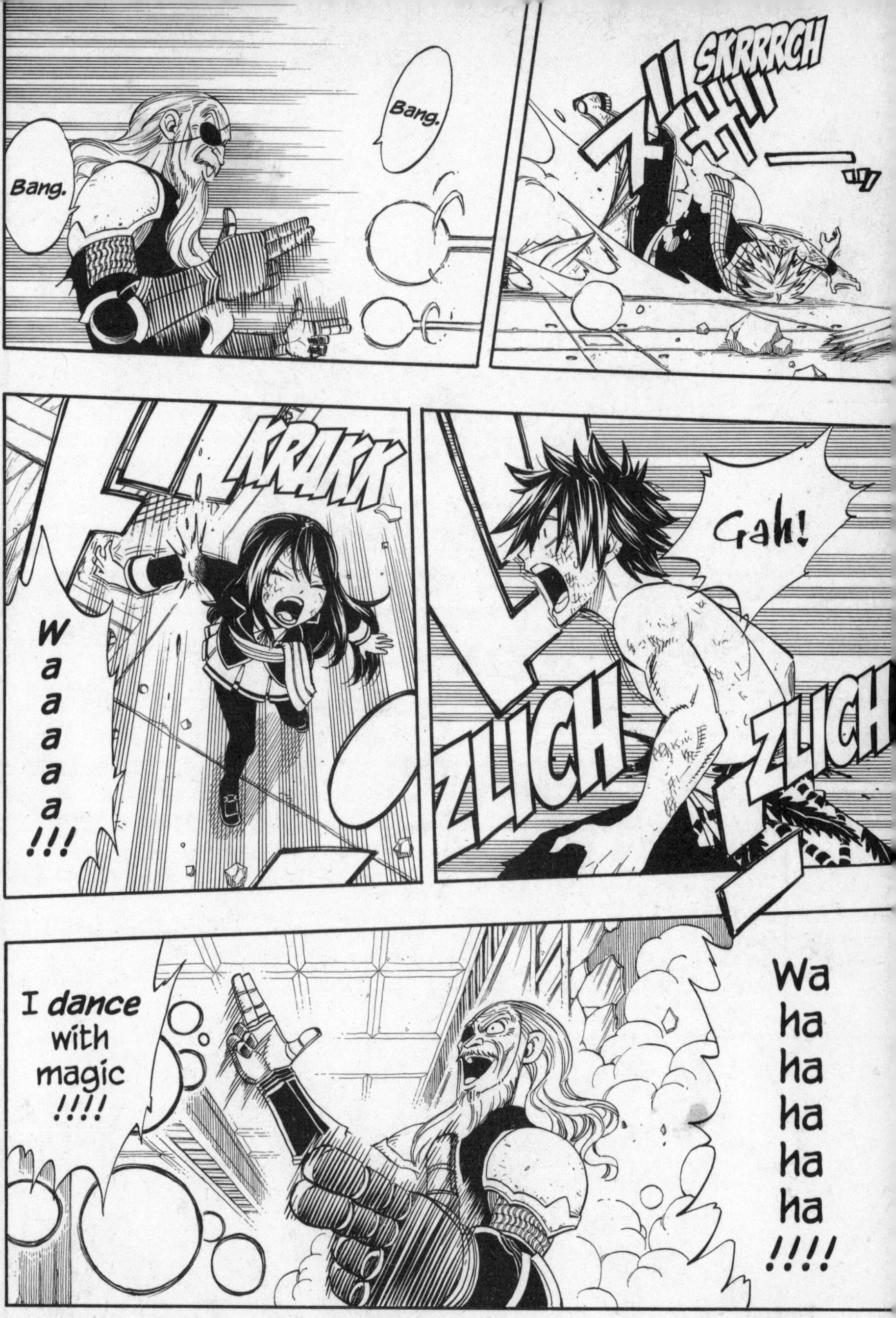
SKRRRCH
Bang.
Bang.
Gah!
ZLICH
ZLICH
KRAKK
Waaaaaa!!!
Wahahahahaha!!!!
I dance with magic!!!!

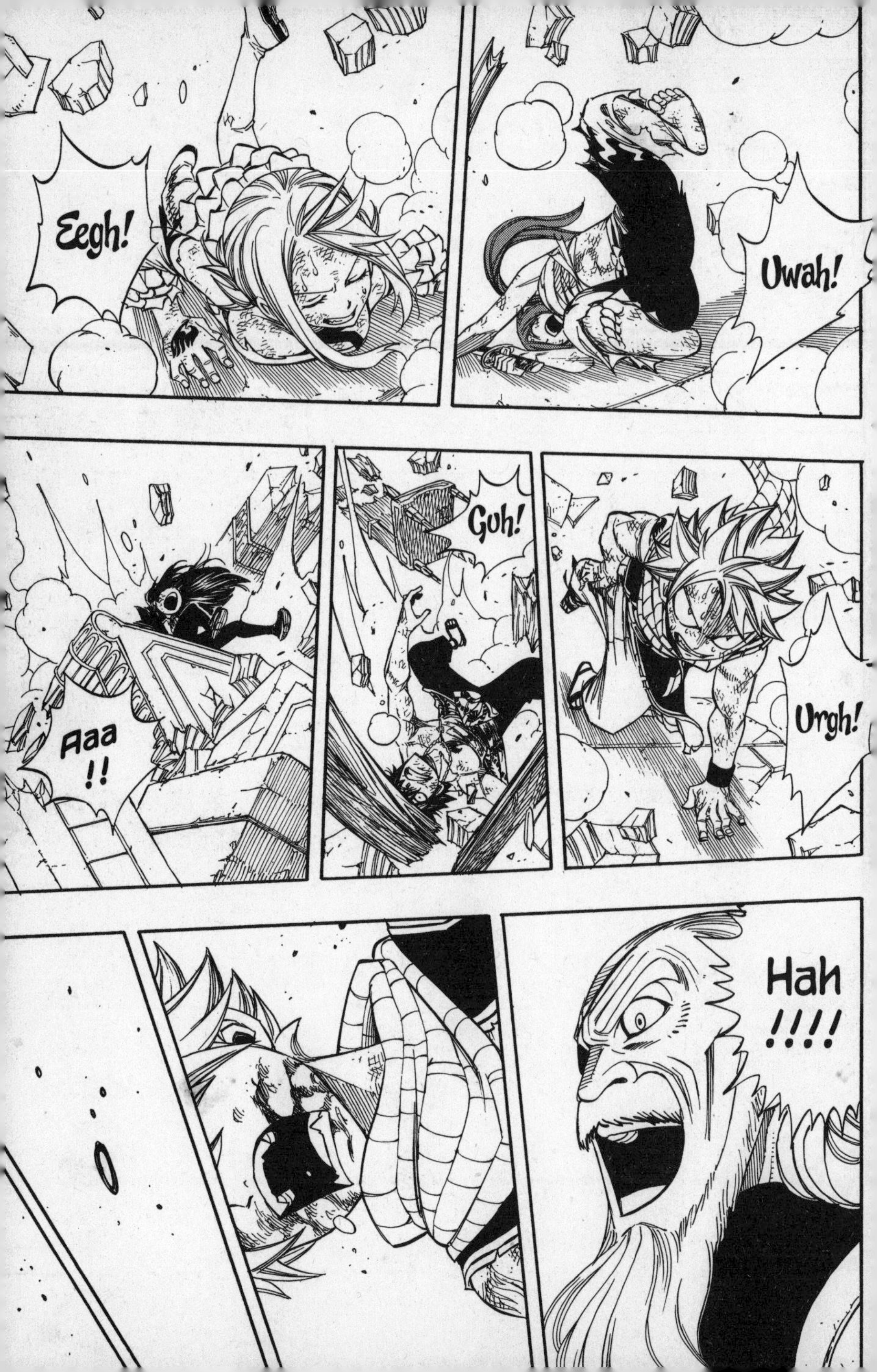
Uwah!
Eegh!
Urgh!
Guh!
Aaa !!
Hah !!!!

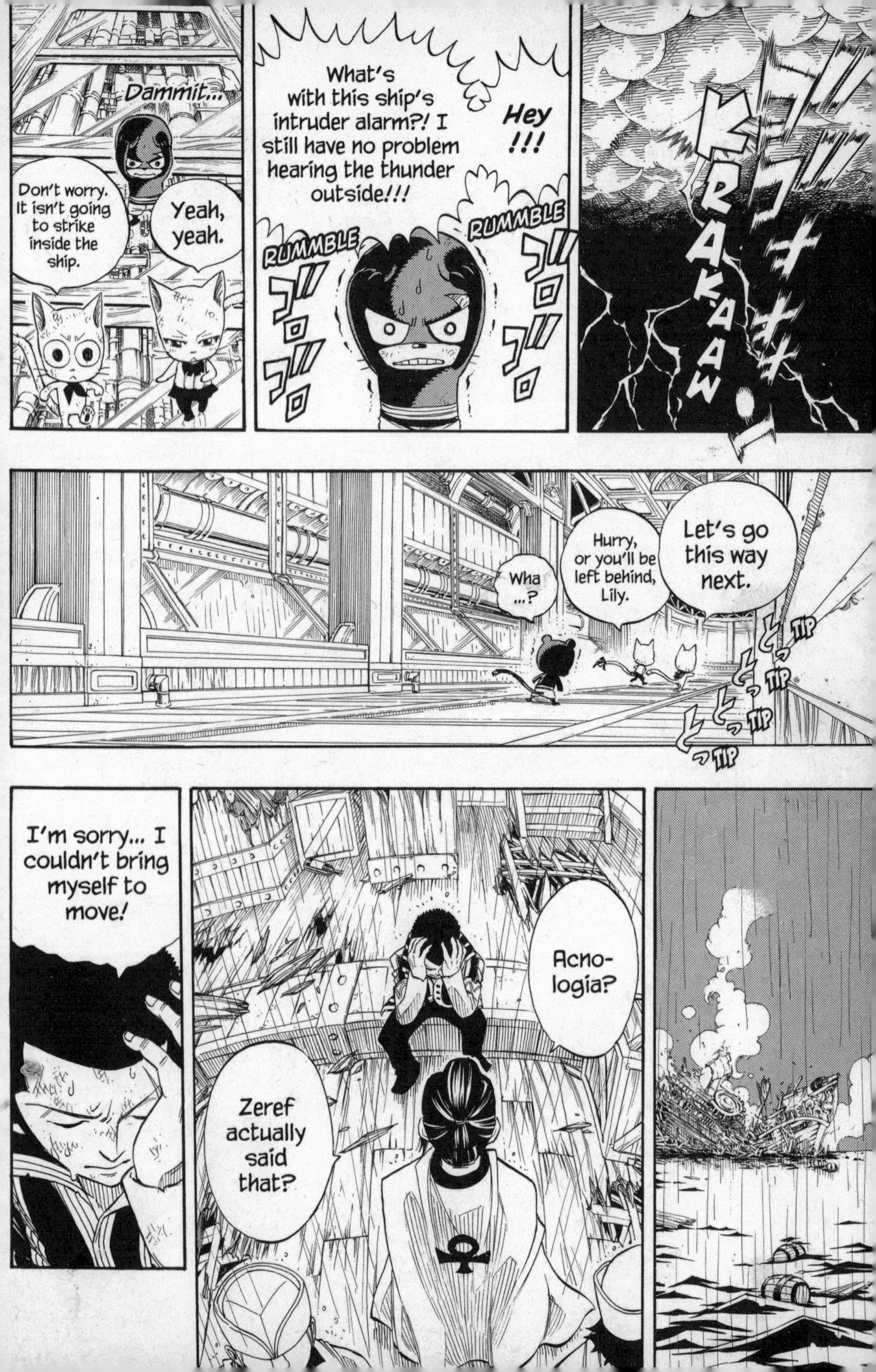
KRAKAAAW
Hey!!!
What's with this ship's intruder alarm?! I still have no problem hearing the thunder outside!!!
RUMMBLE
RUMMBLE
Dammit...
Yeah, yeah.
Don't worry. It isn't going to strike inside the ship.
Let's go this way next.
Hurry, or you'll be left behind, Lily.
Wha ...?
TIP
TIP
TIP
TIP
Acno-logia?
Zeref actually said that?
I'm sorry... I couldn't bring myself to move!

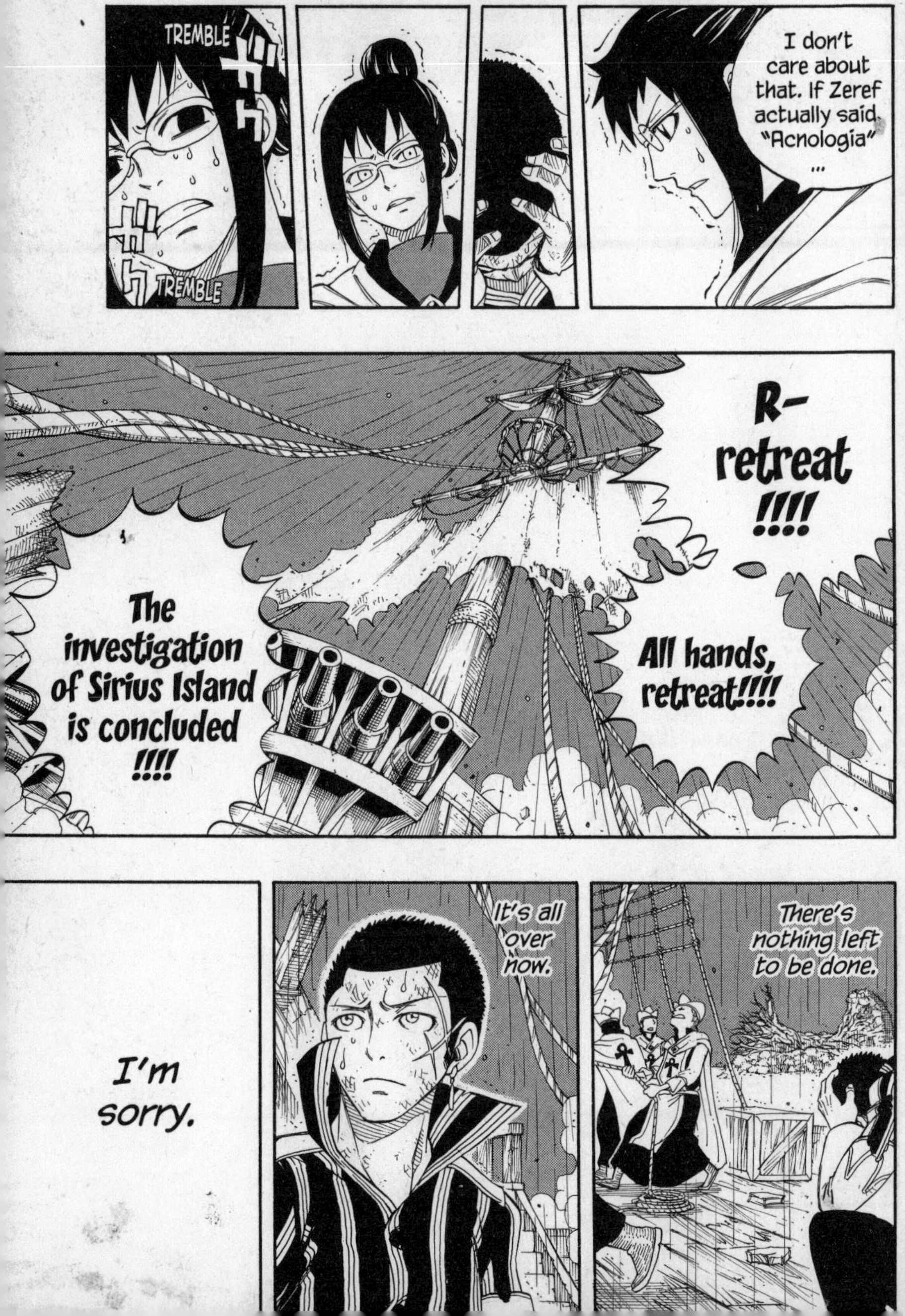
I don't care about that. If Zeref actually said "Acnologia" ...
TREMBLE
TREMBLE
R-retreat!!!!
All hands, retreat!!!!
The investigation of Sirius Island is concluded!!!!
There's nothing left to be done.
It's all over now.
I'm sorry.

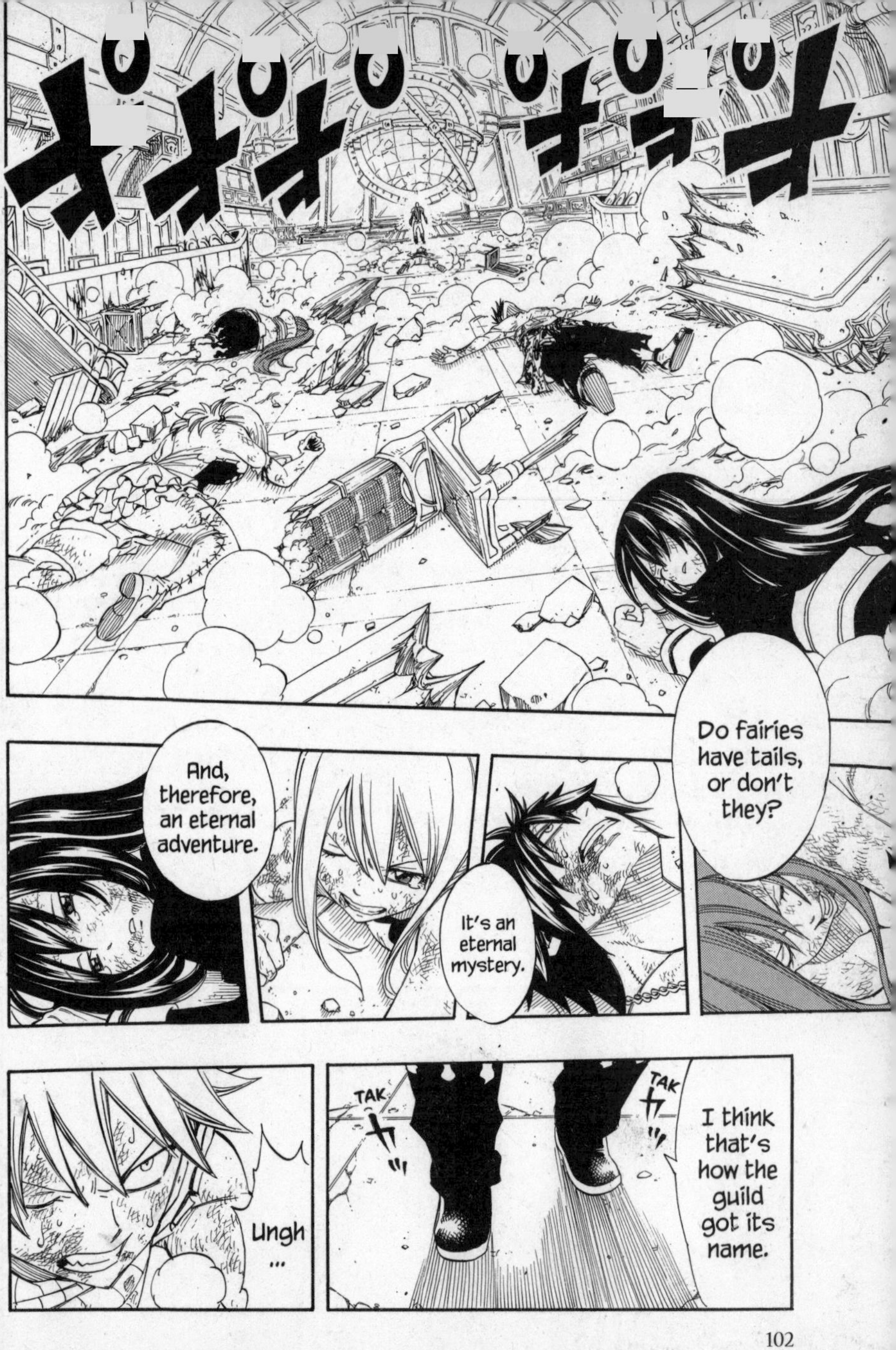

Do fairies have tails, or don't they?
It's an eternal mystery.
And, therefore, an eternal adventure.
TAK
I think that's how the guild got its name.
TAK
Ungh ...

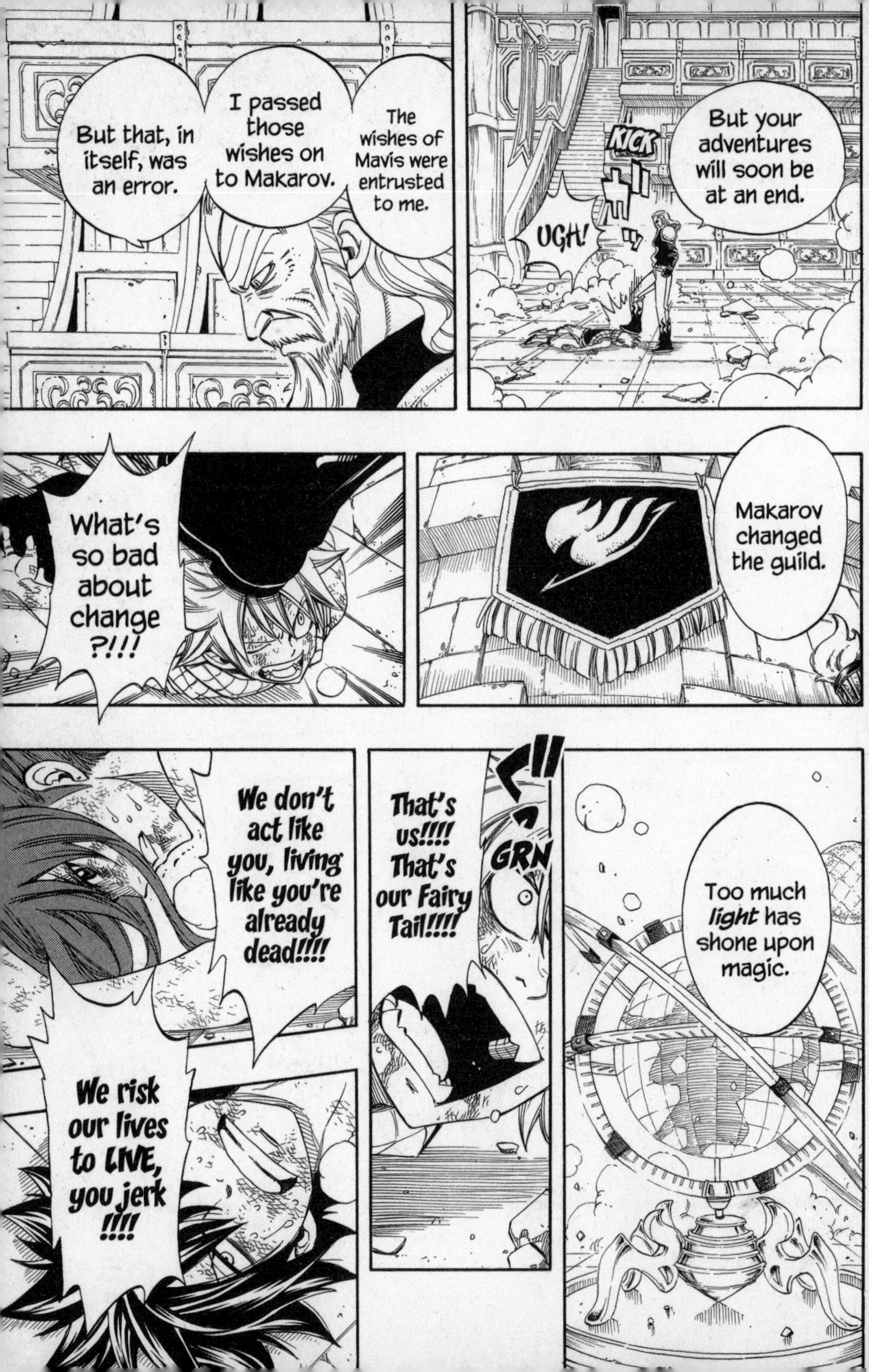
But your adventures will soon be at an end.
KICK
UGH!
The wishes of Mavis were entrusted to me.
I passed those wishes on to Makarov.
But that, in itself, was an error.
Makarov changed the guild.
What's so bad about change?!!!
Too much *light* has shone upon magic.
GRN
That's us!!!! That's our Fairy Tail!!!!
We don't act like you, living like you're already dead!!!!
We risk our lives to LIVE, you jerk!!!!

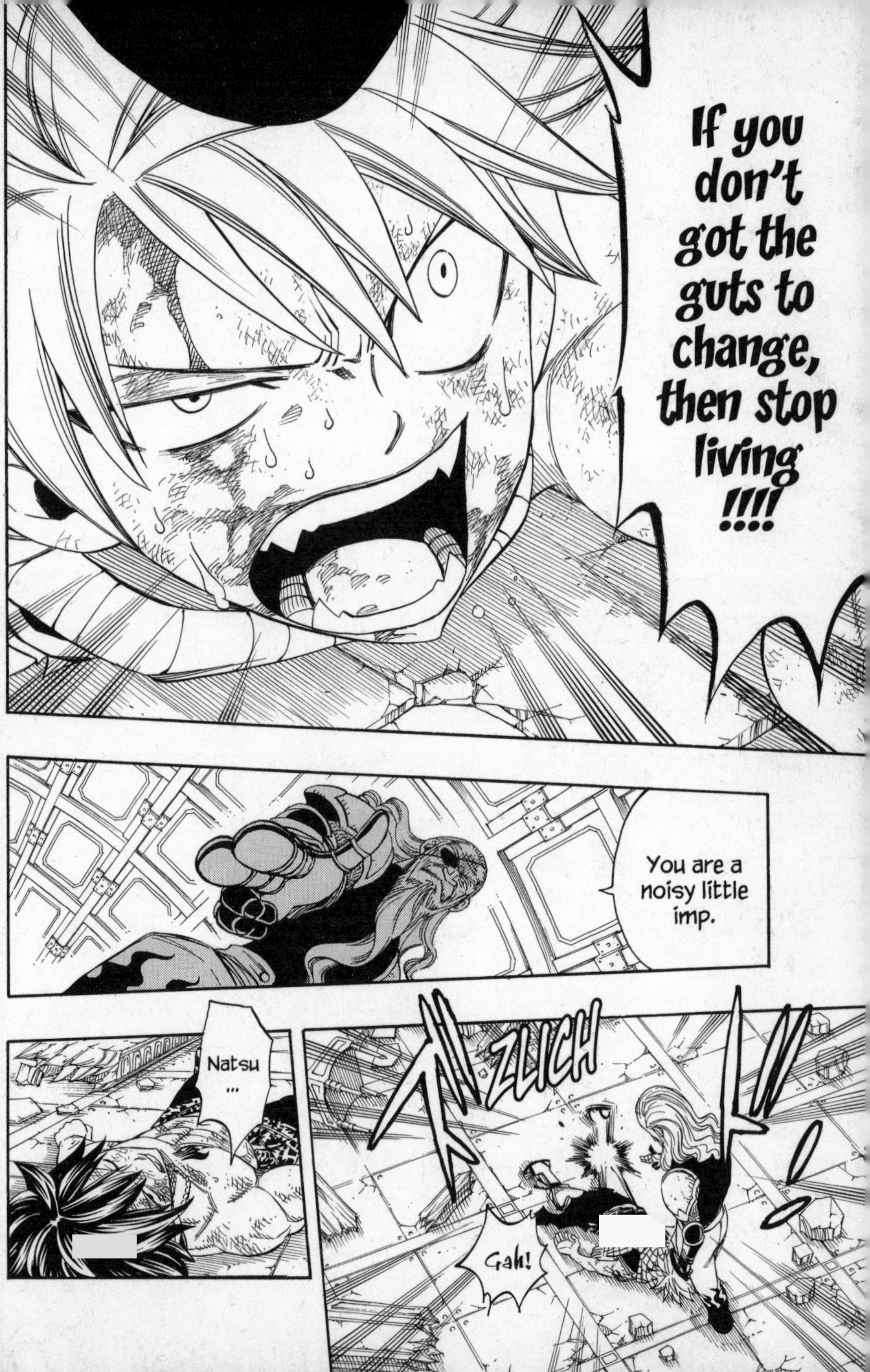
If you don't got the guts to change, then stop living!!!!
You are a noisy little imp.
ZLICH
Gah!
Natsu ...

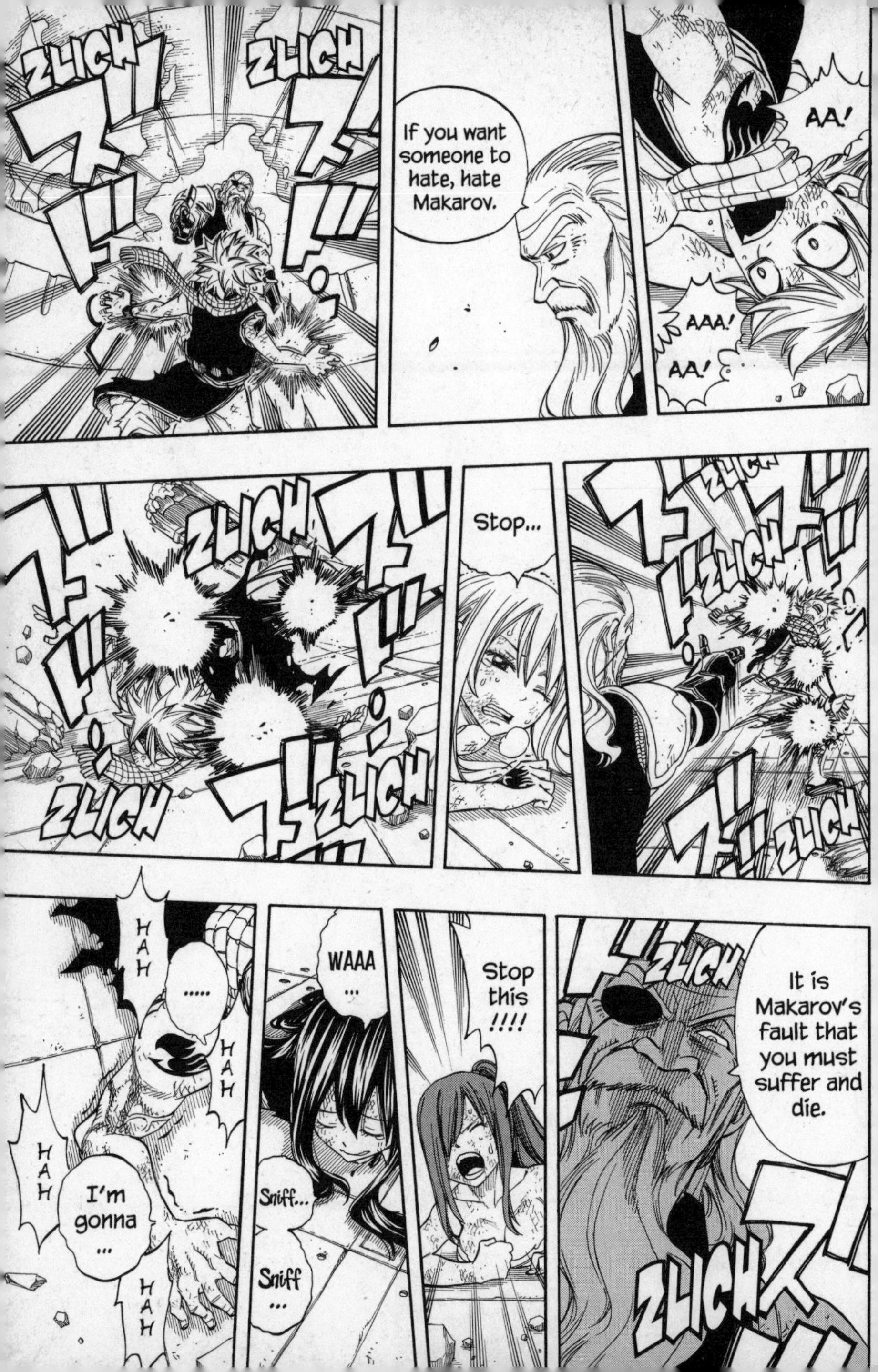

AA!
AAA!
AA!
If you want someone to hate, hate Makarov.
ZLICH
ZLICH
ZLICH
ZLICH
ZLICH
Stop...
ZLICH
ZLICH
ZLICH
ZLICH
It is Makarov's fault that you must suffer and die.
ZLICH
Stop this !!!!
WAAA ...
Sniff...
Sniff ...
HAH HAH
.....
HAH HAH
HAH HAH
I'm gonna ...
HAH HAH

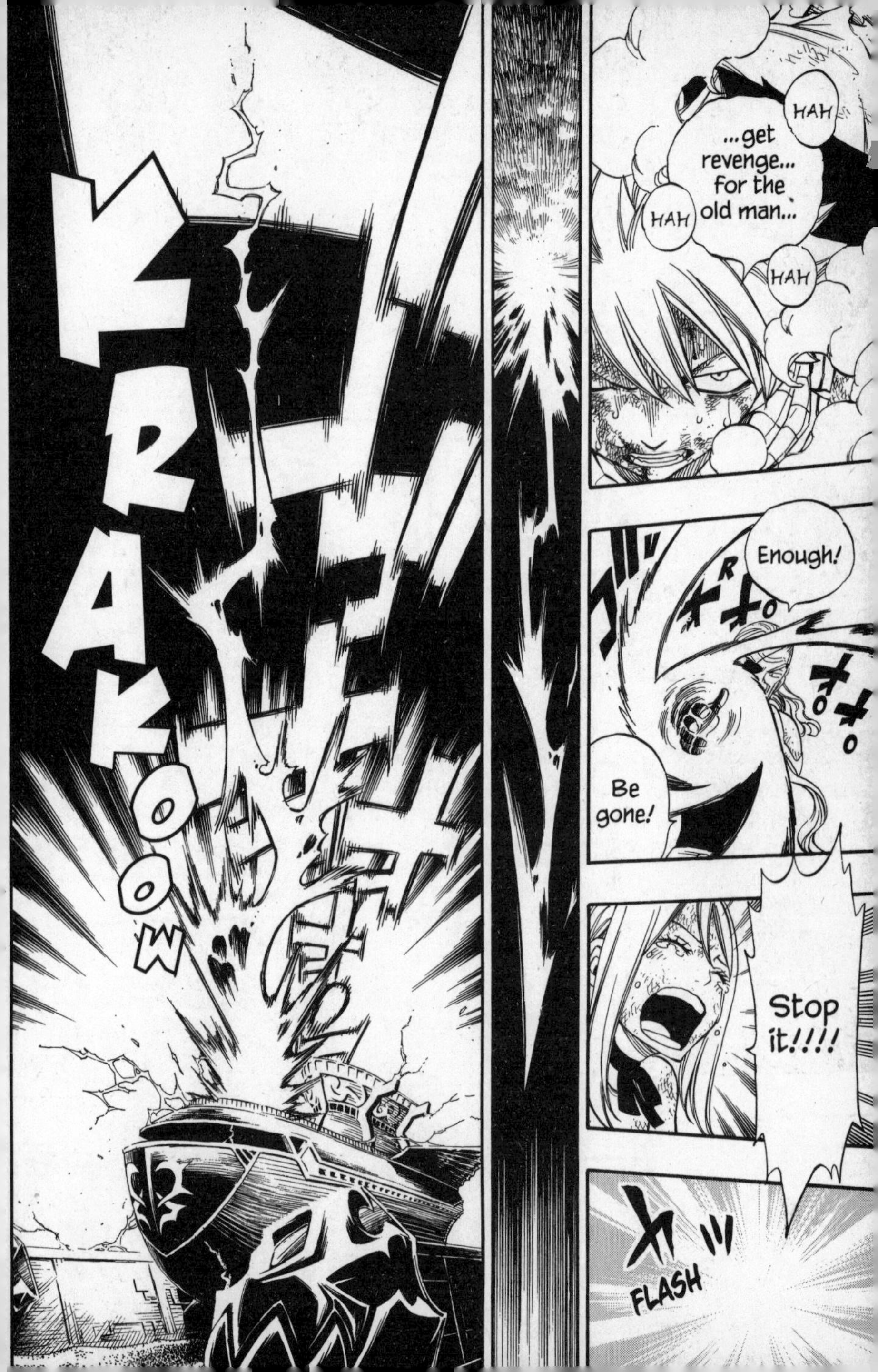
HAH
...get revenge... for the old man...
HAH
HAH
Enough!
Be gone!
Stop it!!!!
FLASH
KRAKOOW

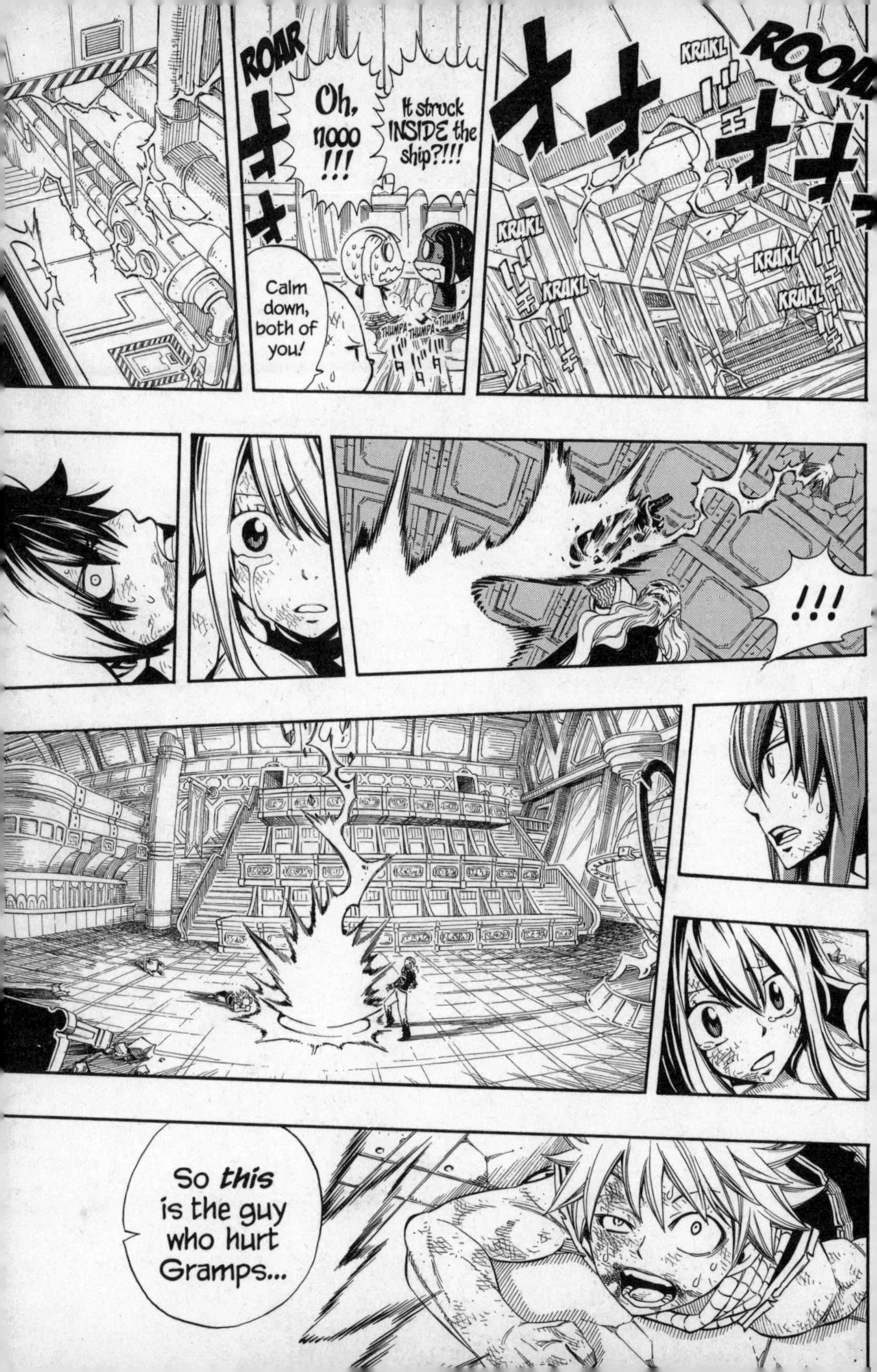
KRAKL
KRAKL
KRAKL
KRAKL
KRAKL
ROAR
It struck INSIDE the ship?!!!
Oh, nooo!!!
Calm down, both of you!
THUMPA THUMPA THUMPA
!!!
So *this* is the guy who hurt Gramps...

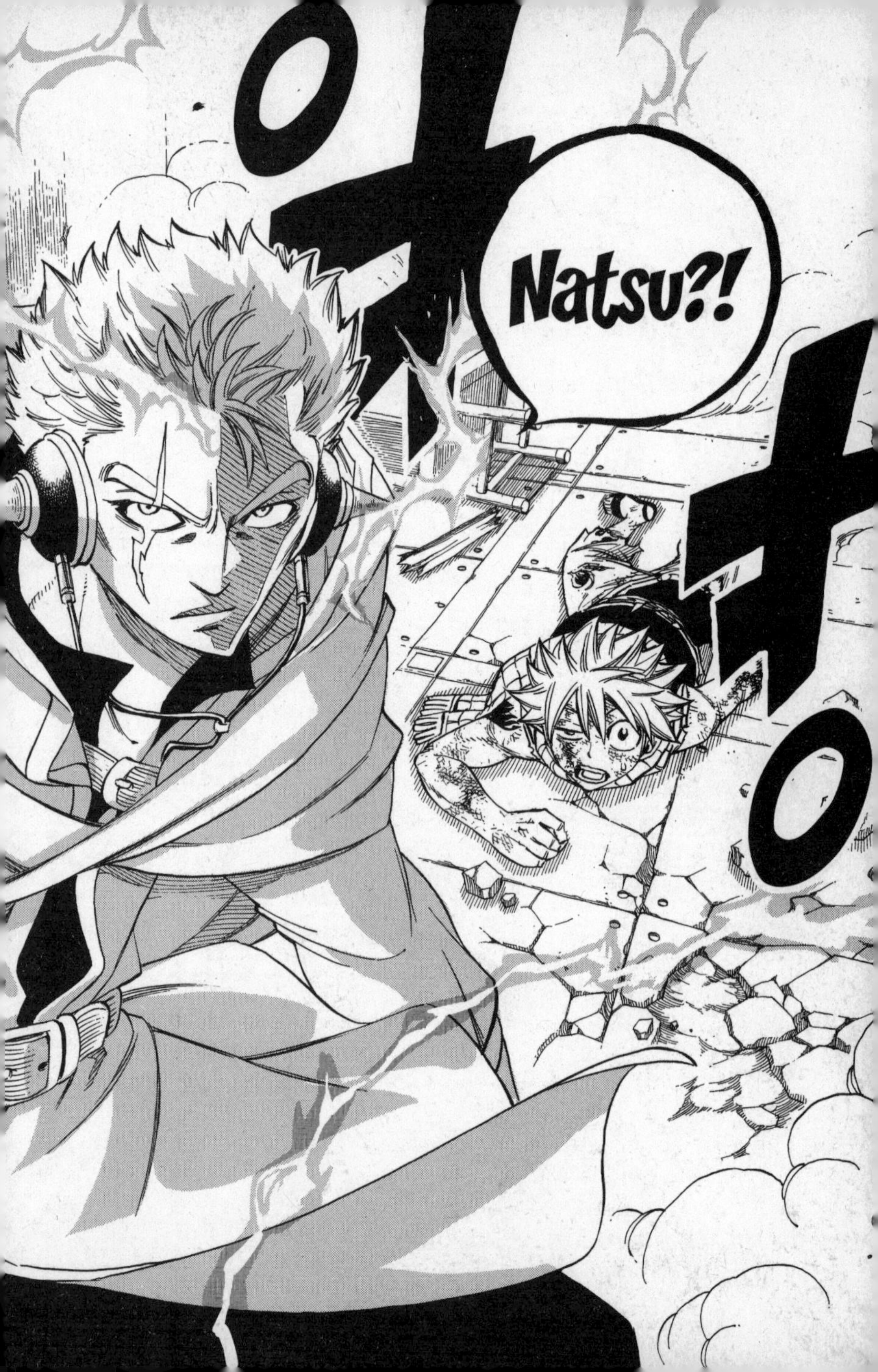
Natsu?!

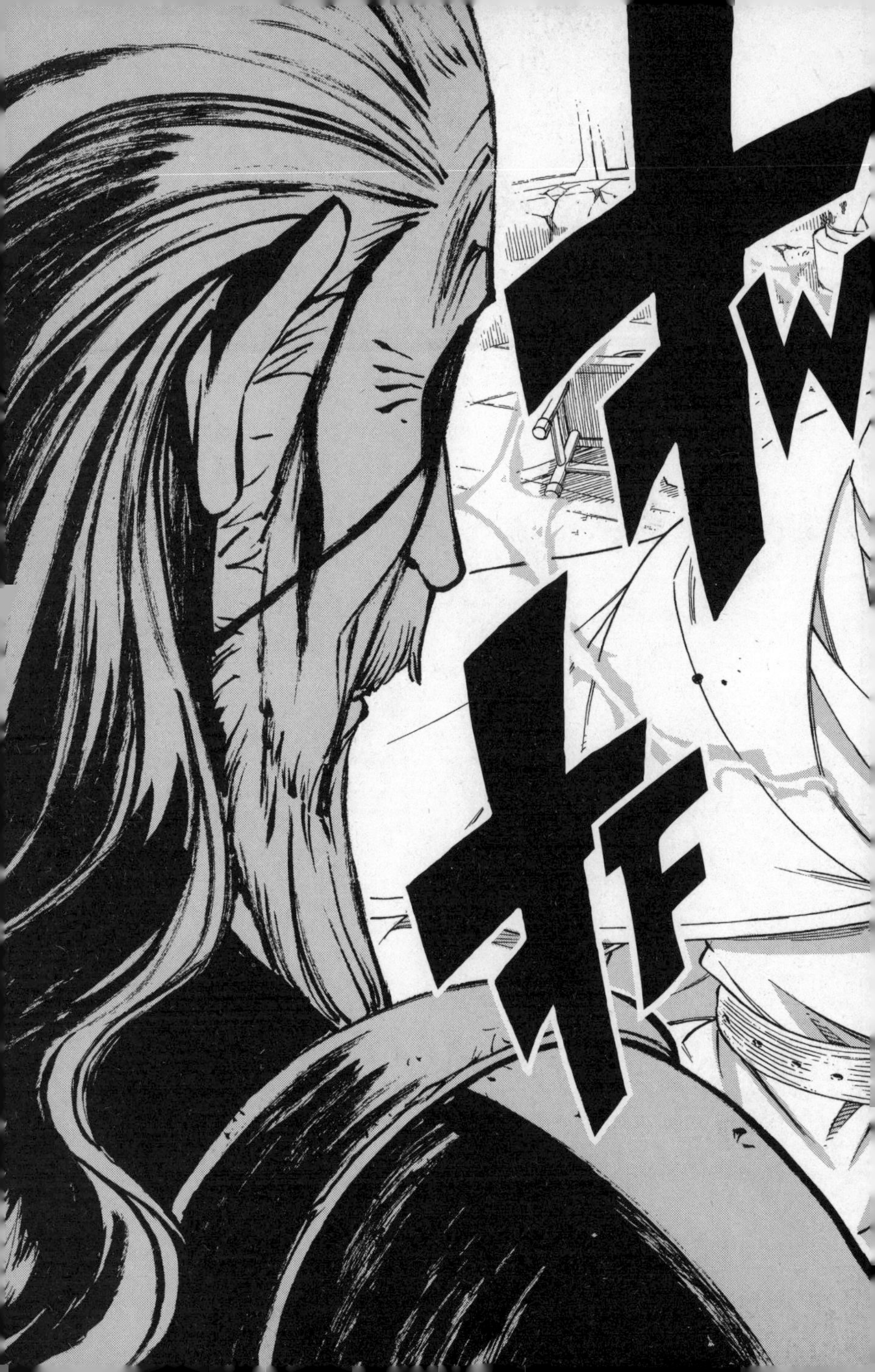

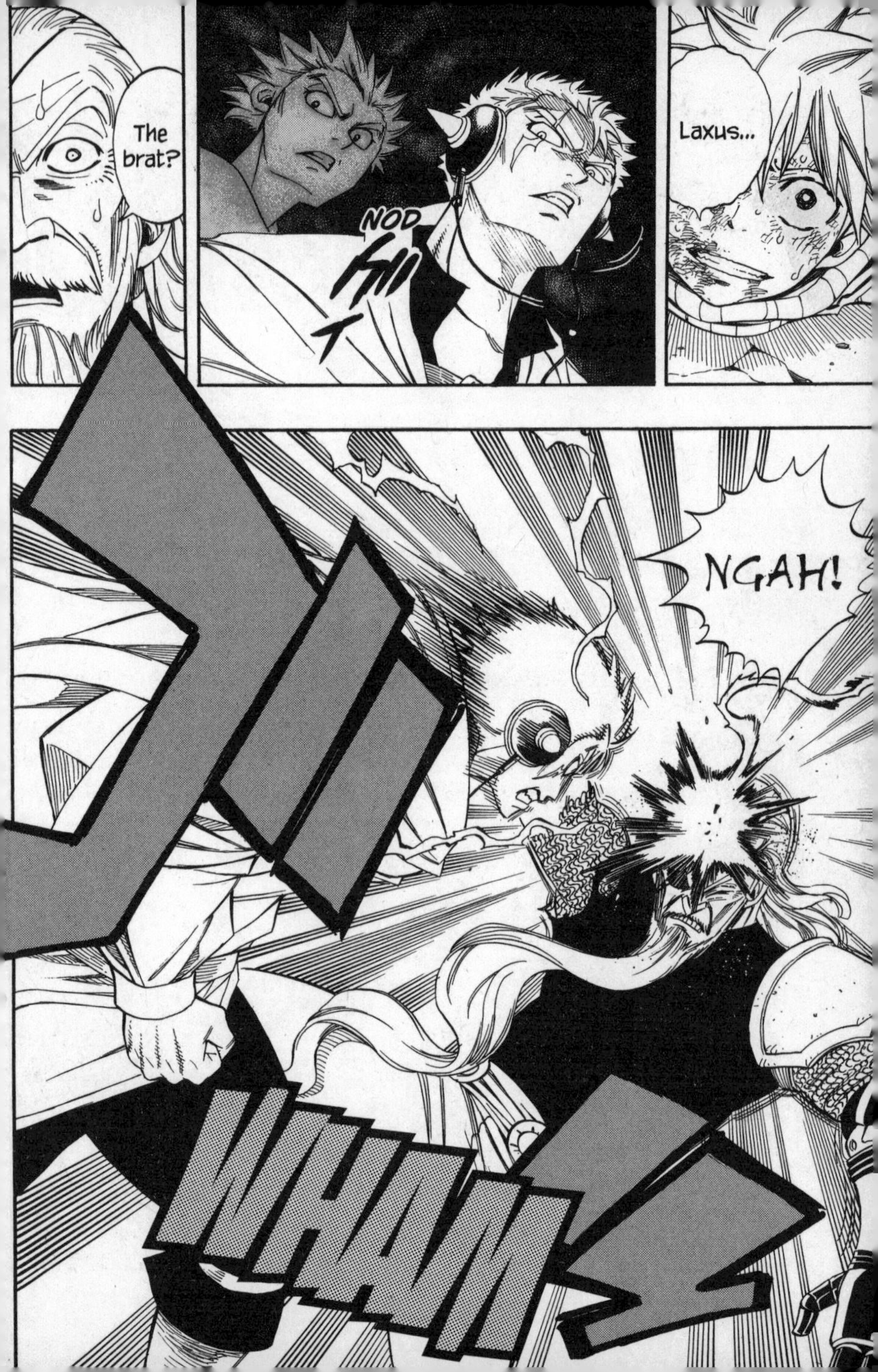
Laxus...
NOD
The brat?
NGAH!

FAIRY TAIL

フェアリーテイル

Chapter 245: The Man Without the Mark

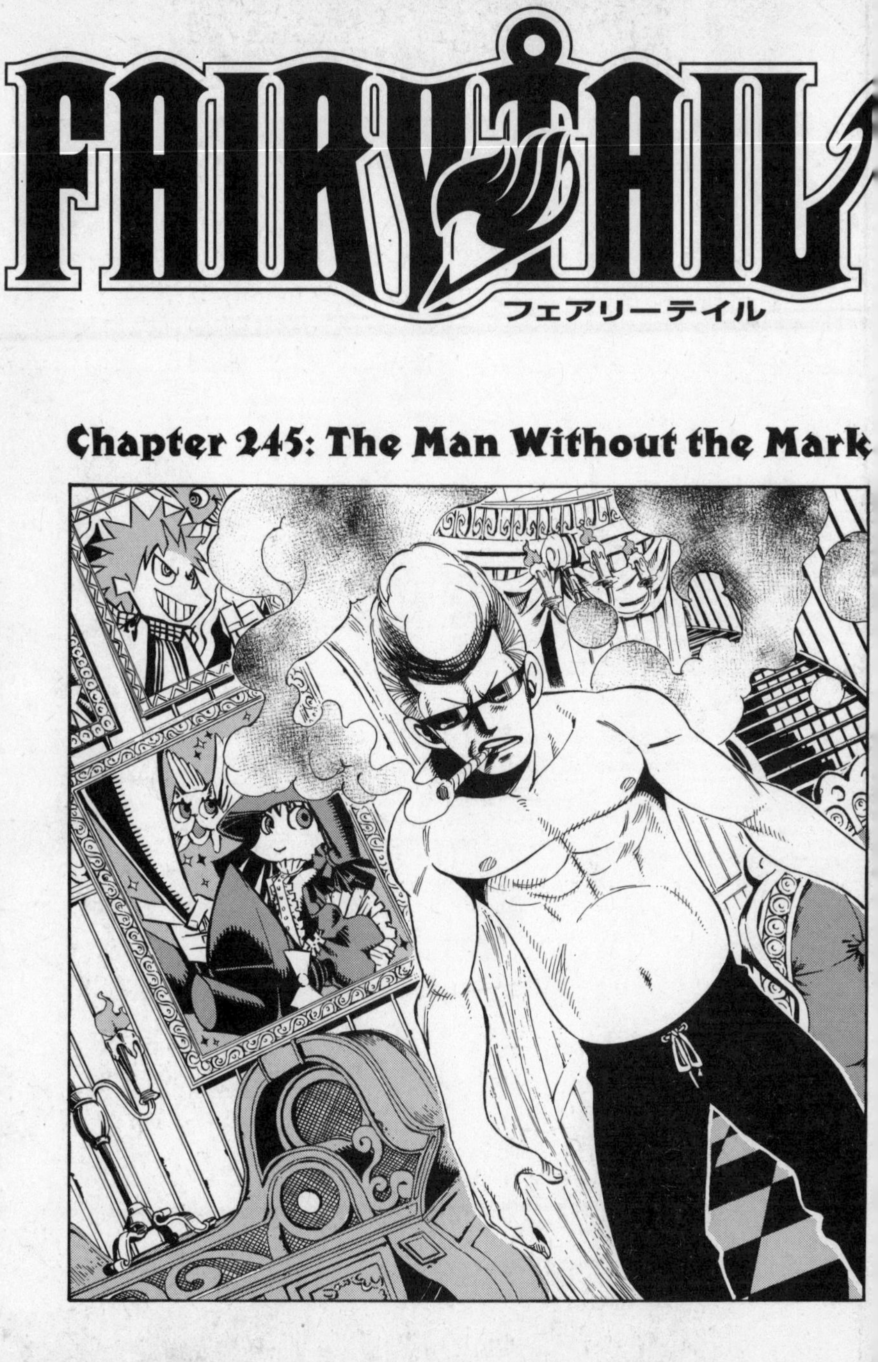

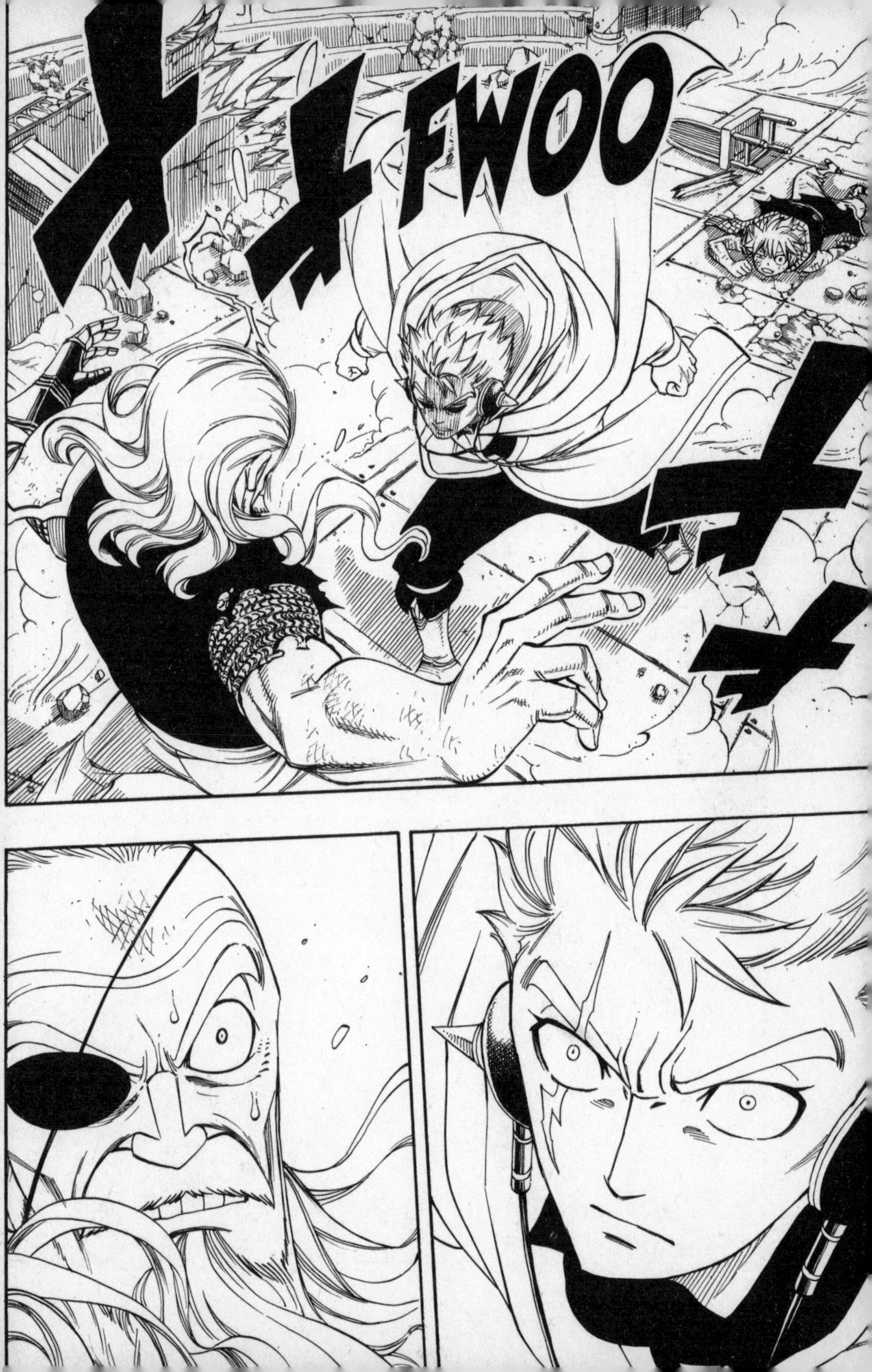
FWOO

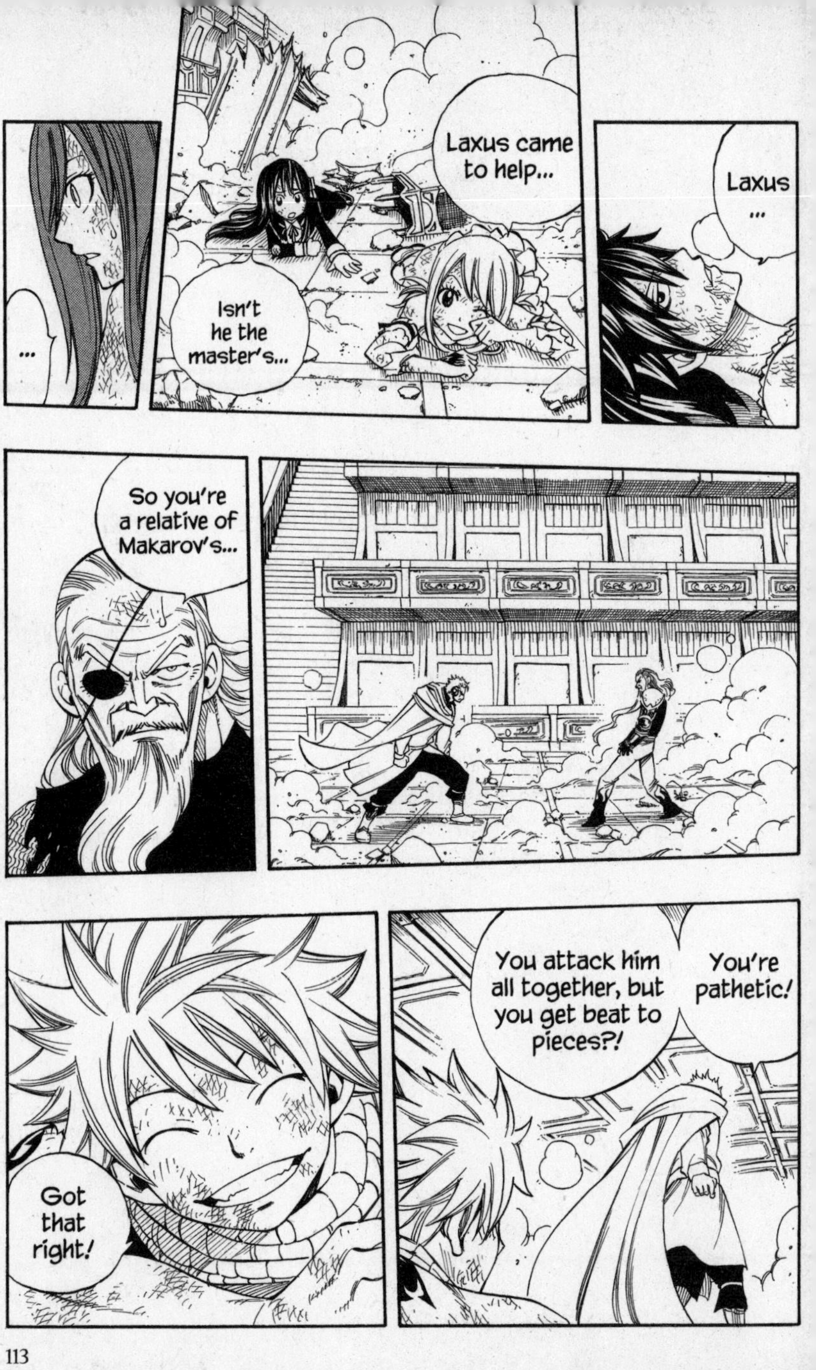

Laxus ...
Laxus came to help...
Isn't he the master's...
...
So you're a relative of Makarov's...
You're pathetic!
You attack him all together, but you get beat to pieces?!
Got that right!

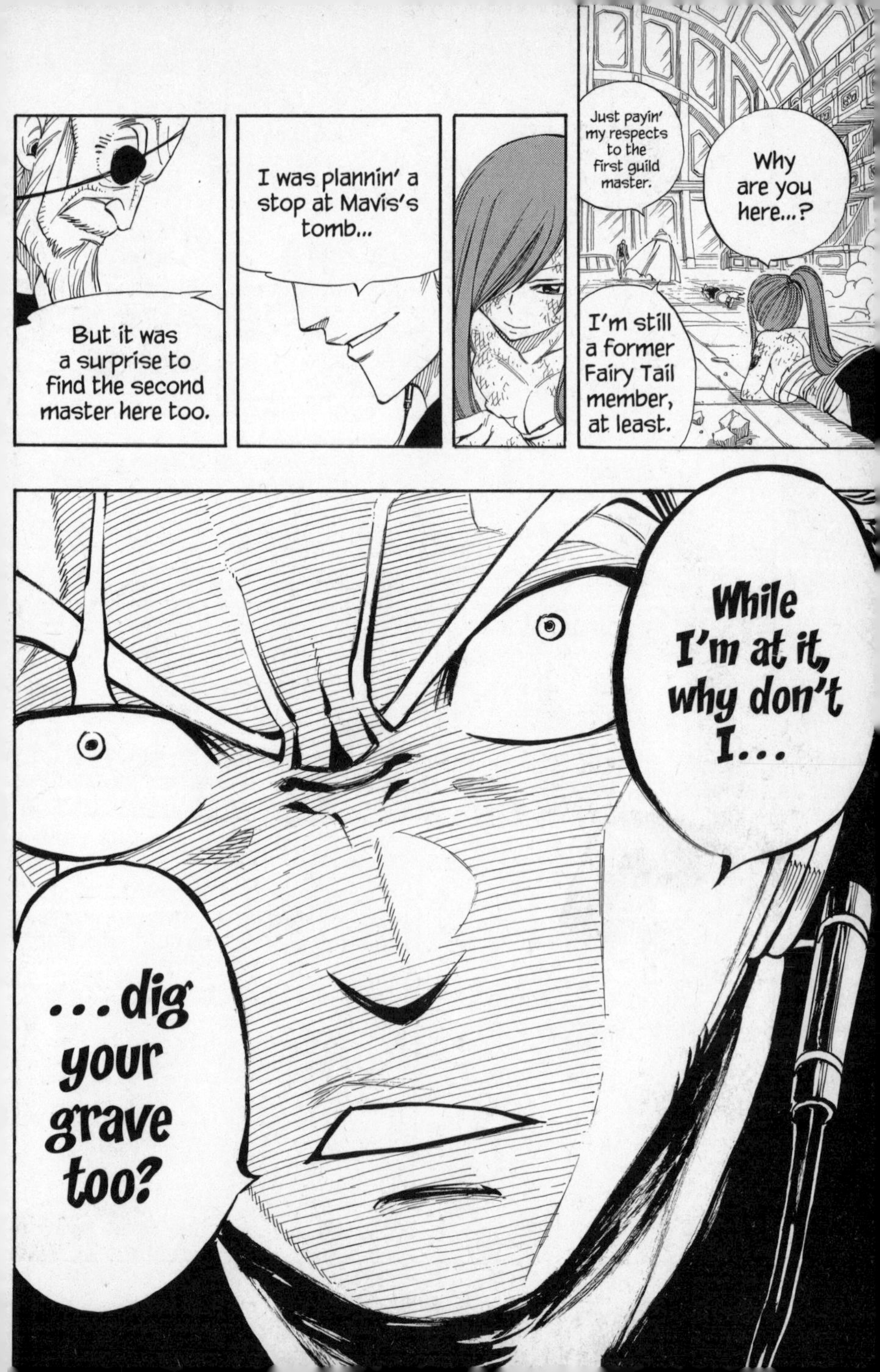
Why are you here...?
Just payin' my respects to the first guild master.
I'm still a former Fairy Tail member, at least.
I was plannin' a stop at Mavis's tomb...
But it was a surprise to find the second master here too.
While I'm at it, why don't I...
...dig your grave too?

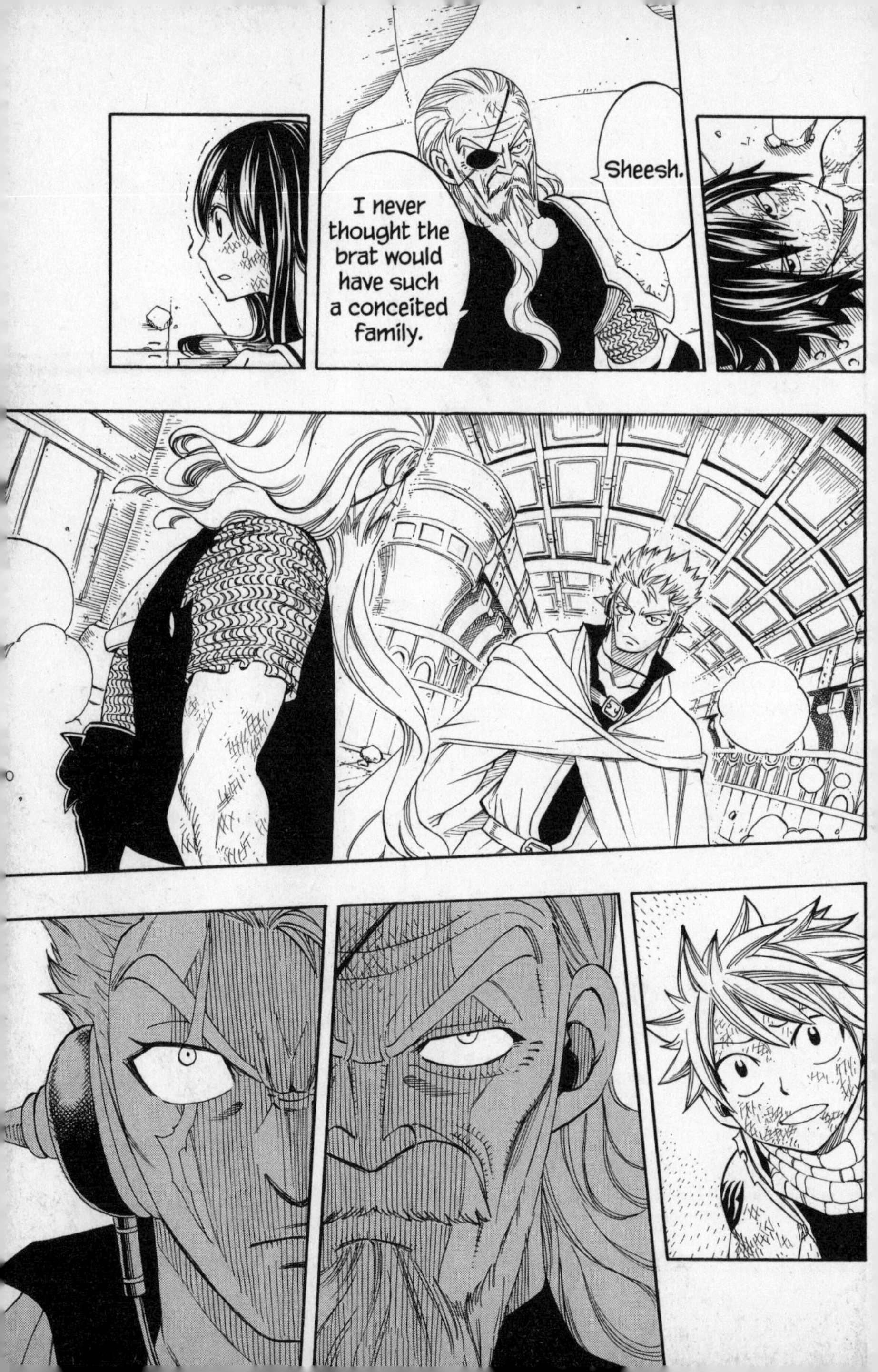
Sheesh.
I never thought the brat would have such a conceited family.

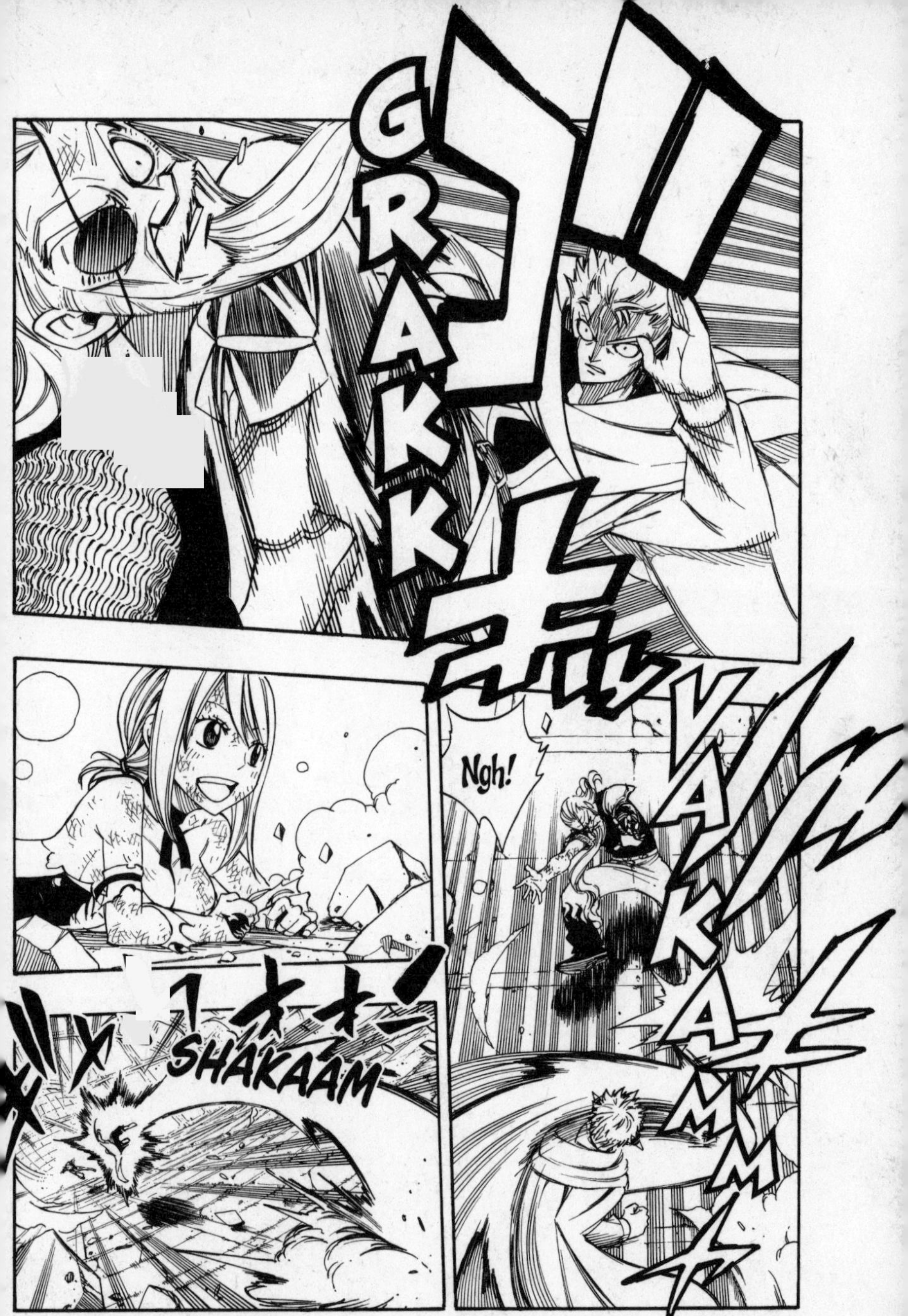
GRAK
Ngh!
VAKAMM
SHAKAAM

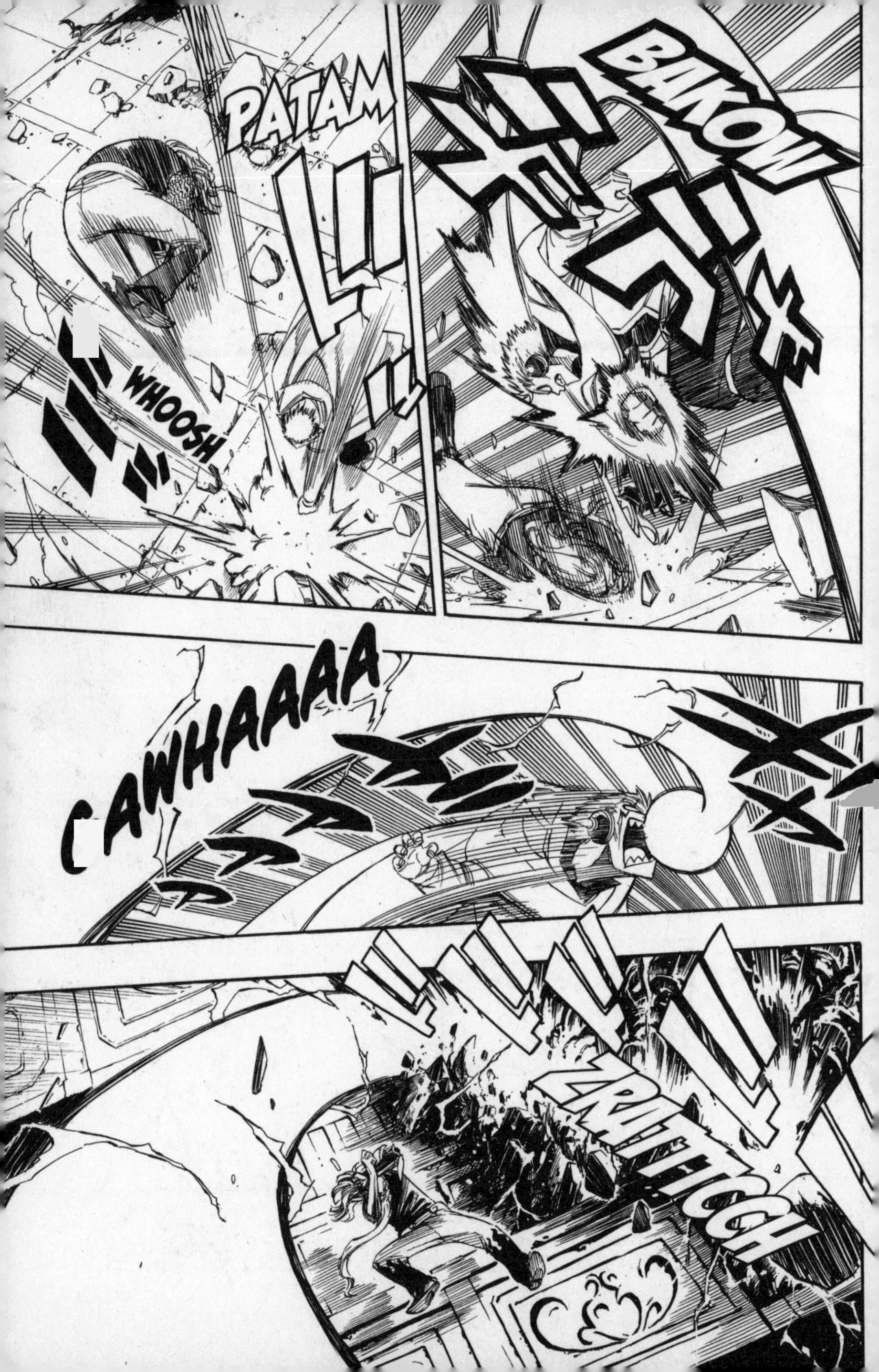
BAKOW
PATAM
WHOOSH
CAWHAAAA

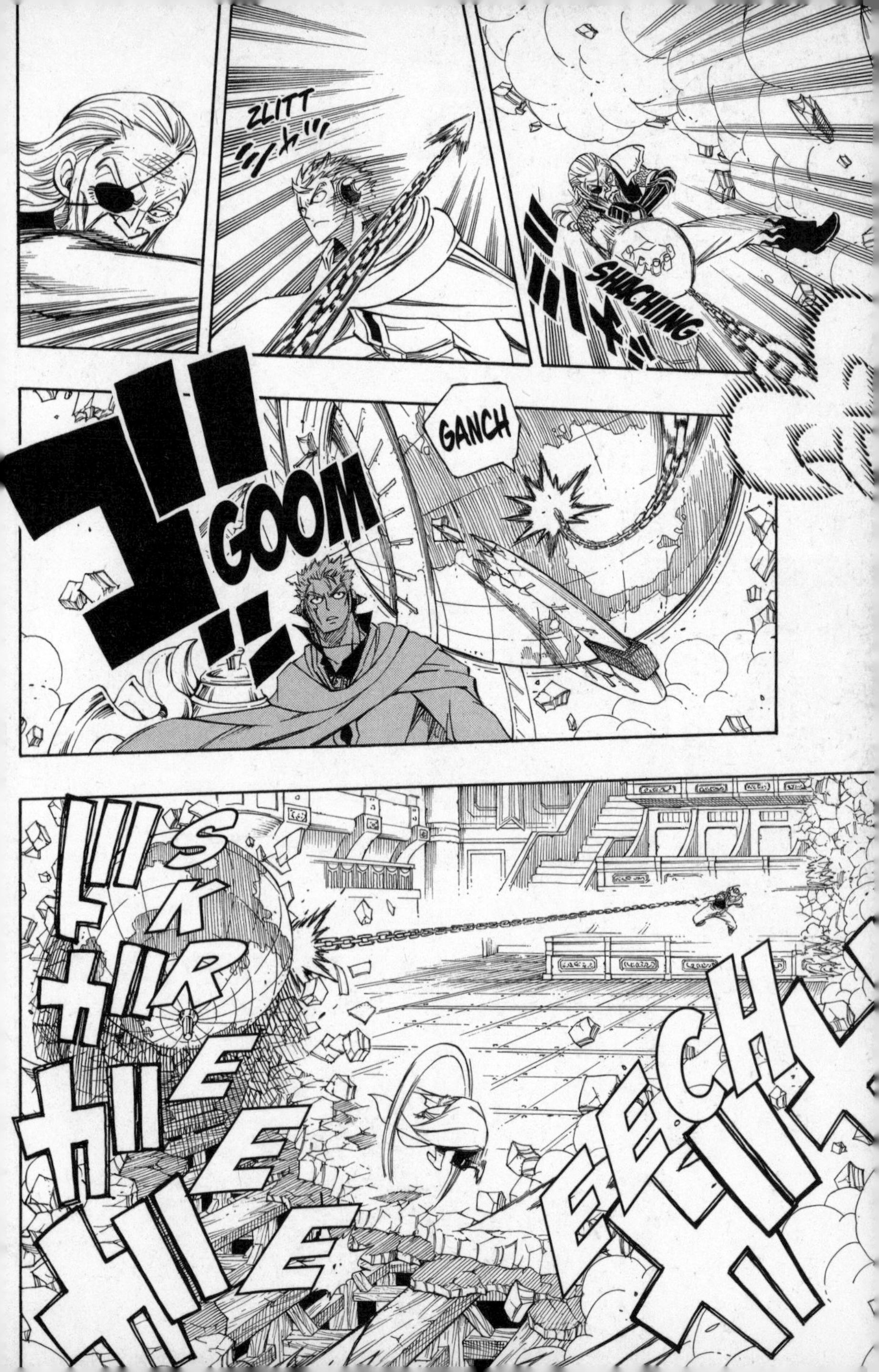
SHACHIIING
ZLITT
GANCH
GOOM
SKREEE
EECH

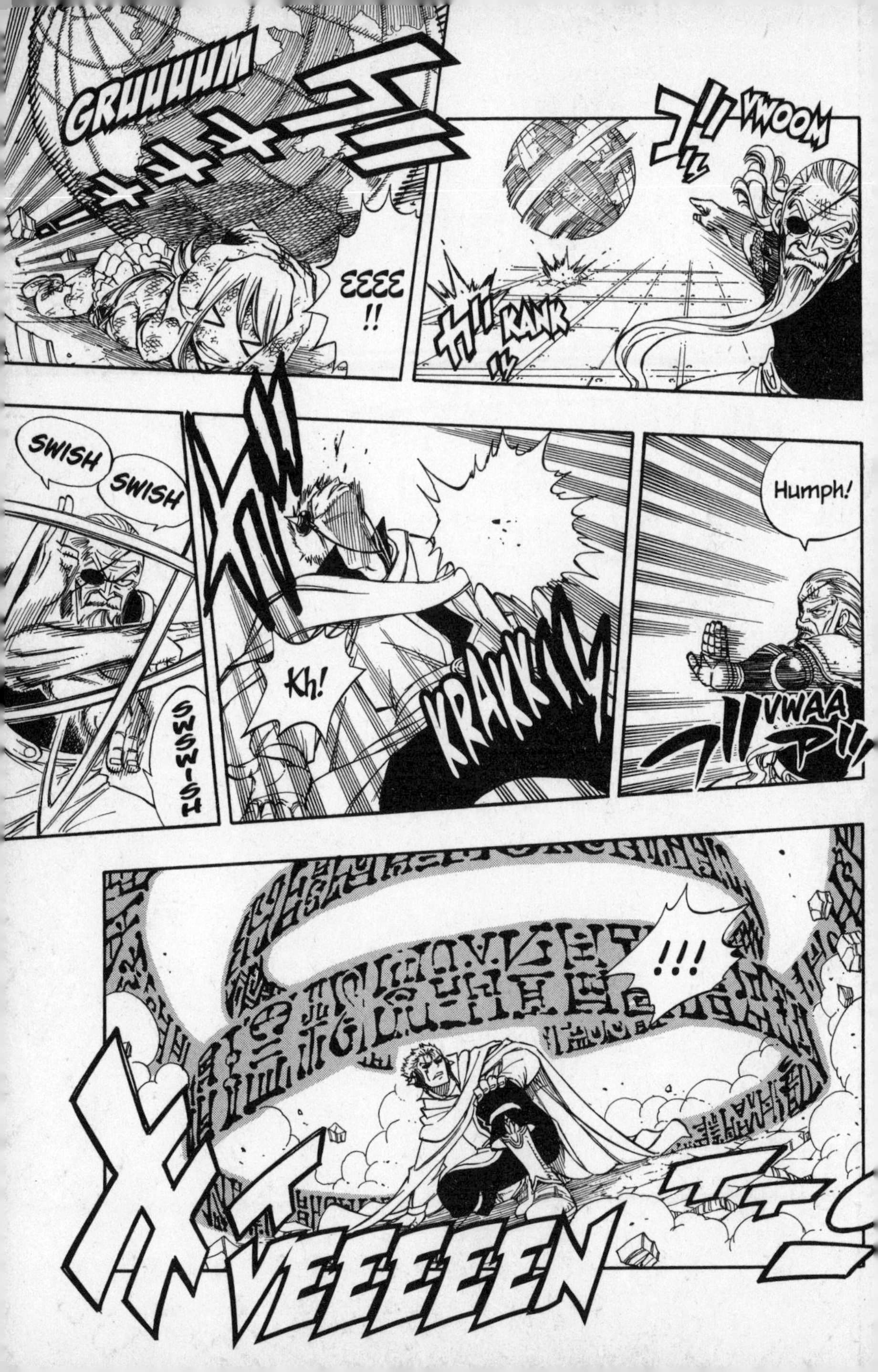
VWOOM
KANK
GRUUUUM
EEEE !!
Humph!
VWAAP!!
Kh!
KRAKK
SWISH
SWISH
SWSWISH
!!!
VEEEEEN

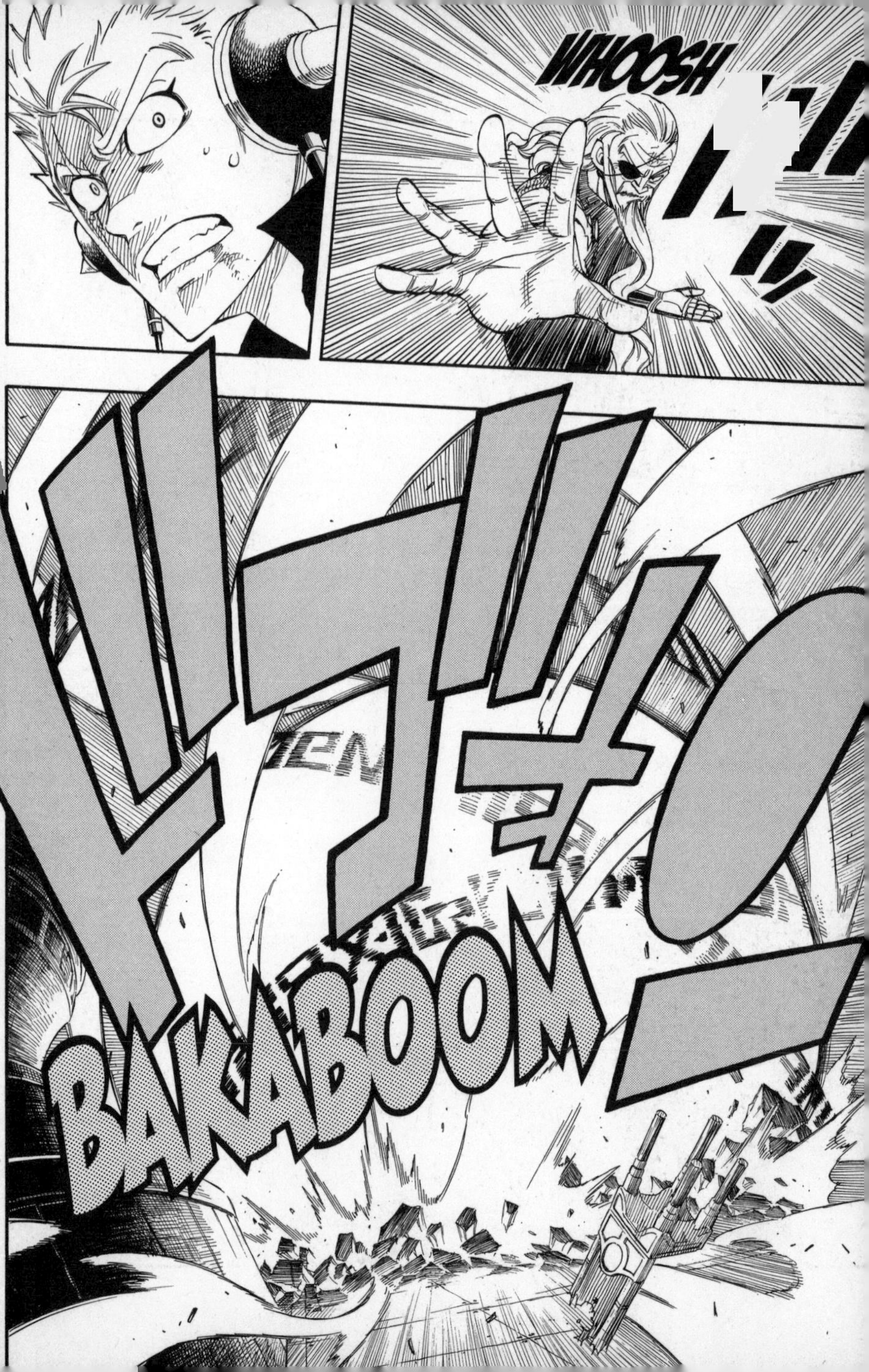
WHOOSH
BAKABOOM

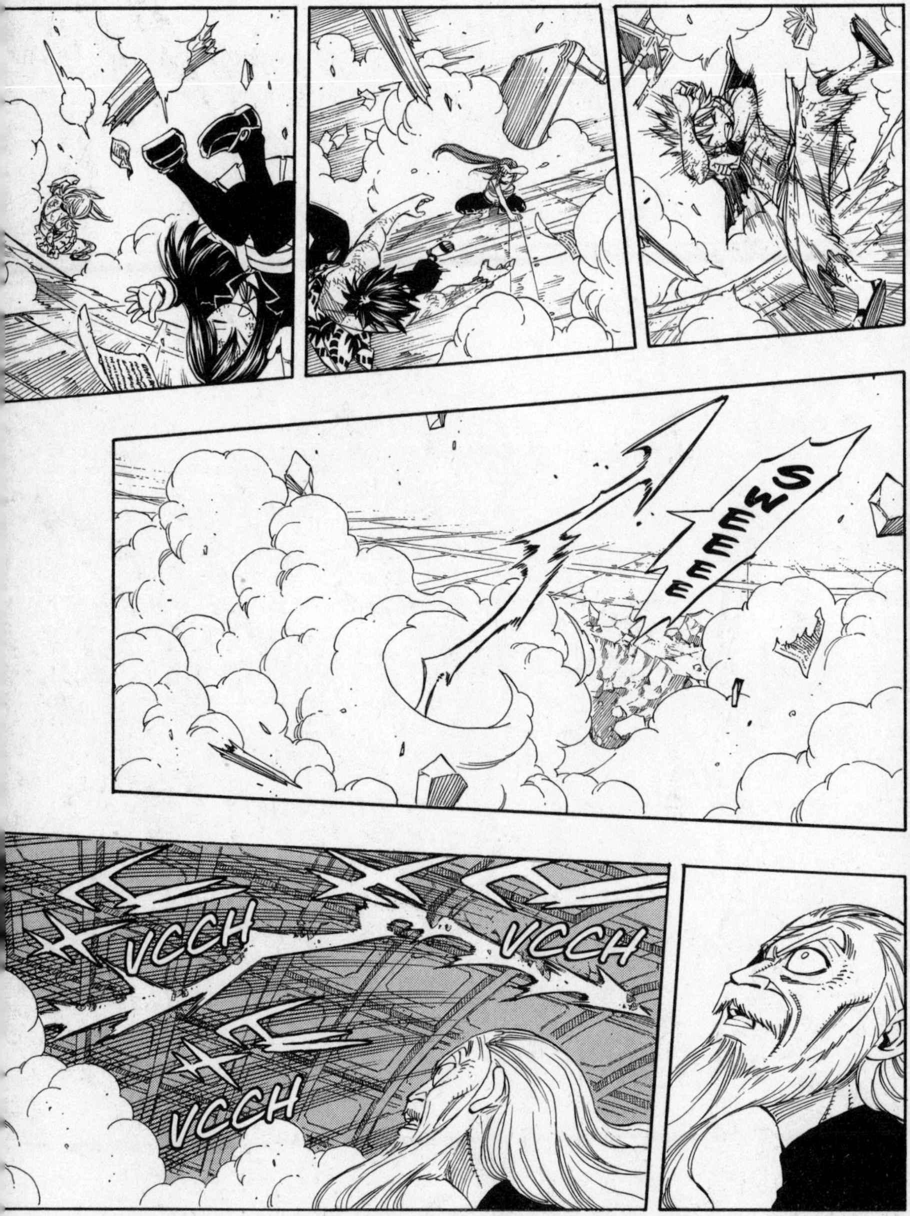
SWEEEE
VCCH
VCCH
VCCH

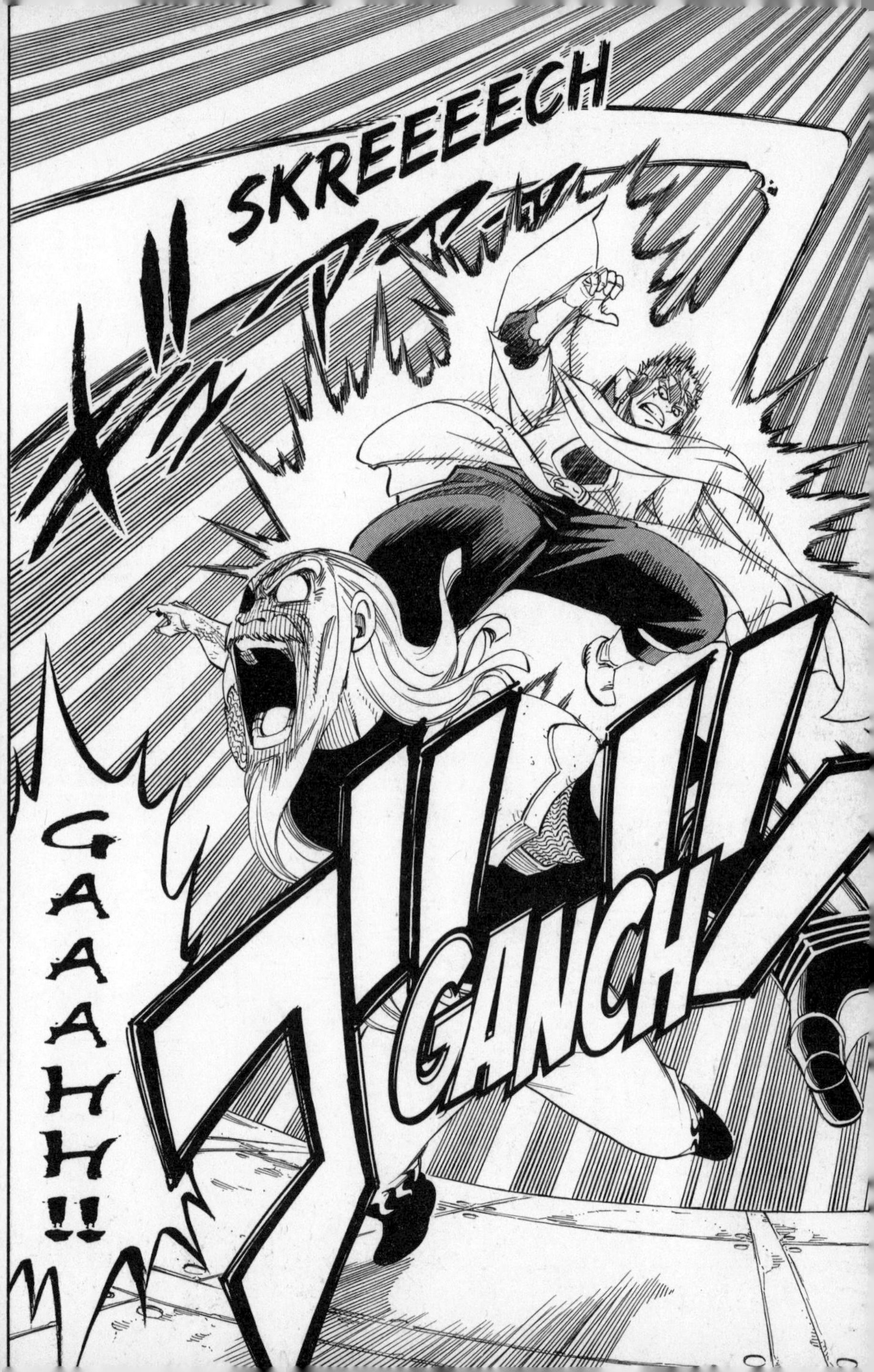
SKREEEEECH
CANCH
GAAAHH!!

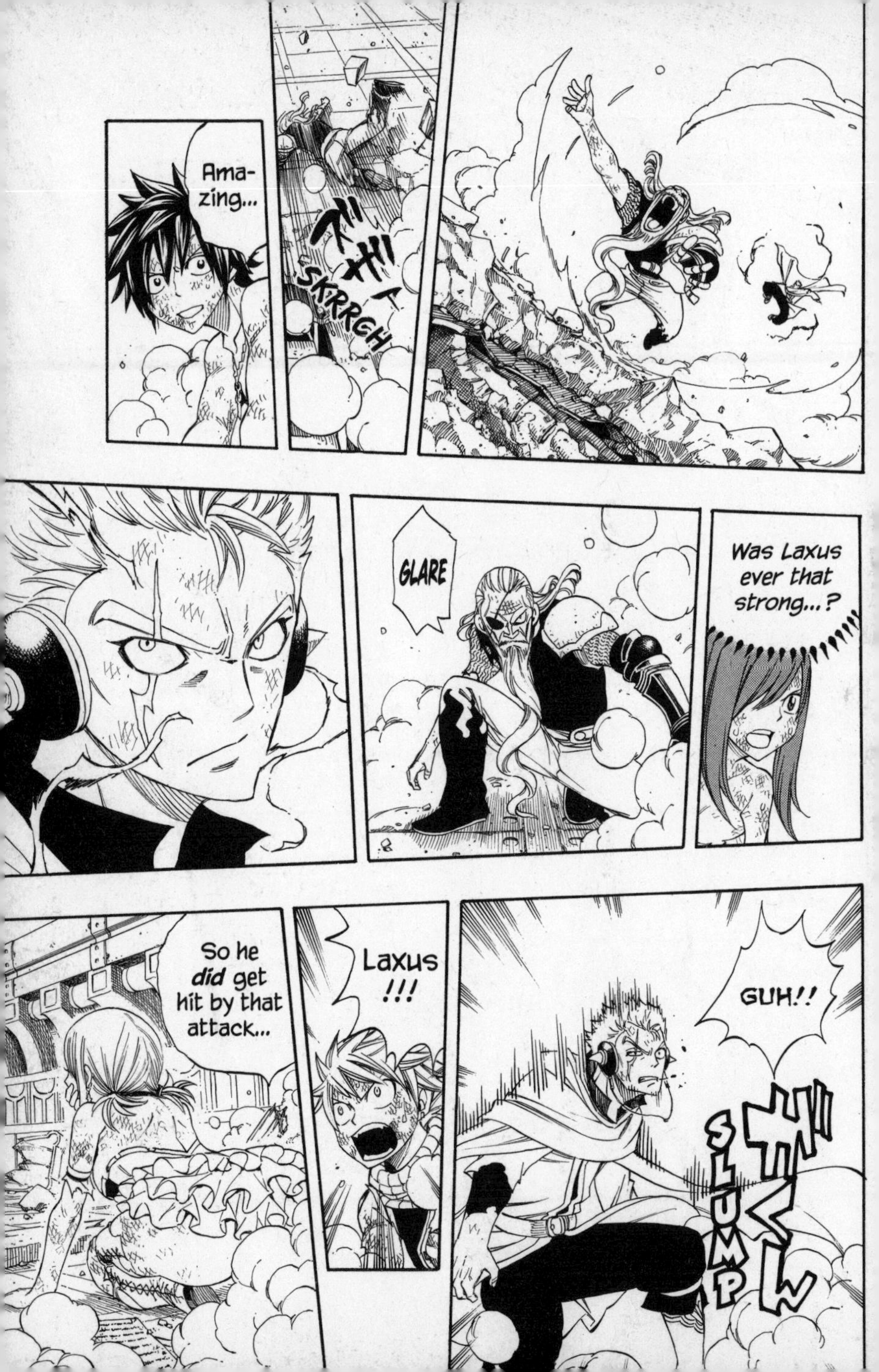
SKRRCH
Ama-zing...
Was Laxus ever that strong...?
GLARE
GUH!!
SLUMP
Laxus !!!
So he *did* get hit by that attack...

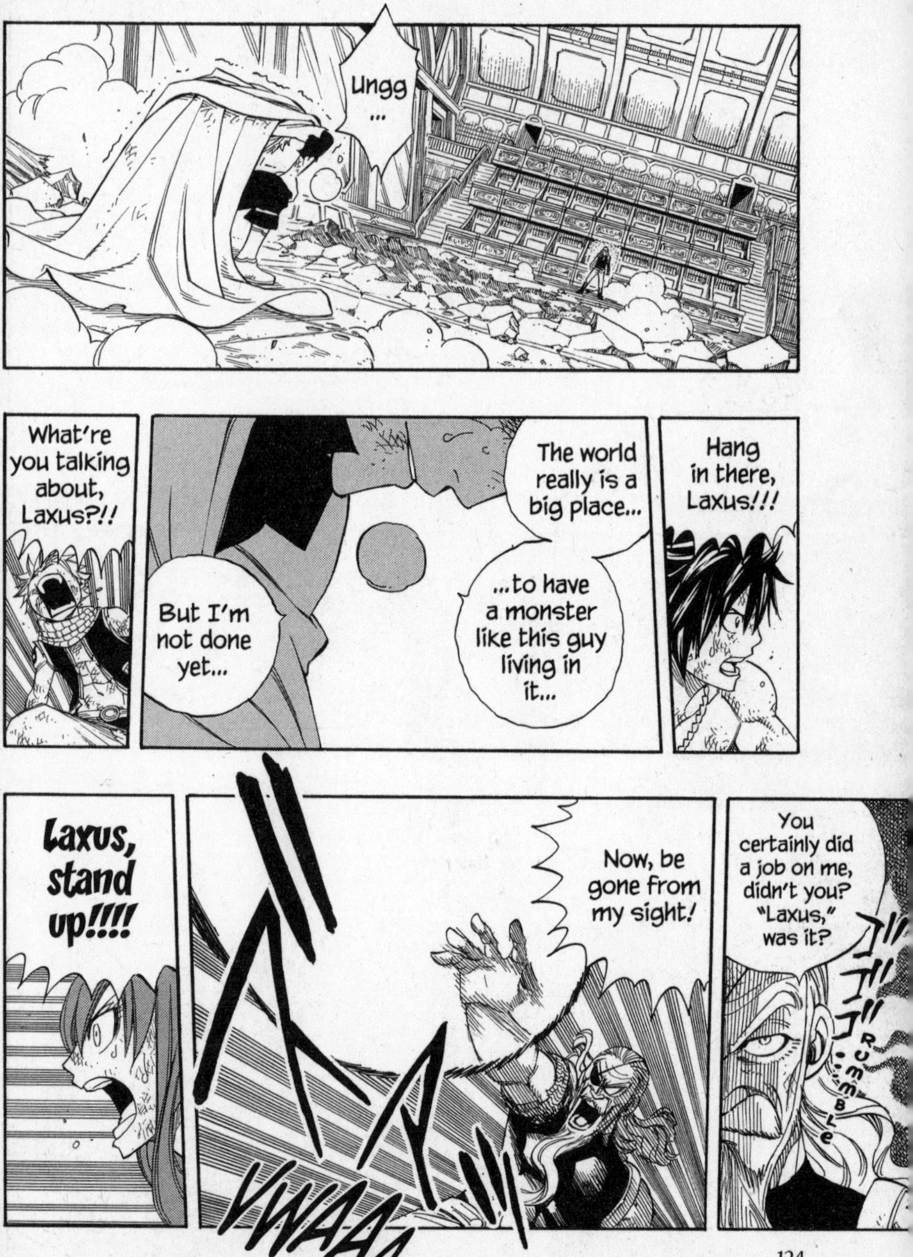
Ungg ...
Hang in there, Laxus!!!
The world really is a big place...
...to have a monster like this guy living in it...
But I'm not done yet...
What're you talking about, Laxus?!!
You certainly did a job on me, didn't you? "Laxus," was it?
RUMBLE
Now, be gone from my sight!
VWAAA
Laxus, stand up!!!!

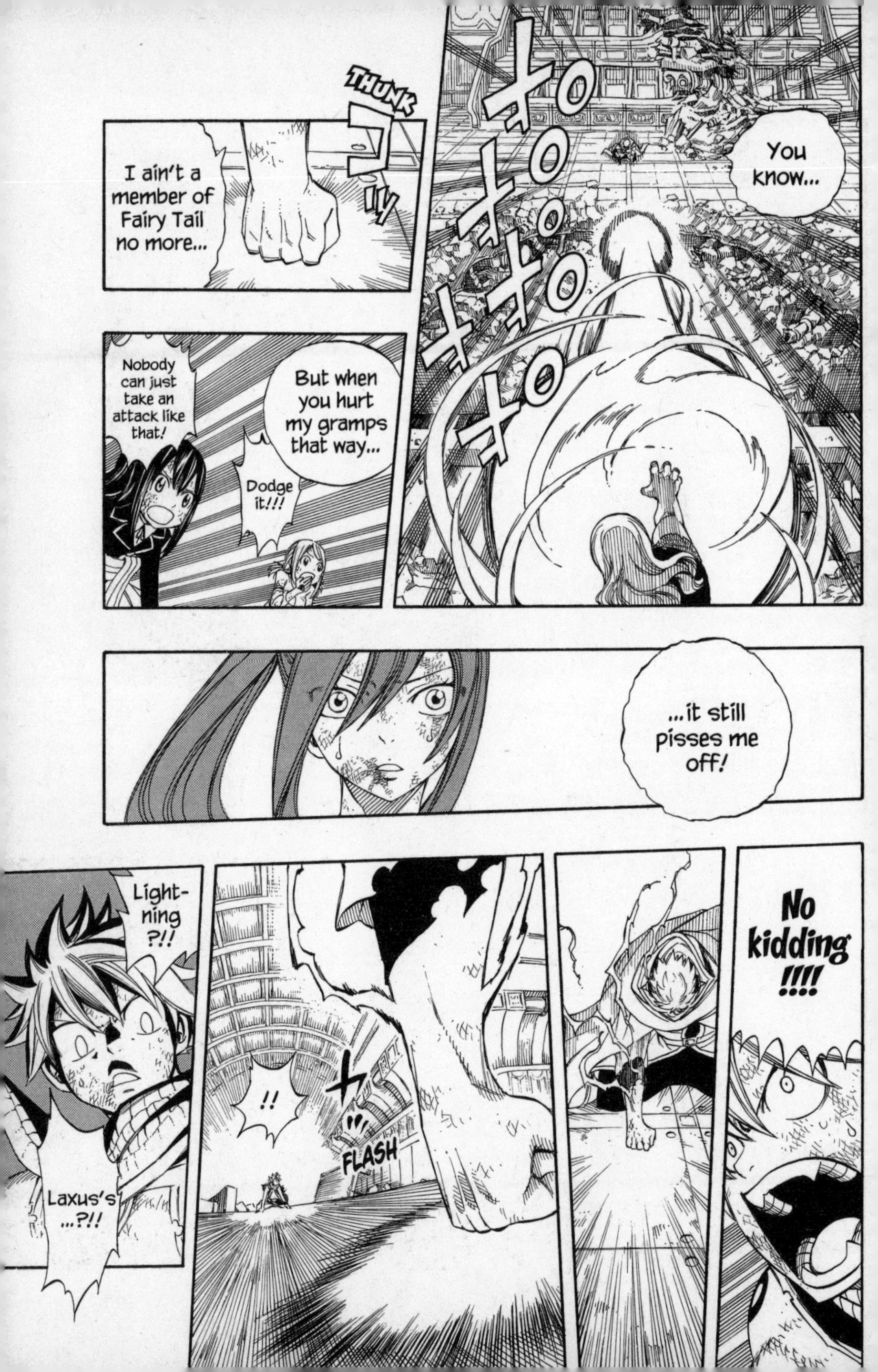
You know...
THUNK
I ain't a member of Fairy Tail no more...
But when you hurt my gramps that way...
Nobody can just take an attack like that!
Dodge it!!!
...it still pisses me off!
No kidding!!!!
FLASH
!!
Light-ning?!!
Laxus's...?!!

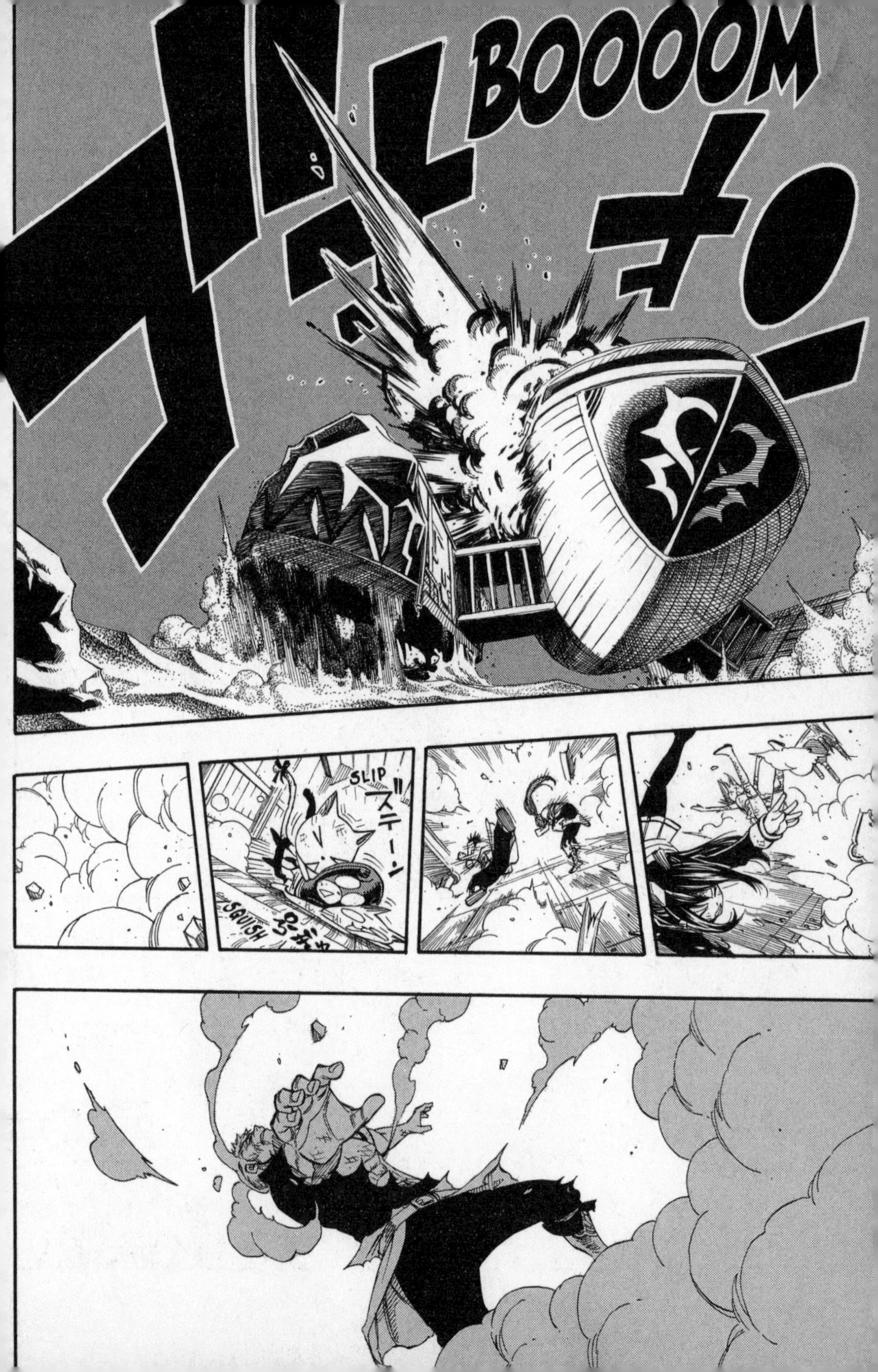
BOOOOM
SLIP
ズテーン
SQUISH

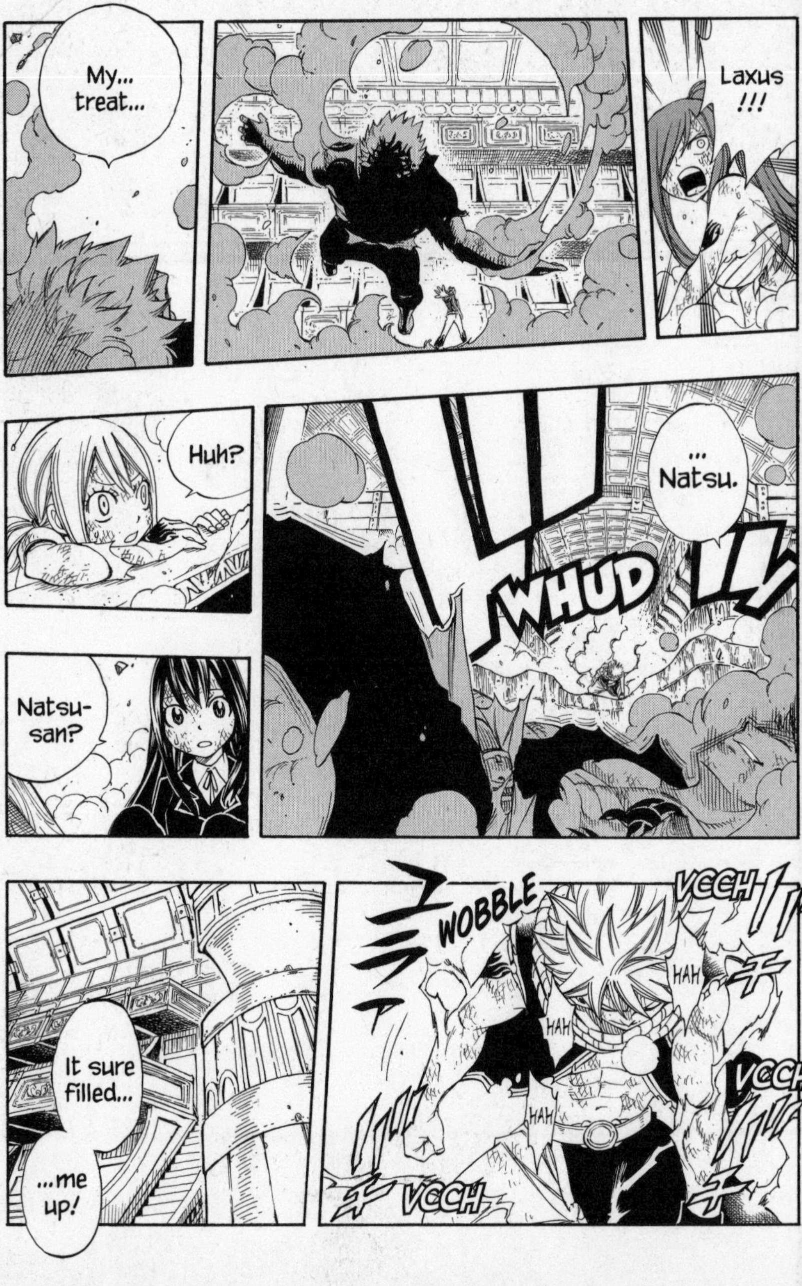
Laxus !!!
My... treat...
... Natsu.
WHUD
Huh?
Natsu-san?
VCCH
WOBBLE
HAH
HAH
VCCH
HAH
VCCH
It sure filled...
...me up!

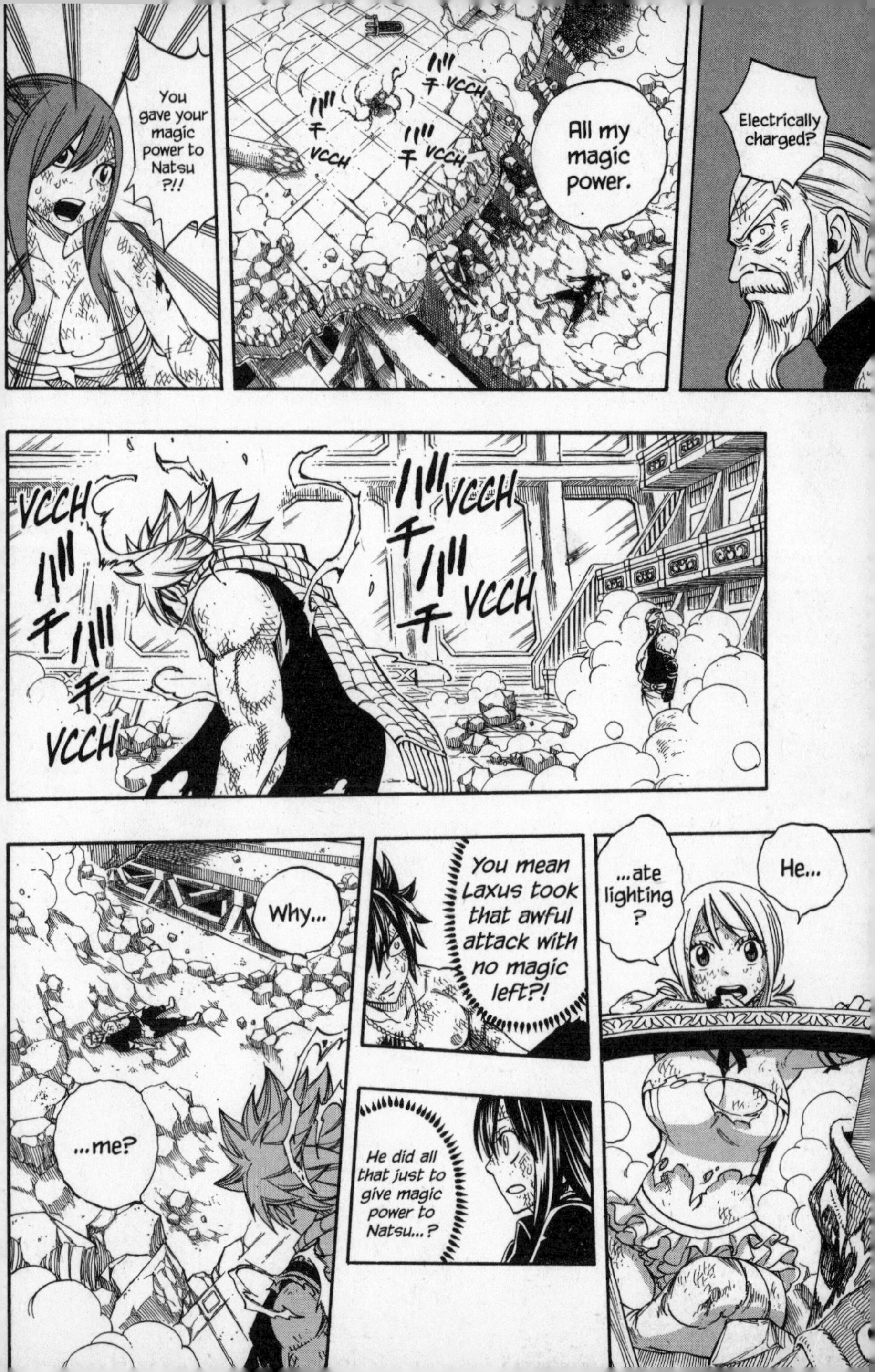
Electrically charged?
All my magic power.
VCCH
VCCH
VCCH
You gave your magic power to Natsu ?!!
VCCH
VCCH
VCCH
VCCH
He...
...ate lighting ?
You mean Laxus took that awful attack with no magic left?!
He did all that just to give magic power to Natsu...?
Why...
...me?

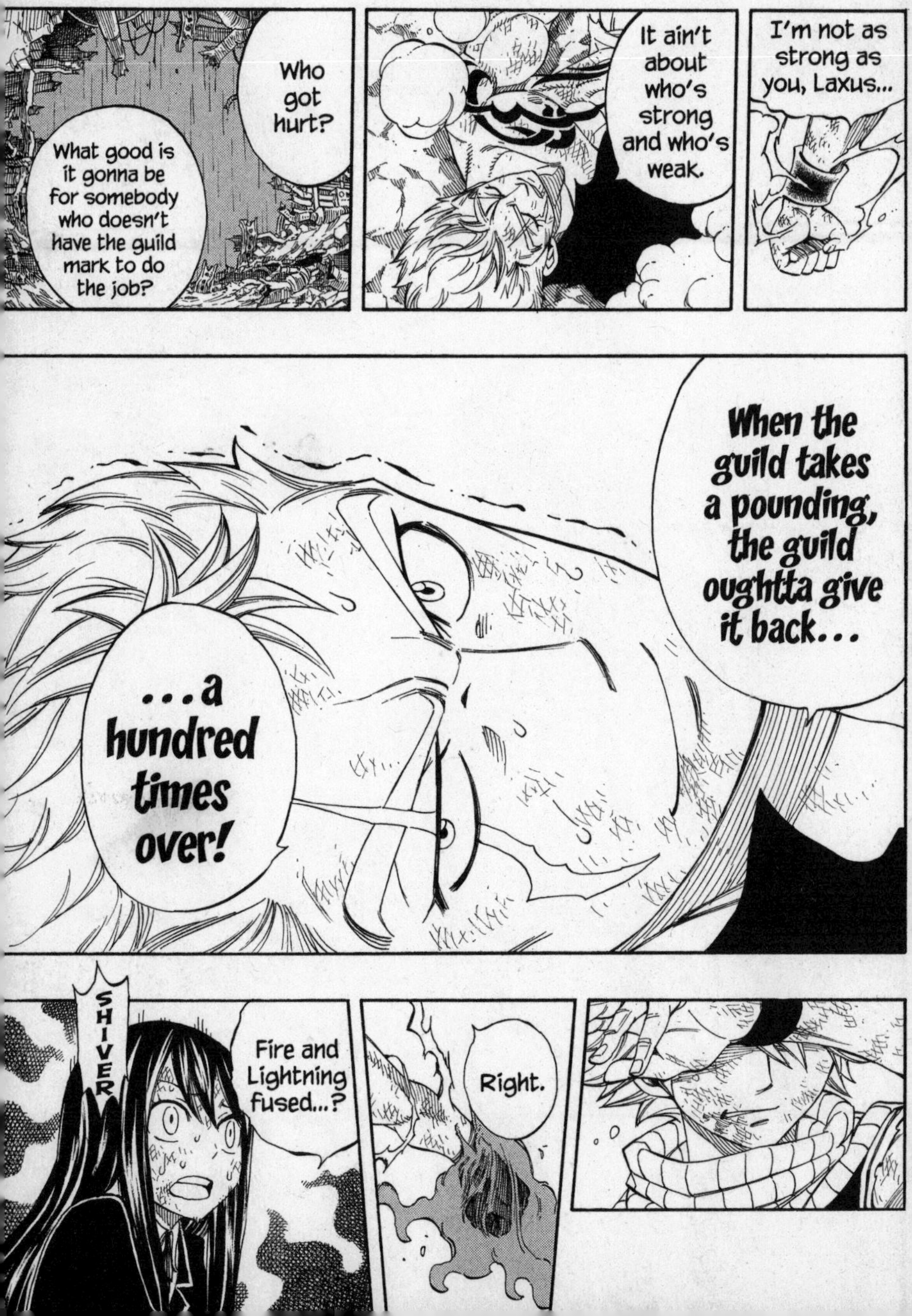
I'm not as strong as you, Laxus...
It ain't about who's strong and who's weak.
Who got hurt?
What good is it gonna be for somebody who doesn't have the guild mark to do the job?
When the guild takes a pounding, the guild oughtta give it back...
...a hundred times over!
Right.
Fire and Lightning fused...?
SHIVER

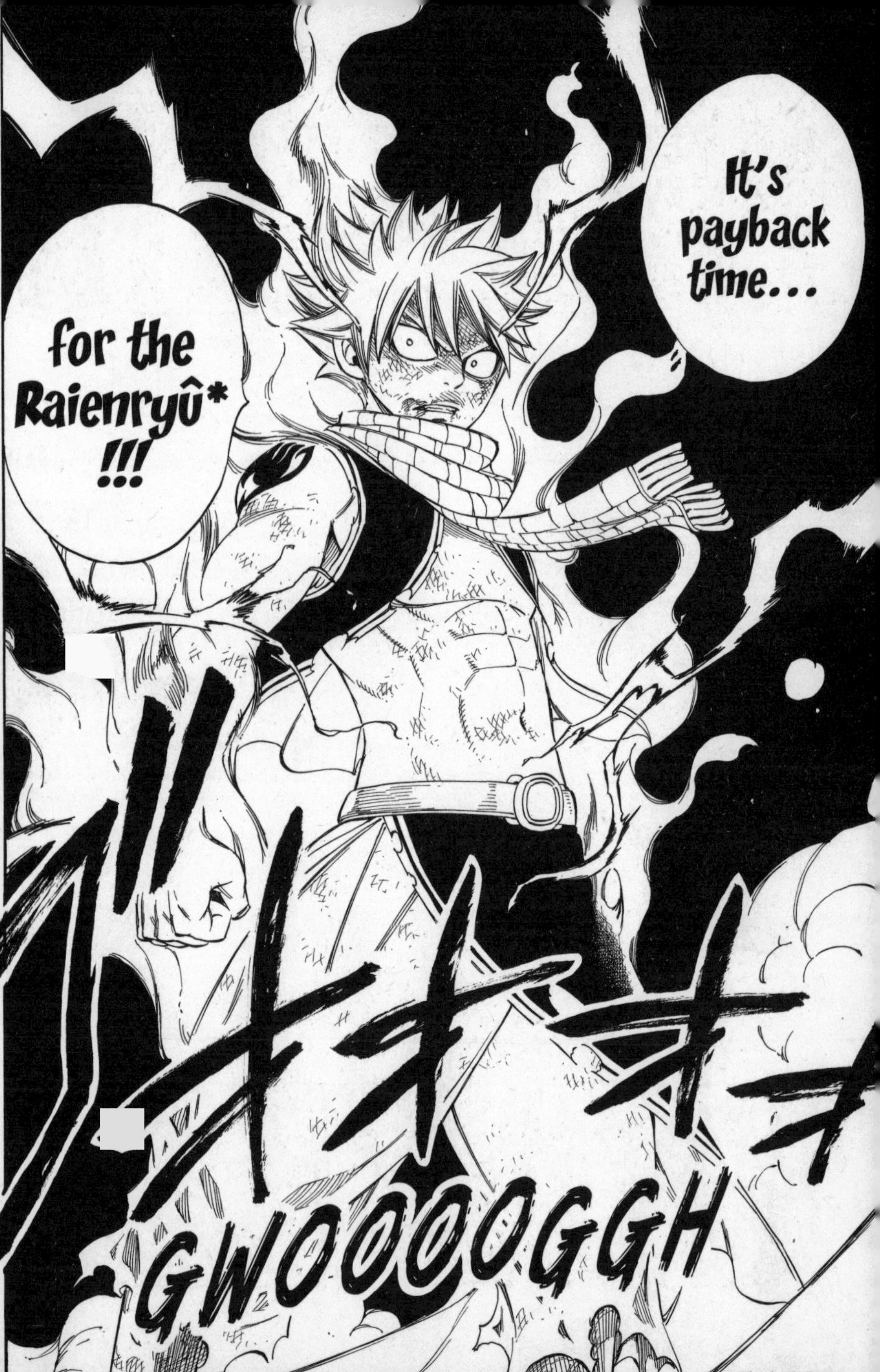
It's payback time...
for the Raienryû* !!!
GWOOOOOGGH

*Thunder-Fire Dragon

FAIRY TAIL

フェアリーテイル

Chapter 246: The Region of the Depths

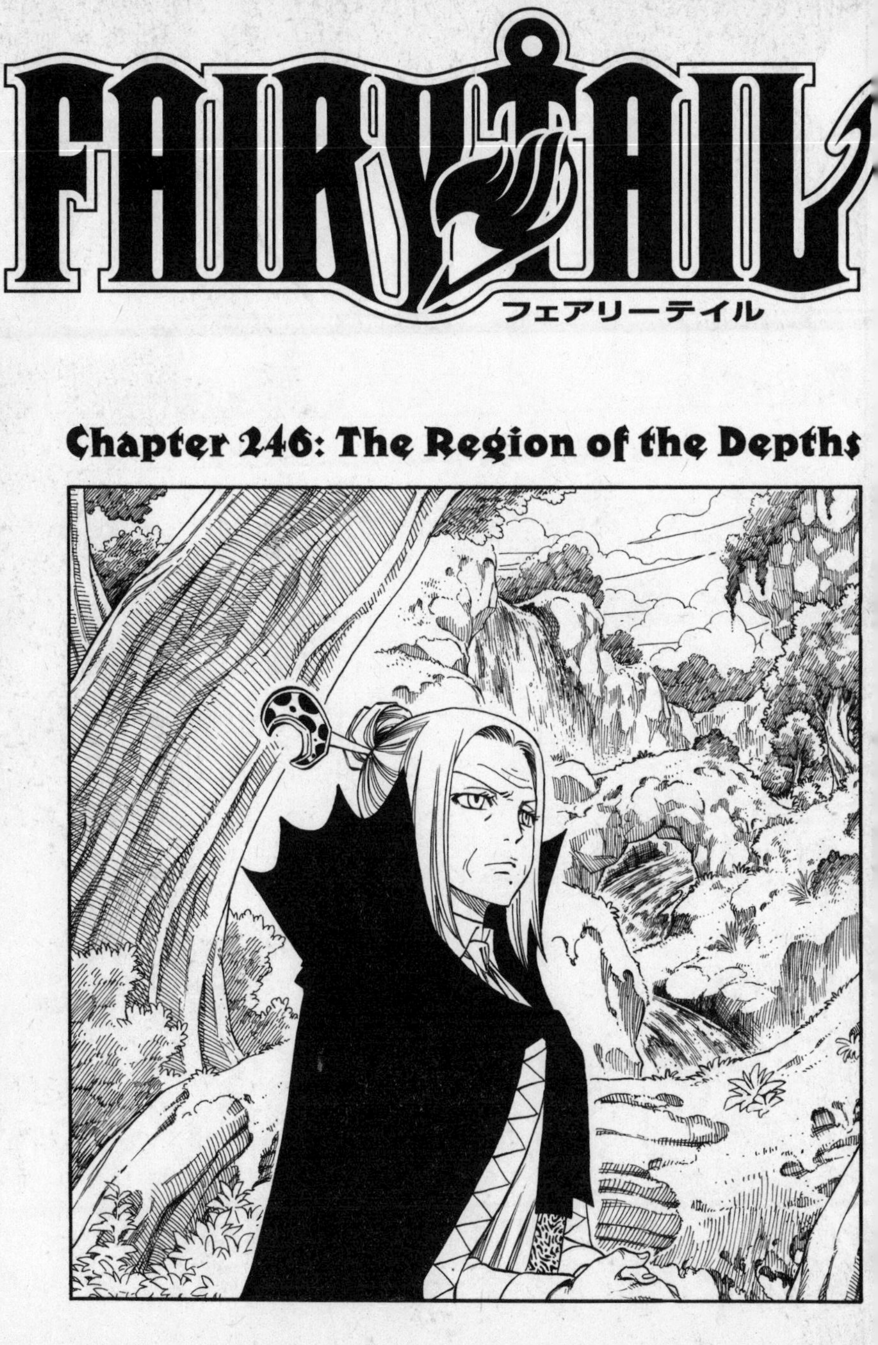

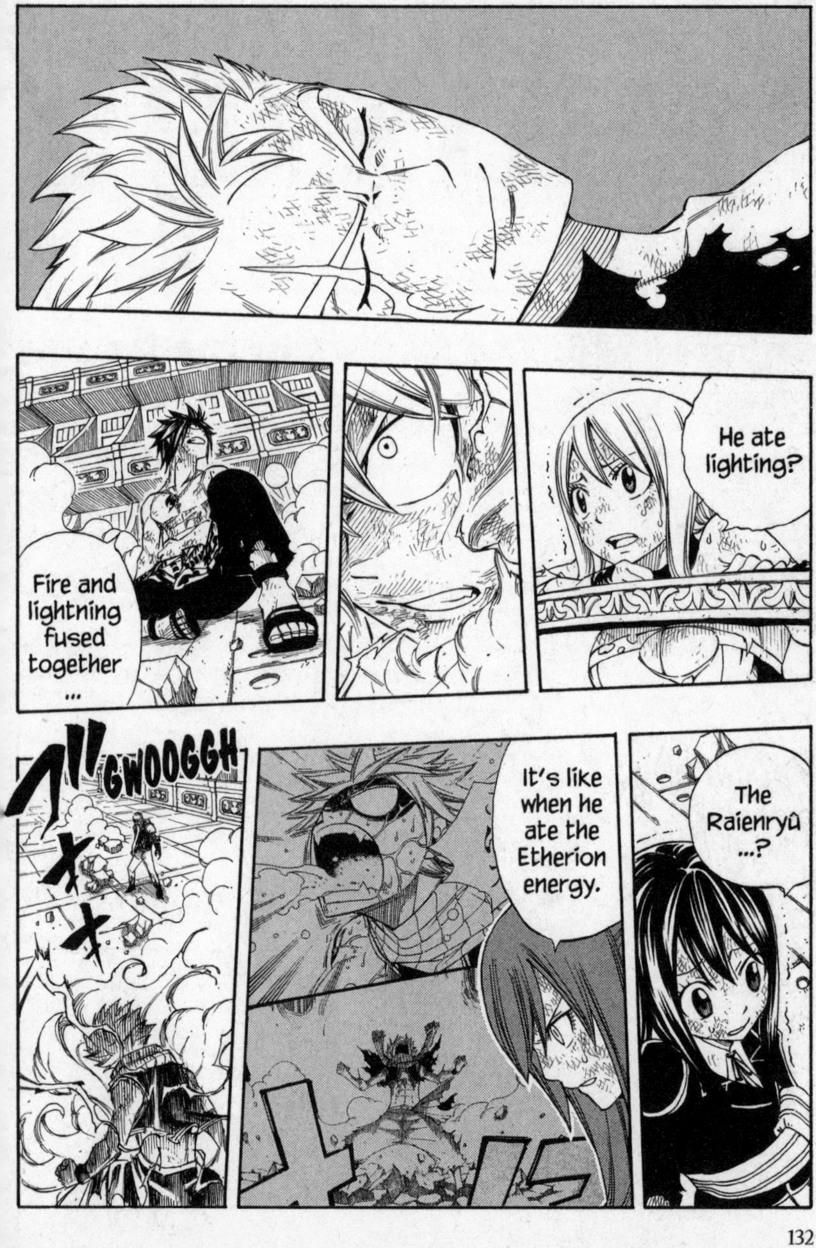
He ate lighting?
Fire and lightning fused together ...
The Raienryû ...?
It's like when he ate the Etherion energy.
GWOOGGH

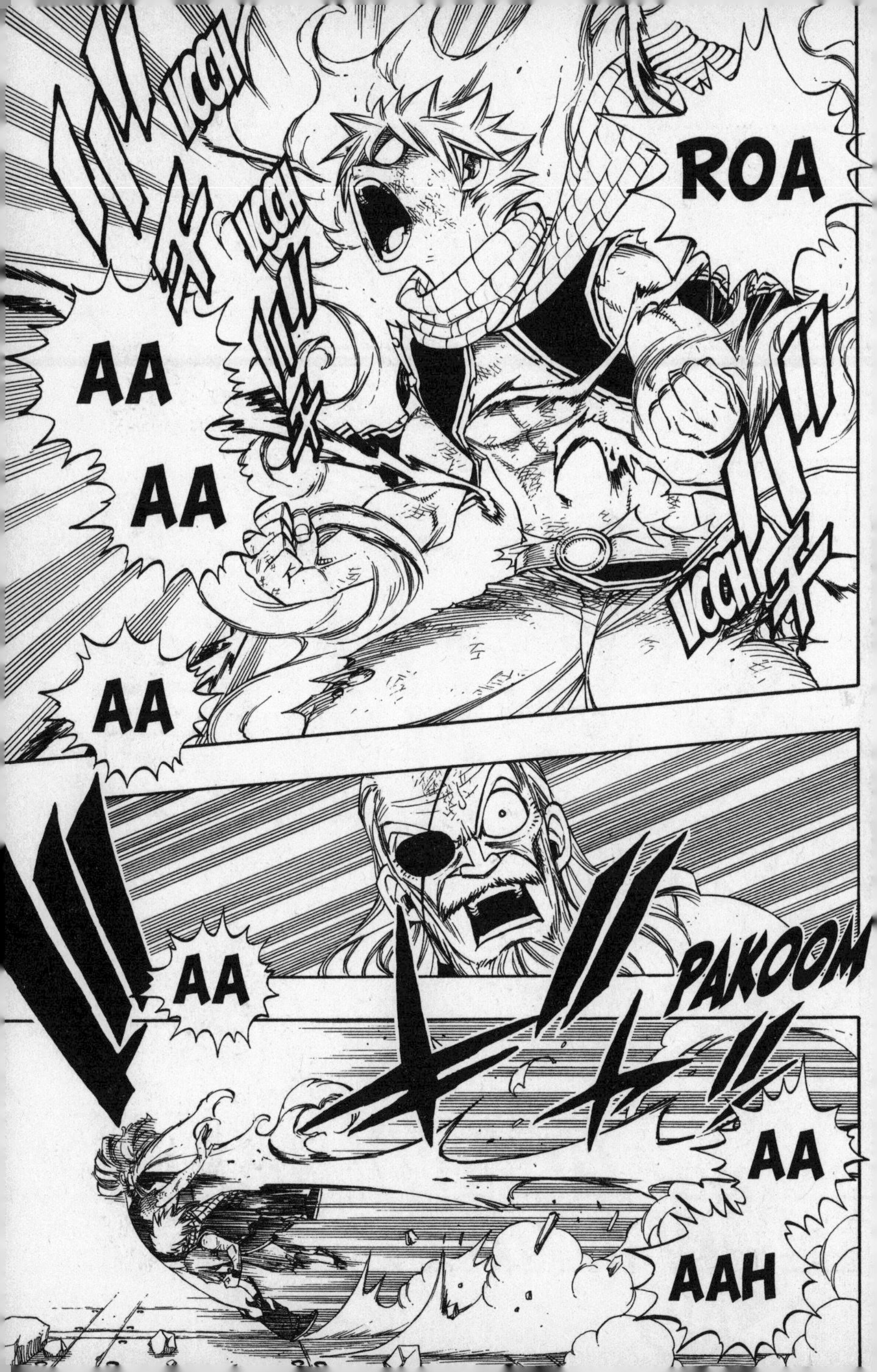
ROA
AA
AA
AA
AA
VCCH
VCCH
VCCH
PAKOOM
AA
AAH

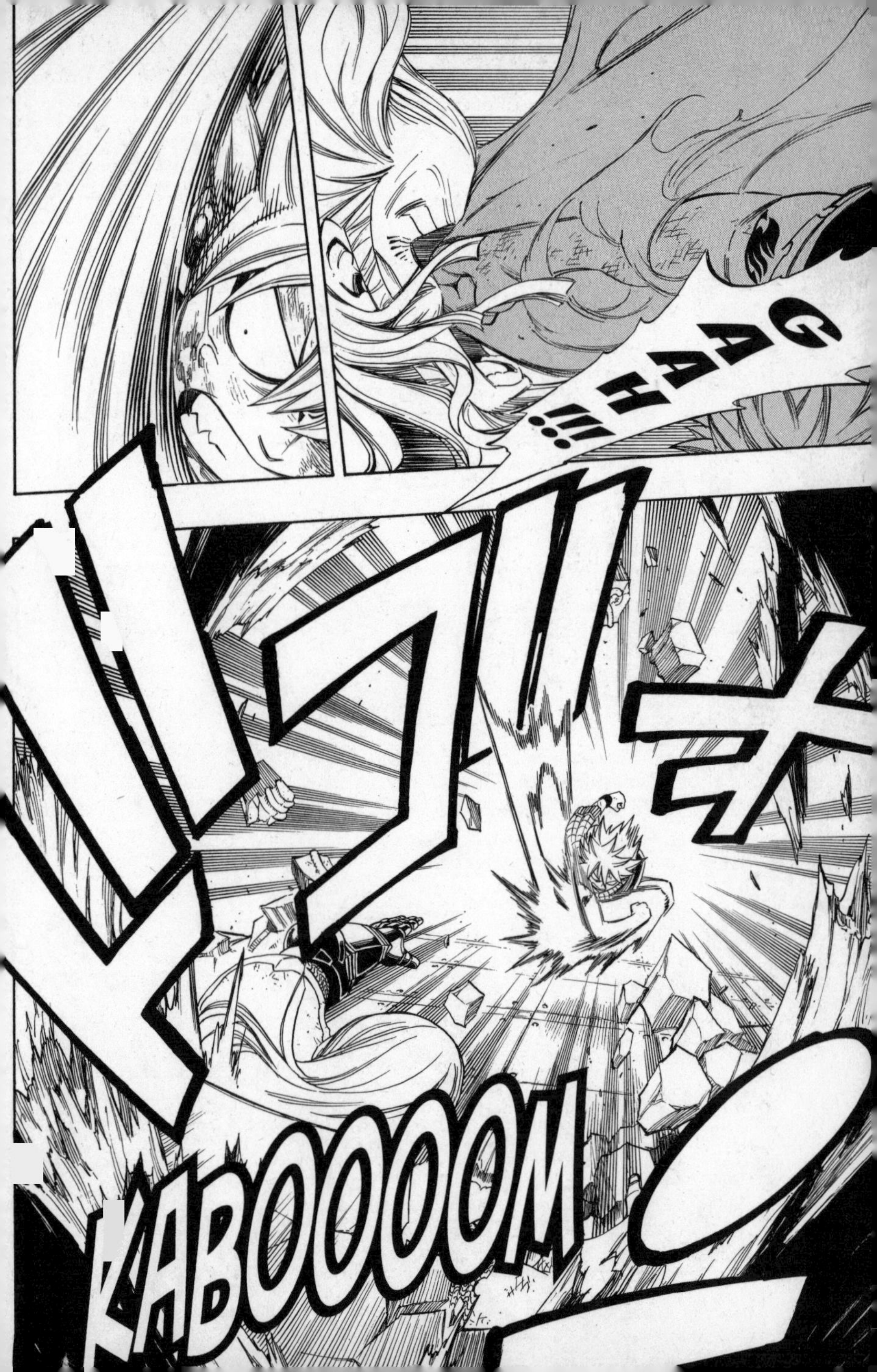
GAAH!!!
KABOOOOM

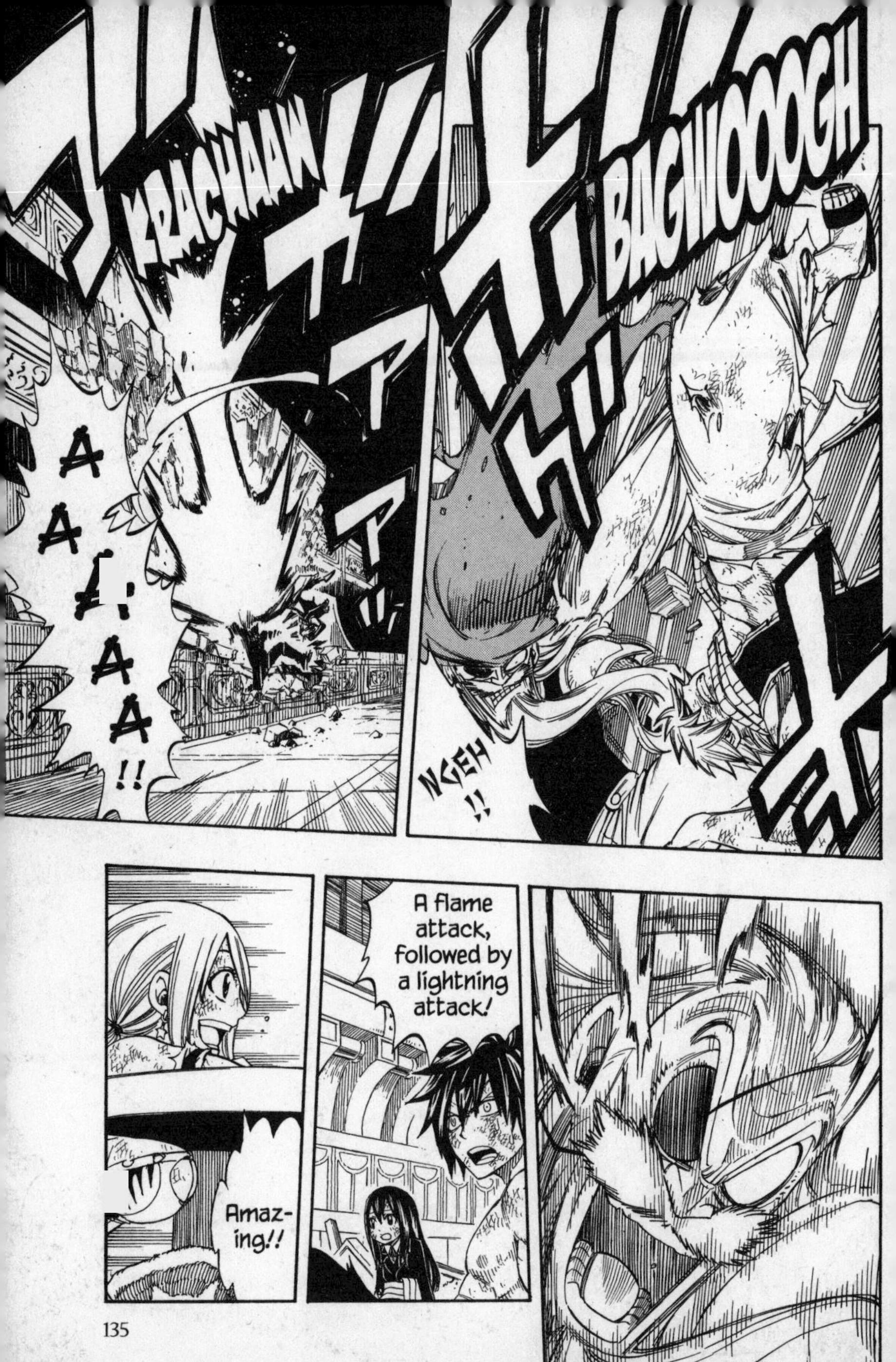
BAGWOOOGH
NGEH!!
KRACHAAW
AAAAAA!!
A flame attack, followed by a lightning attack!
Amaz-ing!!

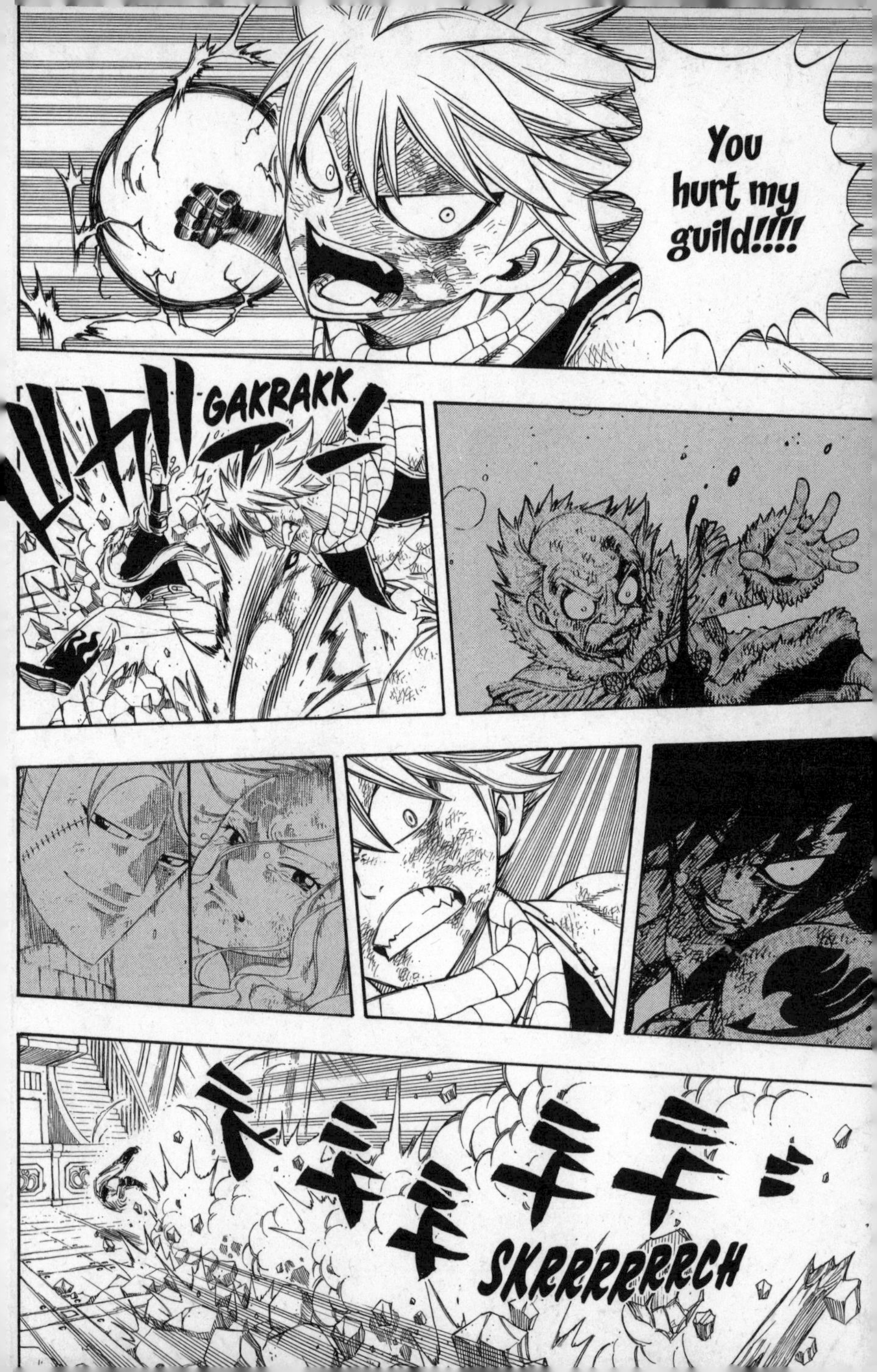
You hurt my guild!!!!
GAKRAKK
SKRRRRRRCH

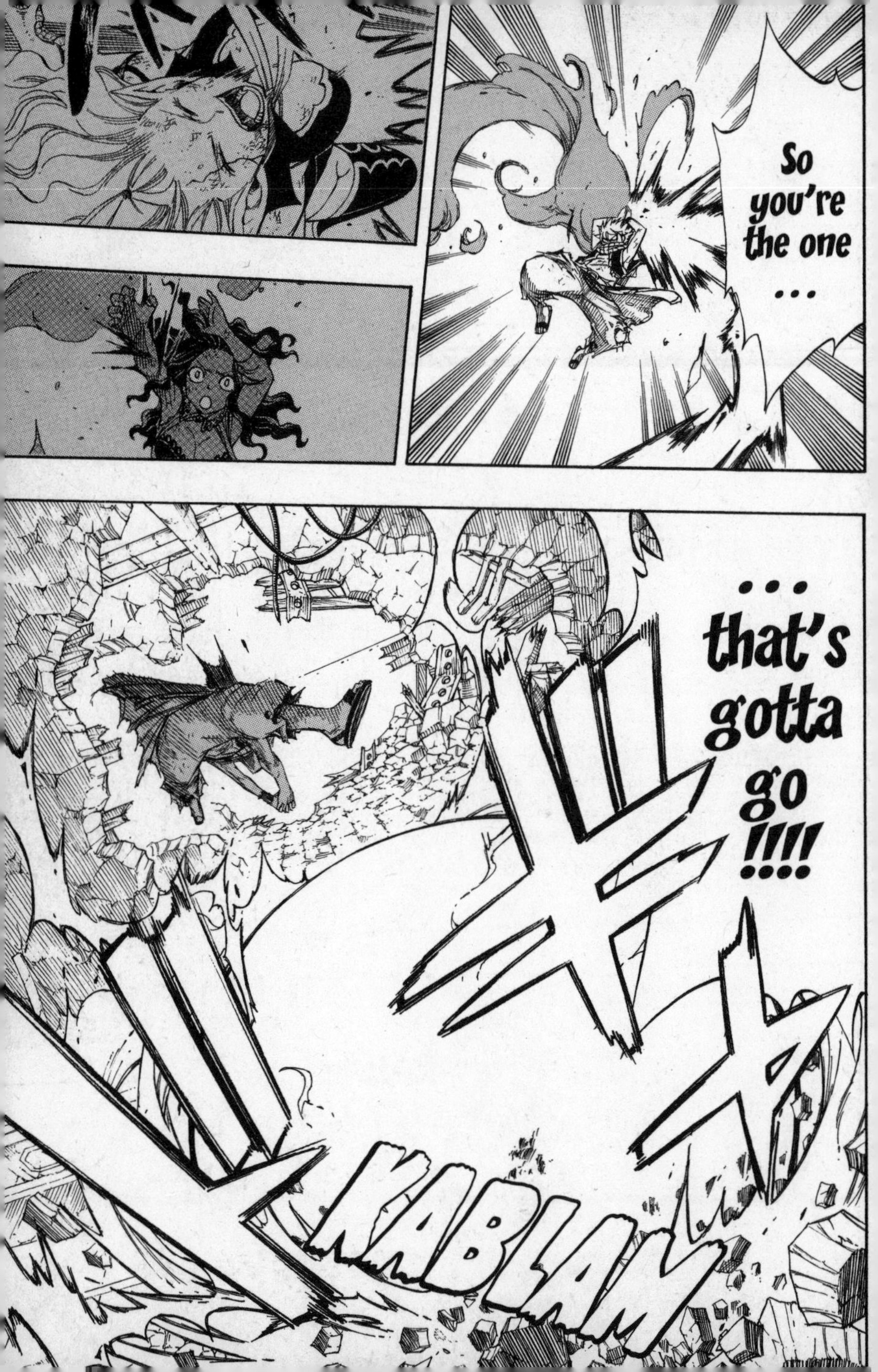
So you're the one …
… that's gotta go !!!!
KABLAM

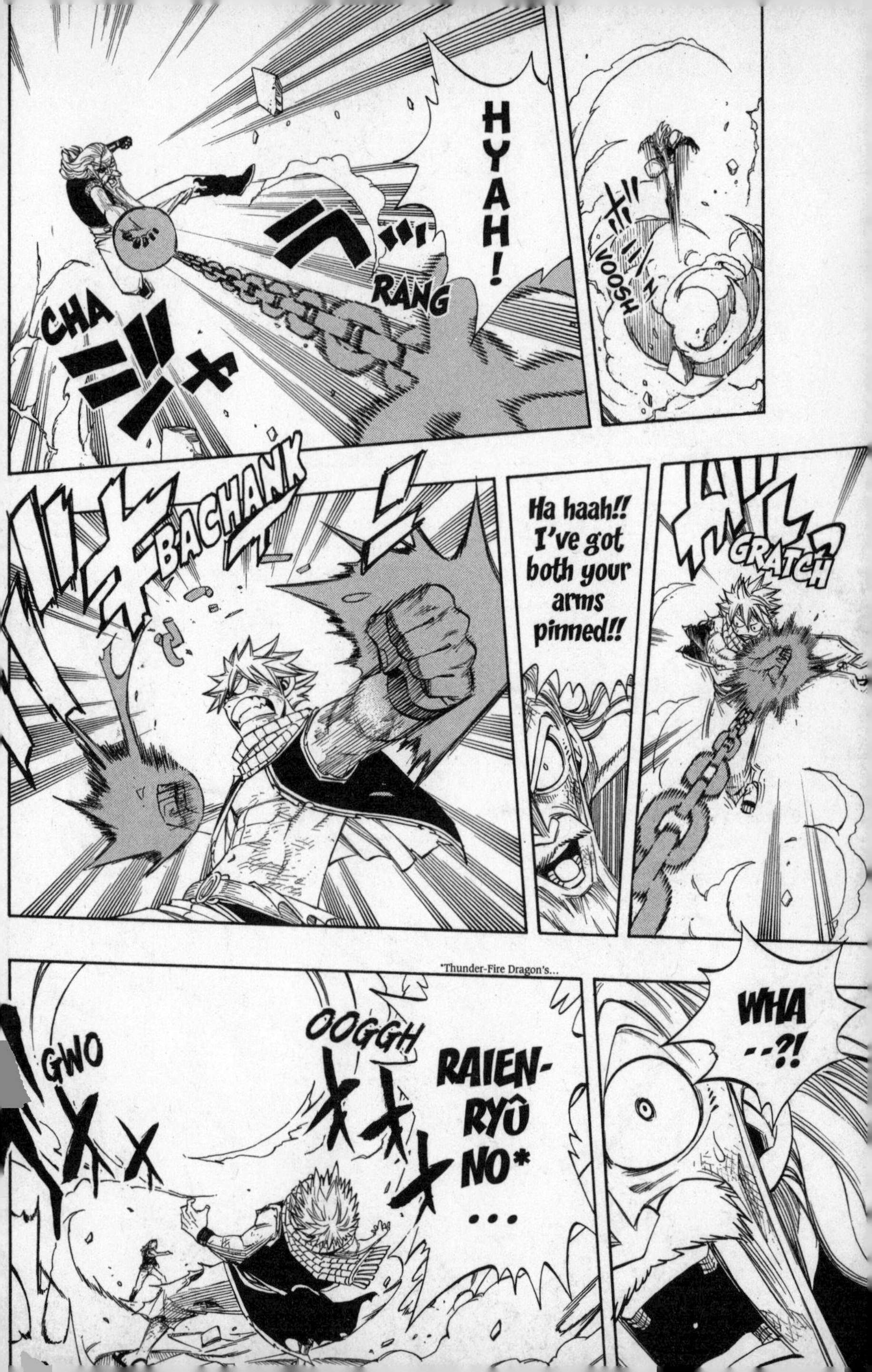
WOOSH
HYAH!
RANG
CHA
GRATCH
Ha haah!! I've got both your arms pinned!!
BACHANK
WHA--?!
RAIEN-RYÛ NO*...
OOGGH
GWO
*Thunder-Fire Dragon's...

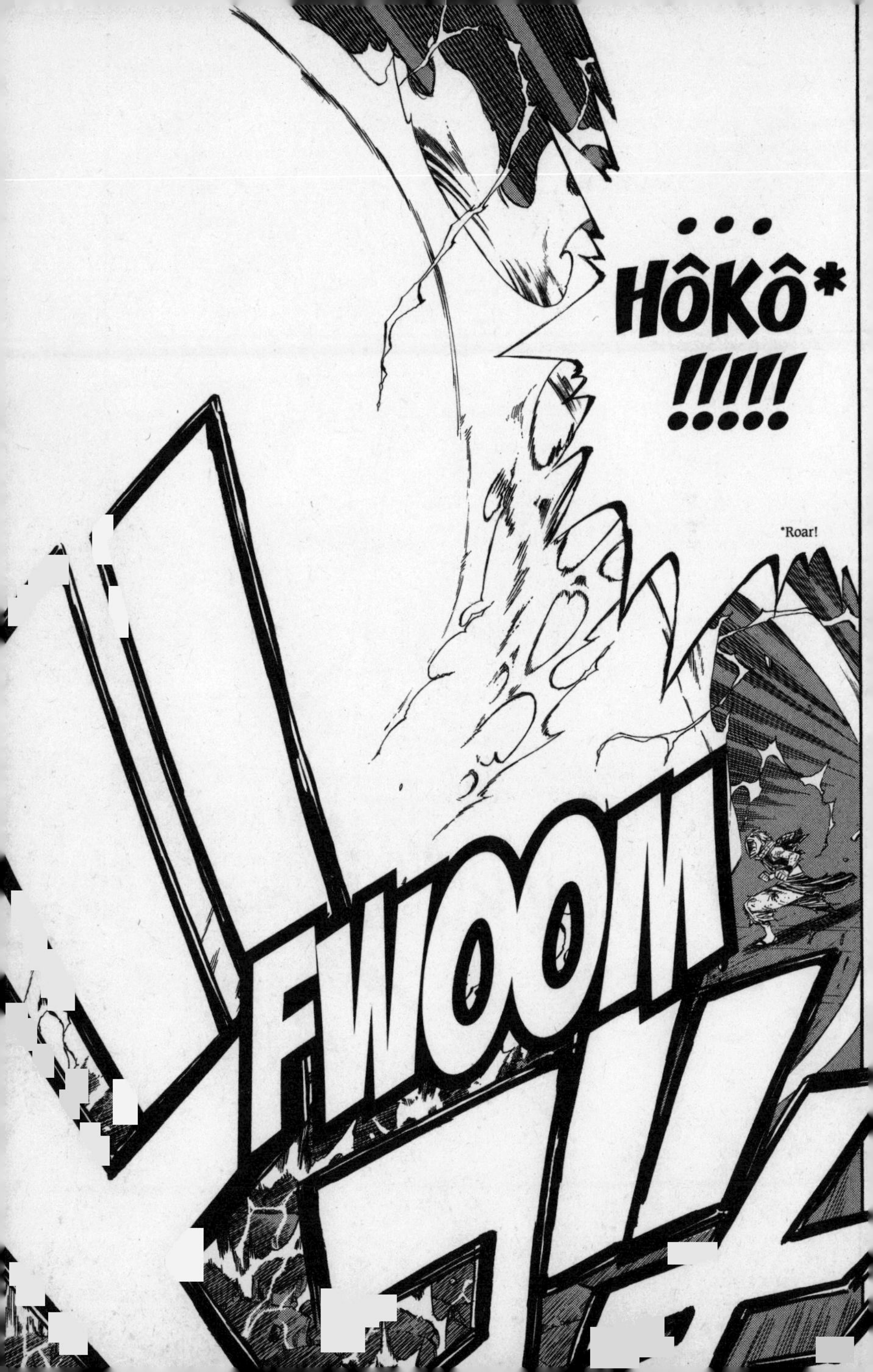
HÔKÔ*
!!!!!
FWOOM
*Roar!

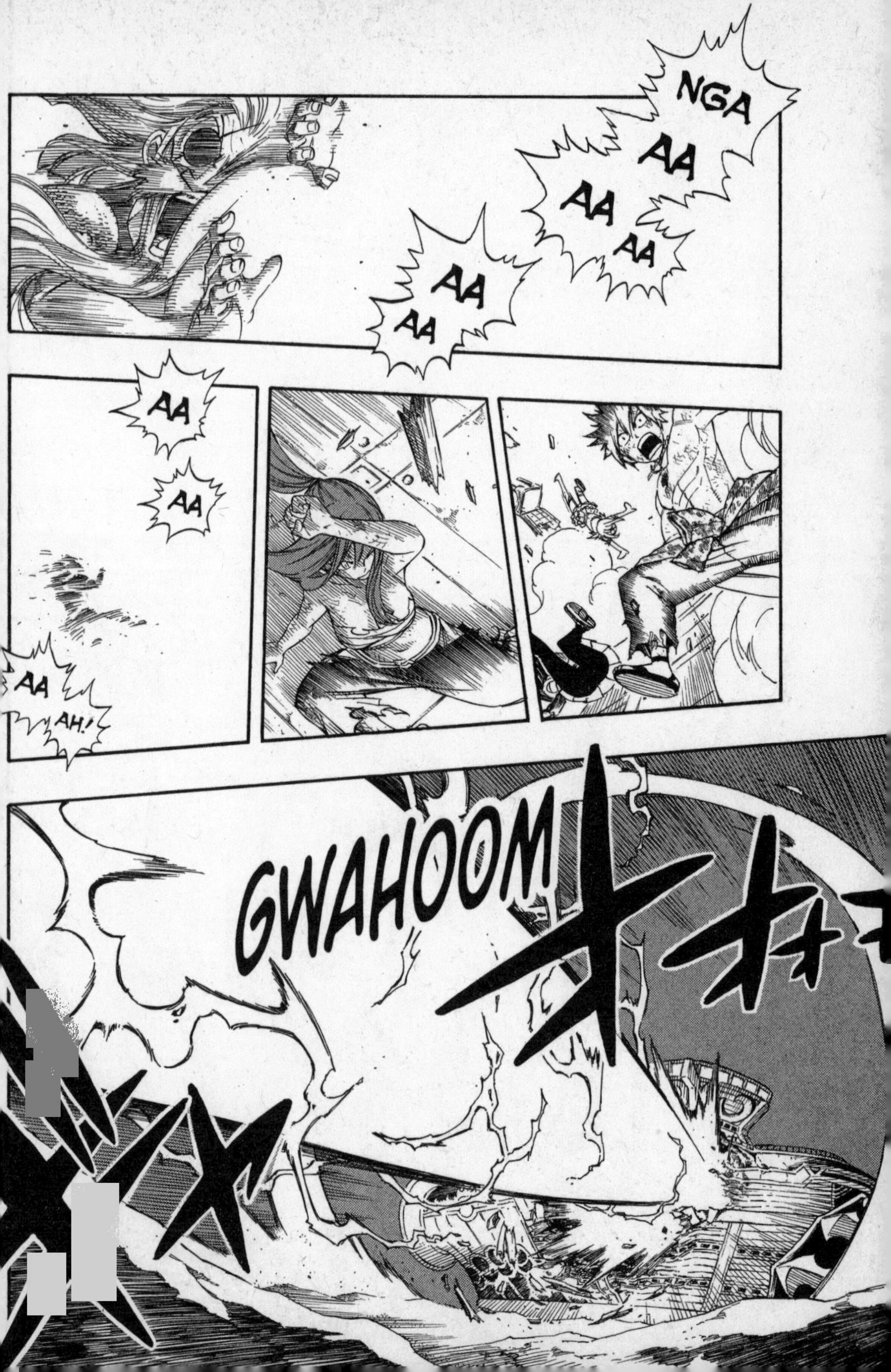
NGA
AA
AA
AA
AA
AA
AA
AA
AA
AH!
GWAHOOM

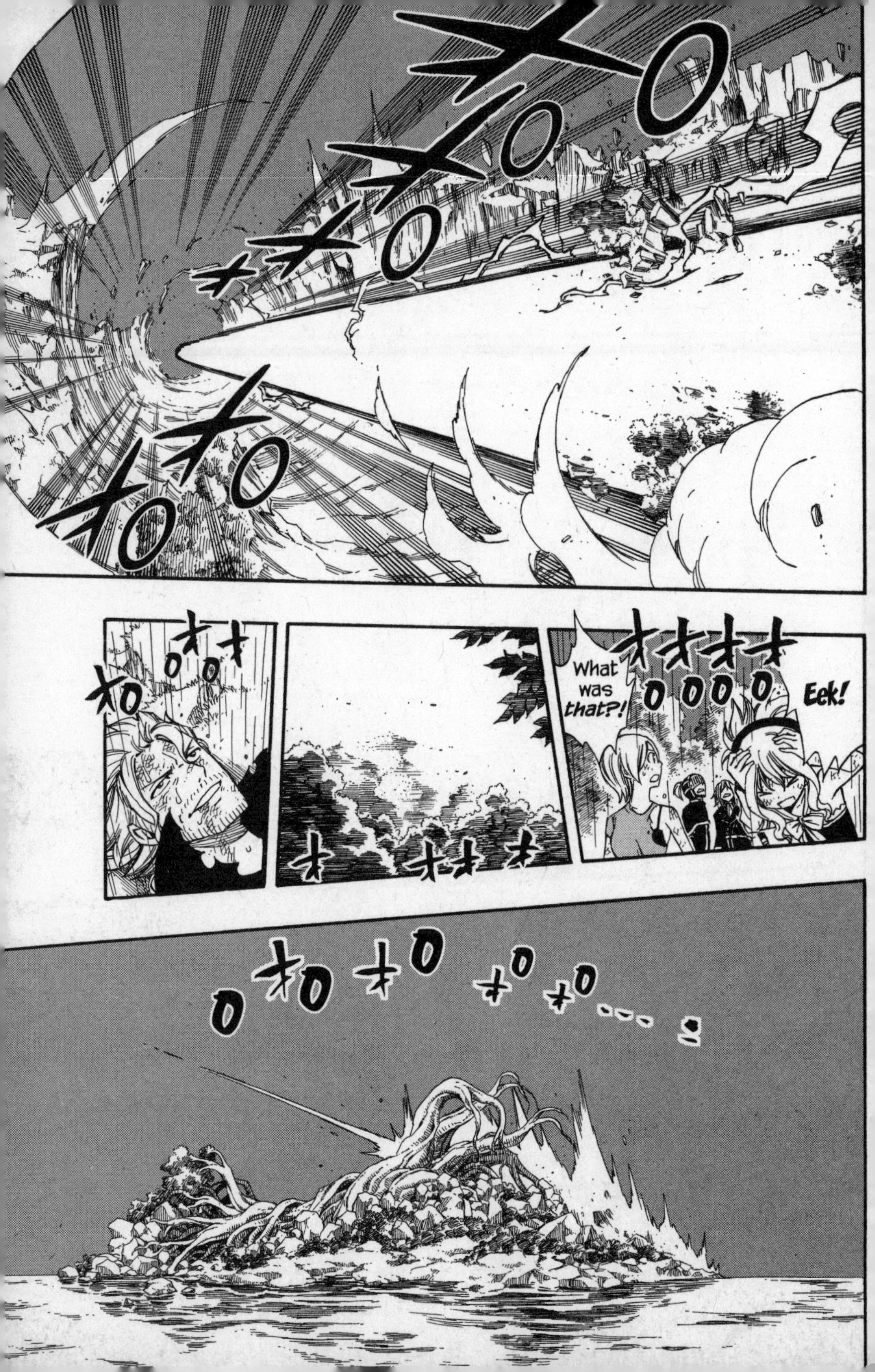
Eek!
What was that?!

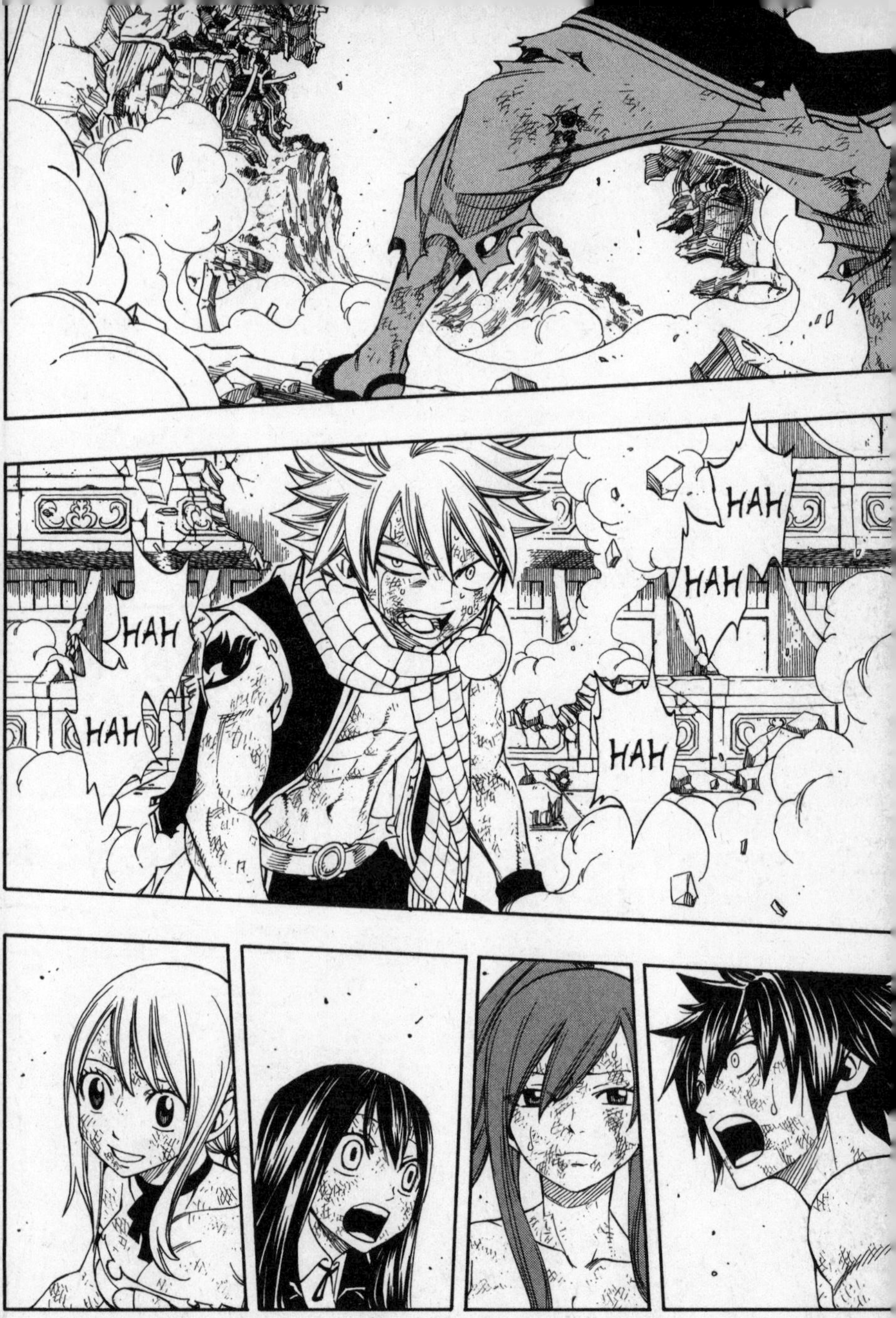
HAH
HAH
HAH
HAH
HAH

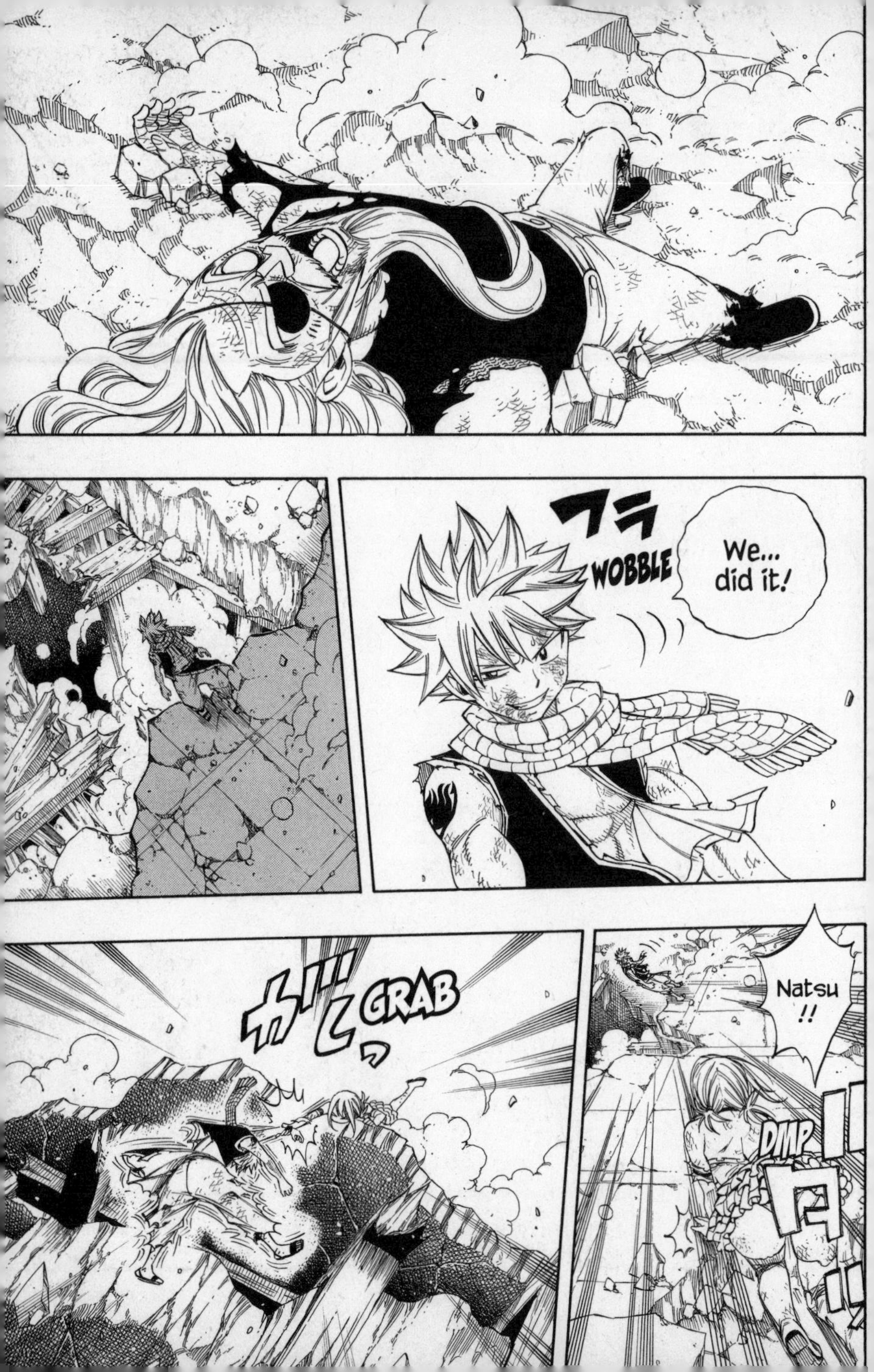
フラ
WOBBLE
We... did it!
Natsu !!
DMP
ガしっ
GRAB

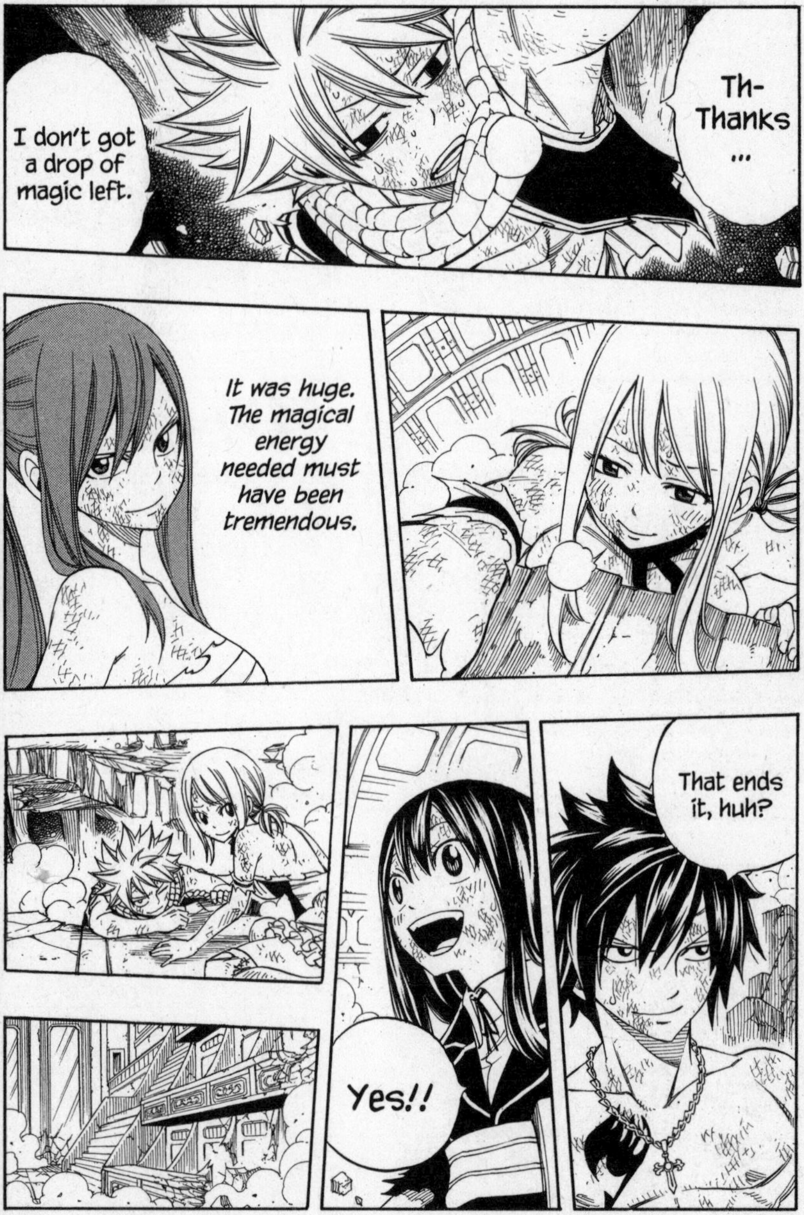
Th- Thanks ...
I don't got a drop of magic left.
It was huge. The magical energy needed must have been tremendous.
That ends it, huh?
Yes!!

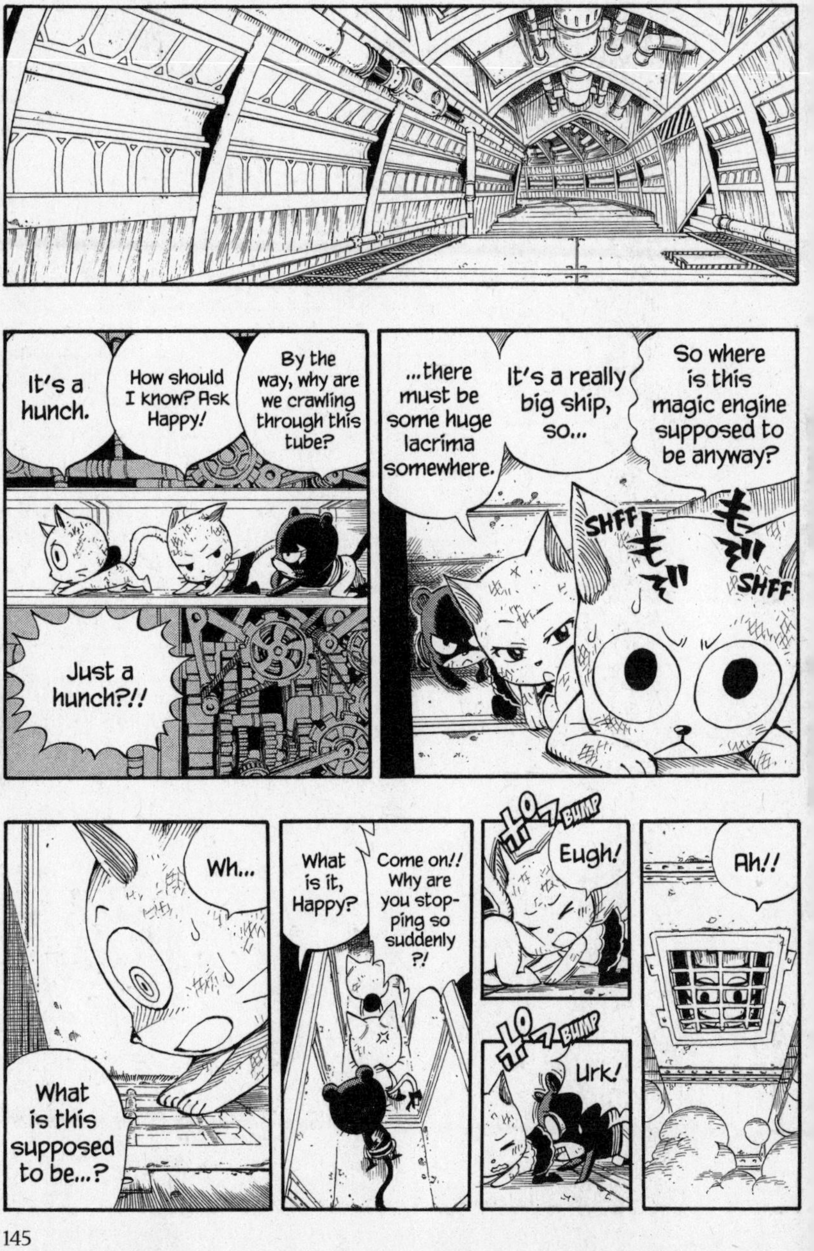
So where is this magic engine supposed to be anyway?
It's a really big ship, so...
...there must be some huge lacrima somewhere.
SHFF
SHFF
By the way, why are we crawling through this tube?
How should I know? Ask Happy!
It's a hunch.
Just a hunch?!!
Ah!!
BUMP
Eugh!
BUMP
Urk!
Come on!! Why are you stopping so suddenly?!
What is it, Happy?
Wh...
What is this supposed to be...?

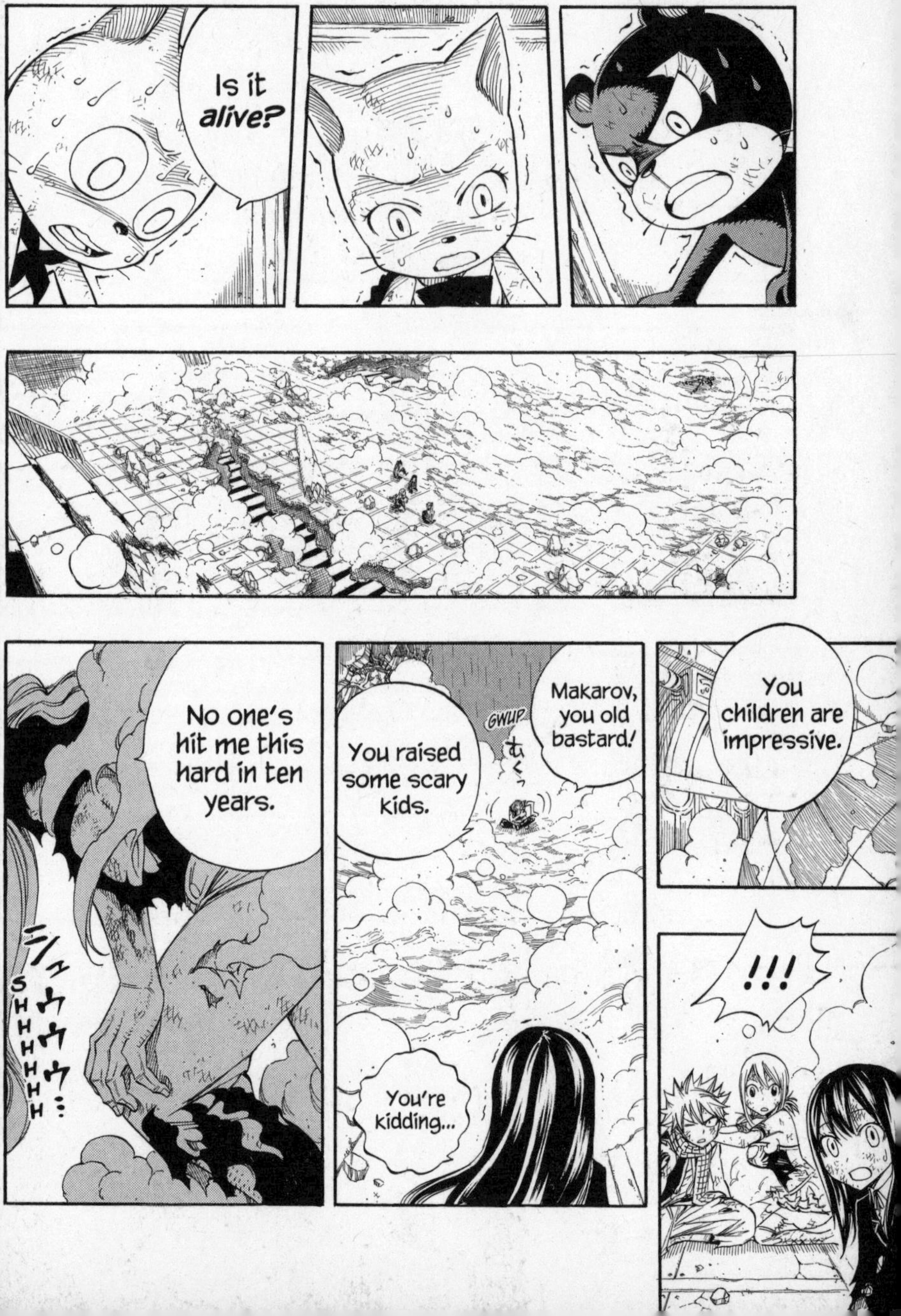
Is it alive?
You children are impressive.
!!!
Makarov, you old bastard!
GWUP
むくっ
You raised some scary kids.
You're kidding...
No one's hit me this hard in ten years.
シュウウウ…
SHHHHHH

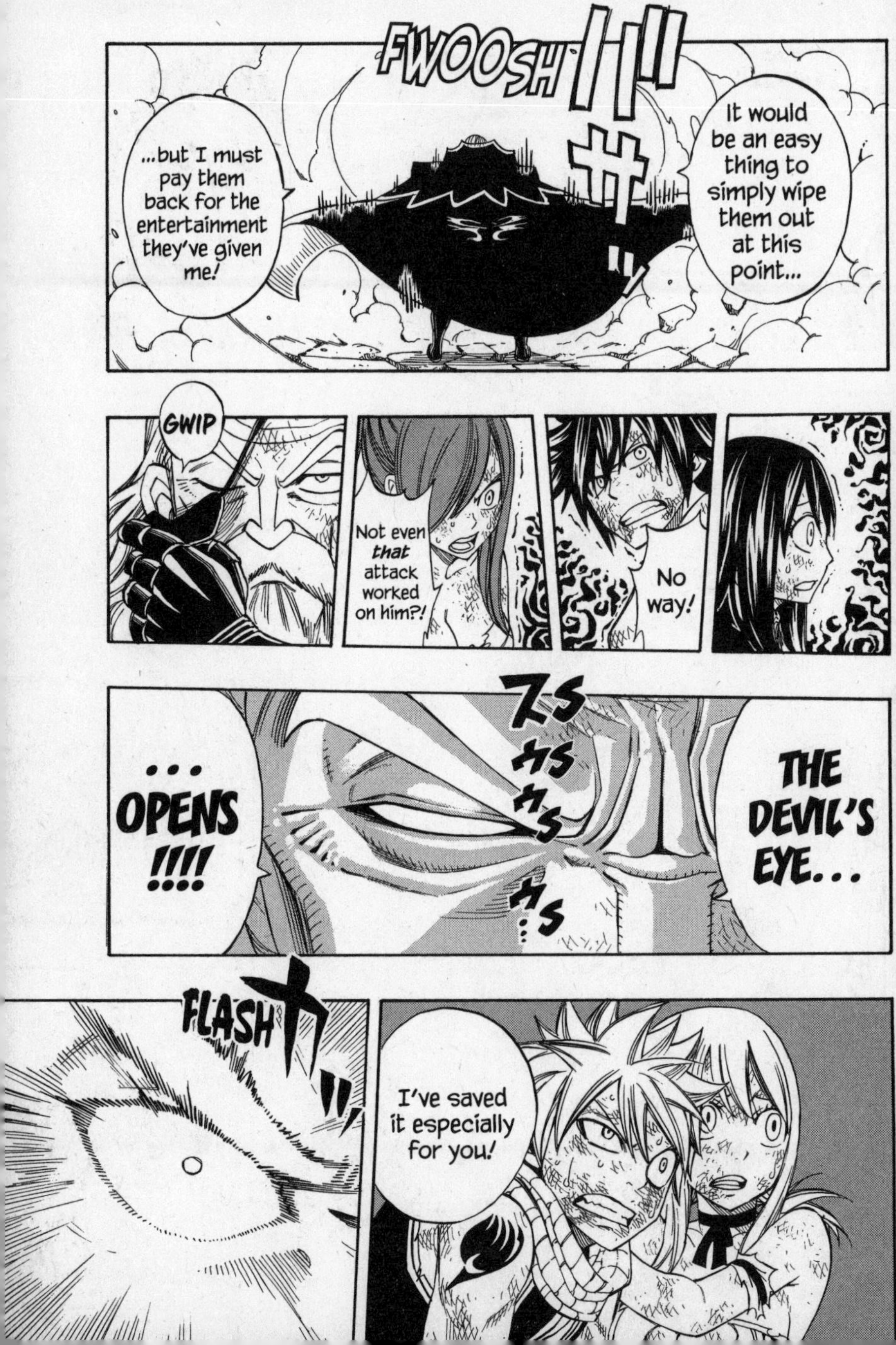
FWOOSH
It would be an easy thing to simply wipe them out at this point...
...but I must pay them back for the entertainment they've given me!
No way!
Not even *that* attack worked on him?!
GWIP
THE DEVIL'S EYE...
...OPENS!!!!
I've saved it especially for you!
FLASH

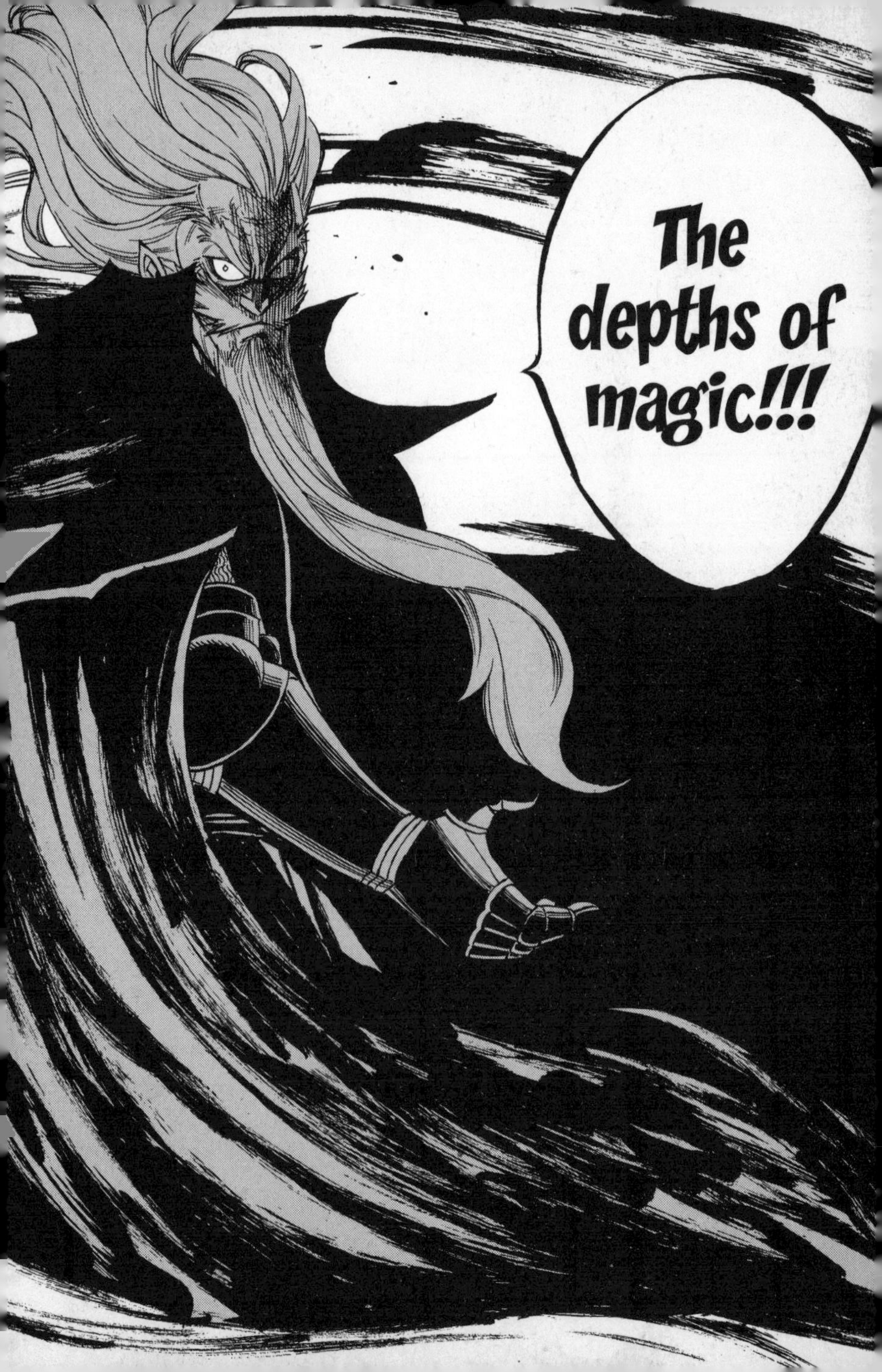
The depths of magic!!!

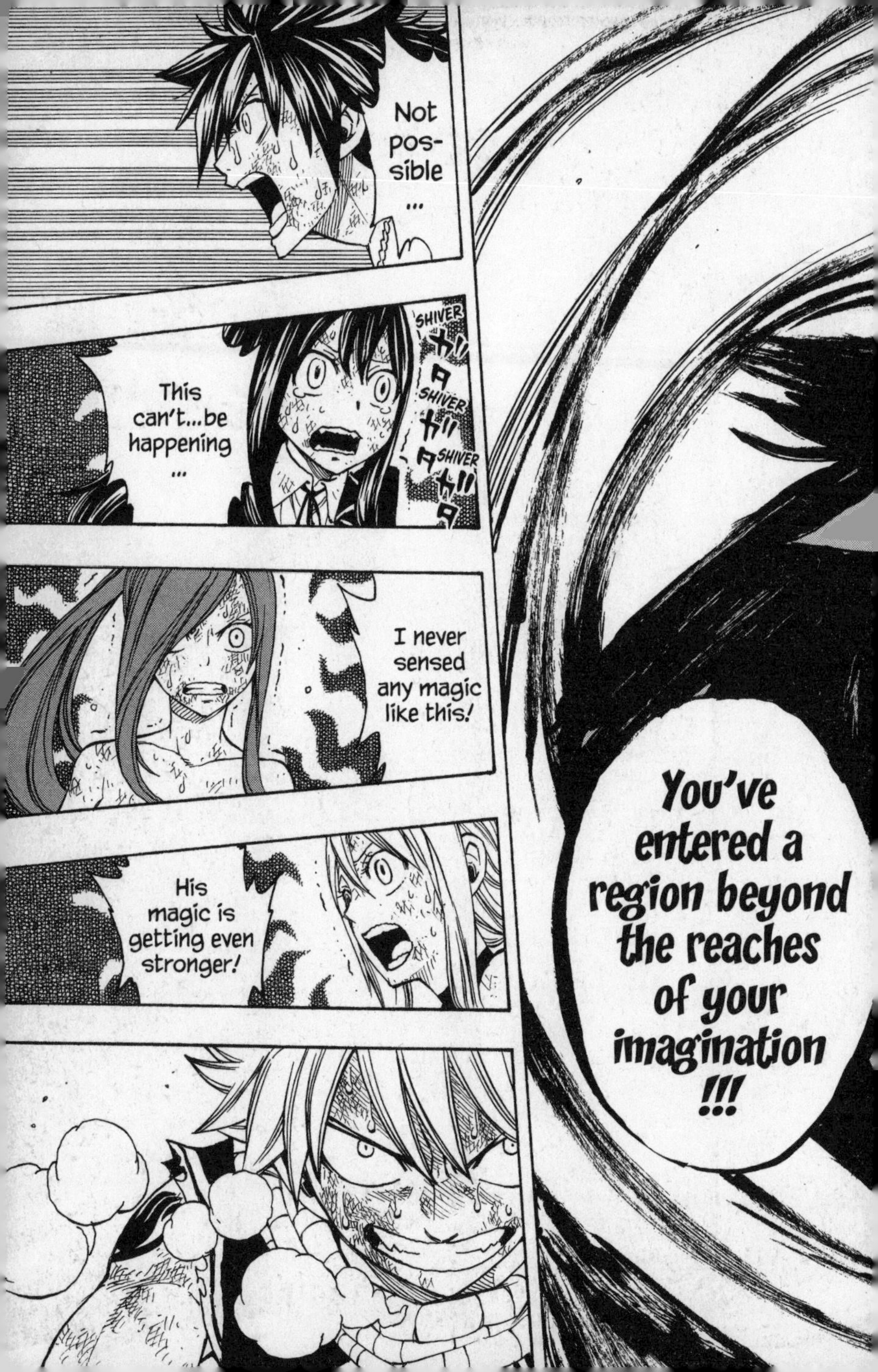
You've entered a region beyond the reaches of your imagination !!!
Not pos-sible ...
SHIVER ガタ
SHIVER ガタ
SHIVER ガタ
This can't...be happening ...
I never sensed any magic like this!
His magic is getting even stronger!

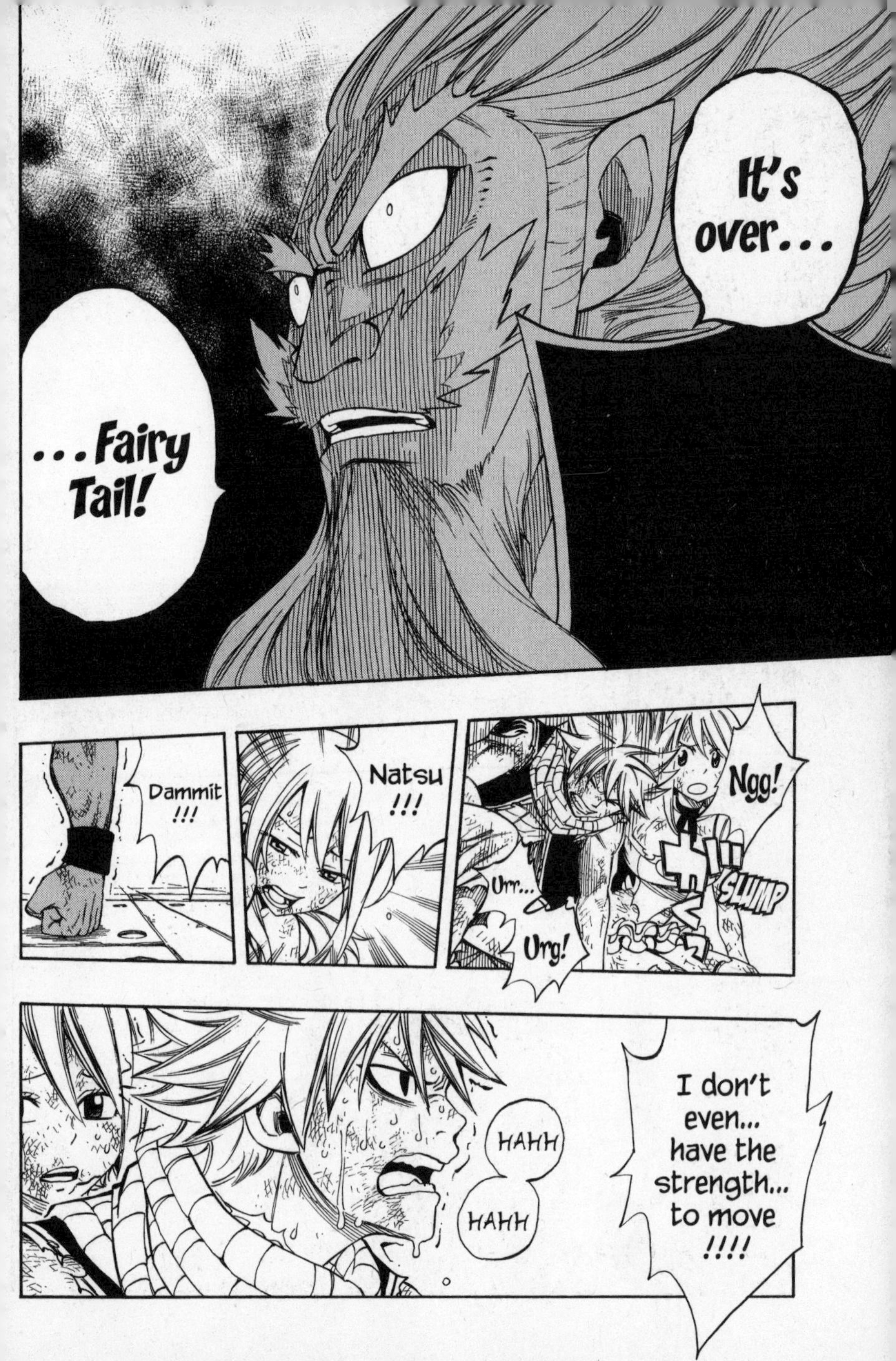
It's over...
...Fairy Tail!
Ngg!
SLUMP
Urr...
Urg!
Natsu !!!
Dammit !!!
I don't even... have the strength... to move !!!!
HAHH
HAHH

FAIRY TAIL

フェアリーテイル

Chapter 247: Just Look How Close

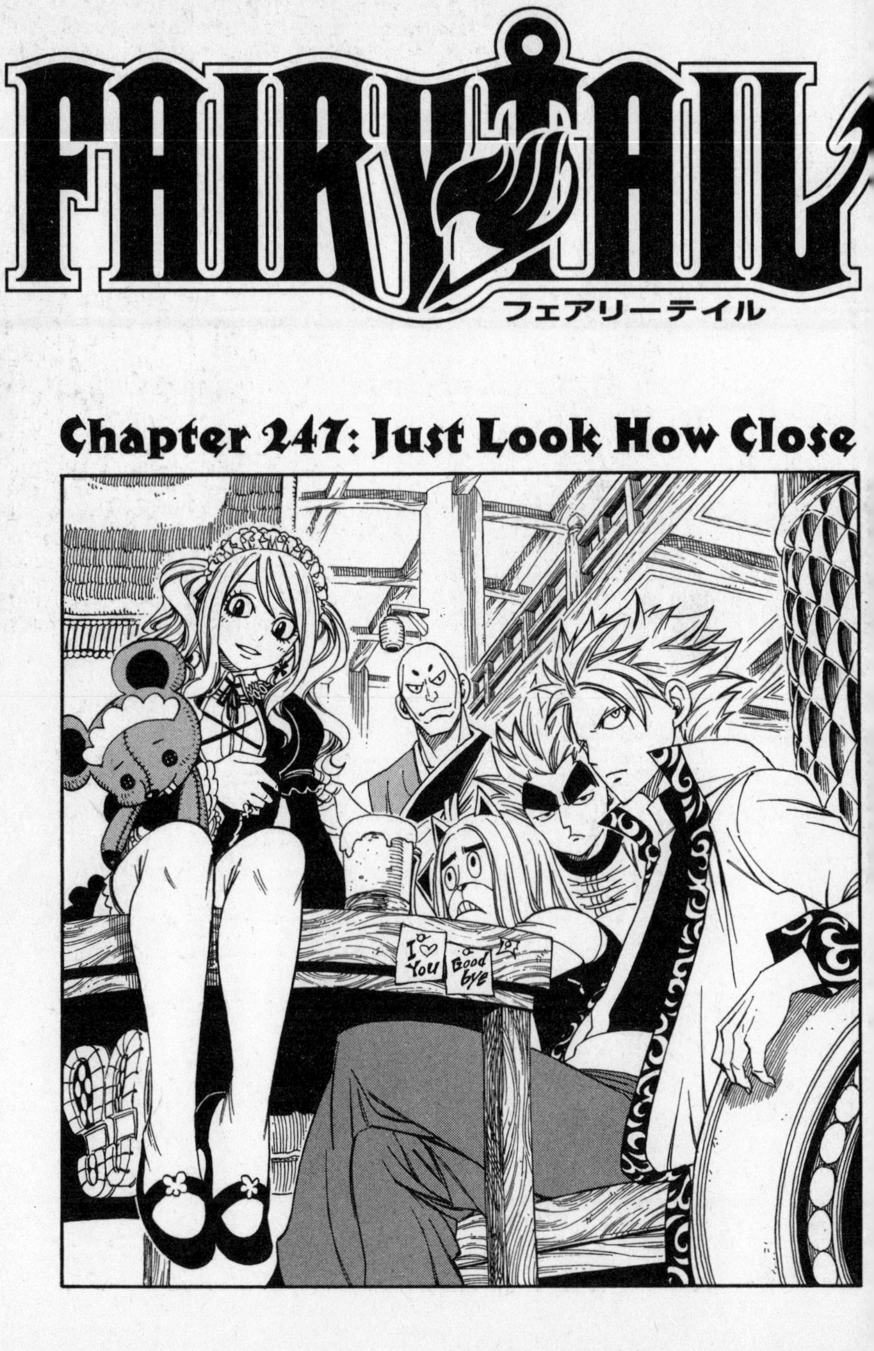
I ♡ YOU
Good bye

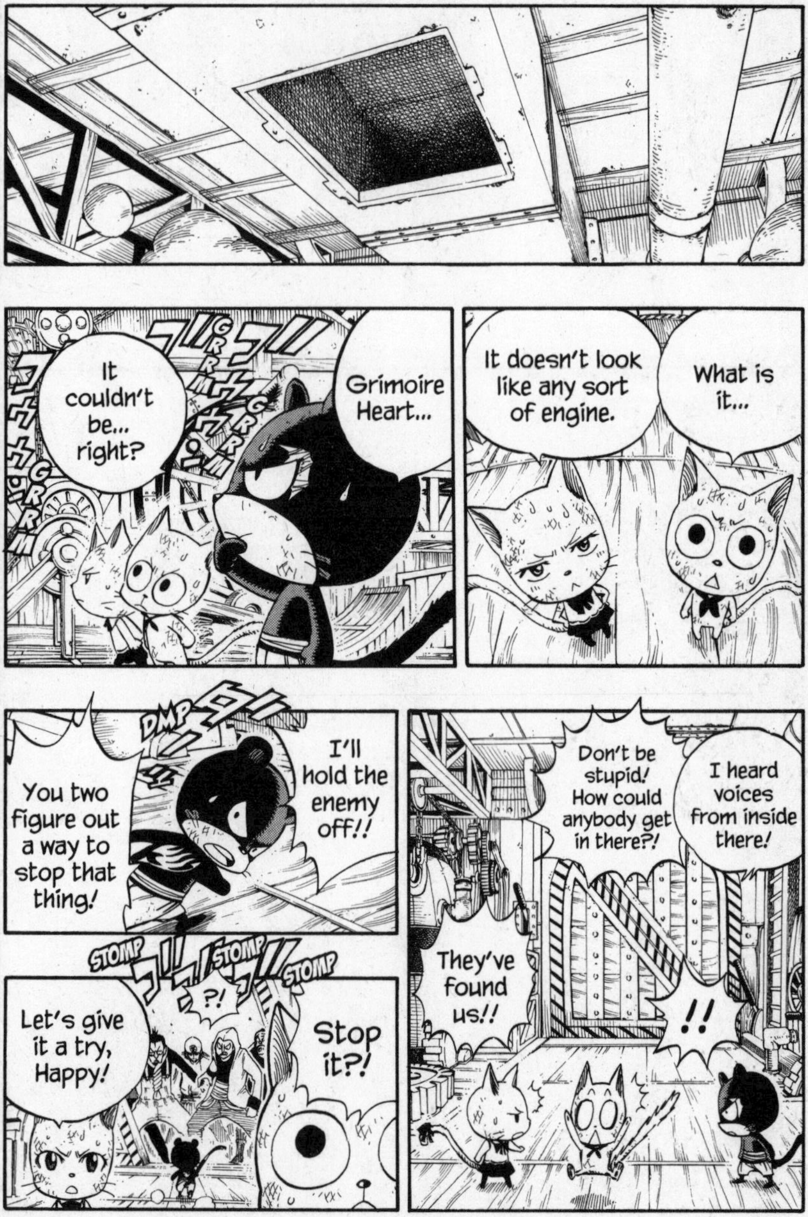
What is it...
It doesn't look like any sort of engine.
Grimoire Heart...
GRRM
GRRM
It couldn't be... right?
GRRM
I heard voices from inside there!
Don't be stupid! How could anybody get in there?!
!!
They've found us!!
DMP
I'll hold the enemy off!!
You two figure out a way to stop that thing!
STOMP
STOMP
STOMP
Stop it?!
?!
Let's give it a try, Happy!

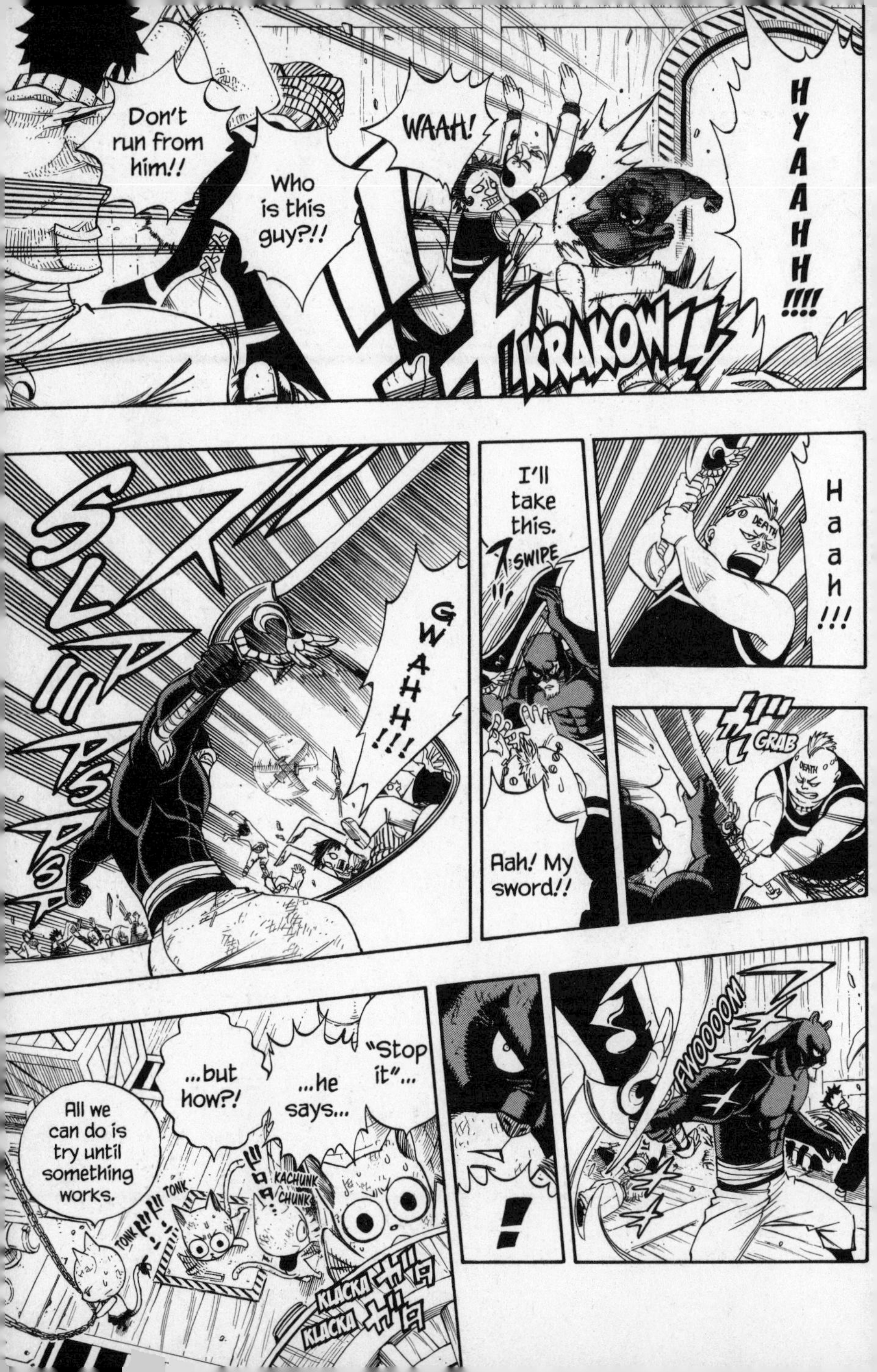
HYAAAHH!!!!
KRAKOW!!
WAAH!
Who is this guy?!!
Don't run from him!!
Haah!!!
GRAB
I'll take this.
SWIPE
Aah! My sword!!
GWAHHH!!!
FWOOOOM
!
"Stop it"...
...he says...
...but how?!
KACHUNK CHUNK
TONK
All we can do is try until something works.
KLACKA
KLACKA

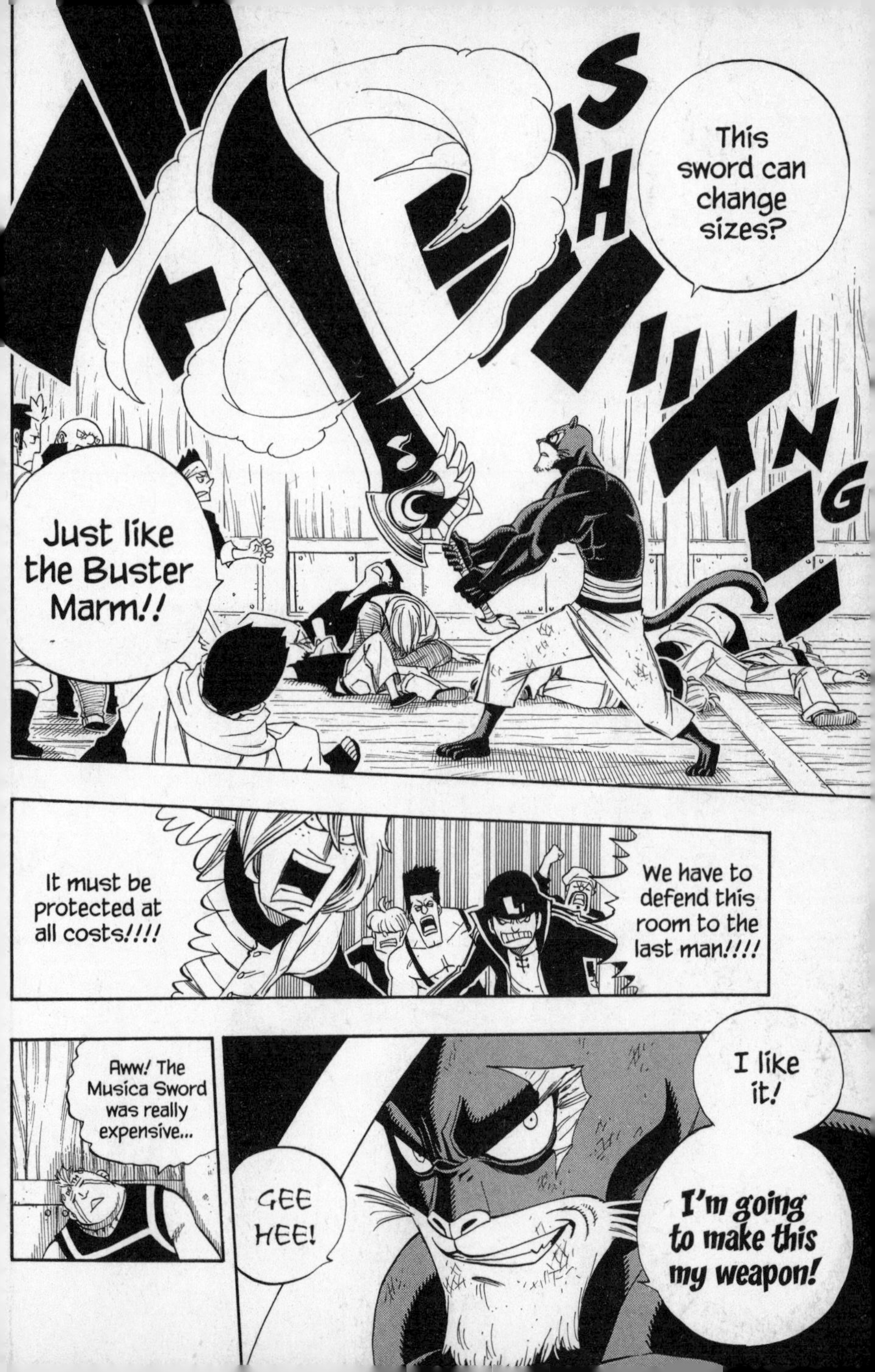
SHIIIING
This sword can change sizes?
Just like the Buster Marm!!
We have to defend this room to the last man!!!!
It must be protected at all costs!!!!
I like it!
I'm going to make this my weapon!
GEE HEE!
Aww! The Musica Sword was really expensive...

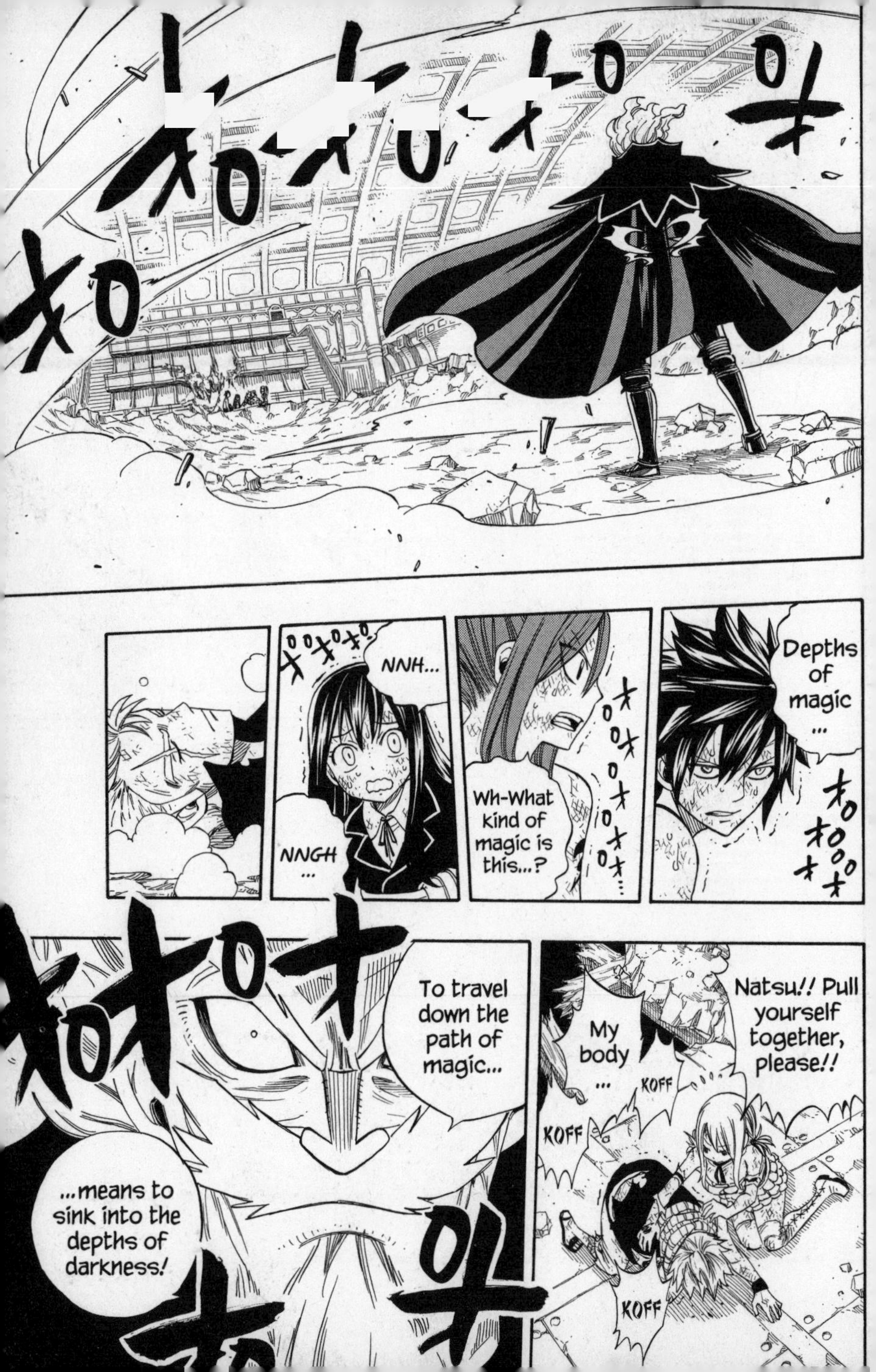

Depths of magic ...
Wh-What kind of magic is this...?
NNH...
NNGH ...
Natsu!! Pull yourself together, please!!
My body ...
KOFF
KOFF
KOFF
To travel down the path of magic...
...means to sink into the depths of darkness!

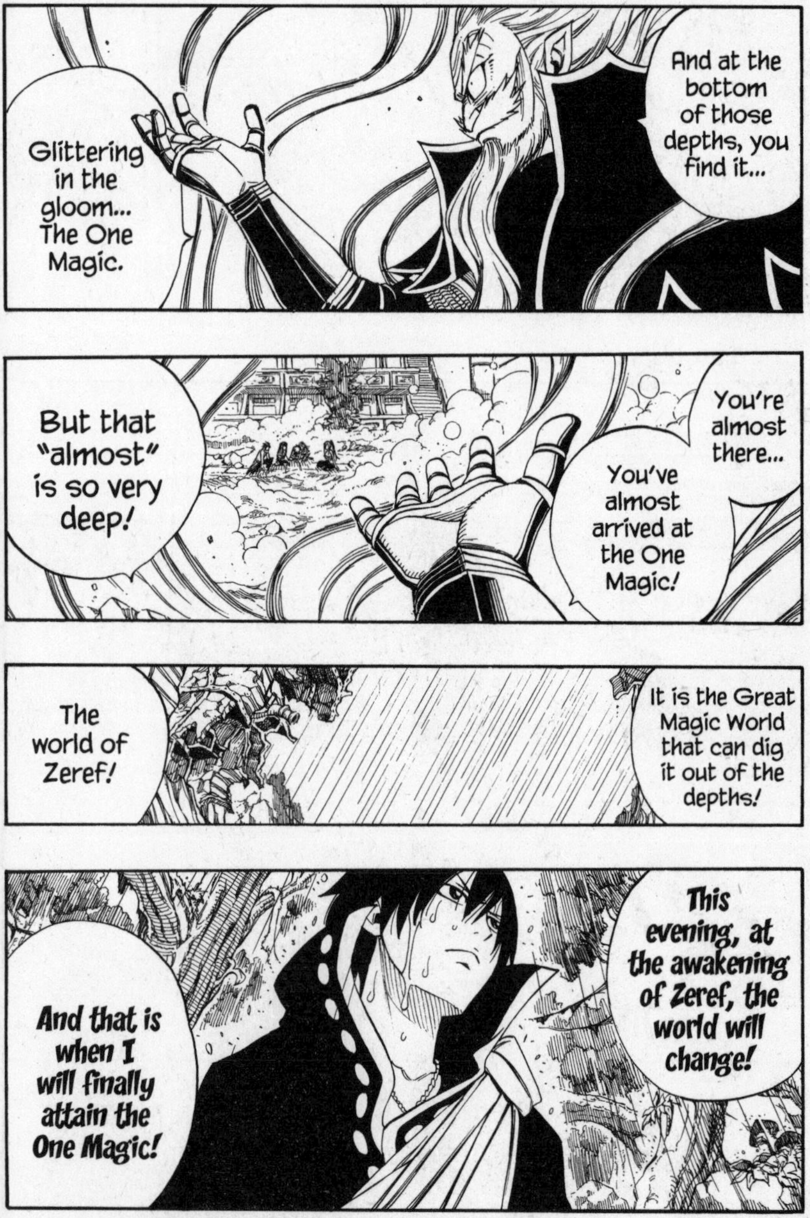
And at the bottom of those depths, you find it...
Glittering in the gloom... The One Magic.
You're almost there...
You've almost arrived at the One Magic!
But that "almost" is so very deep!
It is the Great Magic World that can dig it out of the depths!
The world of Zeref!
This evening, at the awakening of Zeref, the world will change!
And that is when I will finally attain the One Magic!

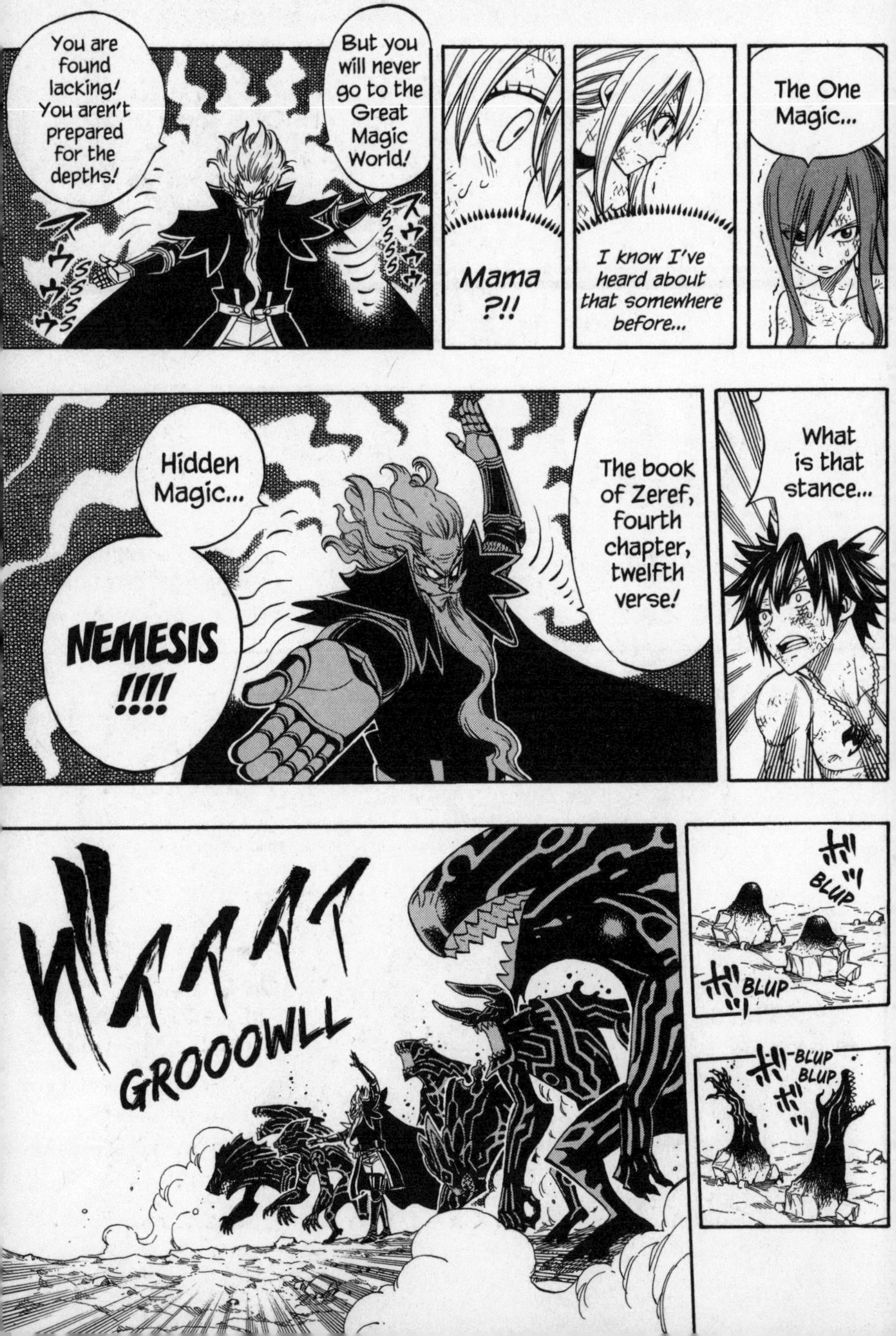
The One Magic...
I know I've heard about that somewhere before...
Mama ?!!
But you will never go to the Great Magic World!
You are found lacking! You aren't prepared for the depths!
SSSS
SSSS
What is that stance...
The book of Zeref, fourth chapter, twelfth verse!
Hidden Magic...
NEMESIS !!!!
BLUP
BLUP
BLUP BLUP
GROOOWLL

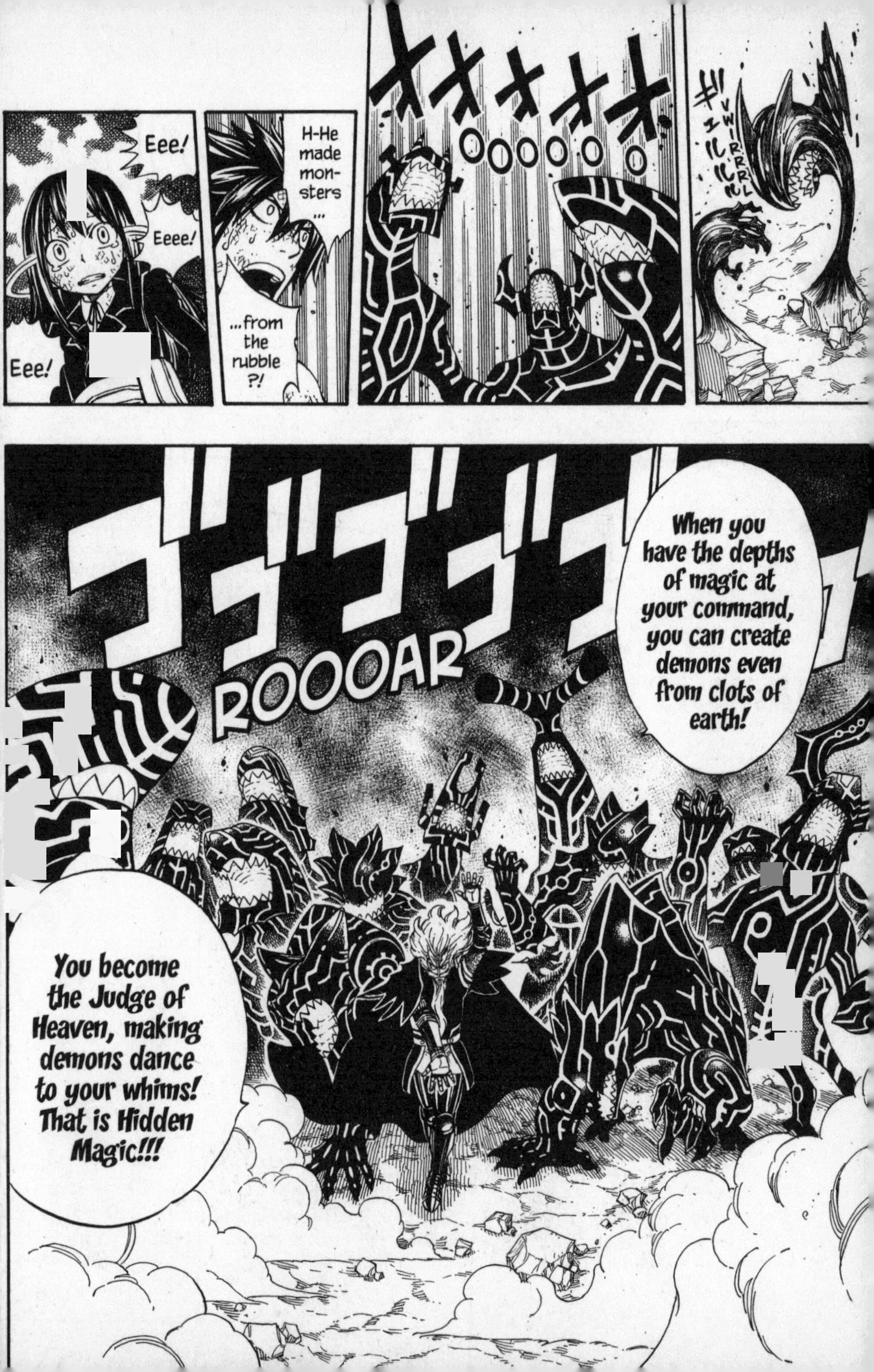
VWIRRRL
OOOOOO
H-He made monsters...
...from the rubble?!
Eee!
Eeee!
Eee!
ROOOAR
When you have the depths of magic at your command, you can create demons even from clots of earth!
You become the Judge of Heaven, making demons dance to your whims! That is Hidden Magic!!!

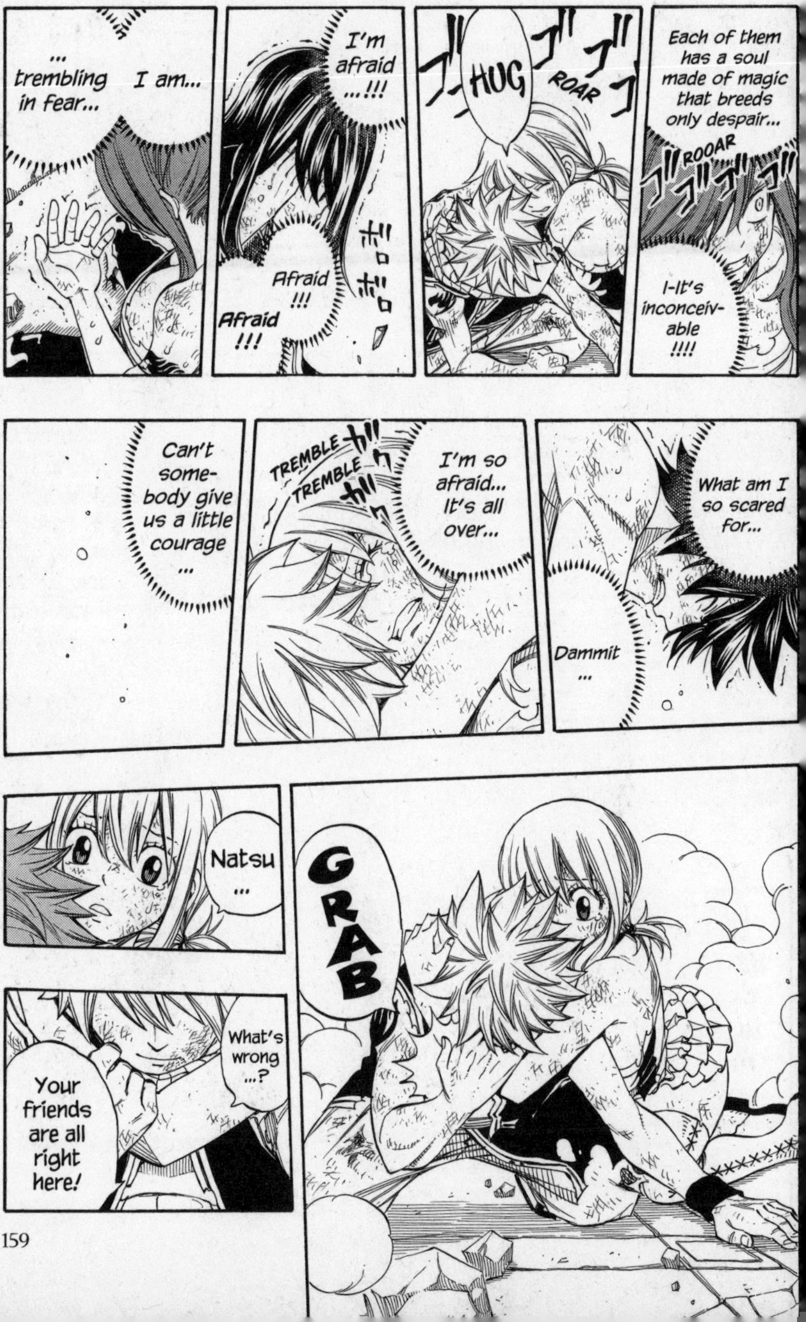

Each of them has a soul made of magic that breeds only despair...
ROOAR
I-It's inconceivable !!!!
HUG
ROAR
I'm afraid ...!!!
Afraid !!!
Afraid !!!
I am...
... trembling in fear...
What am I so scared for...
Dammit ...
I'm so afraid... It's all over...
TREMBLE
TREMBLE
Can't somebody give us a little courage ...
GRAB
Natsu ...
What's wrong ...?
Your friends are all right here!

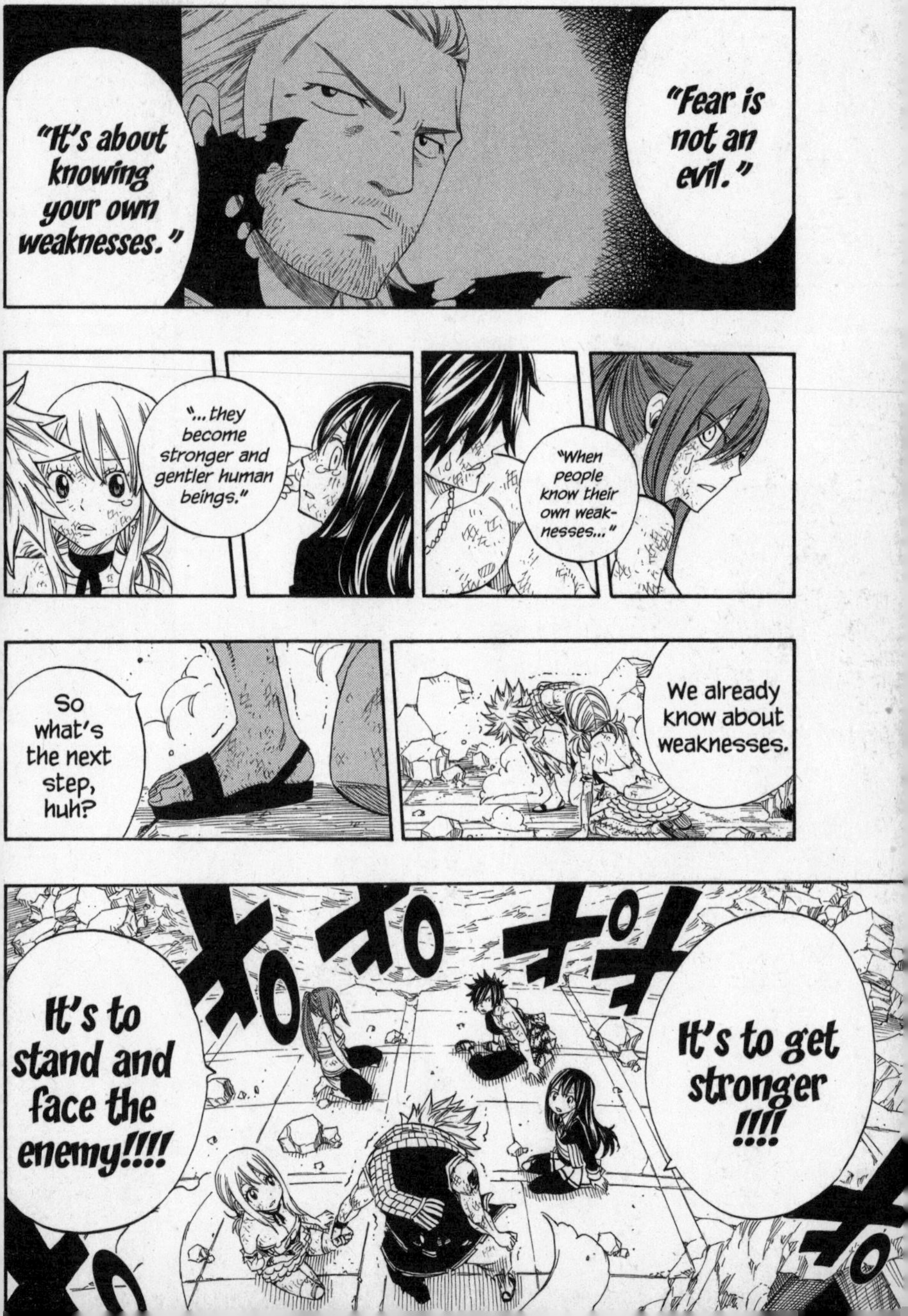
"Fear is not an evil."
"It's about knowing your own weaknesses."
"When people know their own weaknesses..."
"...they become stronger and gentler human beings."
We already know about weaknesses.
So what's the next step, huh?
It's to get stronger!!!!
It's to stand and face the enemy!!!!

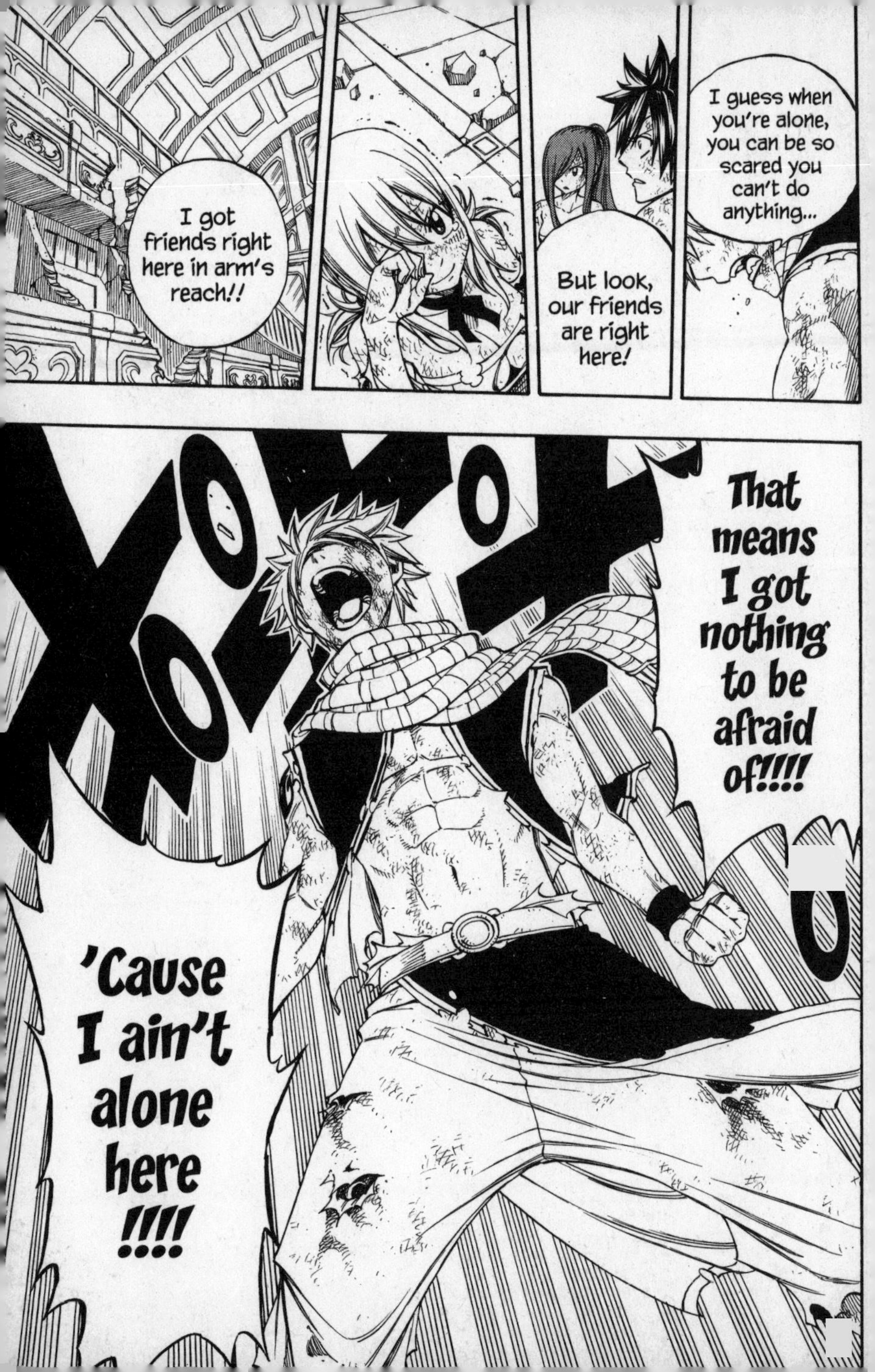
I guess when you're alone, you can be so scared you can't do anything...
But look, our friends are right here!
I got friends right here in arm's reach!!
That means I got nothing to be afraid of!!!!
'Cause I ain't alone here!!!!

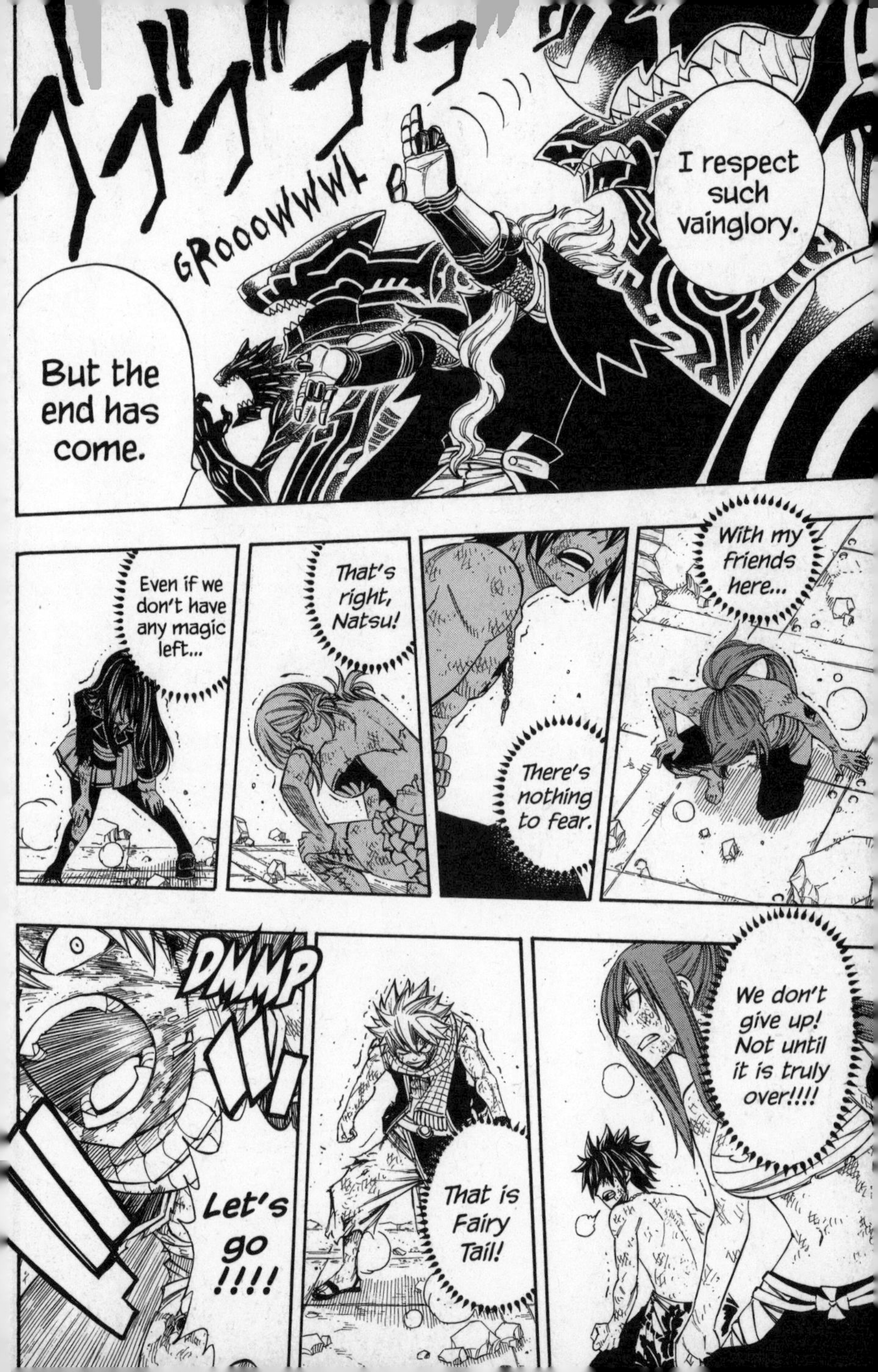
I respect such vainglory.
GROOOWWWL
But the end has come.
With my friends here...
There's nothing to fear.
That's right, Natsu!
Even if we don't have any magic left...
We don't give up! Not until it is truly over!!!!
That is Fairy Tail!
DMMP
Let's go !!!!

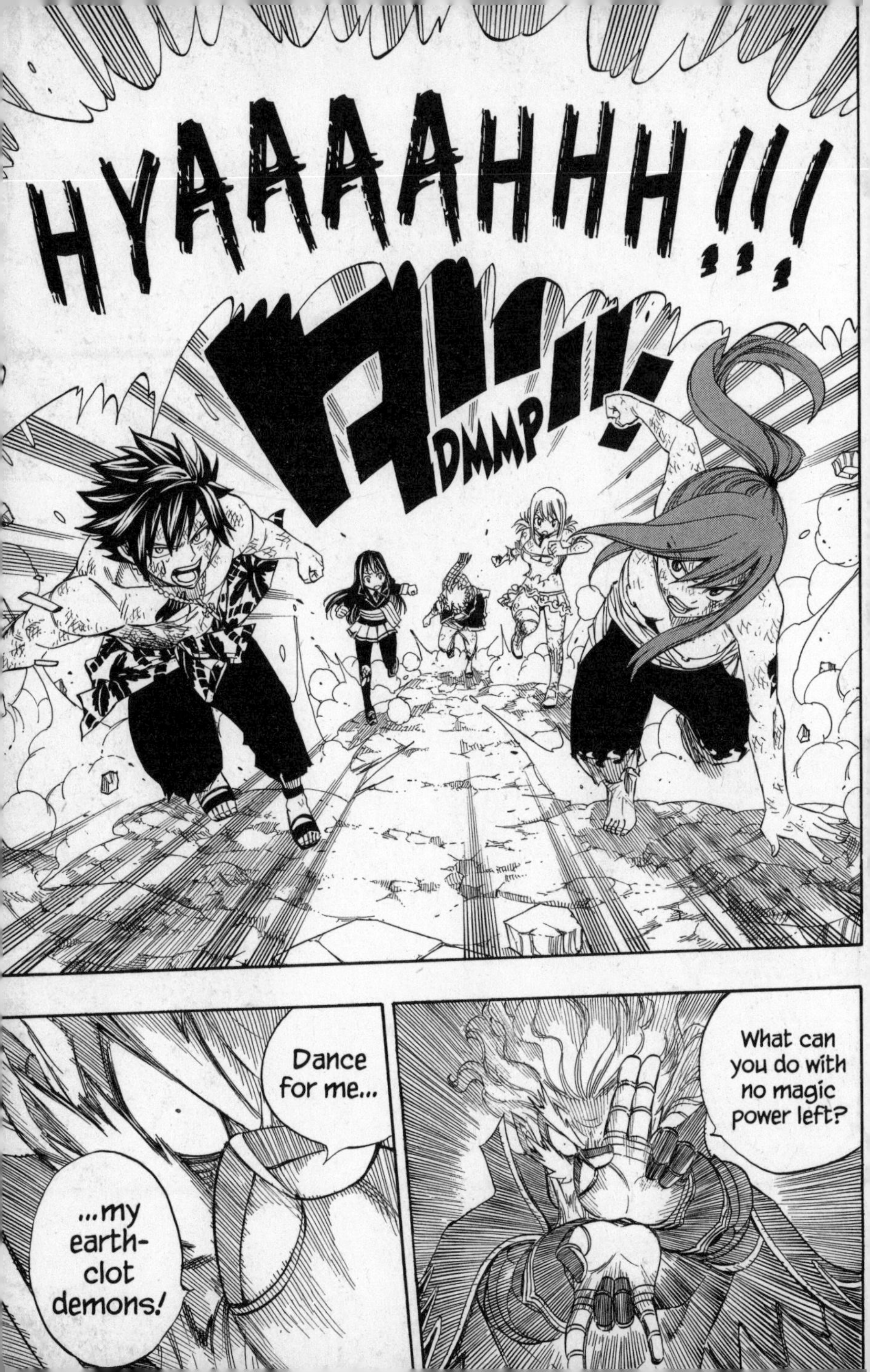

HYAAAAHHH!!!
DMMP
What can you do with no magic power left?
Dance for me...
...my earth-clot demons!

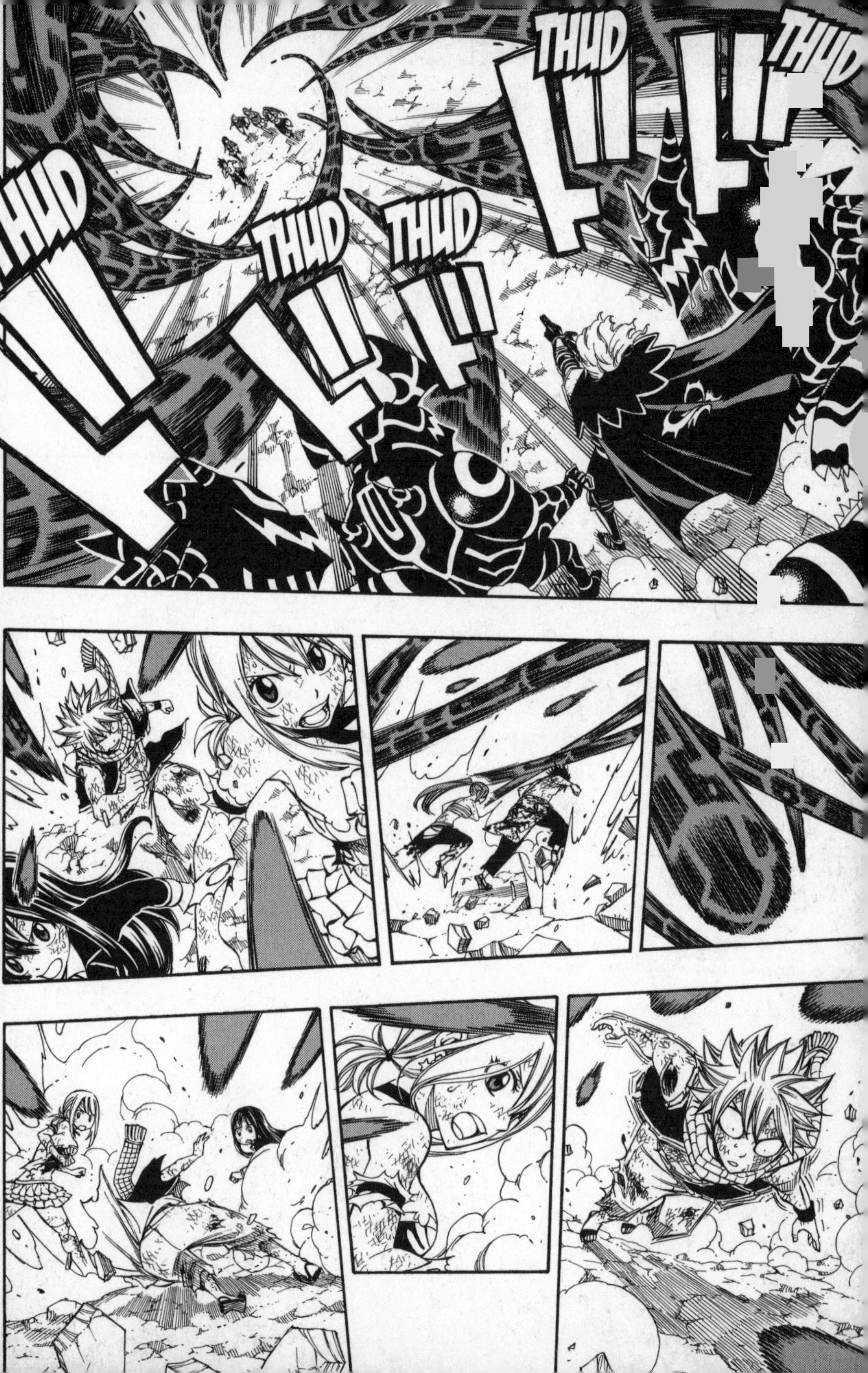
THUD
THUD
THUD
THUD
THUD

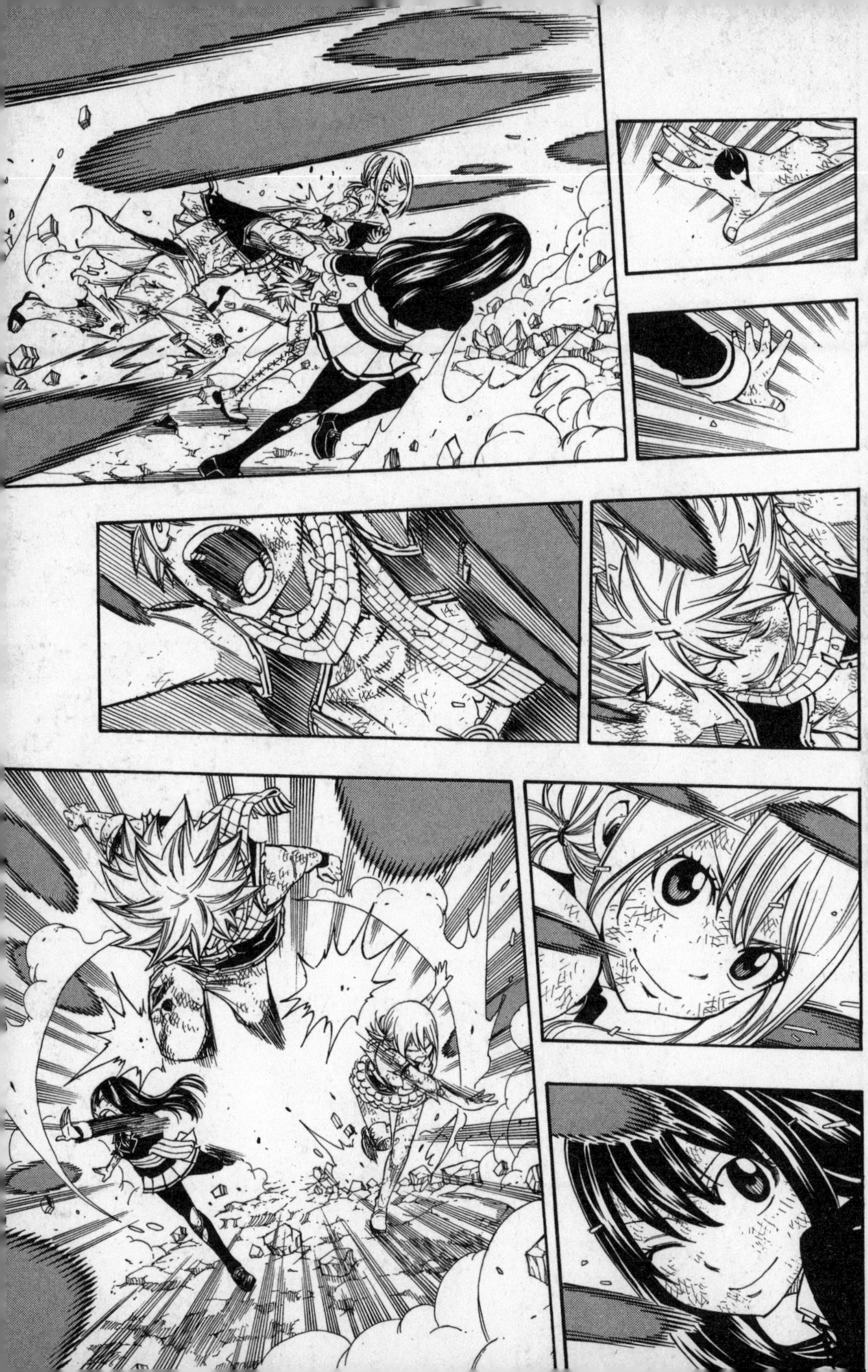

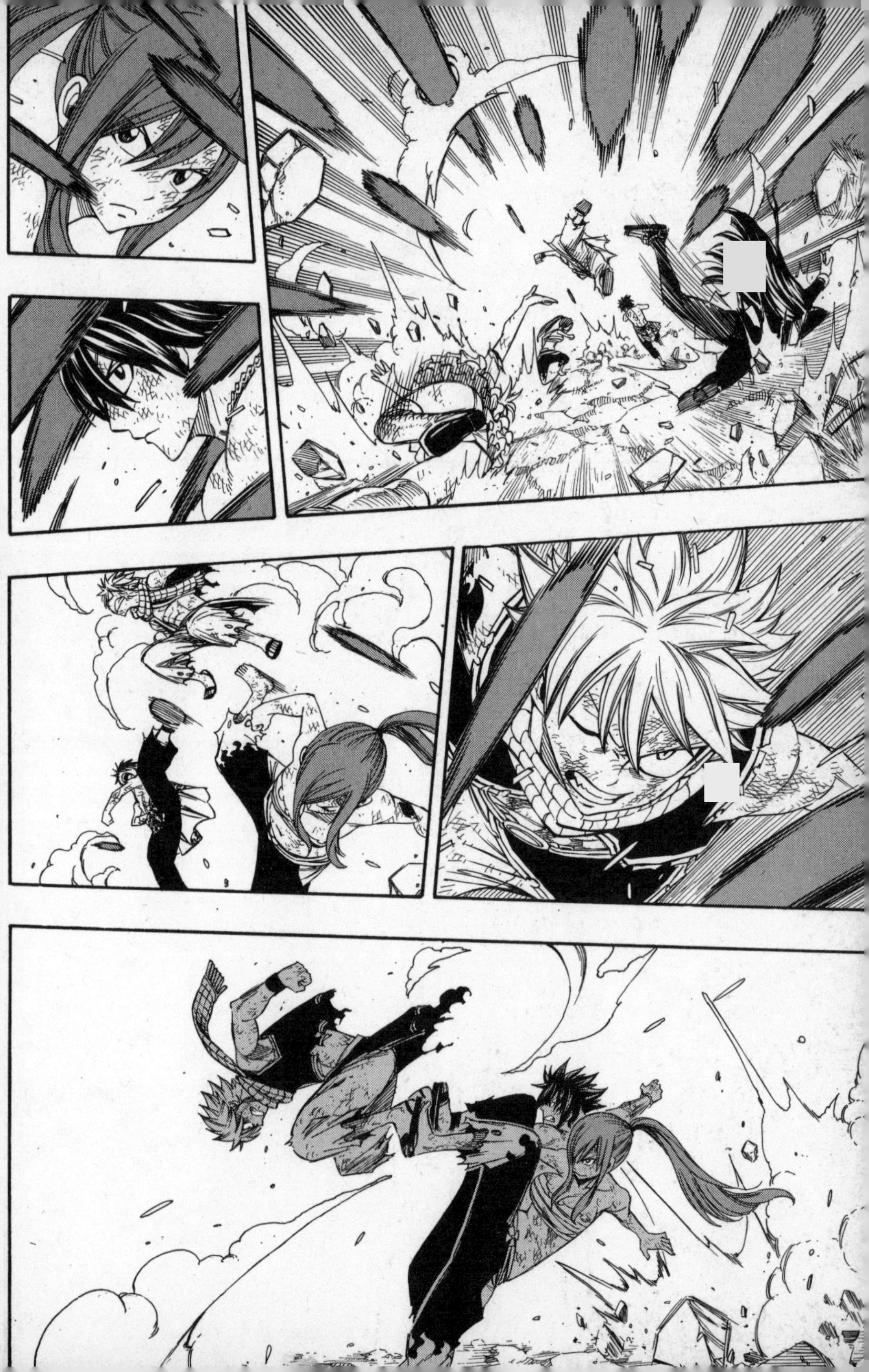

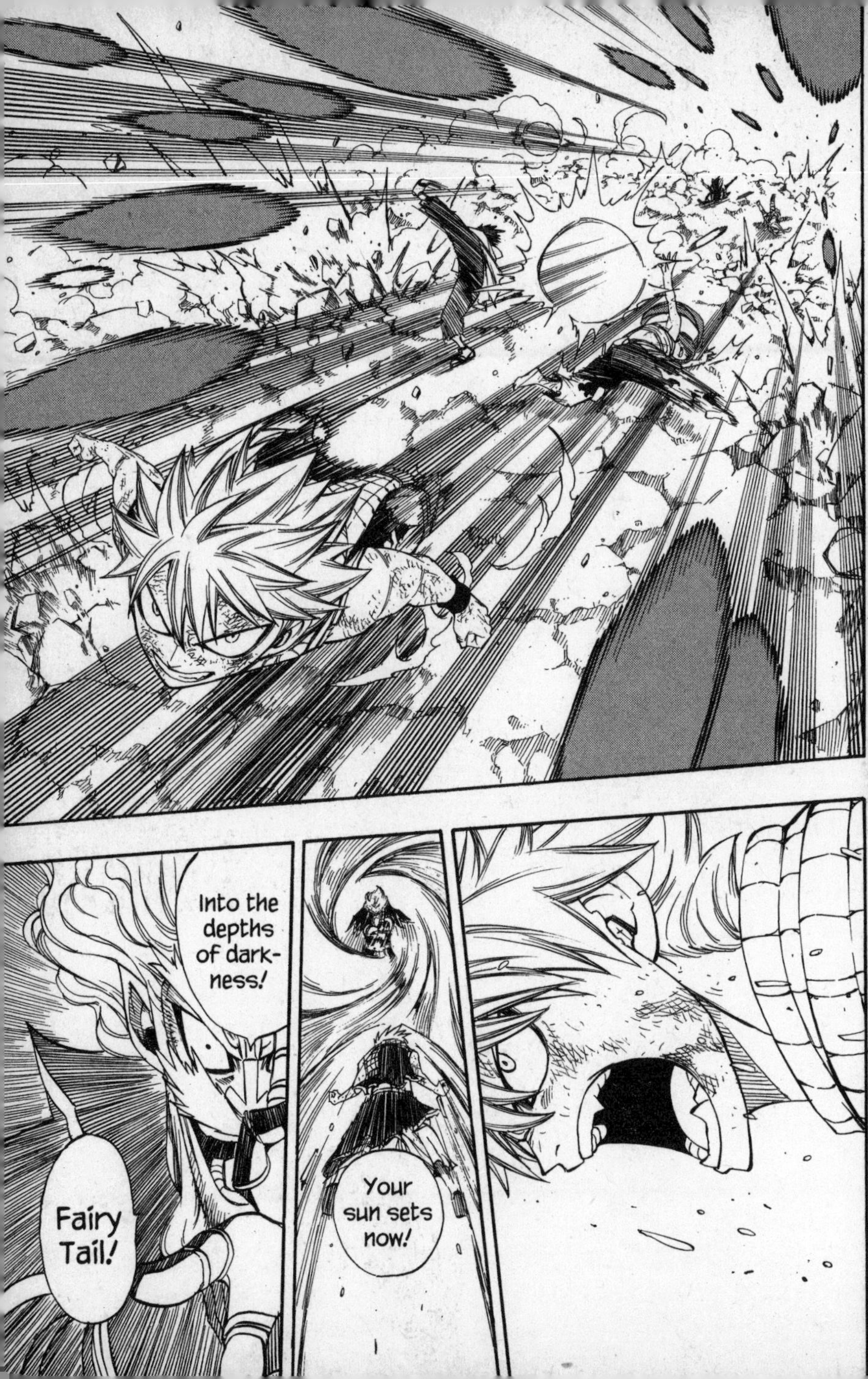
Your sun sets now!
Into the depths of darkness!
Fairy Tail!

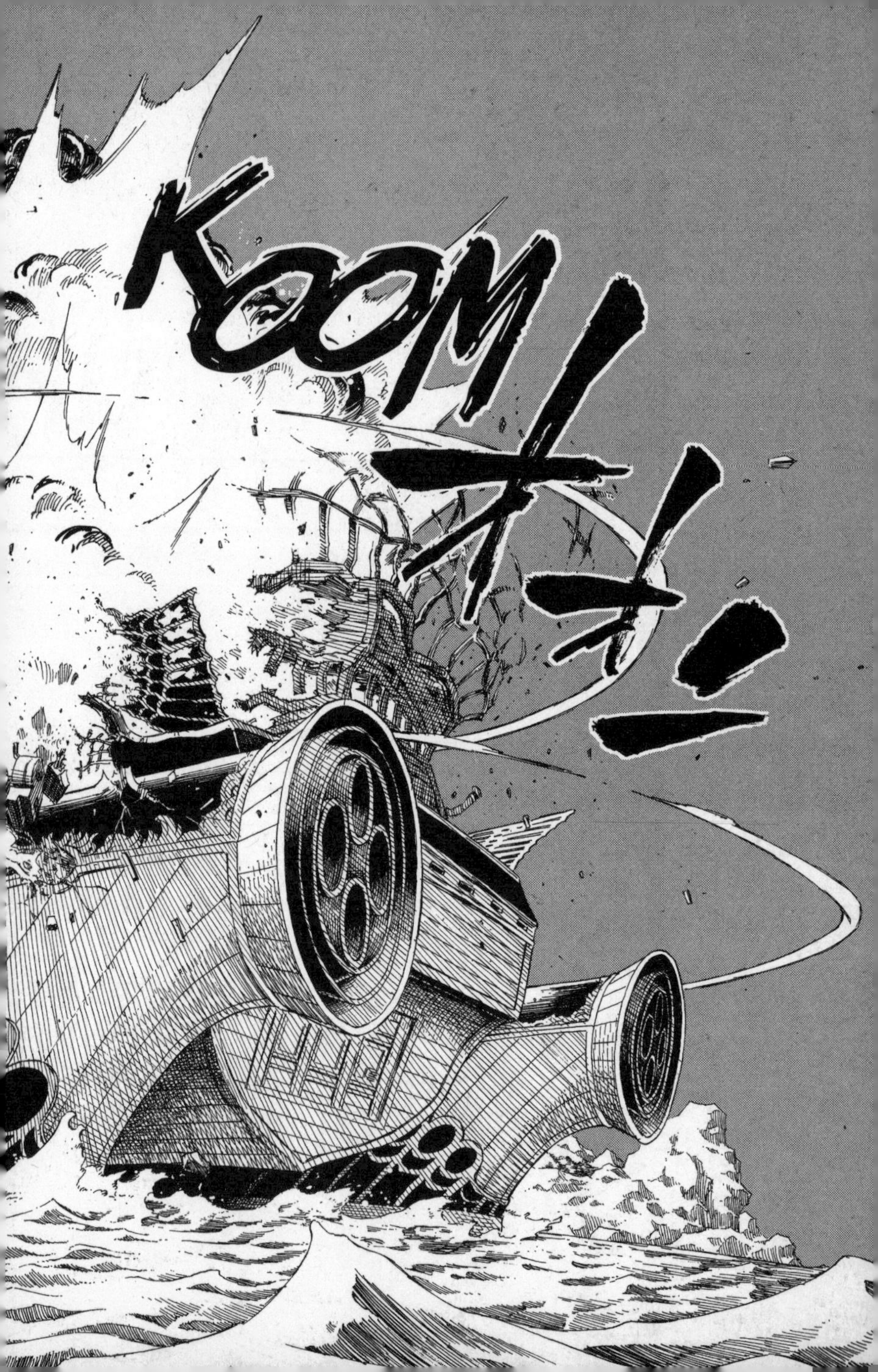
KOOM!

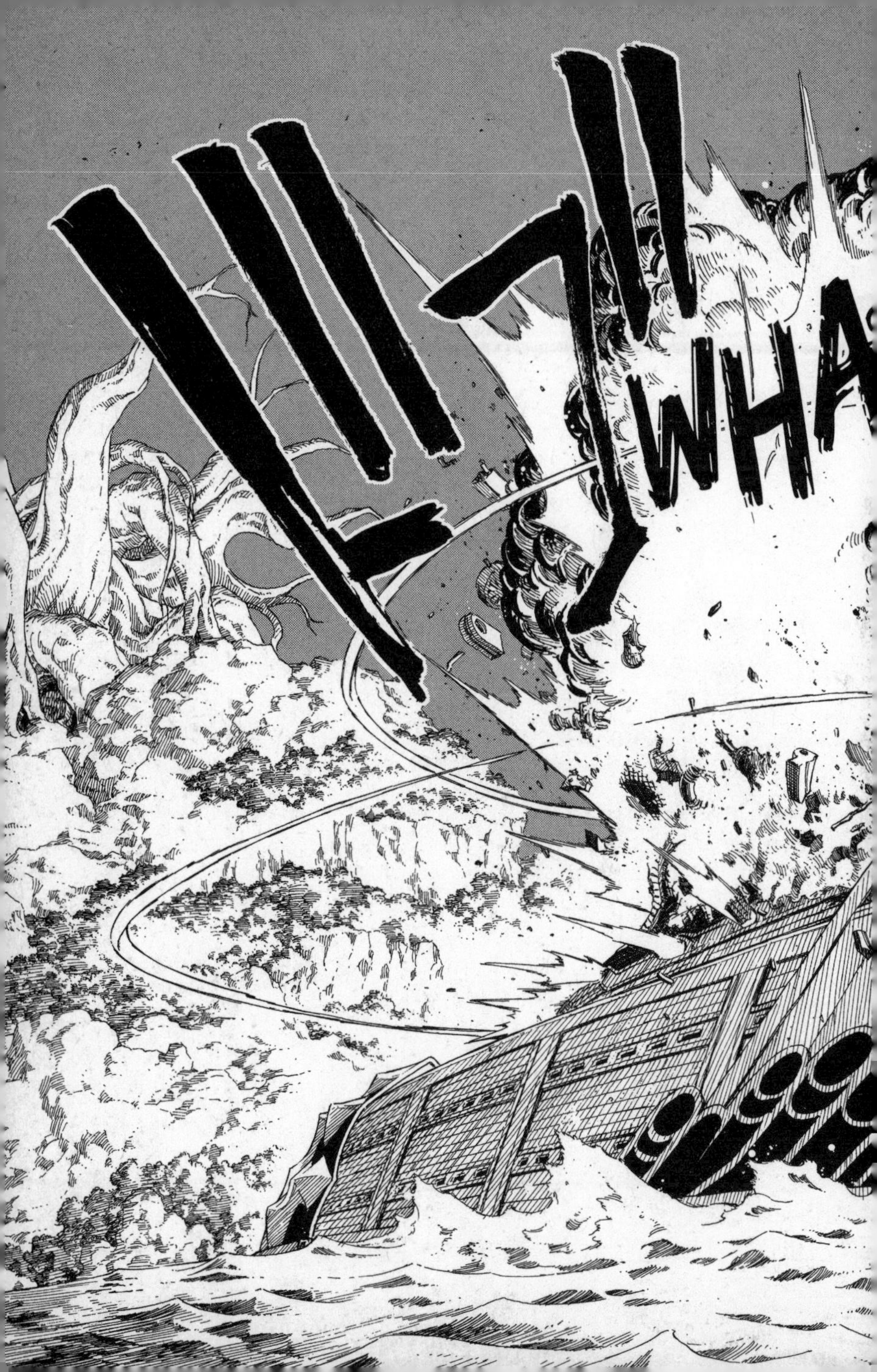
WHA

The Fairy Tail Guild is looking for illustrations! Please send in your art on a postcard or at postcard size, and do it in black pen, okay? Those chosen to be published will get a signed mini poster! ♪ Make sure you write your real name and address on the back of your illustration!

SPECIAL REJECTED COLLECTION 2

FAIRY TAIL GUILD d'ART

No way! I'm not giving that to anybody!!

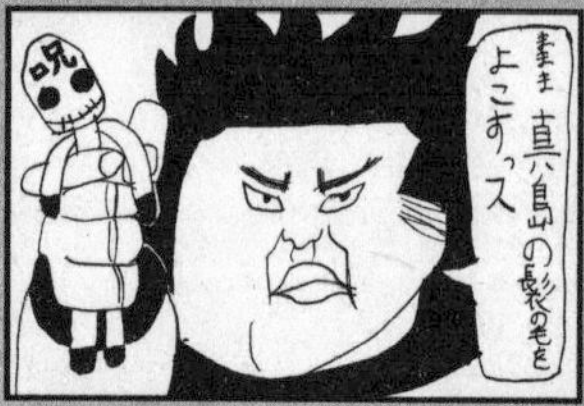

Fukuoka Prefecture, Takuma Kondo

I-Is that right...? I feel sorry for you...

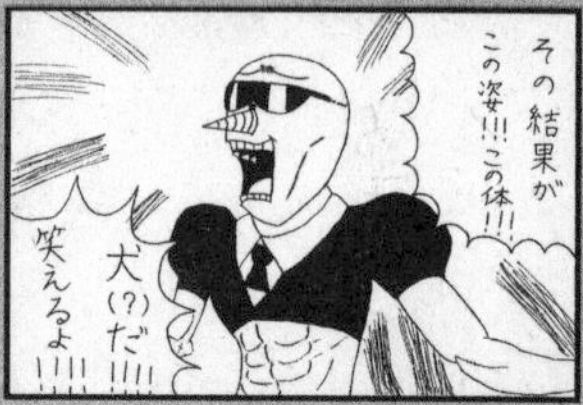
その結果がこの姿!!!この体!!!
犬(?)だ!!!
笑えるよ!!!!

Kanagawa Prefecture, Nattsu

Okayama Prefecture, Hide Norita

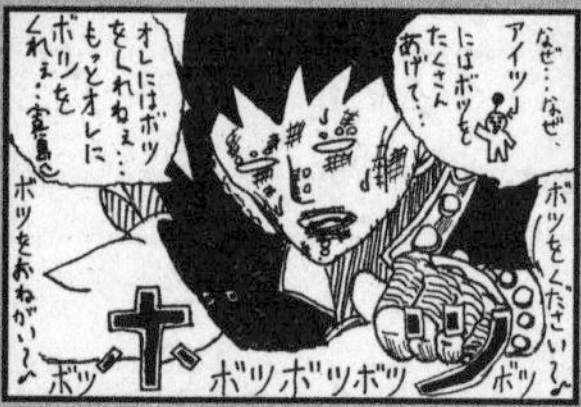
ボツボツボツ

I never thought anybody would try that hard to be rejected...

Aichi Prefecture, Yukimi Umemura

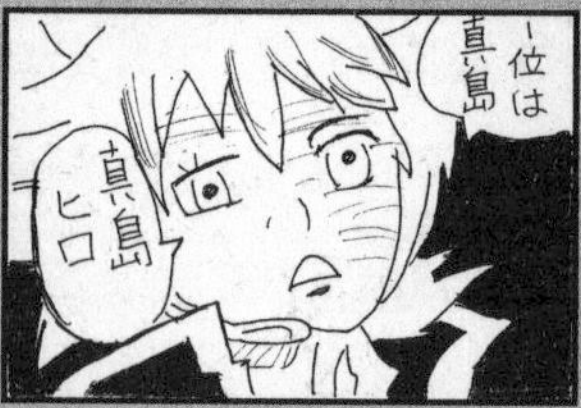
一位は真島
真島ヒロ

Eh? Number-one what? I'm kind of happy... and kind of scared...

Congratulations, Blue Note!

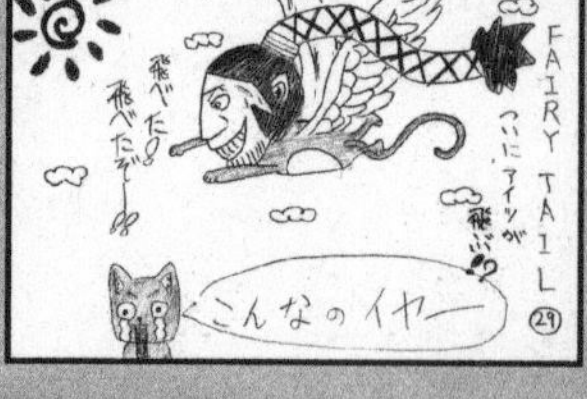
FAIRY TAIL
ついにアイツが飛ぶ!?
飛べた!飛べたぞ!
こんなのイヤー

I'm really fond of how Azuma is drawn a lot smaller than everyone else!

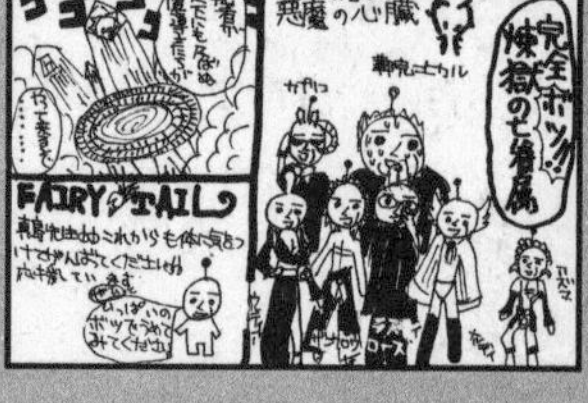
悪魔の心臓
FAIRY TAIL

Aichi Prefecture, Shunsuke Sugawara

Kanagawa Prefecture, Nattsu

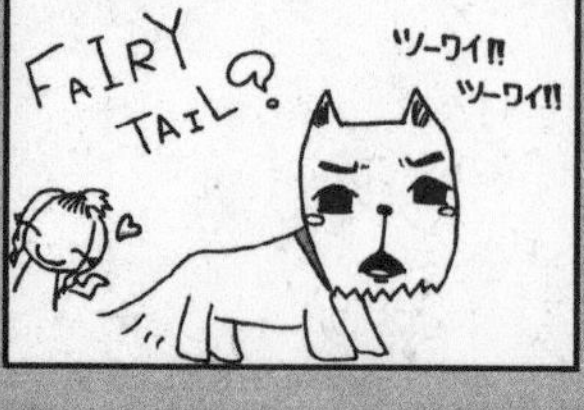
FAIRY TAIL
ツーワイ!!
ツーワイ!!

You're kidding! It's the arrival of the stray dog!

Kyoto, Fuuka Uenishi

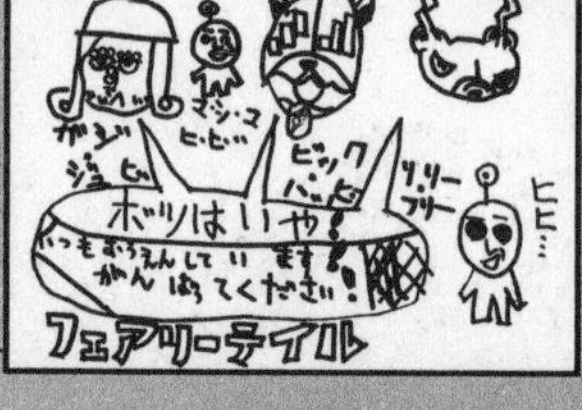
ボツはいや!
ヒヒ…
フェアリーテイル

Cats + Raijin Tribe!! I never even dreamed of this...

Send to Hiro Mashima, Kodansha Comics, 451 Park Ave. South, 7th Floor, New York, NY 10016

FAIRY TAIL
フェアリーテイル

Chapter 248: Dawn on Sirius Island

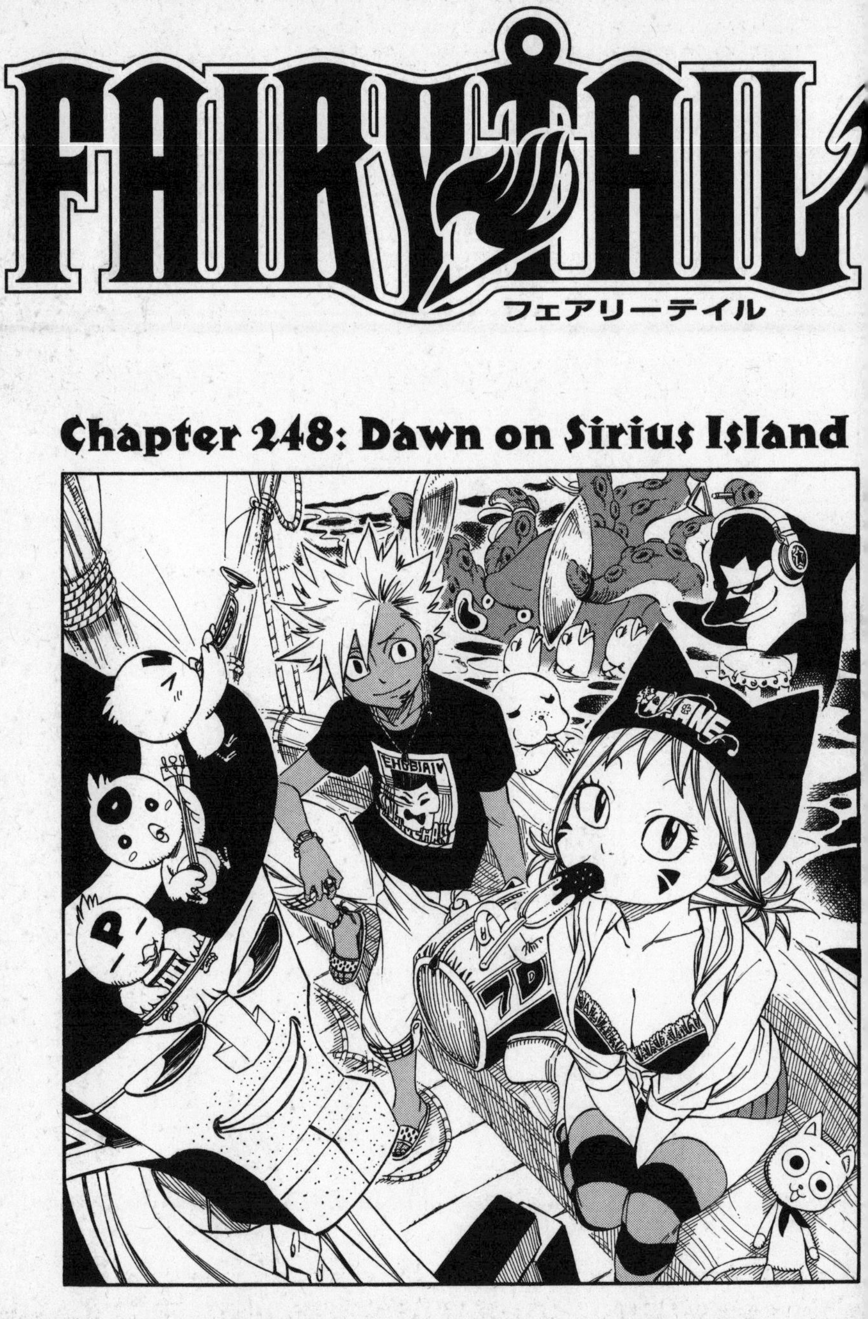

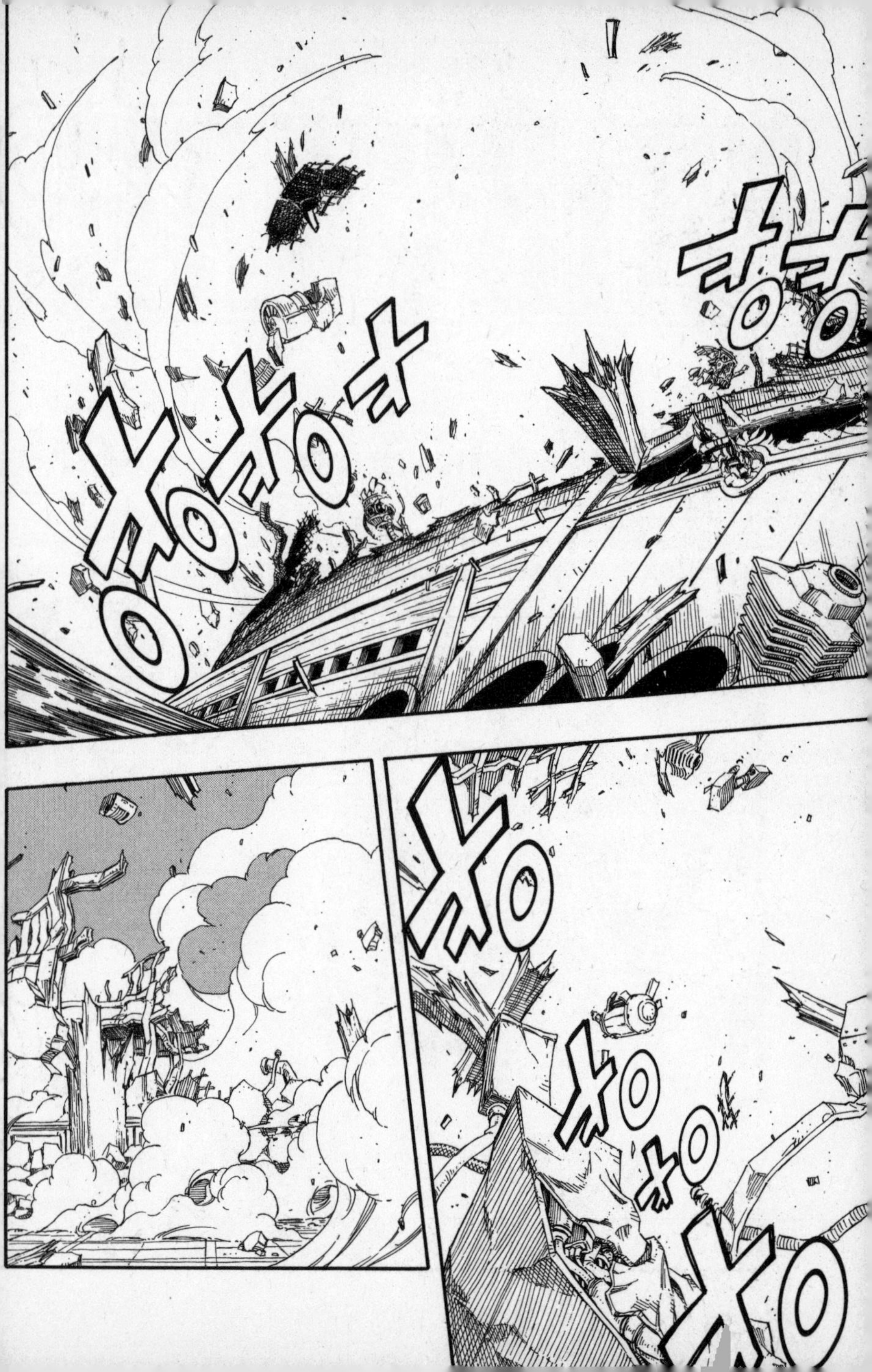

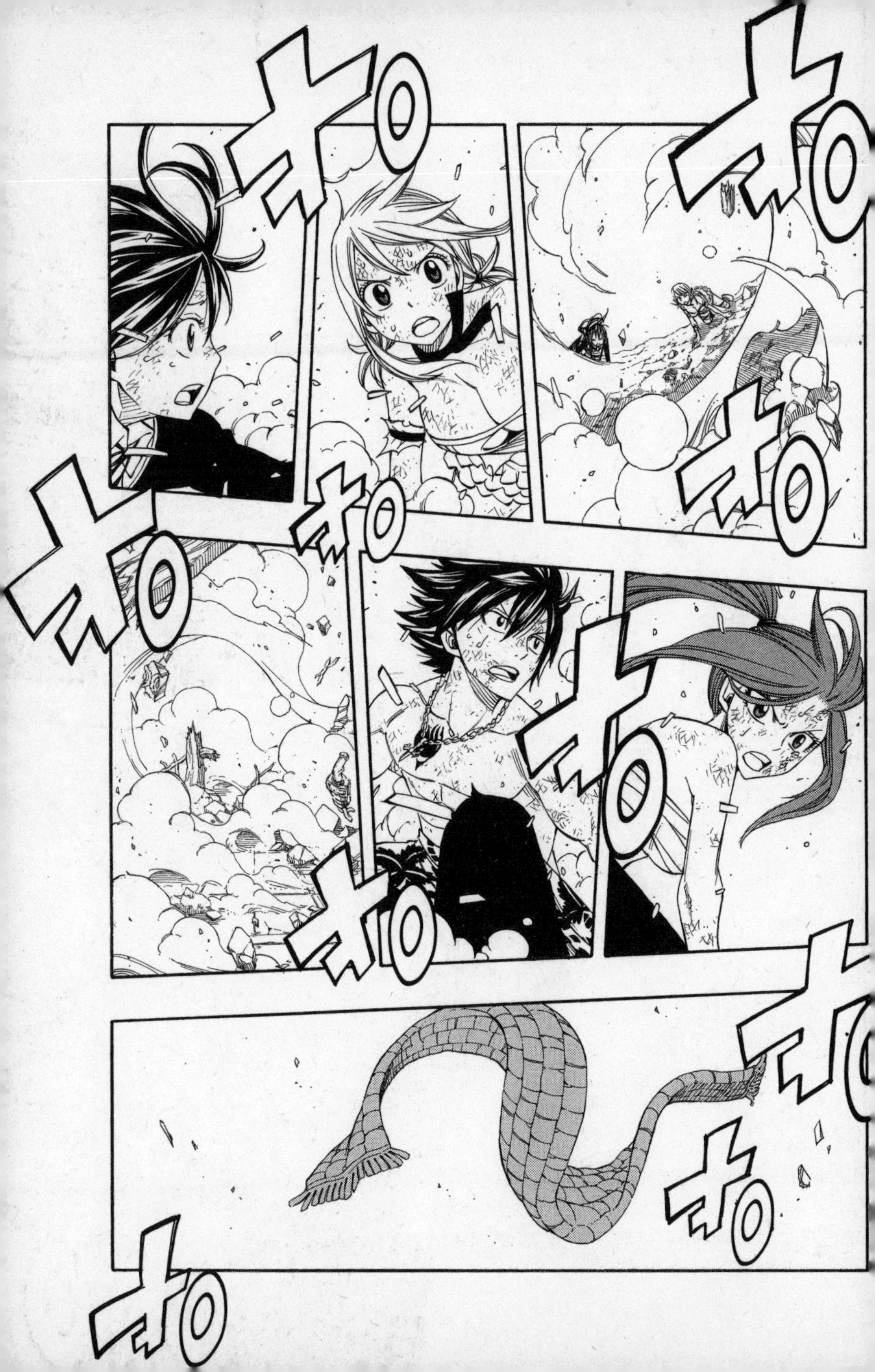

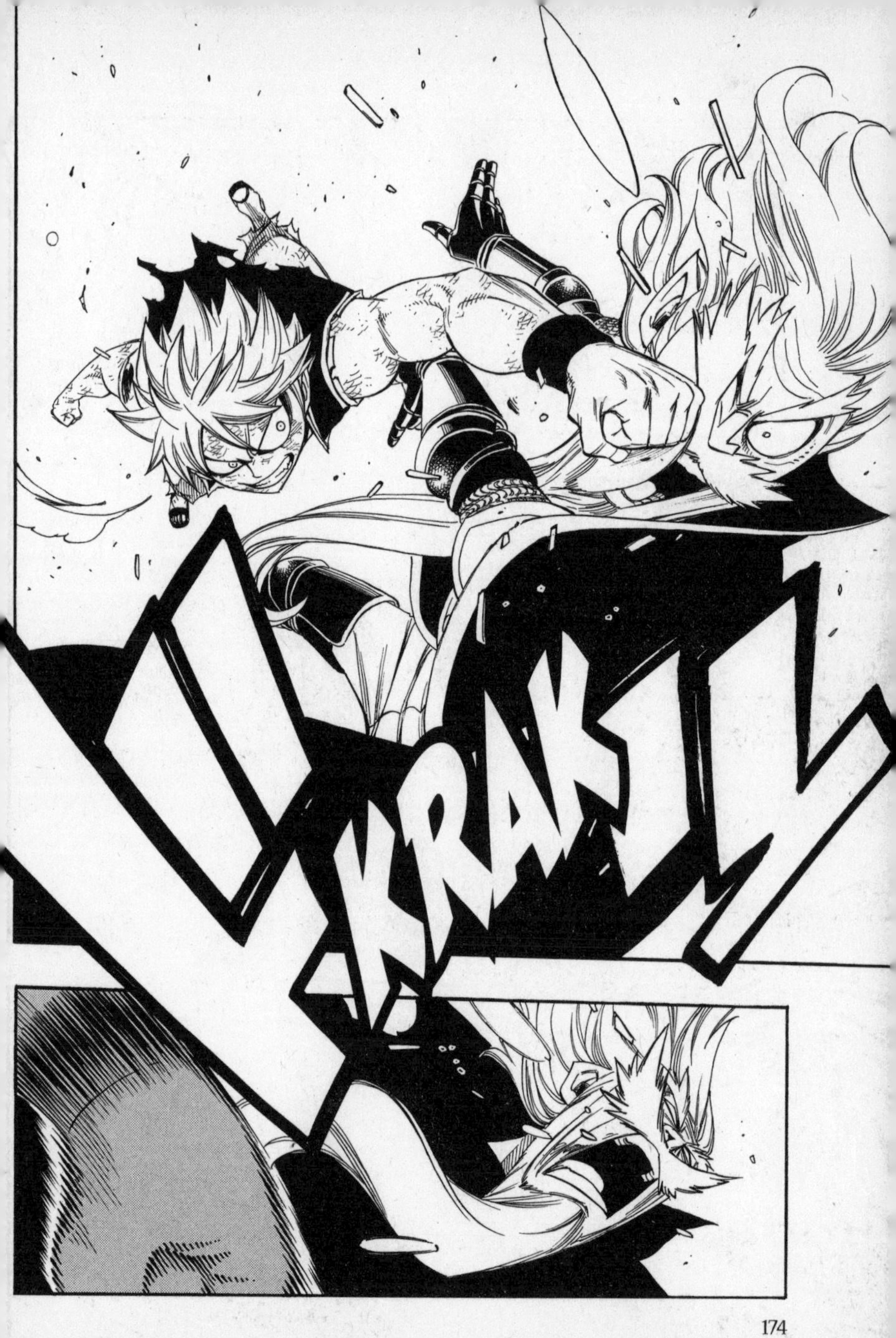
KRAK!

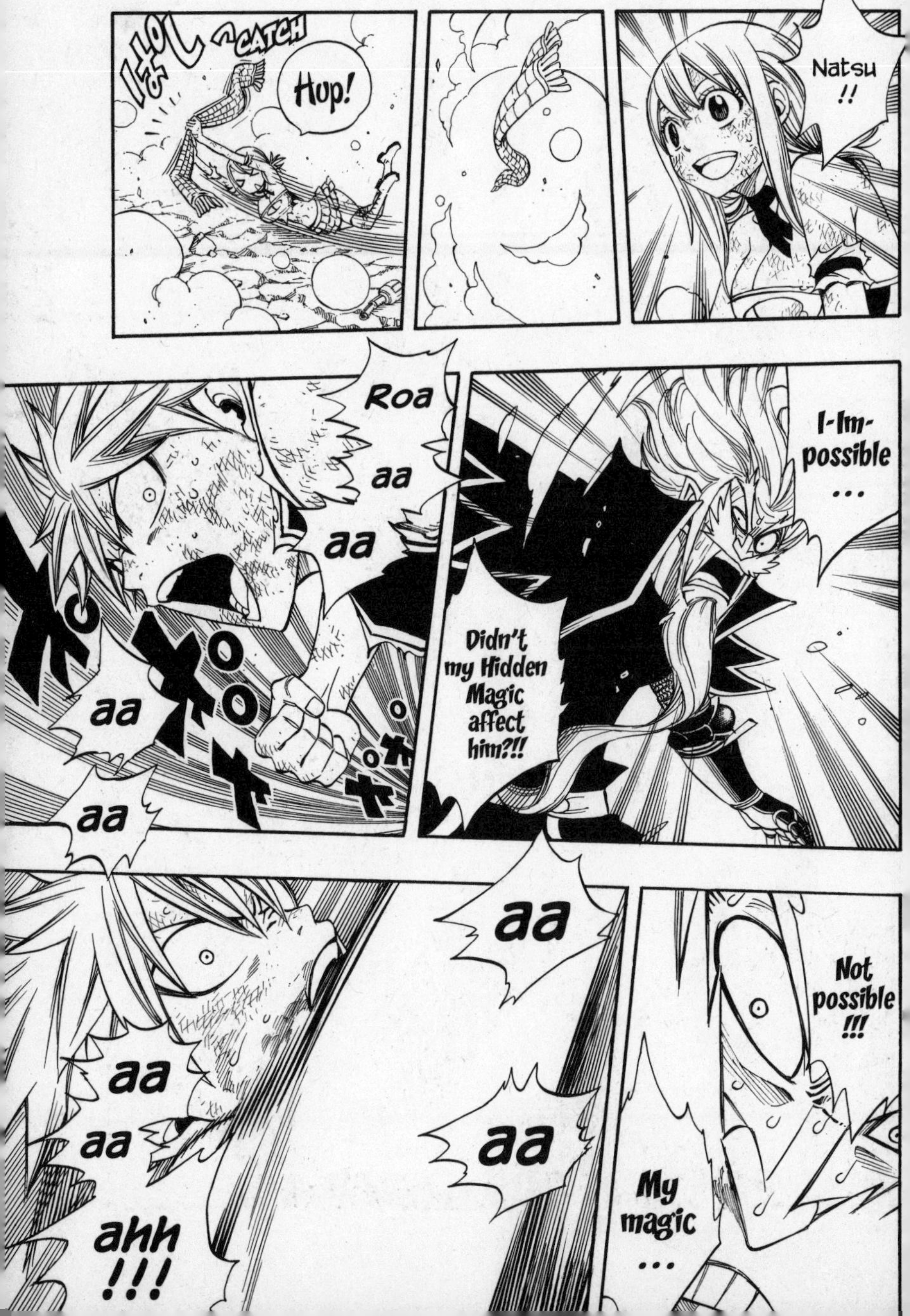
Natsu !!
CATCH
Hup!
I-Im-possible ...
Didn't my Hidden Magic affect him?!!
Roa
aa
aa
aa
aa
Not possible !!!
My magic ...
aa
aa
aa
aa
ahh !!!

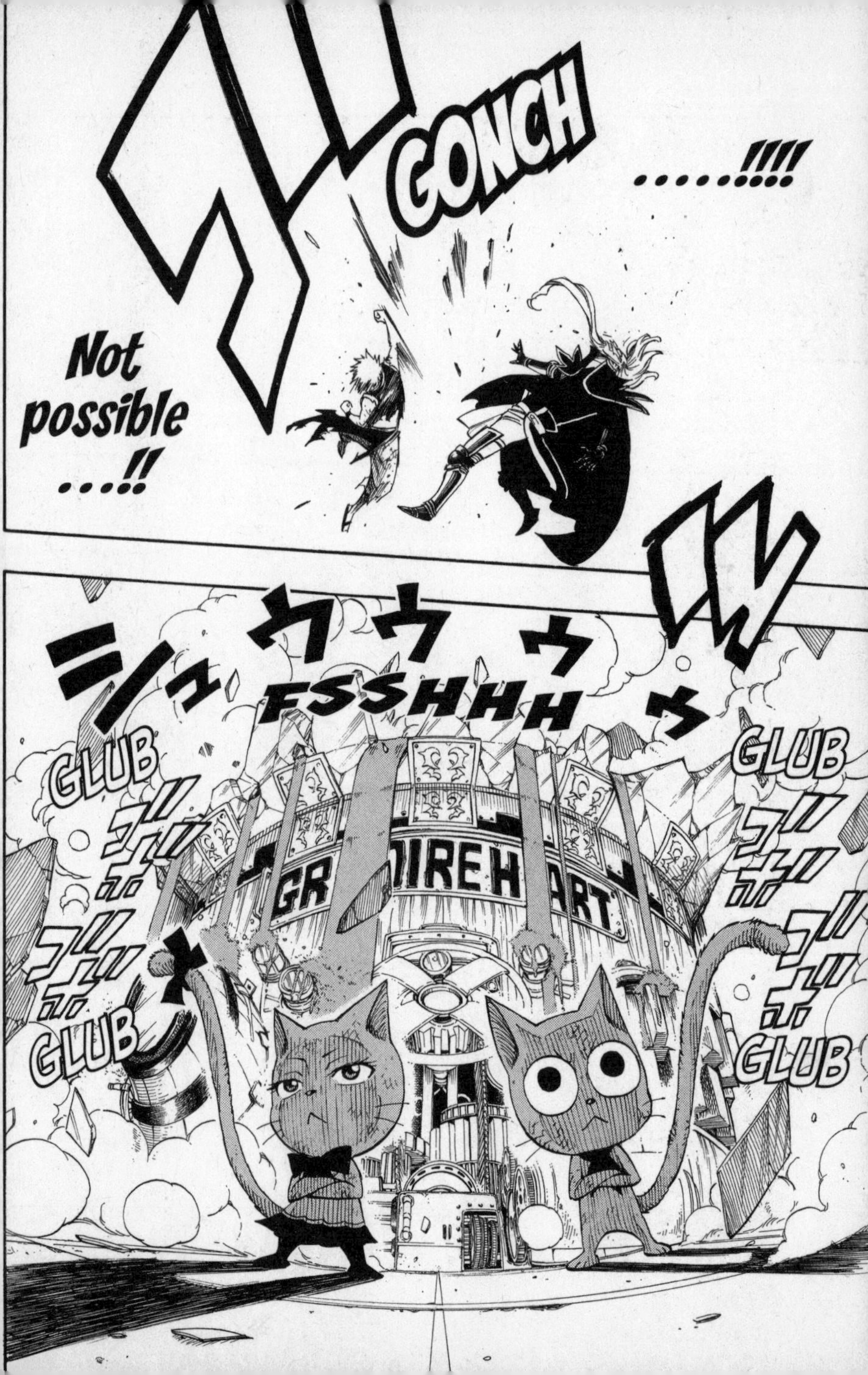

......!!!!
GONCH
Not possible ...!!
FSSHHH
GLUB
GLUB
GLUB
GLUB

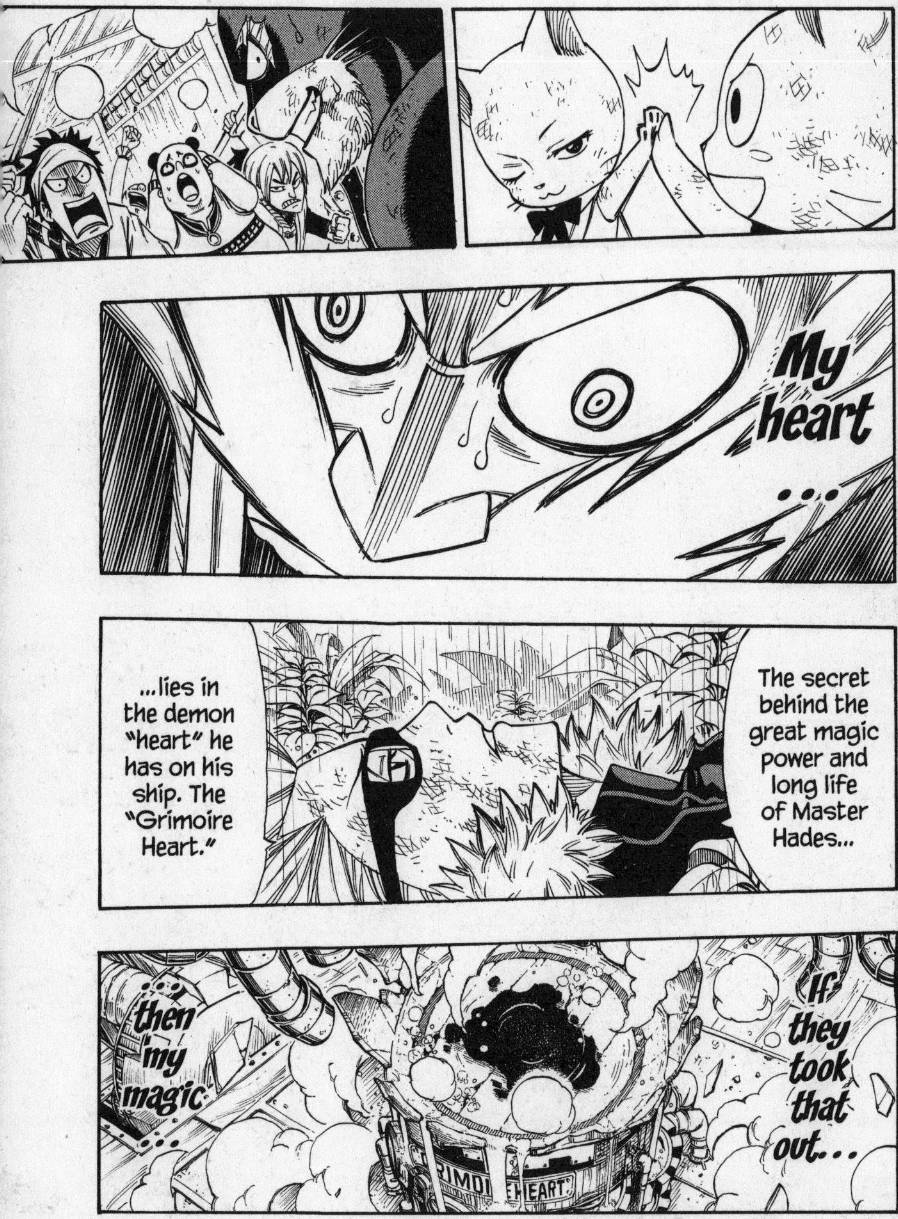
My heart...
The secret behind the great magic power and long life of Master Hades...
...lies in the demon "heart" he has on his ship. The "Grimoire Heart."
If they took that out...
...then my magic

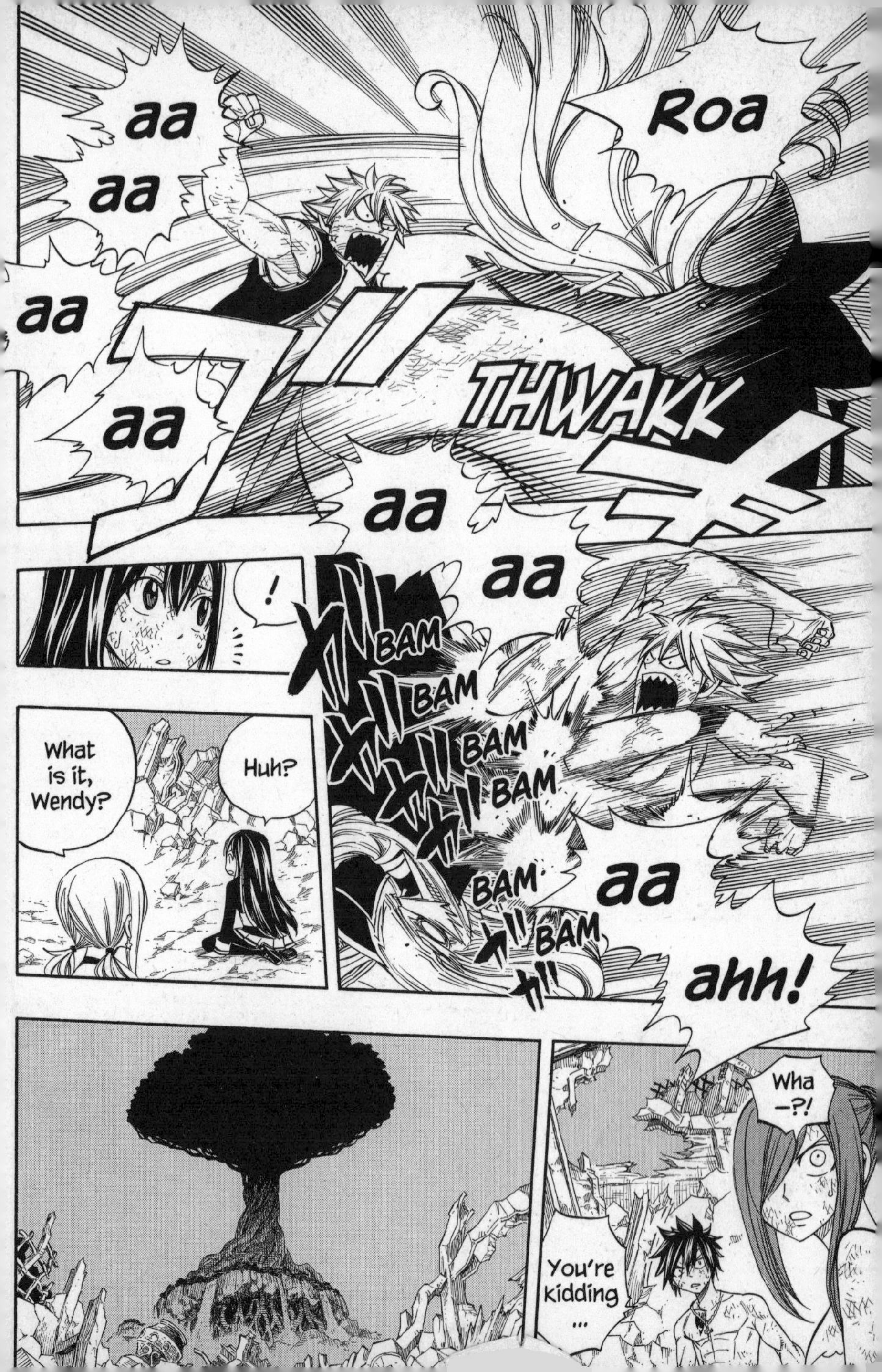
Roa
aa
aa
aa
aa
THWAKK
aa
aa
BAM
BAM
BAM
BAM
BAM
BAM
aa
ahh!
!
Huh?
What is it, Wendy?
Wha—?!
You're kidding ...

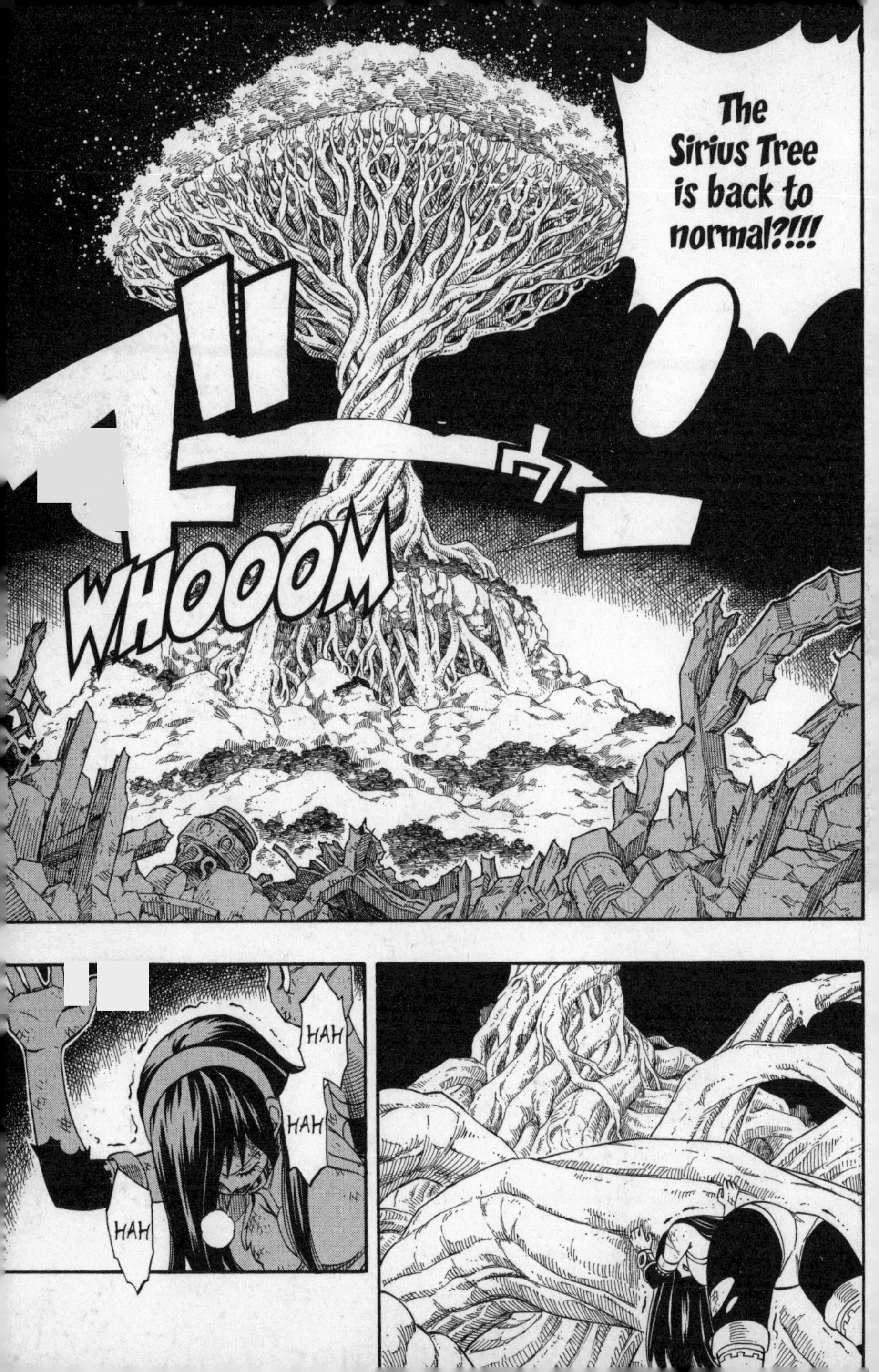
The Sirius Tree is back to normal?!!!
WHOOOM
HAH
HAH
HAH

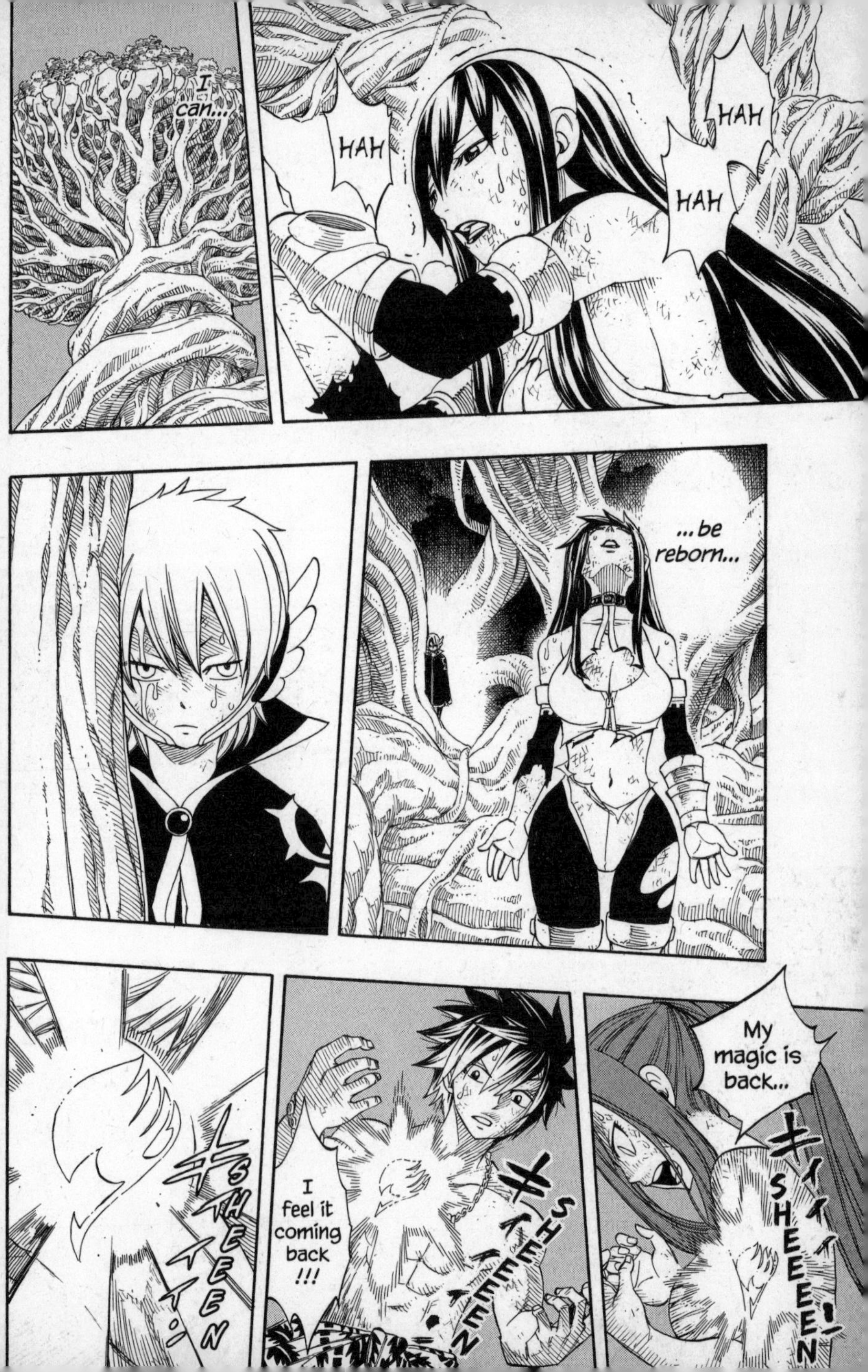
HAH
HAH
HAH
I can...
...be reborn...
My magic is back...
SHEEEEEN!
I feel it coming back!!!
SHEEEEEN
SHEEEEN

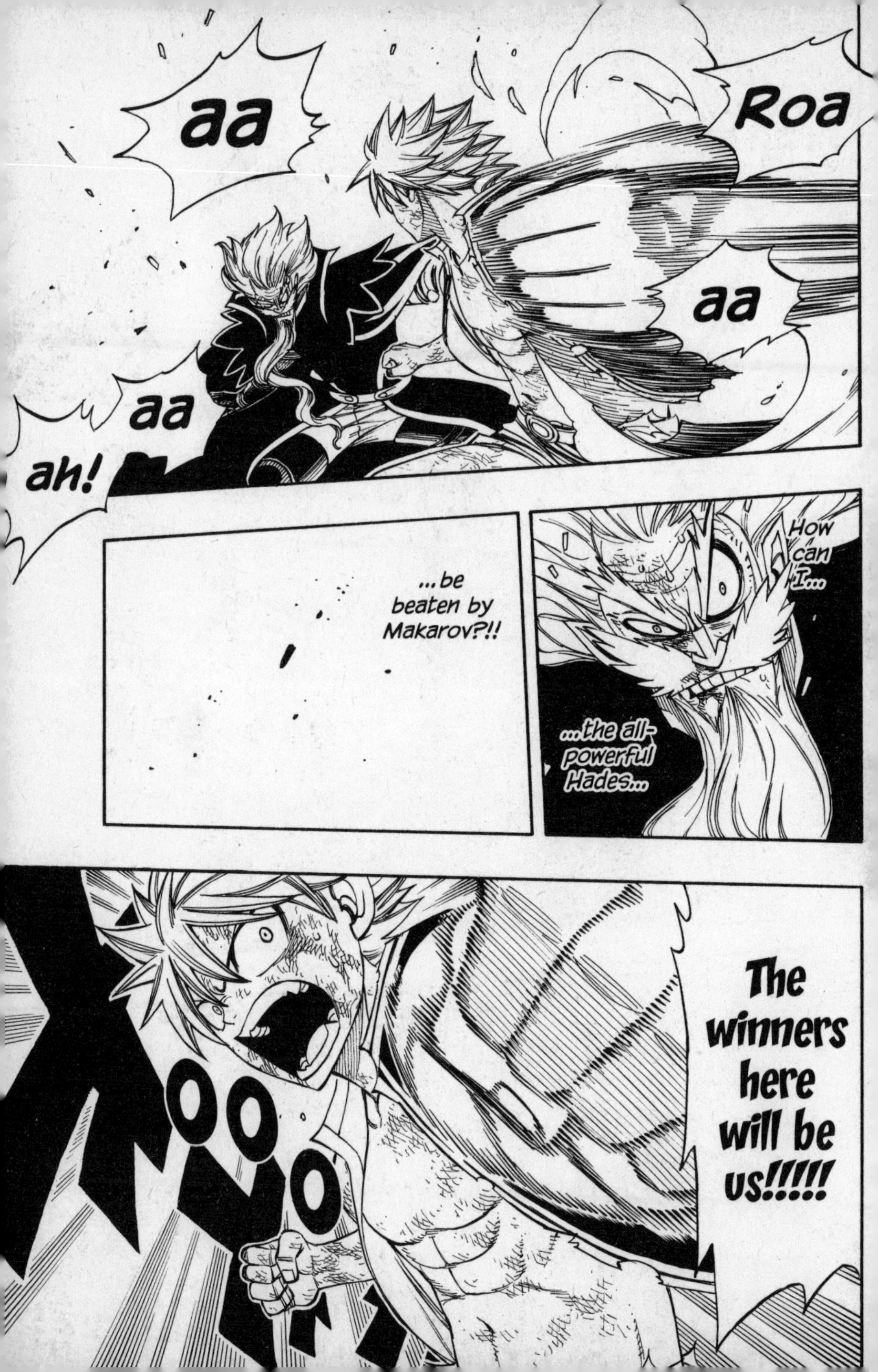
Roa
aa
aa
aa
ah!
How can I...
...the all-powerful Hades...
...be beaten by Makarov?!!
The winners here will be us!!!!!

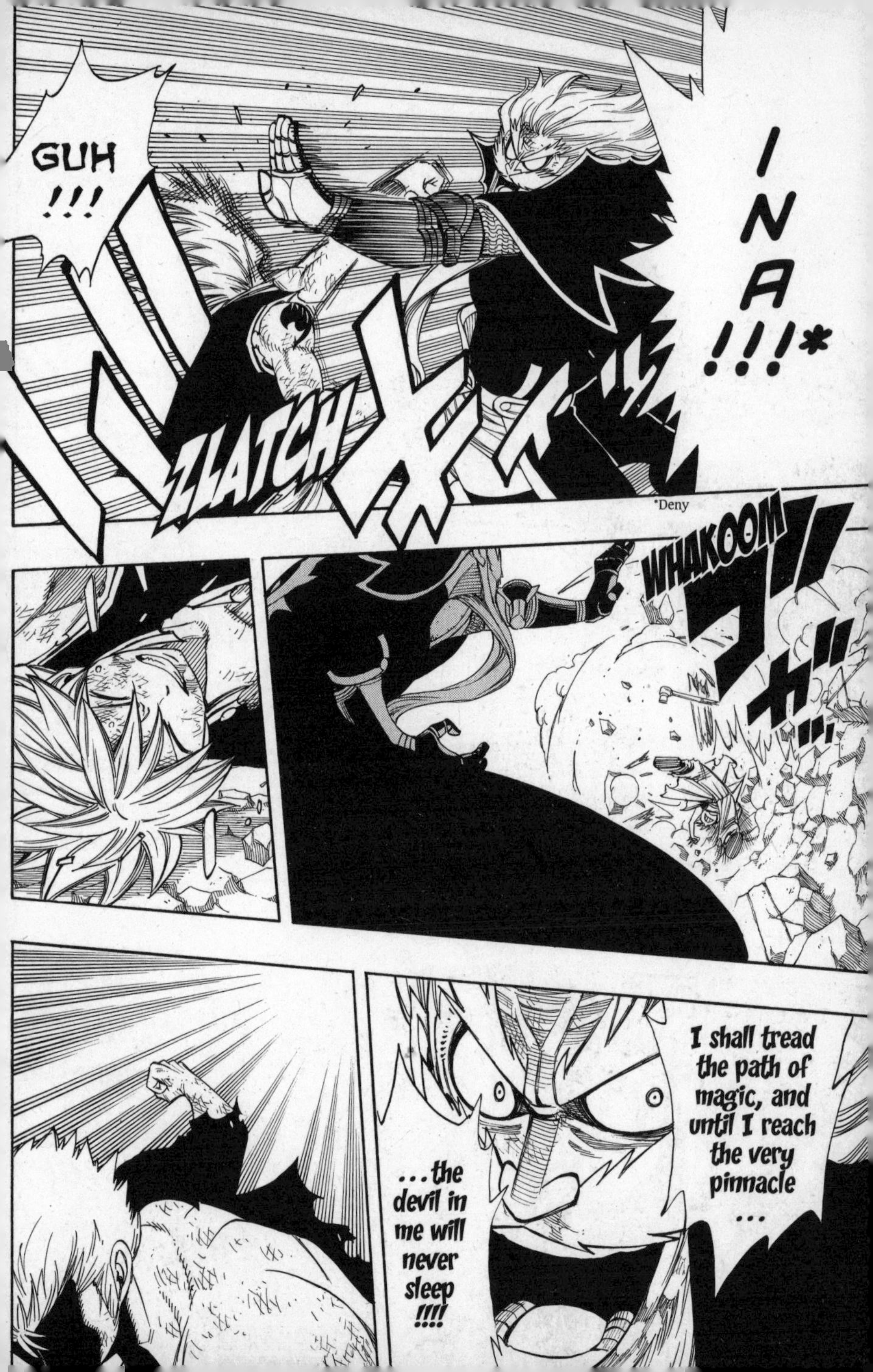
INA!!!*
GUH !!!
ZLATCH
*Deny
WHAKOOM
I shall tread the path of magic, and until I reach the very pinnacle ...
...the devil in me will never sleep !!!!

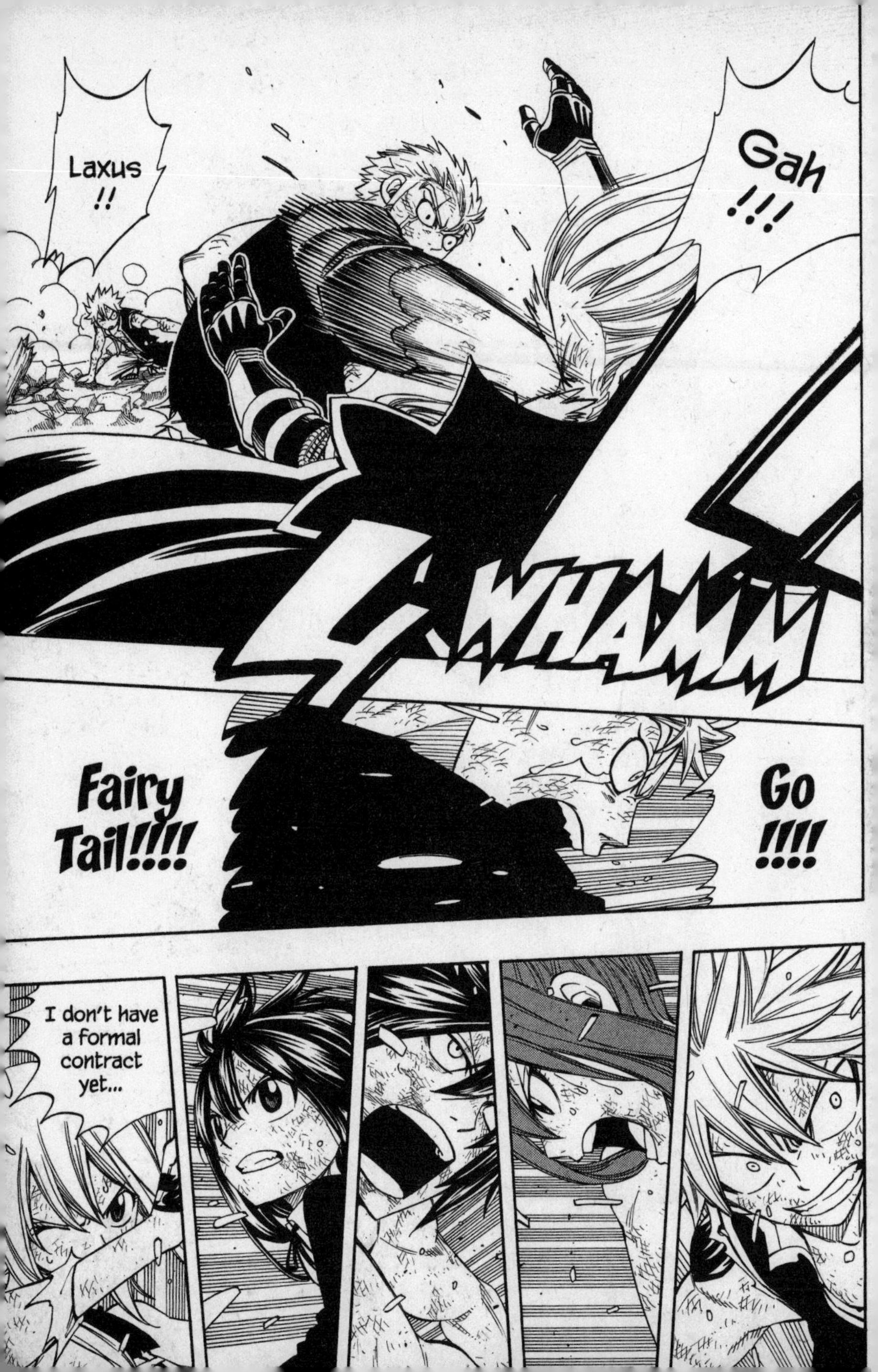
Gah!!!
Laxus!!
WHAMM
Go!!!!
Fairy Tail!!!!!
I don't have a formal contract yet...

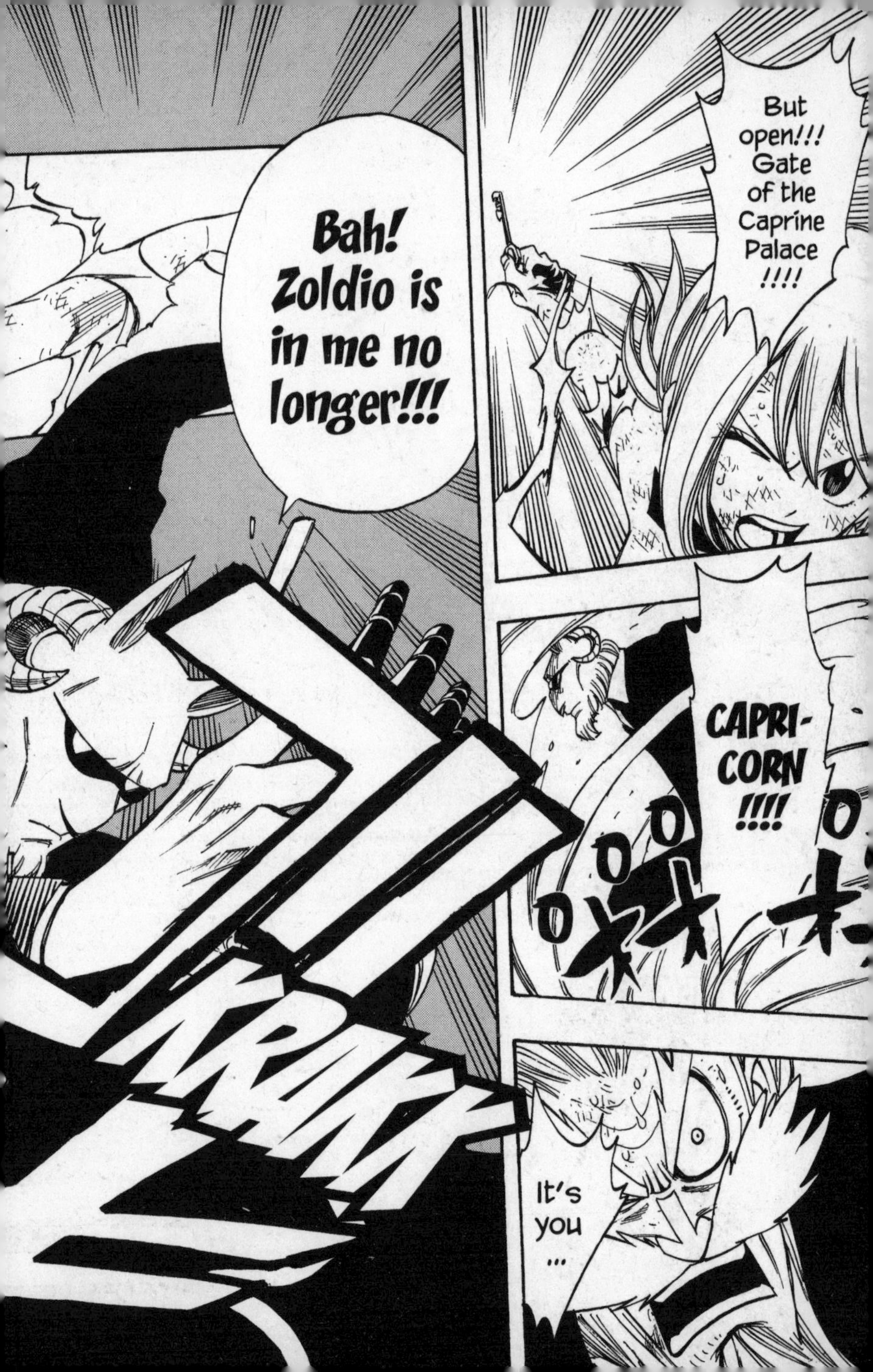

But open!!! Gate of the Caprine Palace !!!!
CAPRI-CORN !!!!
It's you ...
Bah! Zoldio is in me no longer!!!

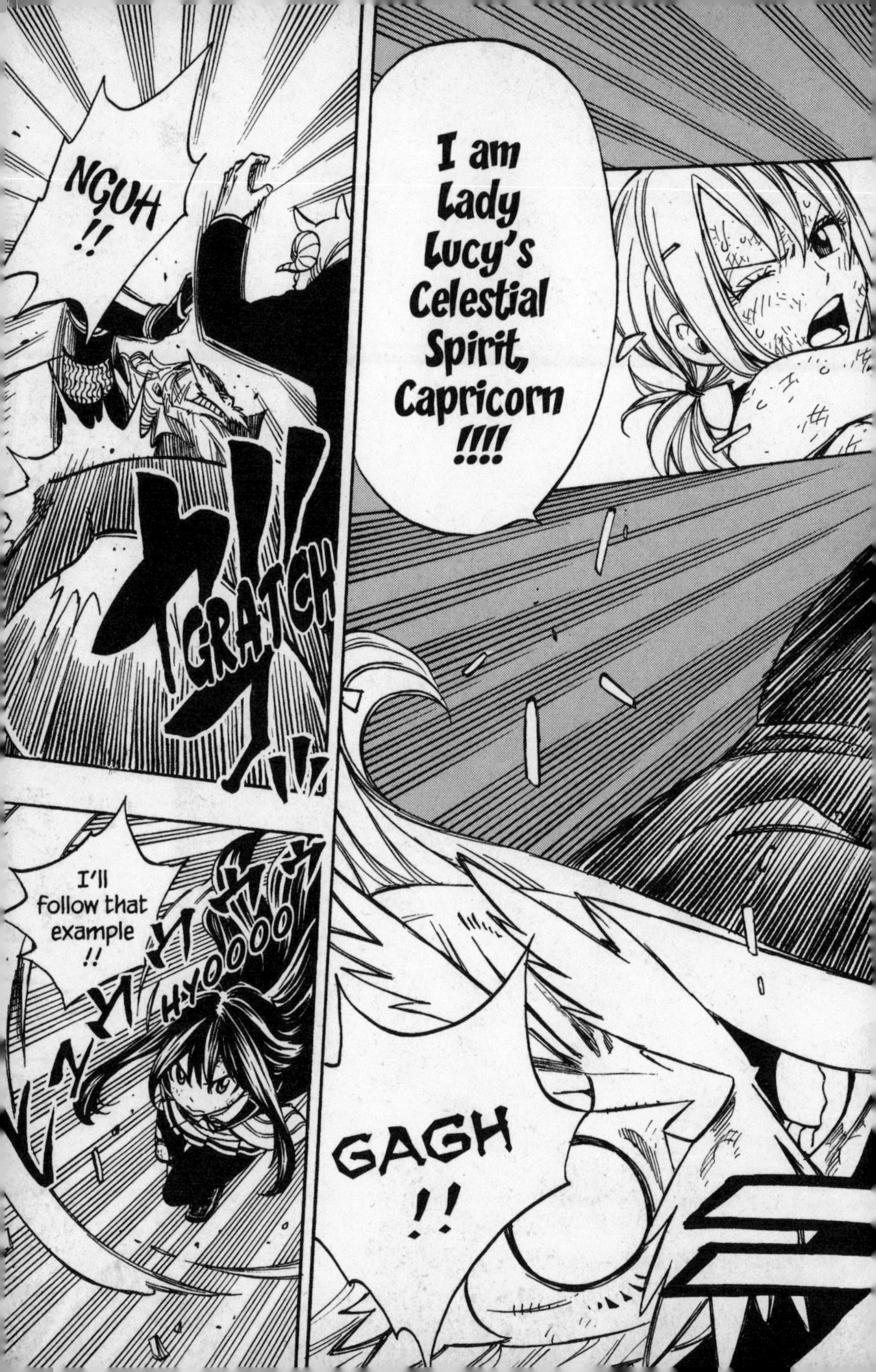

I am Lady Lucy's Celestial Spirit, Capricorn!!!!
GAGH!!
NGUH!!
GRATCH
I'll follow that example!!
HYOOOOO

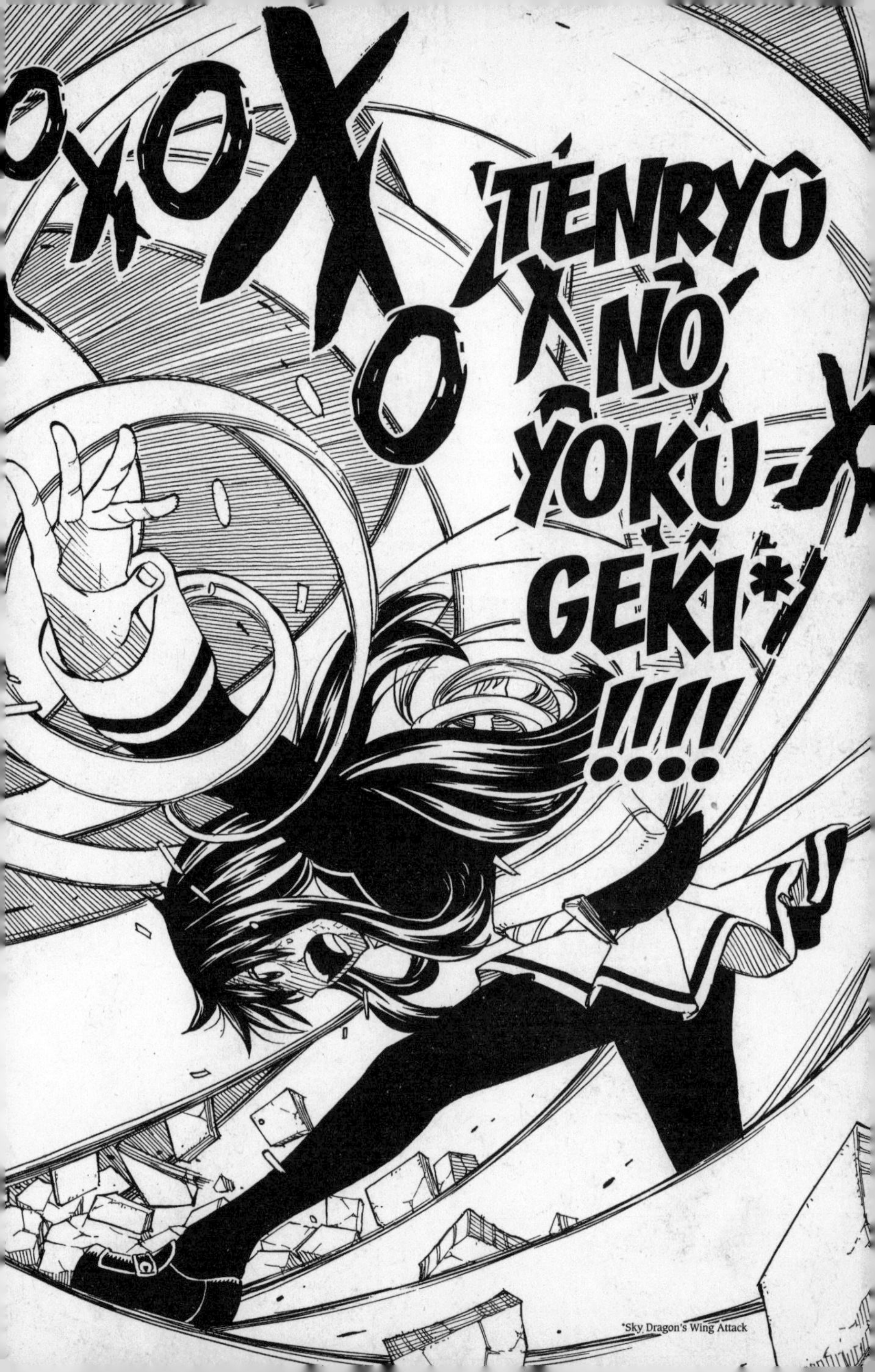
TENRYÛ NO YOKU-GEKI*!!!!

*Sky Dragon's Wing Attack

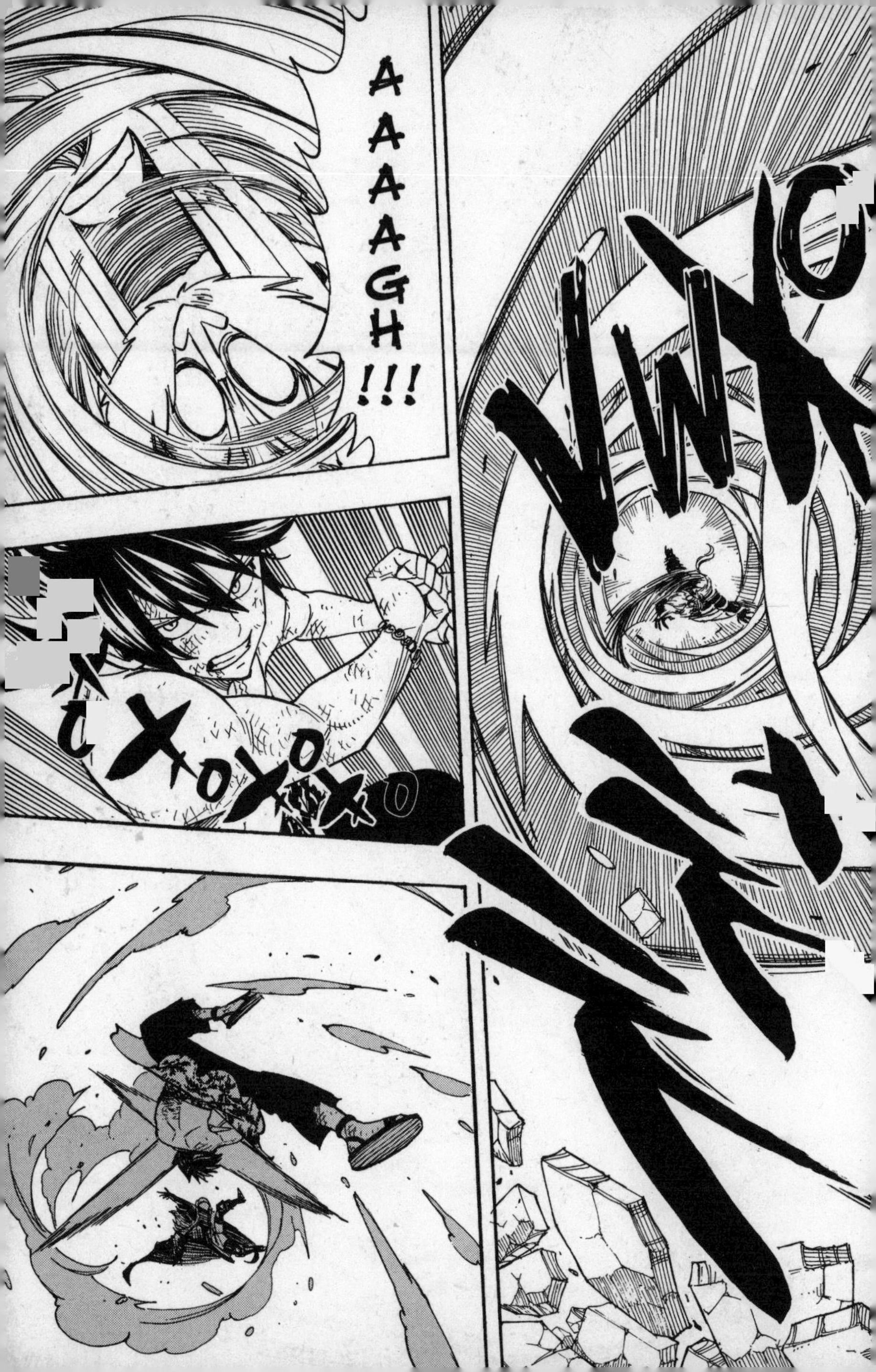
AAAAGH!!!

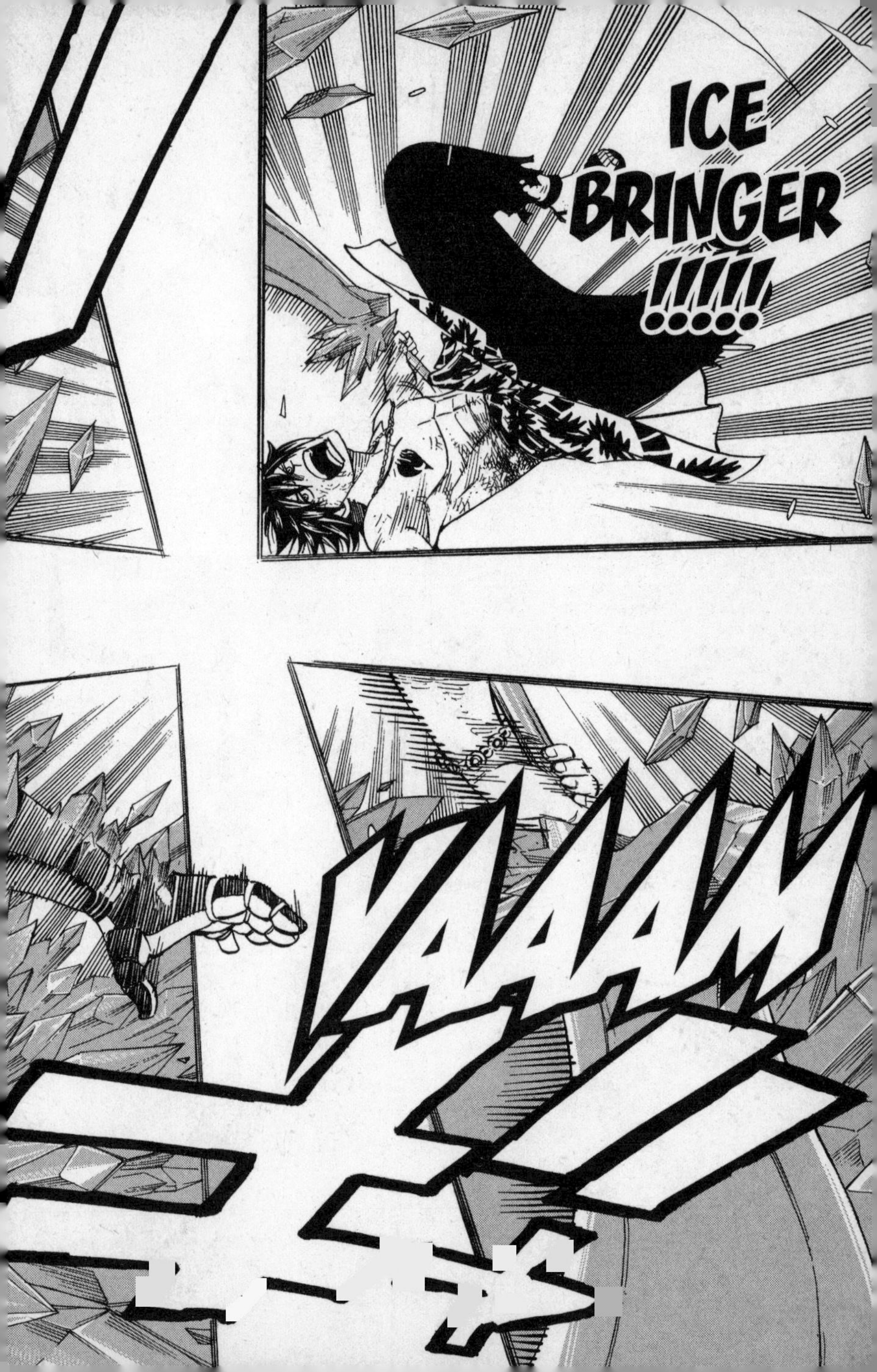
ICE BRINGER!!!!!
VAAAM

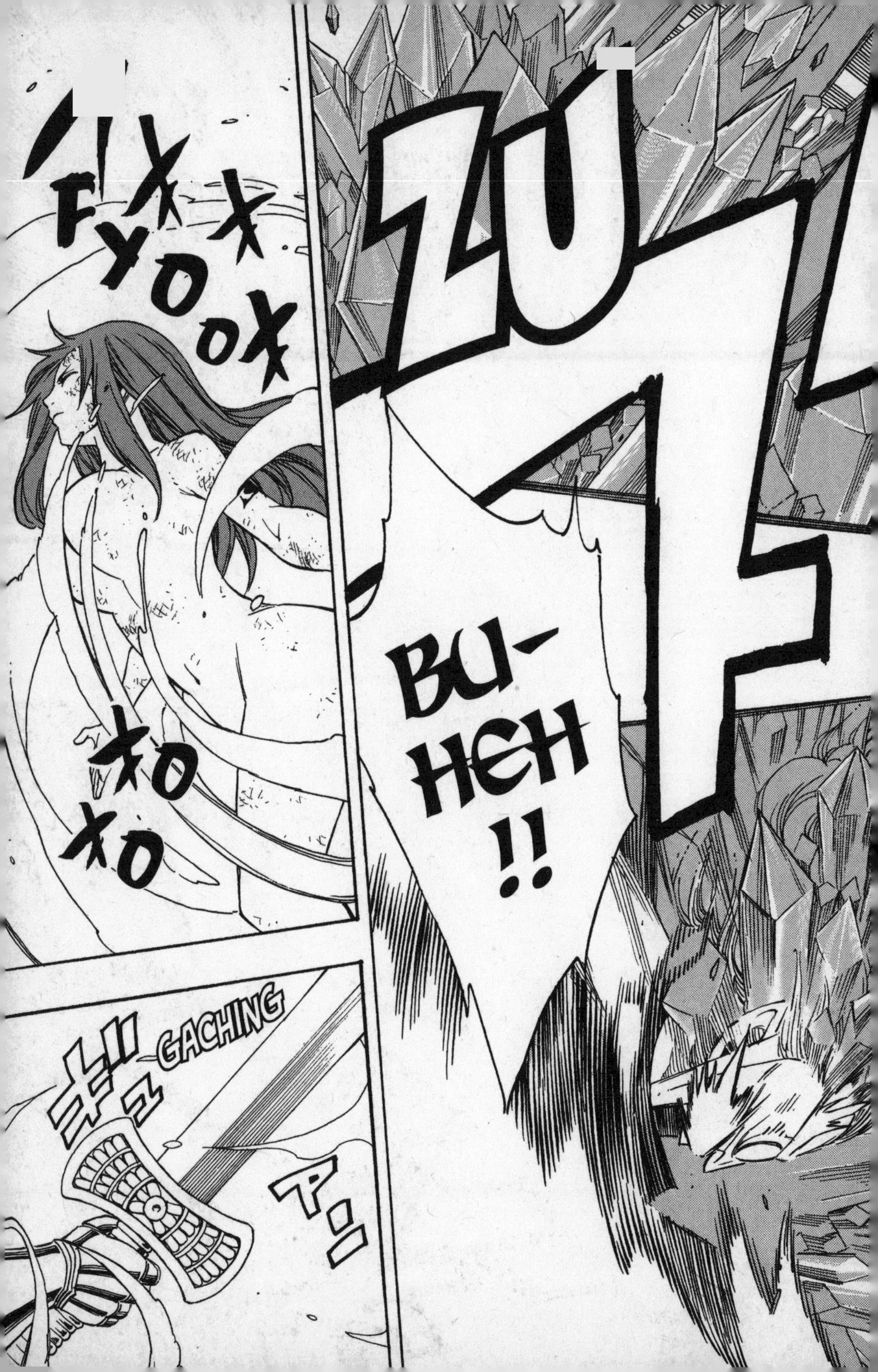
ZUN
BU-HEH!!
FYOOO
ギュ
GACHING

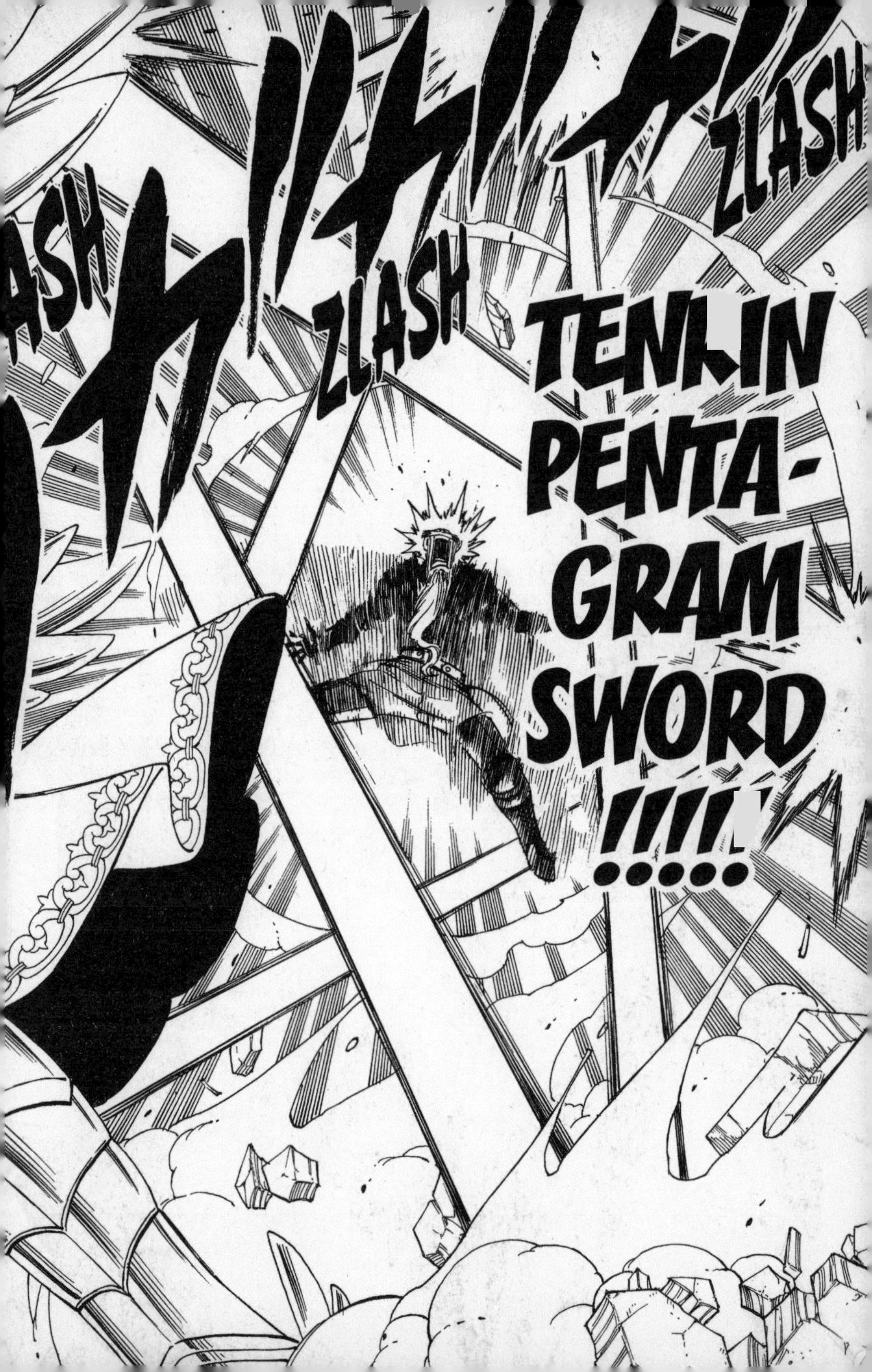
ZLASH
ZLASH
ASH
TENKIN PENTA-GRAM SWORD!!!!!

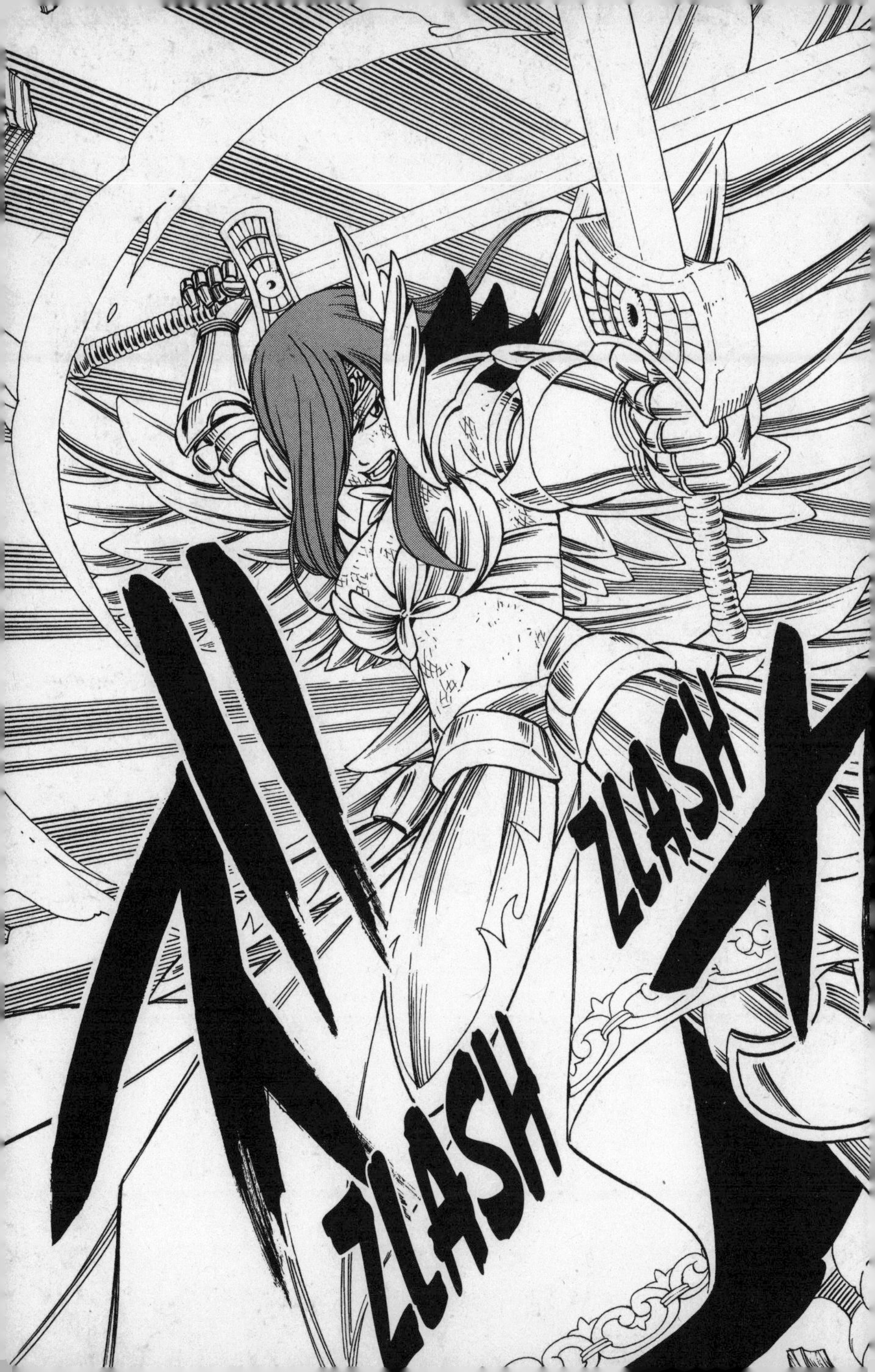
ZLASH
ZLASH

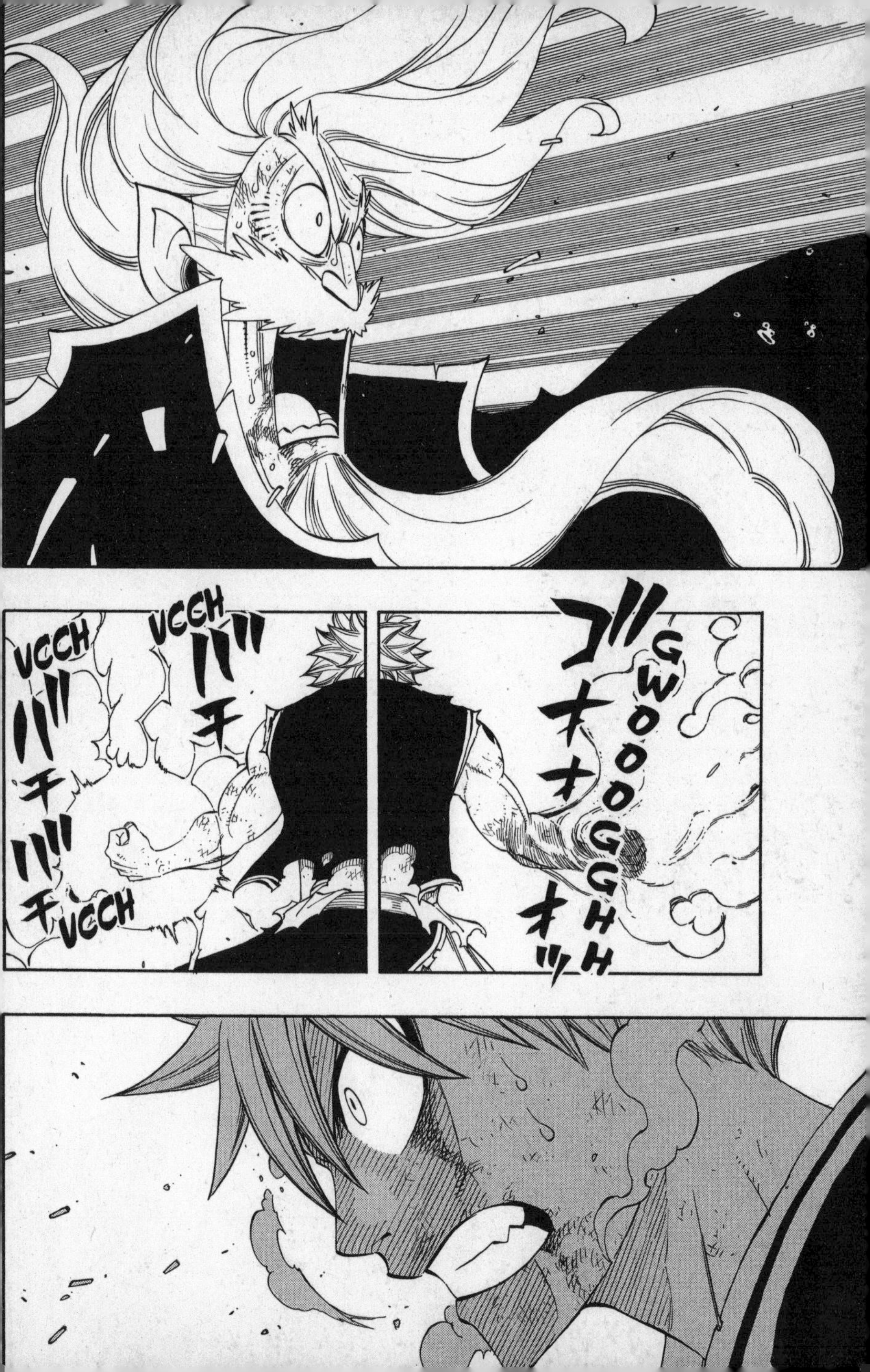
ゴオオオッ
GWOOOOGGHHH
VCCH
バチ
VCCH
バチバチ
VCCH

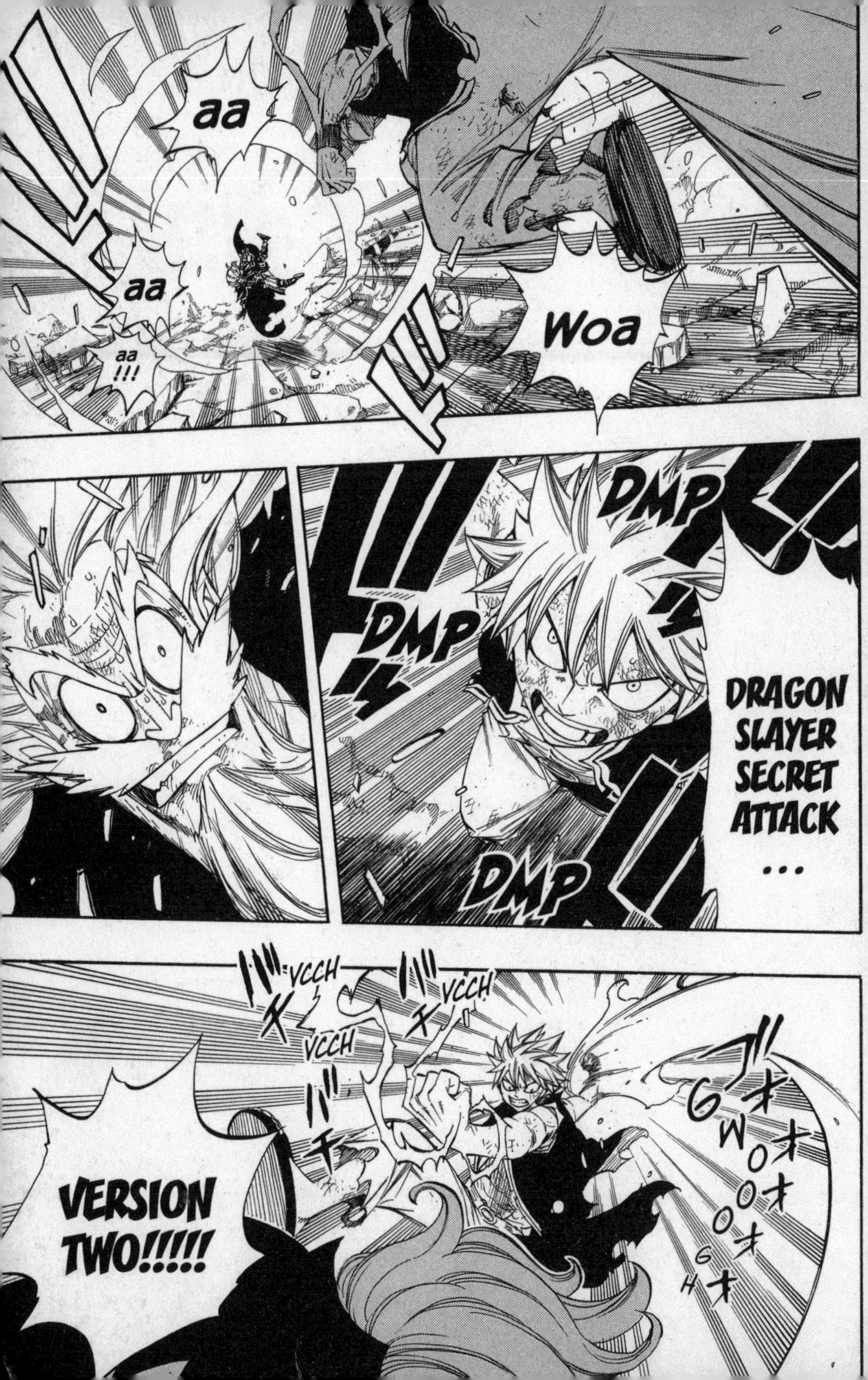
Woa
aa
aa
aa !!!
DMP
DMP
DMP
DRAGON SLAYER SECRET ATTACK ...
VCCH
VCCH
VCCH
GWOOOOGH
VERSION TWO!!!!!

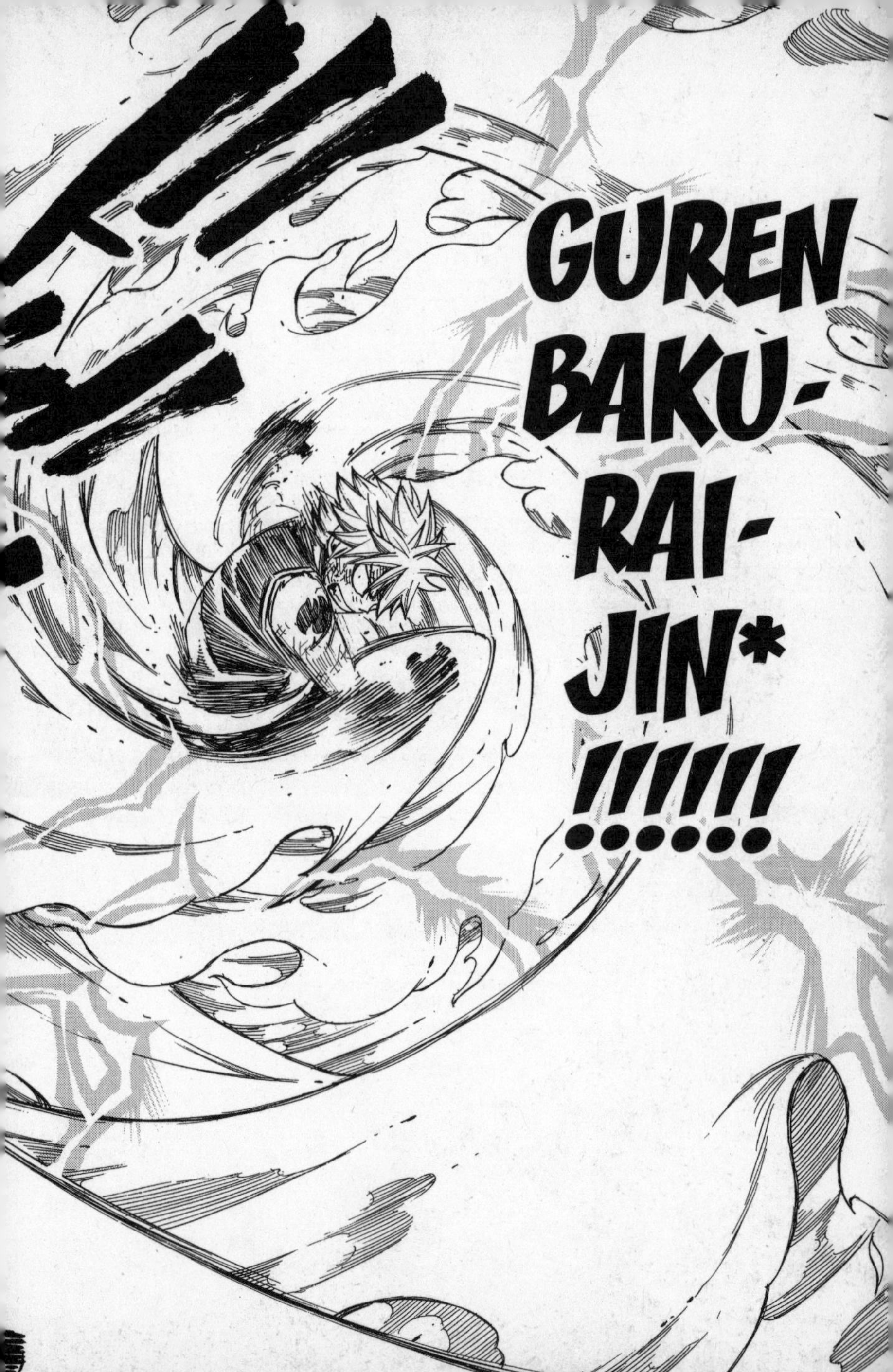
GUREN BAKU-RAI-JIN*!!!!!!

*Blazing Exploding Thunder Sword

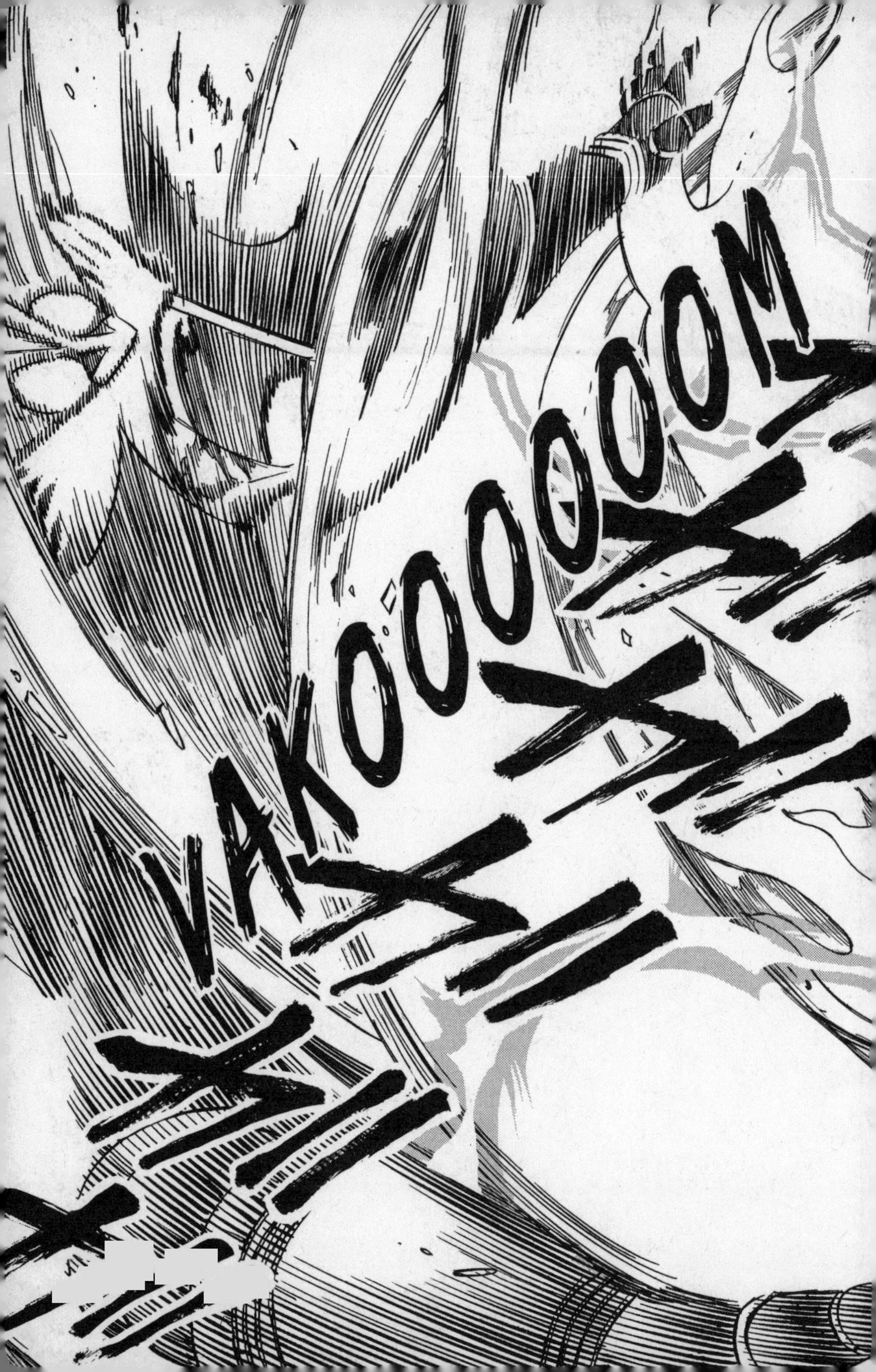
VAKOOOOOOM

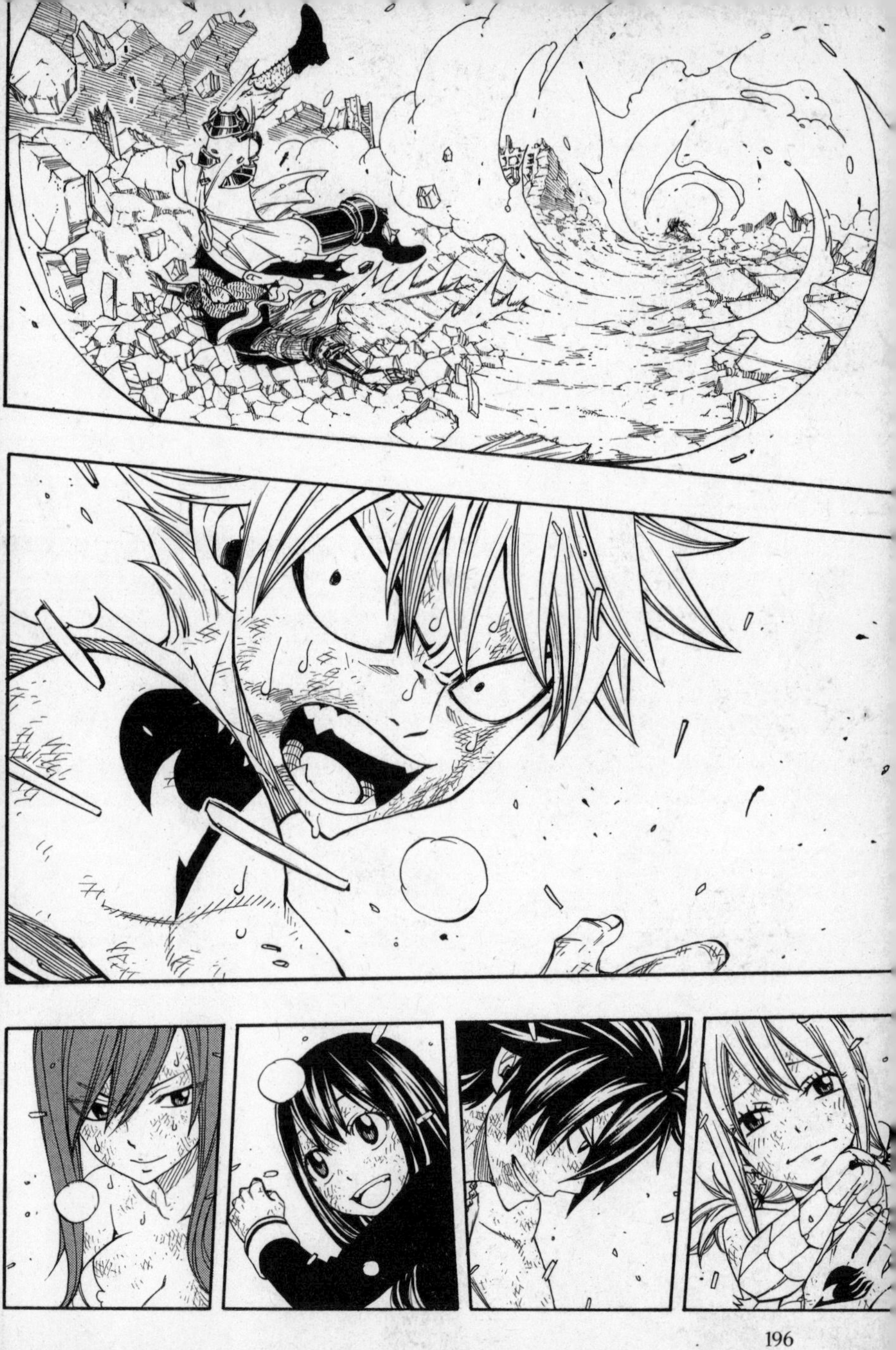

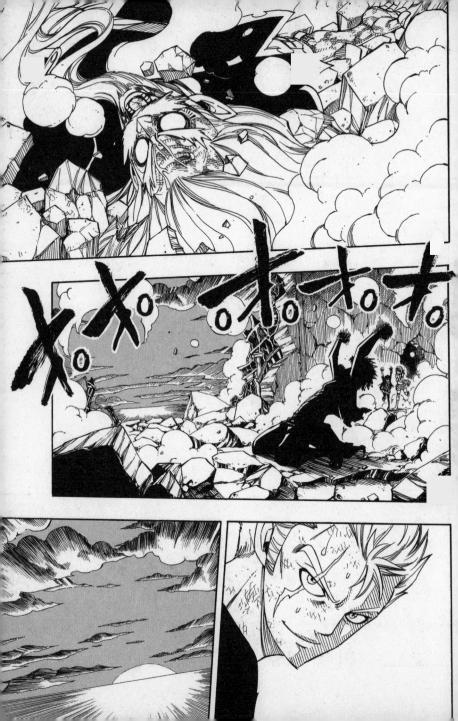

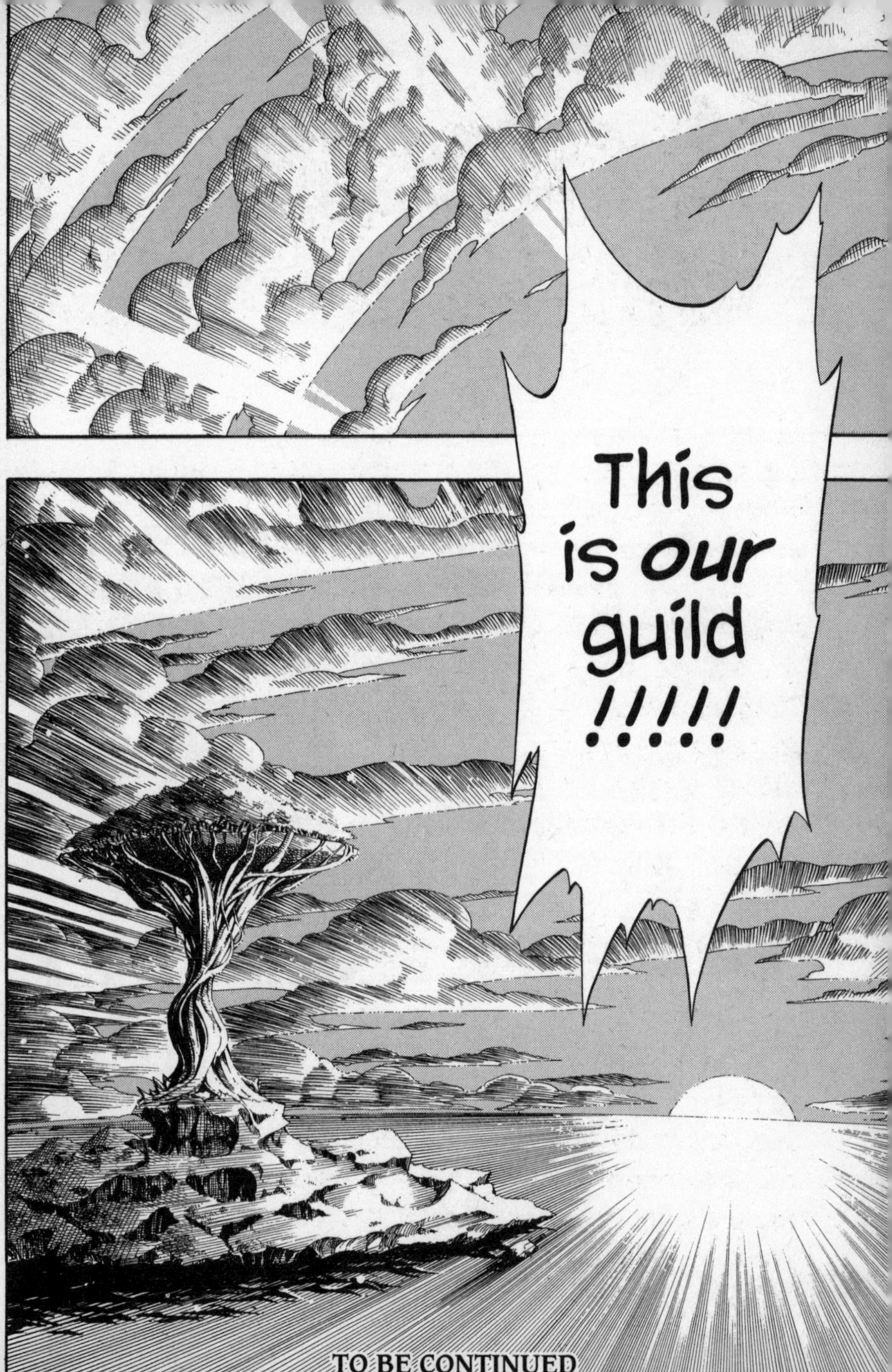
This is *our* guild !!!!!

TO BE CONTINUED

Afterword
あとがき

There were so few bonus pages this time!
I'm sorry!! There was just nothing I could do about it.
Now, I'm sure some of you already noticed, but there
was a different version of Chapter 248 (Dawn on Sirius
Island) in Shonen Magazine than you saw here. In this
volume, I gave everyone really eye-catching double-page
spreads for their ultimate attacks. I cut out one page (of the
Magazine version) and added in nine more pages. It was a
lot of work!! A while back with Chapter 128 (Fantasia), I
did the same thing and made a "director's cut" version of
the chapter. And if timing and conditions work out in the
future, I'd like to do it again. I really love these added-page
versions!
Speaking of add-ons, did you notice that the Edolas
versions of Gajeel and Makarov were a part of the anime
Fairy Tail? They were original episodes not in the manga,
but they were a part of the "cut scenes" that I, through
my tears, had to cut. But now they're reborn in the anime!
I especially think the Edo-Gajeel came out to be a great
character! Edo-Makarov was supposed to be there during
the final plot twist. But the voice actor was the same, and
I'll bet everyone noticed. If you don't understand what I'm
talking about, check out the DVDs!!

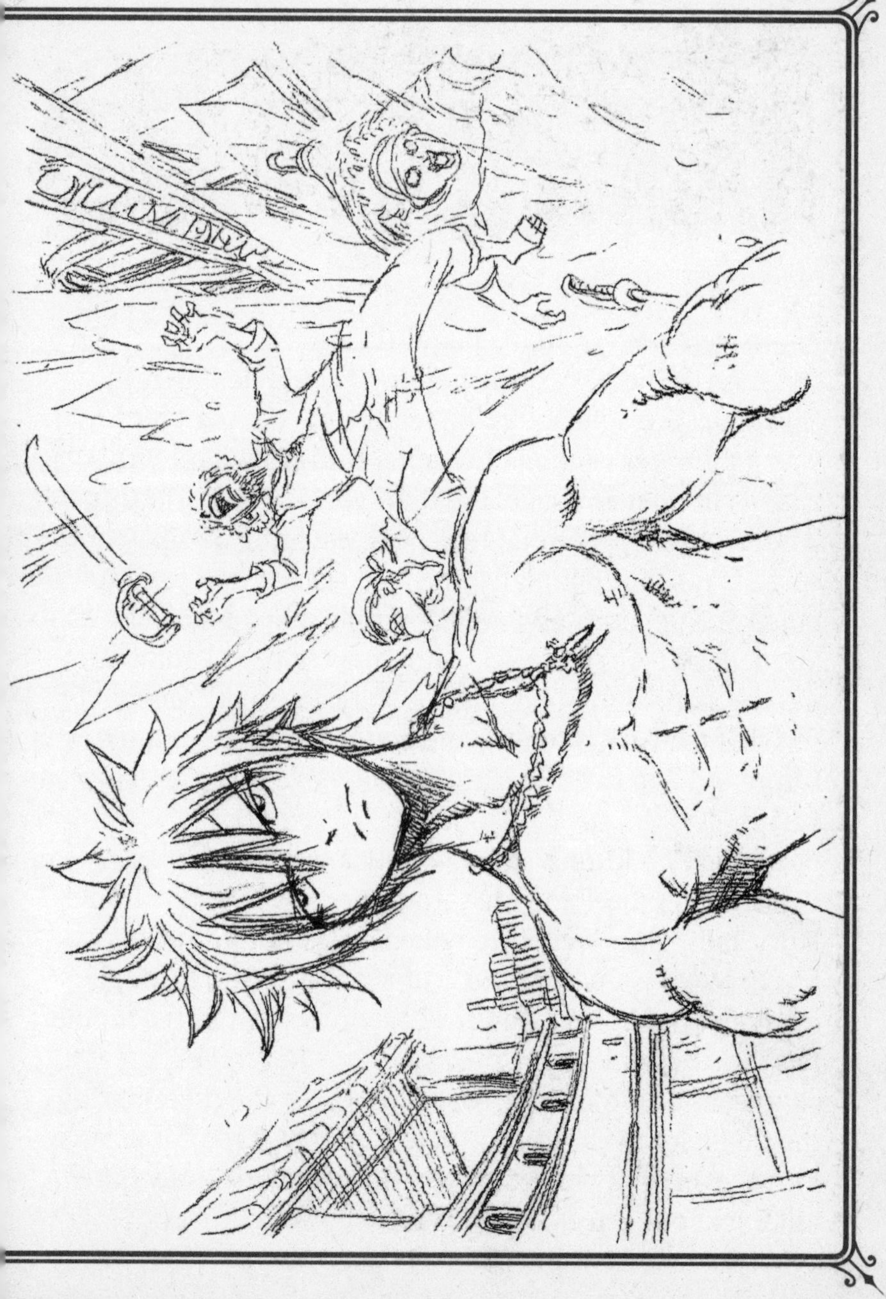

FAIRY TAIL 29

フェアリーテイル

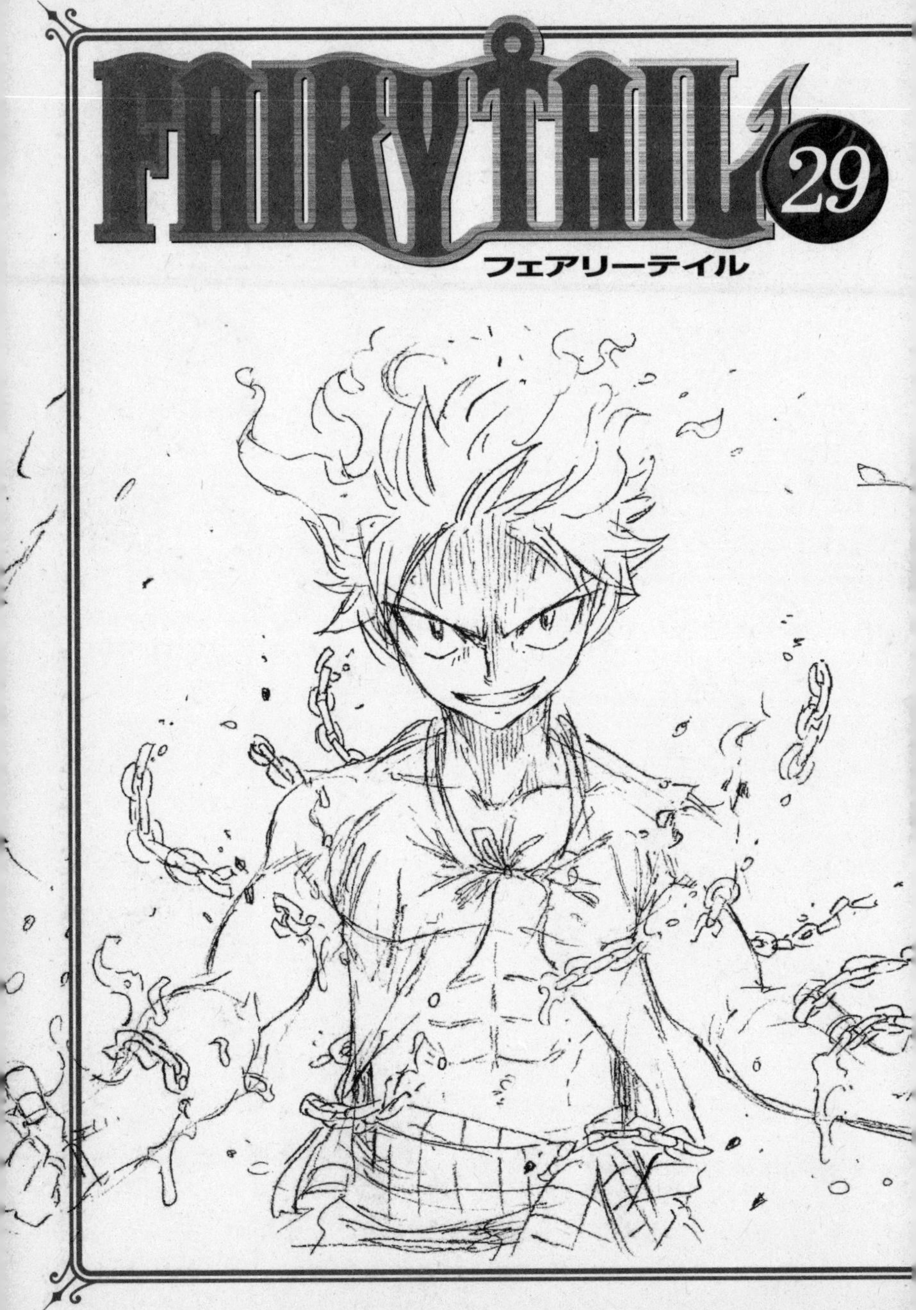

FROM HIRO MASHIMA

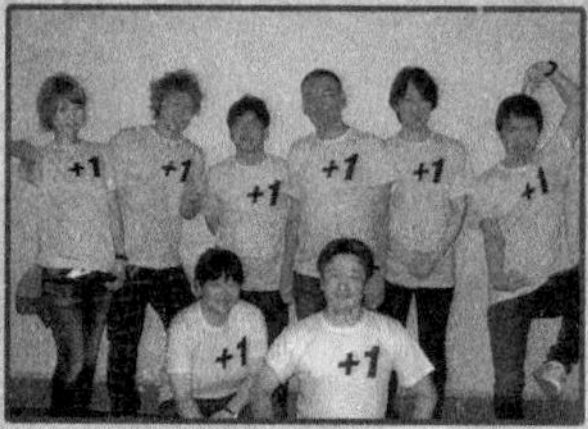

Back row, left to right: Yoshikawa-sensei, me, Morikawa-sensei, Fukumoto-sensei, Seo-sensei, Nishimoto-sensei. Front row, left to right: Yamamoto-sensei, Raiku-sensei.

As a part of a 24-hour TV event, I went to Fukushima for a signing. But I never thought for a second that I'd end up in this T-shirt! We couldn't sing or run around like the other entertainers, but we were determined to do our best to bring even just a smile to the survivors of the earthquake and tsunami with the power of manga. I went there with that in mind.

Original Jacket Design: Hisao Ogawa

Translation Notes:

Japanese is a tricky language for most Westerners, and translation is often more art than science. For your edification and reading pleasure, here are notes on some of the places where we could have gone in a different direction with our translation of the work, or where a Japanese cultural reference is used.

Page 22, Rosenkrone

This attack name is made up of two German words, the word for "rose," and the word for "crown." The Japanese version of manga backs this up with *kanji* of the same meaning.

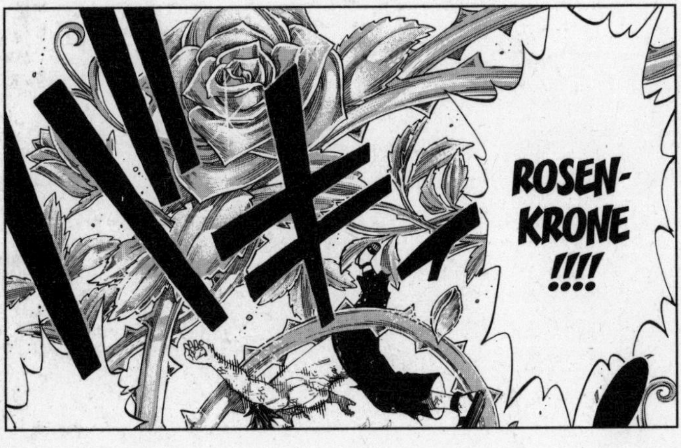
ROSEN-
KRONE
!!!!

Page 114, Gungnir

Gungnir, in mythology, is the spear of the ruler of the Norse Gods, Odin. The spear appears in many songs and legends, as well as in Wagner's opera cycle, The Ring of the Nibelung.

Page 114, Exploding Thunder Sword

The previous "Guren" attack, "Guren Bakuenjin" (Blazing Backflash Sword) has an actual Japanese word, *bakuen*, in the attack name rather than just combination of *kanji* to make a new word. For this one too, *bakurai*, which literally means "exploding thunder," is also an actual Japanese word meaning "depth charge," the weapon that surface ships use against submarines.

Preview of *Fairy Tail*, volume 30

We're pleased to present you with a preview from Fairy Tail, volume 30, available digitally in June 2013 and in print in September. See our Web site (www.kodanshacomics.com) for more details!

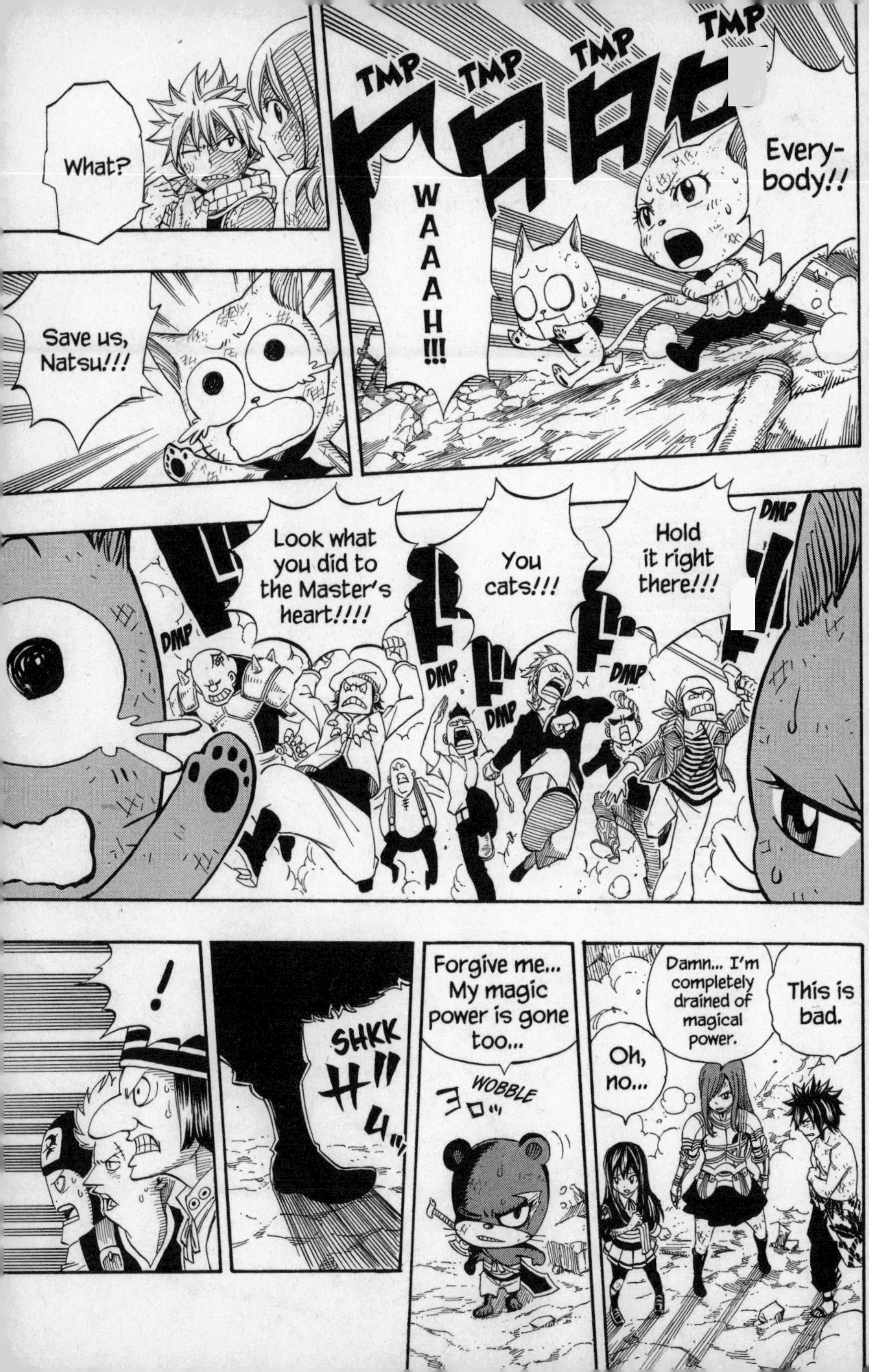
Every-body!!
TMP
TMP
TMP
TMP
WAAAAH!!!
What?
Save us, Natsu!!!
DMP
Hold it right there!!!
You cats!!!
DMP
DMP
DMP
Look what you did to the Master's heart!!!!
DMP
This is bad.
Damn... I'm completely drained of magical power.
Oh, no...
Forgive me... My magic power is gone too...
WOBBLE
SHKK
!

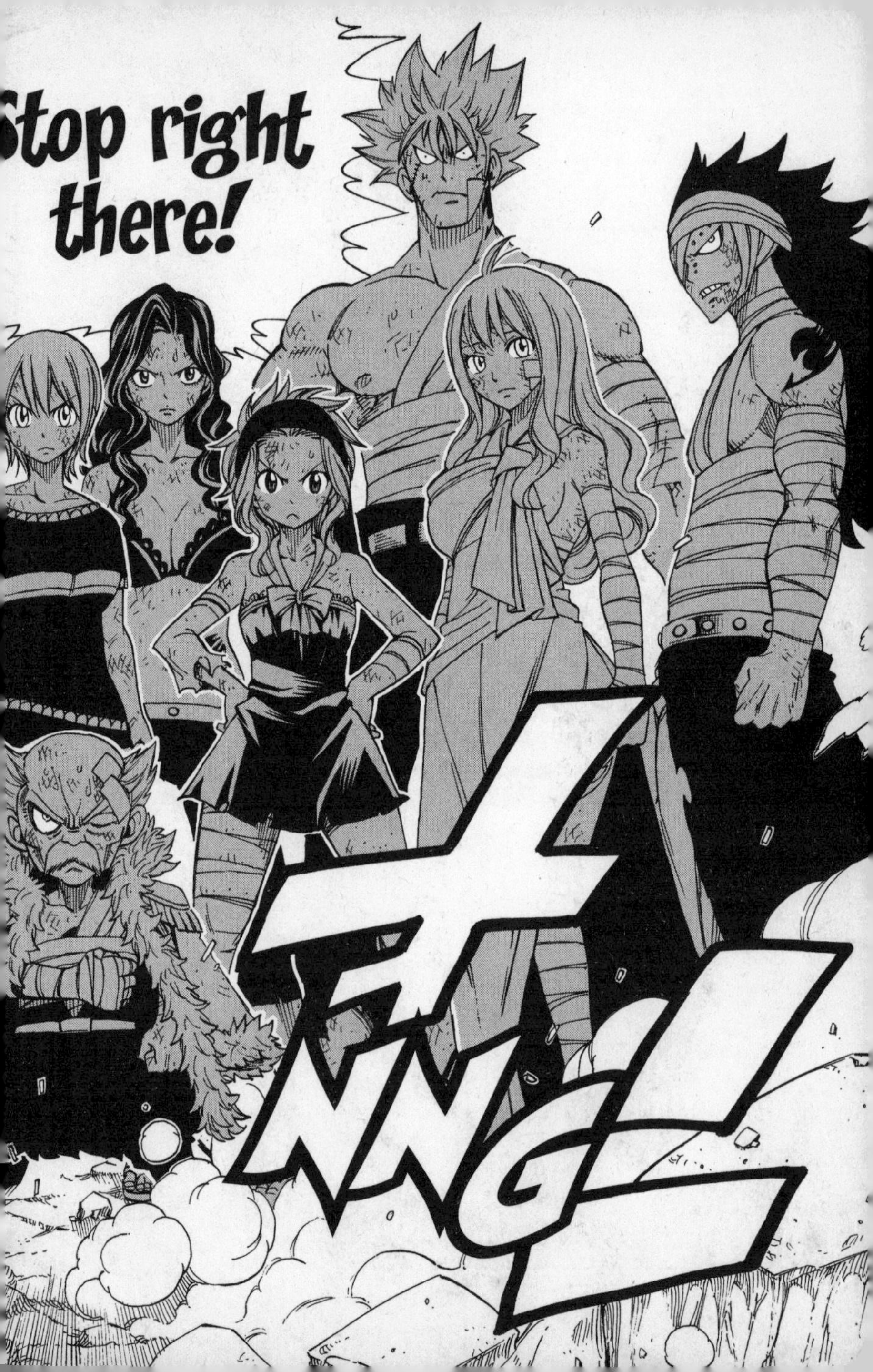
Stop right there!

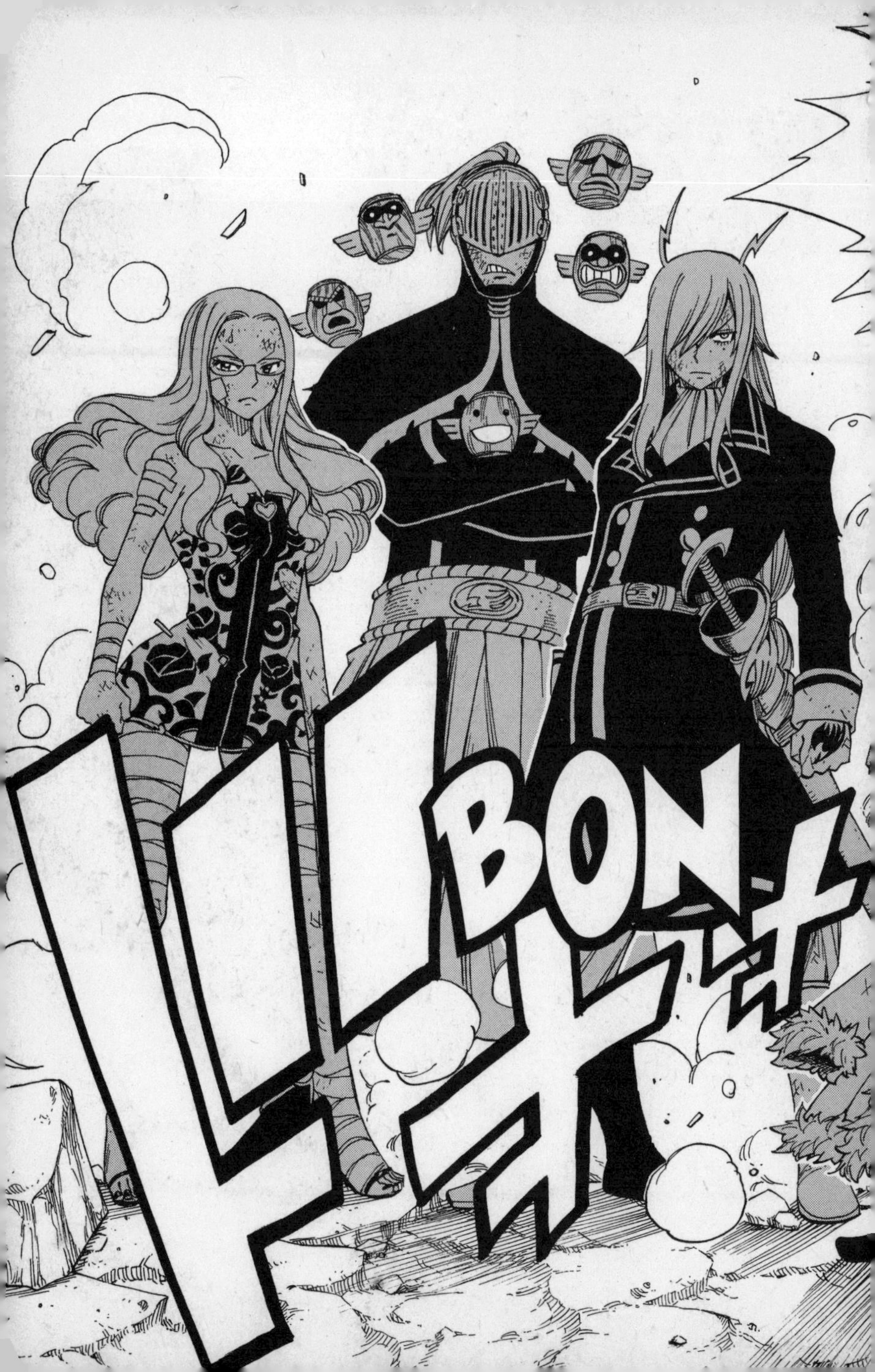
BON!

Fairy Tail volume 29 is a work of fiction. Names, characters, places, and incidents are the products of the author's imagination or are used fictitiously. Any resemblance to actual events, locales, or persons, living or dead, is entirely coincidental.

A Kodansha Comics Trade Paperback Original.

Fairy Tail volume 29 copyright © 2011 Hiro Mashima
English translation copyright © 2013 Hiro Mashima

Published in the United States by Kodansha Comics, an imprint of Kodansha USA Publishing, LLC, New York.

Publication rights for this English edition arranged through Kodansha Ltd., Tokyo.

First published in Japan in 2011 by Kodansha Ltd., Tokyo
ISBN 978-1-61262-406-8

Printed in the United States of America.

www.kodanshacomics.com

9 8 7 6 5 4 3 2 1

Translator: William Flanagan
Lettering: AndWorld Design